Also by Charles Osborne

Frontispiece: Mozart by Dorothea Stock (Dresden, 1789)

THE COMPLETE OPERAS OF MOZART

A CRITICAL GUIDE

BY CHARLES OSBORNE

ATHENEUM

NEW YORK

1978

Library of Congress Cataloging in Publication Data
Osborne, Charles, date
    The complete operas of Mozart.
    Bibliography: p.
    Includes index.
    1. Mozart, Johann Chrysostom Wolfgang Amadeus,
1756-1791. Operas. I. Title.
MT100.M7608   782.1'092'4   78-55623
ISBN 0-689-10886-9

Don't never forget your true and faithfull friend

Wolfgang Amadè Mozart

Vienna, the 24 April, 1787

(Entry by Mozart, in English, in the album of his friend Franz von Jacquin.)

For my mother,
Elsa Louise Osborne

CONTENTS

LIST OF ILLUSTRATIONS

Frontispiece
Mozart by Dorothea Stock (Dresden, 1789)

Following page 30
Four pages from the libretto of *Mitridate*, published in Milan, 1770.
Costume designs by Heinrich Lefler for a production of *Zaide* in Vienna, 1902.

Following page 192
A page of the manuscript of *Die Entführung aus dem Serail*: part of the final *allegro* of Osmin's aria, 'Solche hergelauf'ne Laffen'.
Title-page from an early piano score of *Die Entführung aus dem Serail*.
Costume designs by Franz Gaul for a production of *Der Schauspieldirektor* in Vienna, 1880.
Title-page from an early piano score of *Le nozze di Figaro*.
Silhouettes of Ann Storace and Francesco Benucci, the first Susanna and Figaro.
Costume designs by Alfred Roller for Gustav Mahler's production of *Le nozze di Figaro* in Vienna, 1902.
Engravings of scenes from *Le nozze di Figaro* by J. H. Ramberg, 1827.
Costume designs by Heinrich Lefler for Gustav Mahler's production of *Così fan tutte* in Vienna, 1900.
Title-page from an early piano score of *Così fan tutte*.
Title page from an early piano score of *La clemenza di Tito*.
Costume designs by Franz Gaul for a production of *La clemenza di Tito* in Vienna, 1888.

Following page 240
Title-pages from two early piano scores of *Die Zauberflöte*.
Stage designs by Karl Friedrich Schinkel for a production of *Die Zauberflöte* in Berlin, 1829.
'Monostatos and Pamina' by Moritz von Schwind (1869). Part of Schwind's fresco of scenes from *Die Zauberflöte* in a loggia of the Vienna State Opera House.

INTRODUCTION

THREE OF MOZART'S operas – *Don Giovanni, Le nozze di Figaro* and *Die Zauberflöte* – have always been among the most popular in the entire operatic repertoire; their composer needs no introduction. Within recent years, they have been joined by *Così fan tutte*, and a handful of other operas by Mozart is also now to be encountered fairly regularly in the opera houses of Europe and America. However, throughout his lifetime Mozart composed no fewer than twenty operas, and began two more, and it is possible to see most of these staged or to hear them on record or tape. In this book I have set out to provide, for the music lover coming fresh to any of them, an introduction to all of the operas, setting each in its historical context and discussing the music and the provenance of the libretto.

When, some years ago, I wrote a similar book on the operas of Verdi, I thought it would be useful to the reader if I were to provide linking passages of biography. I have adopted the same method here: in the case of Mozart who wrote his first operas as a child and his last within weeks of his death, but who also, in the space of a tragically brief lifetime, composed masterpieces of symphonic and chamber music, the biographical element has loomed even larger than in the Verdi book.

The sources I have consulted are mentioned in footnotes and in a bibliography at the end of the volume. I must acknowledge the helpfulness of libraries and other institutions in Vienna, Salzburg, Munich and London, and of countless individuals who have lightened my task.

C. O.

I

Die Schuldigkeit des ersten Gebots

part one of a sacred *Singspiel*

K. 35

Dramatis personae:

A lukewarm but later ardent Christian	(tenor)
The Spirit of Christianity	(tenor)
Worldliness	(soprano)
Divine Mercy	(soprano)
Divine Justice	(soprano)

LIBRETTO by Ignaz von Weiser

TIME: unspecified

PLACE: a garden, with a small wood nearby

FIRST PERFORMED in the Knights' Hall of the Palace of the Archbishop of Salzburg, 12 March, 1767. (Part II, with music by Michael Haydn, was performed on 19 March, and Part III, with music by Anton Kajetan Adlgasser, on 26 March.) The cast comprised Anton Franz Spitzeder (Spirit of Christianity); Maria Magdalena Lipp (Divine Mercy); Maria Anna Fesemayer (Worldliness); Maria Anna Braunhofer (Divine Justice); Joseph Meissner (the Christian).

Die Schuldigkeit des ersten Gebots

11 years old

I

IT IS PROBABLE that more people have visited the birthplace of Mozart in Salzburg (Getreidegasse No. 9) than that of any other composer. It is certain that more have made pilgrimages to the grave of any other composer, for the exact whereabouts of Mozart's grave in Vienna are unknown. The spirit of music is still palpable in the city of Vienna: the music of Mozart, of course, but also of Haydn, Beethoven, Schubert, the Strauss family, Mahler, Lehár, Richard Strauss and Berg. Salzburg, however, remains the city of Mozart, and Mozart alone. As a young man, Mozart's chief desire was to get away from it and to make his fortune in Vienna. But the music he wrote as a young man, the serenades, divertimenti, the violin concertos and the early piano concertos, all are imbued with a fresh, spring-like gaiety of spirit that even today still seems to characterize the lovely (and, out of festival time, quiet) town on the Salzach river, with the Bavarian alps to the west, and the idyllic lakes and mountains of Upper Austria to the east.

Wolfgang Amadeus Mozart was born in Salzburg on 27 January, 1756. His father, Leopold Mozart, was a violinist and composer in the service of the Prince Archbishop of Salzburg, and had written a treatise on violin-playing, *Versuch einer gründlichen Violinschule*, which was published a few months after the birth of Wolfgang, the seventh and last of his children. His wife, Anna Maria Pertl, was from the nearby town of St Gilgen on the Wolfgangsee. Leopold's ambition was to become, in due course, Kapellmeister, or leading musician, in the Archbishop's Court. It was an ambition he was never to achieve. By the time Wolfgang reached his eighth year, Leopold had become Vice-Kapellmeister, a post he occupied until his death. But by this time Leopold's ambition had altered, for he had discovered young Wolfgang to be a musical prodigy.

Wolfgang and his sister Maria Anna were the only survivors of the seven children. Maria Anna, or 'Nannerl' as she was called by the family, was four and a half years older than Wolfgang; when she was seven her father began to give her lessons on the clavier. It was soon found that the three-year-old boy liked to sit at the keyboard, picking out thirds and showing obvious delight in the harmonies thus produced. In his fourth year, his father began to teach him simple pieces to play, and, as Nannerl was to recall many years later, 'he learned a piece in an hour, and a minuet in half an hour, so that he could play it faultlessly and with the greatest delicacy, and keeping exactly in time. He made such progress that at the age of five he was already composing little pieces, which he played to his father who wrote them down'.[1]

Leopold was so excited by his youngest child's precocious musicianship that he became determined to make a famous musician of the boy. Doubtless his motives were impure, in the sense that they were mixed. Motives usually are. A child prodigy must have represented an enormous financial asset to a hard-pressed family, and Leopold was to squeeze the utmost commercial advantage out of his son's genius while he was still a child and thus a phenomenon. But it is also surely true that he believed his son's gifts to be God-given, and saw it as his duty to make them known to the world. Mozart's biographers have speculated as to whether the composer might have lived beyond the tragically brief span of less than thirty-six years had he not spent his childhood being dragged across Europe on exhausting concert tours, and exposed to the dangers of smallpox, scarlet fever and other diseases, most of which he contracted at one time or another. Perhaps he would have lived longer, but we know from his letters that he himself enjoyed his hectic, exciting childhood and his travels to foreign countries, and also that, although music was his entire life, he was a high-spirited, amiable child, and no infant prig. He received his entire education, in music and in the humanities, from his father; and, as one of his father's Court colleagues, the trumpeter and violinist Johann Schachtner, was later to recall, 'it was of small matter to him what he was given to learn; he simply wanted to learn, and he left the choice to his dearly loved father as to what field he was to work in'. Two fascinating and indeed moving stories of the young Wolfgang come from Schachtner, in a long letter he wrote to Nannerl some months after Wolfgang's death. One of them describes the baby composer:

I once went with your father to your house, after the Thursday service. We found the four-year-old Wolfgängerl busy with his pen.
Papa: What are you doing?
Wolfgang: Writing a clavier concerto; it will soon be done.
Papa: Let me see it.
Wolfgang: It's not finished yet.
Papa: Never mind, let me see it. It must be something very fine.
His father took it from him and showed me a smudge of notes. (Little Wolfgängerl, knowing no better, dipped the pen to the bottom of the inkwell each time, and so, when he put it to the paper a drop of ink was bound to fall

[1] Quoted in *Mozart: a documentary biography* by Otto Erich Deutsch (London, 1965).

off; but that did not disturb him; drawing the palm of his hand across it, he wiped it away and wrote on.)

At first we laughed at what seemed such nonsense, but your father then began to observe the theme, the notes and music; he stared long at the sheet, and then tears of joy and delight fell from his eyes. 'Look, Herr Schachtner,' he said, 'how correct and orderly it is; only it can't be used, for it is so very difficult that no one could play it.' Wolfgängerl said: 'That's why it's a concerto, you must practise till you get it right, look, this is how it goes.' He began to play and managed to get just enough out of it for us to see what he intended. At that time he had the firm conviction that playing concertos and working miracles were the same thing.[1]

Schachtner's other story concerns Wolfgang's prowess as a violinist, at the age of six. Another colleague, Wenzl, had brought to the Mozarts six trios he had composed, about which he wanted Leopold's advice. The trios were played, Wenzl on first violin, Schachtner second violin, with Leopold Mozart playing the base line on the viola.

Wolfgängerl begged to be allowed to play the second violin, but your father refused him this foolish request, because he had never had instruction on the violin, and your father thought that he could not possibly play anything. Wolfgang said: 'You don't need to have studied in order to play second violin,' whereupon your father insisted that he go away and not bother us any more. Wolfgang began to weep bitterly and slunk off with his little violin [a toy which he had recently got as a present in Vienna]. I asked them to let him play with me. Your father eventually said: 'Play with Herr Schachtner, but so softly that we can't hear you, or you will have to go.' And so it was settled, and Wolfgang played with me. I soon noticed with astonishment that I was quite superfluous, I quietly put my violin down and looked at your father.[2]

After he had been teaching Wolfgang and Nannerl for three years, Leopold Mozart decided the time had come to 'proclaim to the world a prodigy that God has vouchsafed to be born in Salzburg',[3] and made plans to embark upon the first of those journeys which were to occupy so much of Wolfgang's time for the next ten years. The best way to make him known abroad was to introduce him to the various courts of Europe, the nearest one to Salzburg being the court of the Bavarian Elector, Maximilian Josef III, in Munich. Accordingly Leopold and the two children set off on 12 January, 1762, about two weeks before Wolfgang's sixth birthday. The children's accomplishments included playing both clavier and violin, while Wolfgang could also play the organ, conduct, sing (he had appeared some months earlier in Salzburg in an opera composed by Johann Ernst Eberlin for the Archbishop's

[1] Quoted in *Life of Mozart* by Otto Jahn (London, 1882).
[2] Jahn, op. cit.
[3] Quoted in *Mozart and His Times* by Erich Schenk (London, 1960).

name day), and, of course, compose. The Mozarts' three-week stay in Munich was successful enough to encourage Leopold to plan a longer journey later in the year, to Vienna and the court of Maria Theresa, by way of Passau and Linz.

This time, the entire family travelled. In Passau Leopold succeeded in persuading the new Bishop, Count Josef Maria Thun-Hohenstein, to give a hearing to Wolfgang. The Bishop rewarded the lad with one ducat, which, however one computes its modern value, was not a generous sum! The family continued their journey by sailing down the Danube to Linz. Another passenger on the boat was Count Herberstein, Dean of the Cathedral at Passau, who befriended them. At Linz the Mozarts stayed at the Dreifaltigkeit (Trinity) Inn in the Hofgasse, kept by the Kiener sisters, 'two spinsters who, since the death of their parents, have taken charge of the house and who are so fond of my children that they do everything they possibly can for us'.[1] It was in this inn that Wolfgang gave his first public performance, on 1 October, 1762, when he was heard by Count Leopold Schlick, the Governor of Upper Austria, and his wife, and also by the young Count Karl Hieronymous Pálffy, Court Councillor in the Ministry of Commerce in Vienna. These aristocrats urged the Mozarts to proceed to Vienna as quickly as possible, where they would be assured of a warm welcome at Maria Theresa's court; indeed Pálffy, who preceded them to Vienna, was the first to inform the capital of the *Wunderkind* from Salzburg.

The journey down the Danube by passenger boat to Vienna continued, with stops at Mauthausen, Ybbs and Stein, then through the beautiful wine country of the Wachau to the Danube Canal Pier, Vienna. Wolfgang so entranced the customs officer by playing the violin for him, that the man asked permission to visit the family in Vienna, and allowed their baggage to pass free of duty. Once settled in their quarters in the Tiefer Graben, Leopold lost no time in setting about achieving introductions to the aristocracy, with the help of the friends he had already made, and three days after their arrival the children performed at the Palace of Count Thomas Vinciguerra Collalto which is in the square Am Hof, next to the Jesuit Church. Within the next few days they met Count Johann Wilczek, the Vice-Chancellor Count Franz Colloredo, the young Countess Friderike Waldstein, the Hungarian Chancellor Count Pálffy (father of the young count they had met in Passau), Bishop Esterházy and many others. 'All the ladies are in love with my boy,' Leopold wrote to his friend Hagenauer. 'We are already being talked of everywhere, and when, on the 10th, I was alone at the

---

[1] Leopold Mozart in a letter to Lorenz Hagenauer, his friend and landlord in Salzburg: Linz, 3 October, 1762. The Mozart family's letters are published in *Die Briefe Mozarts und seiner Familie* (edited by Ludwig Schiedermair: Munich, 1914) and in English translation in *The Letters of Mozart and his Family* (edited by Emily Anderson: London, 1938).

opera, I heard the Archduke Leopold from his box say a number of things to another box, namely that there was a boy in Vienna who played the clavier most excellently.'[1]

On 13 October the children performed at the palace of Schönbrunn before the Empress Maria Theresa, her consort the Emperor Francis I, and their daughter, the seven-year-old Marie Antoinette, future Queen of France. An eyewitness account of the occasion reveals that Wolfgang was greatly charmed by Marie Antoinette. 'When he was taken to the apartments of the Empress Maria Theresa and shown around by the little princes and princesses, he had the misfortune to slip, for he was unaccustomed to walking on such polished floors. None was quicker to spring to his aid than the little Archduchess Marie Antoinette. This so touched his heart that he went straightway to the Empress and extolled the Princess's kindness.'[2] And Leopold wrote to Hagenauer: 'Their Majesties received us with such extraordinary graciousness that, when I shall tell of it, people will declare that I have made it up. Suffice it to say that Wolferl jumped up on the Empress's lap, threw his arms around her neck, and kissed her heartily.'[3]

The round of aristocratic engagements continued. The day after their presentation at Schönbrunn, the family visited the Countess Maria Theresia Kinsky (*née* Marchesa Rofrano: a family name familiar to admirers of Strauss and Hofmannsthal's *Der Rosenkavalier*),[4] and then went on to the palace of the Lord High Steward, Count Anton von Ulfeld, where they met the Count's daughter Wilhelmine, the wife of Count Franz Joseph Thun. The following week the Mozarts were summoned again to Schönbrunn where the children gave a concert, after which Wolfgang complained of a pain around his waist which a doctor diagnosed as a kind of scarlet fever, but which later researchers believe to have been a nodular rash. He was seriously ill for almost two weeks, and on his recovery gave a concert in the house of Doctor Johann von Bernhard, Professor of Medicine at Vienna University, the physician who had attended him. More contacts with the upper classes were made, with Count Harrach at his palace on the street called Freyung, with the French Ambassador who invited the family to Versailles, and with the Imperial Paymaster who handed Leopold an honorarium of one hundred ducats and courteously invited the Mozarts to remain longer in Vienna. At the invitation of the Pálffys, they spent two weeks in Pressburg (now Bratislava in Czechoslovakia), and finally, on New

---

[1] 16 October, 1762.

[2] Quoted in Schenk, op. cit.   [3] 16 October, 1762.

[4] The previous evening they had been the guests of Prince Joseph Friedrich von Saxe-Hildburghausen at the Rofrano Palace (now the Auersperg Palace). In *Der Rosenkavalier*, it is not only Oktavian's family name, Rofrano, which has Mozartian connections, but also his pet name, 'Quinquin', which was the nickname of Count Franz Esterhàzy in whose memory Mozart wrote his Masonic Mourning Music, K. 477.

Year's Eve, left Vienna in a new carriage which Leopold had bought, arriving back in Salzburg on 5 January, 1763.

Wolfgang fell ill almost immediately with acute rheumatism, but six months later the entire family set forth again, this time on a grand tour of Europe which was to last three and a half years. They travelled in their recently acquired carriage, accompanied by their nineteen-year-old servant, Sebastian Winter; their first stop was Munich where Wolfgang performed before the Bavarian nobility, at the palace of the Elector. In Augsburg, Leopold inserted an advertisement in the local newspaper, in the form of a letter to the editor, ostensibly from a resident of Vienna:

> Conceive if you can of a girl aged eleven years who plays the most difficult sonatas of the greatest masters on the clavichord or harpsichord with the most distinct execution, with almost incredible ease, and in the best taste. That alone would be enough to astonish many persons. But we are transported with utter amazement when we see a boy of six years sitting at a harpsichord, and hear him not only playing the same sonatas, trios and concertos manfully, not at all like a child, but also hear him improvising from his head, now cantabile, now with chords, for whole hours at a time, and producing the best ideas in contemporary taste, or reading at sight to accompany symphonies, arias and recitatives at grand concerts. Tell me, does this not exceed all powers of the imagination? And yet it is the pure truth![1]

The Mozarts gave three public concerts at the Hotel Zu den Drei Königen, but the financial results were disappointing. Travelling through Ulm towards Stuttgart, they learned at Plochingen, where they had stopped to change horses, that Duke Karl Eugen of Württemberg and his court were not at Stuttgart but at the Duke's palace at Ludwigsburg. They made their way to Ludwigsburg, but were not received by the Duke. His Kapellmeister, the composer Jomelli, arranged a performance in his own house in the presence of a few of the court musicians, after which the Mozarts proceeded to Schwetzingen, the summer residence of the Elector Palatine, Karl Theodor, whose principal residence was at Mannheim. In Schwetzingen, Wolfgang heard for the first time the famous Mannheim Orchestra which was renowned for its precision, its virtuoso execution and its expressiveness. Leopold wrote to Hagenauer: 'The orchestra is undeniably the best in Germany. It consists altogether of people who are young and of good character, not drunkards, gamblers or dissolute rascals, so that both their conduct and their playing are admirable.'[2]

The tour continued. From Schwetzingen they proceeded to Heidelberg, then on to Mannheim, Worms, and Mainz. From Mainz they made a detour by boat to Frankfurt am Main where they gave a concert at the residence of Count van Pergen, the Imperial Envoy. The

[1] Quoted in Schenk, op. cit.   [2] 19 July, 1763.

fourteen-year-old Goethe was present at the concert with his father; sixty-seven years later he was to say to his biographer Eckermann, 'I still remember quite clearly the little fellow with his wig and sword'.[1] After visiting several towns in the vicinity of Mainz, the family went on to Coblenz where they were heard by the Elector and the Coblenz nobility. In Aachen they met Princess Amalia, sister of Frederick III of Prussia, who invited them to Berlin. But, as Leopold noted,[2] 'she herself has no money, and her whole equipage and court retinue resemble a physician's suite as closely as one drop of water another. If the kisses she gave my children, Wolfgang especially, had all been louis d'or, we should be quite happy.'

Travelling through the Austrian Netherlands to Brussels where they wasted a month loitering at the court of Prince Charles of Lorraine ('This Prince spends his time hunting, guzzling and drinking, and in the end it appears that he has no money'[3]), the Mozarts eventually reached Paris on 18 November, 1763, where Leopold made the most of the letters of introduction he had accumulated in Salzburg, Vienna and *en route*. For the five months they remained in Paris, they were able to stay at the palace of Count van Eyck, the Bavarian Minister, whose wife, a daughter of Count Arco of Salzburg, proved a very good friend to them. Leopold made the acquaintance of Melchior Grimm, an influential critic, Encyclopédist and key figure in the Enlightenment,who publicized the children, especially Wolfgang, and arranged their first concert. At a court dinner at Versailles, the Mozarts met the royal family: Louis XV, his Queen and his children and, of course, Madame de Pompadour. La Pompadour was less amiable than the Queen. When Wolfgang attempted to kiss her, she pushed him away, which caused him to exclaim: 'Who does she think she is, not wanting to kiss me. The Empress Maria Theresa herself kissed me!'[4]

Once the Mozart children had been received at court, the French nobility began to take notice of them, and even to compete for the privilege of inviting them to their houses. Minor irritations in Paris included a throat ailment to which Wolfgang succumbed for some days, and the defection of their servant Sebastian to the Prince of Fürstenberg. But their Paris concerts were financially successful, and encouraged by this Leopold decided to continue on to London. After resting in Calais for a few days, looking at the sea and watching the ebb and flow of the tides for the first time in their lives, the Mozarts braved the Channel crossing. 'Thank God we have safely crossed the Maxglanerbach, but not without making a heavy contribution to it in vomiting.'[5] Their first

[1] *Gespräche mit Goethe* (Leipzig, 1908), II, p. 178.   [2] 17 October, 1763.
[3] Leopold Mozart to Hagenauer, 4 November, 1763.
[4] Schenk, op. cit.
[5] Leopold Mozart to Hagenauer, 25 April, 1764. The Maxglanerbach is a very small stream in the Salzburg suburb of Maxglan.

night in London was spent at the White Bear in Piccadilly, after which they took rooms at the house of a hairdresser named John Cousins in Cecil Court (now No. 19), St Martin's Lane. Almost immediately they were invited to court, for the twenty-seven-year-old George III and his German Queen were great lovers of music, and the Queen was a competent player on the harpsichord.

On April 27th, we were with the King and Queen in the Queen's Palace in St James's Park [Buckingham House, on the site of today's Buckingham Palace] so that by the fifth day of our arrival we were already at court. The present was only twenty-four guineas, which we were given immediately we left the King's apartment, but the graciousness with which both their Majesties received us can hardly be described. In short, their informal and friendly manner made us forget that they were King and Queen of England. At all the other courts we have been received with the greatest courtesy, but the welcome we have had here exceeds all the others. A week later, as we were walking in St James's Park, the King and Queen drove past in their carriage, and although we were all dressed differently they recognized us and greeted us. The King opened the window, leaned out and saluted us, and especially our Wolfgang, nodding and waving to us.[1]

The following month Wolfgang and Nannerl gave a second concert at court, at which he played at sight pieces by Abel, Johann Christian Bach, Handel and Wagenseil, and accompanied the Queen who sang an aria. The Mozarts met the Italian singers and musicians of the King's Theatre, Haymarket, and their principal composer, Johann Christian Bach, son of the great Johann Sebastian. They met, too, the English composers associated with the English opera at Covent Garden, among them Dr Thomas Arne. A public concert at which the children played a concerto for two harpsichords was so successful that Leopold took in one hundred guineas, and a few weeks later Wolfgang played at a concert in aid of the Lying-in Hospital which had just been established. When Leopold caught a severe cold, the family moved to 'a spot outside the town, whither I was carried in a sedan chair, to improve my appetite and build up my strength in the fresh air. It has one of the most beautiful views in the world. There are gardens wherever I look, and in the distance splendid castles.'[2] This rustic paradise was the village of Chelsea, and the house in which the Mozarts lived for seven weeks is now 182, Ebury Street, Pimlico. In this house Wolfgang composed his first three symphonies,[3] works which reveal the influence of Johann Christian Bach towards whom he was always to feel the warmest regard.

Returning to the metropolis, the Mozarts took up residence in the

[1] Leopold to Hagenauer, 28 May, 1764.
[2] Leopold to Hagenauer, 9 August, 1764.
[3] K. 16, K. 17, K. 19. K is for Köchel, the nineteenth-century Austrian musicographer who catalogued Mozart's works.

house of a Mr Thomas Williamson in Thrift Street, Soho (now cockneyfied into Frith Street). Wolfgang composed six sonatas, for clavier with either flute or violin,[1] which were published and dedicated to the Queen, who responded with a gift of fifty guineas. More public concerts followed, the last of them in May, 1765, at Hickford's Great Room in Brewer Street, Soho. These brought in less money than Leopold expected, and he hinted obscurely at the reason why 'we are not being treated more generously':

> I did not accept a proposal which was made to me. But what is the point of my saying more about a matter on which I have come to a decision after mature consideration and many sleepless nights, and which is now finished with, as I will not bring up my children in so dangerous a place, where most of the inhabitants have no religion, and where one sees only evil examples to follow. You would be amazed if you saw the way children are brought up here, to say nothing of certain religious matters.[2]

By now the Mozarts had exhausted London. An advertisement in the *Public Advertizer*[3] informs us that Wolfgang and Nannerl gave a series of performances in the Swan and Harp Tavern, Cornhill, every day from twelve to three, admission 2s. 6d., and that 'the two children will also play with four hands on the same keyboard, covering it with a cloth so that they cannot see the keys'. On 1 August after a stay of fifteen months, the family left England. They had intended to return to Salzburg via Paris and Milan, but the Dutch Ambassador in London persuaded them to visit The Hague, as the Princess of Weilburg, sister of the Prince of Orange, was extremely eager to meet Wolfgang. They had beautiful weather and a good wind for their crossing to Calais where they collected their own carriage again, and proceeded to Lille. They were forced to remain in Lille for four weeks as Wolfgang was ill with what his father described as a very bad cold, after which Leopold himself became ill. Early in September they crossed the Dutch border, travelling through Ghent and Antwerp to The Hague.

The court and public appearances at The Hague followed the usual pattern, but it was here that both children became seriously ill with what appears to have been a form of typhoid fever. First Nannerl, then Wolfgang succumbed. Each was ill for about a month with fever and delirium, their lives were thought to be in great danger, and Wolfgang lay in a coma for several days. His recovery was slow, and his father wrote that he was emaciated and changed almost beyond recognition. By mid-January, however, all was well, and the children were able to resume their performances. In Amsterdam, Wolfgang for the first time conducted one of his own symphonies, K. 22, which he had composed at The Hague. In May they were back in Paris, which they left two months

---

[1] K. 10–15.   [2] 19 March, 1765.   [3] 9 July, 1765.

later to return home via Dijon, Lyons, Geneva, Lausanne, Berne, Zürich, Donaueschingen (where they found their former servant Sebastian, who had become personal valet to the Prince Joseph Wenzel von Fürstenberg), Augsburg and Munich. The plan to visit Milan had been abandoned. On Sunday 30 November, 1766, the Mozarts arrived back in Salzburg.

The children, mentally and physically exhausted, must have been relieved and happy to be home, although Wolfgang, once the initial excitement of seeing his old friends and colleagues had worn off, must also have felt very unsettled after his travels. Salzburg no doubt seemed small and not exactly lively compared with, for instance, Paris and London. But he returned to his studies and continued to compose. Early in 1767, he was given the opportunity to compose his first opera, which he completed at the beginning of March.

That statement must immediately be qualified. Wolfgang was invited to compose only one of three acts, and the work was not precisely an opera. During Lent, when the secular theatres and opera houses had to close, it was the practice for the ecclesiastical chapels to circumvent this irksome ban on performance by producing so-called oratorios to German texts of pious religious sentiment. It was also not unknown for more than one composer to be commissioned, so that a work might consist of several acts or movements, each by a different composer.

II

That an eleven-year-old child should be given so important a commission as to share with two leading Salzburg composers the composition of a sacred *Singspiel* or oratorio shows that the Archbishop must have been impressed by the reports which had reached him of the achievements abroad of the *Wunderkind*. The text of the work was written by someone identified on the title-page of the printed libretto simply as 'J.A.W.' There is a copy of the libretto in the Studienbibliothek, Salzburg, the title-page of which reads as follows:

The Obligation

of the first and foremost Commandment[1] (Mark 12, v. 30)

And thou shalt love the Lord thy God with all thy heart, and with all thy soul, and with all thy mind, and with all thy strength.

In three parts

set forth for consideration

by J. A. W.

[1] 'Gebottes': the accepted modern spelling is 'Gebots'.

Part One set to music by Herr Wolfgang Motzard,[1]
      aged 10 years
Part Two by Herr Johann Michael Heiden,[2]
      Concertmaster to His Serene Highness
Part Three by Herr Anton Cajetan Adlgasser, Chamber
      Composer and Organist to His Serene Highness

Printed in Salzburg by the inheritress of the estate of Johann
Joseph Mayr, Court and Academic Printer and Bookseller, 1767.

Mozart's cataloguer Köchel thought that J. A. W. was probably
Johann Adam Wieland (1710–1774) who in 1767 was the Pastor of
Friedorfing. The leading Mozart scholar of today, Professor Erich
Schenk, Head of the Music Department of the University of Vienna,
states quite categorically that 'the rector of the Benedictine Latin School,
Jakob Anton (Marianus) Wimmer, wrote the three-act oratorio *Die
Schuldigkeit des ersten Gebots*.'[3] But the diary (in Latin) of Father Beda
Hübner, Librarian of St Peter's Abbey, Salzburg, at the time, and
secretary to his uncle the Abbot, tells otherwise:

> 12th March, Thursday. Today after evening prayers there took place at Court
> in the so-called Knights' Hall an oratorio set to music for five persons, that is
> to say three women and two men, namely Herr Meissner and Herr Spitzeder.
> The German text was by Herr Weiser, a merchant and councillor, the music
> by Wolfgang Mozart, a boy of ten years.[4]

Herr Weiser is Ignaz Anton von Weiser (1701–1785), a Salzburg
merchant. He was the half-brother of Maria Theresia Hagenauer, wife
of Leopold's friend and landlord, and he became Mayor of Salzburg in
1772 for a period of three years. The pious purpose of his libretto was
'not only to delight the mind but also to elevate the soul' and to bring it
to salvation. The characters are a lukewarm Christian and the various
abstractions which influence him: Worldliness, Divine Mercy, Divine
Justice, and the Christian Spirit. In Part One, the Christian is stirred into
enthusiasm by these virtues, and enticed from the clutches of worldliness.

---

[1] Mozart's name was spelt variously during his lifetime. Other spellings met with include Mozzard, Mozhart and Mozer.

[2] 'Heiden' is Michael Haydn, younger brother of Joseph, and concert master to the Archbishop.

[3] Op. cit.

[4] The diary is today in the Library of St Peter's Abbey, Salzburg. The extract quoted was published in the Mozart Jahrbuch 1957 (Salzburg, 1958). The information concerning the librettist is also given in the preface to *Die Schuldigkeit* in the *Neue Mozart-Ausgabe*, Serie I, Werkgruppe 4, Band 1 (Bärenreiter, 1958).

III

More than one Mozart commentator asserts that the Hon. Daines Barrington, who produced a report on the child Mozart for the Royal Society in 1770, told the story that, in order to be certain that his father did not help him to compose *Die Schuldigkeit des ersten Gebots*, the Archbishop had Wolfgang locked up in a room in his palace for a week. The story is usually retold only to be refuted. 'Recent investigations', says Schenk,[1] 'make it appear more credible that this incident applies to the *Grabmusik* (K. 42), composed for Easter Week.' But nowhere in his report to the Royal Society does Barrington mention *Die Schuldigkeit*. He merely says, without mentioning a date or even a year, 'I am also informed that the prince of Saltzbourg [*sic*], not crediting that such masterly compositions were really those of a child, shut him up for a week, during which he was not permitted to see anyone, and was left only with music paper, and the words of an oratorio. During this short time he composed a very capital oratorio, which was most highly approved of upon being performed.'[2]

Whether it was *Die Schuldigkeit* or, a few weeks later, the *Grabmusik* (Funeral Music) cantata which was written under such unpromising conditions, there is no doubt that the young Mozart produced these works without parental assistance, and most expeditiously. His music for *Die Schuldigkeit* consists of a Sinfonia or Overture and eight separate numbers, each preceded by recitative. The facts that the work is described as a 'geistliches Singspiel' (Spiritual play with music) and that the libretto contains stage directions suggest that it was intended to be acted, not merely sung as an oratorio. It is unlikely, however, that the first performance, during Lent, would have been staged.

The Sinfonia, scored for strings, oboes, bassoons and horns, is a two-part *allegro*, baroque in style and sentiment. The *recitativo secco* which advances the argument, though hardly dramatic, is for the most part correct and intelligible in declamation. The action begins with the lukewarm Christian asleep in the shrubbery while the personified Spirits of Christianity, Mercy and Justice debate. The first aria, 'Mit Jammer muss ich schauen', is sung by the Spirit of Christianity. The music is dignified and simple and the range moderate, taking the tenor voice no higher than G. Like the other numbers it is a *da capo* piece: its central *andante* section sounds a more personally felt note than the outer *allegri*. The second aria, 'Ein ergrimmter Löwe brüllet', sung by the soprano, Mercy, calls for a certain degree of agility, but one is still conscious that the young composer is deliberately not taxing his probably somewhat unaccomplished singers. Between this and the following number, the recitative, formerly accompanied only by a harpsichord, broadens

[1] Op. cit.
[2] Vol. LX of the Philosophical Transactions of the Royal Society (London, 1771).

and deepens for several bars into fully accompanied recitative, reverting
again to *recitativo secco* before the third aria, 'Erwache, fauler Knecht', for
Justice (soprano), which is a stately yet insistent *andante*. The Christian
having been awakened by Justice's aria, the recitative which follows for
Worldliness, Christianity and himself is mostly *recitativo accompagnato*,
the other instruments being joined by an alto trombone. Worldliness
(soprano) contributes the fourth aria, 'Hat der Schöpfer dieses Leben
samt der Erde uns gegeben', a captivating and appropriately worldly
allegro grazioso. The Christian's aria, 'Jener Donnerworte Kraft', is a
somewhat characterless *andante*, with an obbligato part for the alto
trombone, which was presumably prompted by a reference in the text to
the 'Posaunenschall' or sound of the trombones on the Day of Judgment. The sixth aria, 'Schildre einen Philosophen', sung by Worldliness,
is unremarkable, but the seventh, 'Manches Übel', is a charming and
tender *allegro* for the tenor Spirit of Christianity, and by far the most
accomplished number of the score [Ex. 1]. One is not surprised that
Mozart made use of it again the following year in what one might call his

Ex. 1

first 'real' opera, *La finta semplice*. The first part of *Die Schuldigkeit des ersten
Gebots* ends with an attractive trio for the three virtuous spirits, 'Lasst mir
eurer Gnade Schein'. The Christian has still far to go on the road from
lassitude to zeal, but for the remainder of his journey he will be accompanied not by Mozart but by two other composers.

   The Mozart scholar Edward J. Dent would have both this first stage
work of the young Mozart and its successor *Apollo et Hyacinthus*
'dismissed at once',[1] which seems an oddly unsympathetic judgment.
Even the sensitive and knowledgeable Alfred Einstein[2] advises us not to
'occupy ourselves with the analysis' of these and other works of Mozart's
youth. One is tempted perversely to over-praise in order to redress the
balance. This sacred Singspiel by an eleven-year-old child is no
masterpiece, but it is more than competently put together; also, a certain
tender and individual charm emerges intermittently from a score which,
for the most part, sounds like a skilful imitation of Johann Christian
Bach. It would be difficult to make out a very strong case for staging the
work today, though the London Camden Festival produced it in 1968 in
a double bill with *Il sogno di Scipione*, a later piece of Mozart juvenilia.

   [1] Dent, *Mozart's Operas* (London, 1913).
   [2] Alfred Einstein, *Mozart: his Character, his Work* (London, 1947).

II

Apollo et Hyacinthus

(Musical intermezzo to a Latin Comedy)

K. 38

Dramatis personae:

Oebalus, King of Lacedaemonia	(tenor)
Melia, daughter of Oebalus	(soprano)
Hyacinthus, son of Oebalus	(soprano)
Apollo	(alto)
Zephyrus, friend of Hyacinthus	(alto)
Two priests of Apollo	(bass)

LIBRETTO by Father Rufinus Widl, partly drawn from Ovid's *Metamorphoses*

TIME: mythical antiquity

PLACE: Greece

FIRST PERFORMED in the Great Hall of the University of Salzburg, 13 May, 1767, with Mathias Stadler (Oebalus); Felix Fuchs (Melia); Christian Enzinger (Hyacinthus); Johann Ernst (Apollo); Joseph Vonderthon (Zephyrus); Joseph Bründl (First Priest); Jakob Moser (Second Priest)

MITRIDATE
RE DI PONTO,
DRAMMA PER MUSICA
DA RAPPRESENTARSI
NEL REGIO-DUCAL TEATRO
DI MILANO
Nel Carnovale dell' Anno 1771.
D E D I C A T O
A SUA ALTEZZA SERENISSIMA
I L
DUCA DI MODENA,
REGGIO, MIRANDOLA ec. ec.
AMMINISTRATORE,
E CAPITANO GENERALE
DELLA LOMBARDIA AUSTRIACA
ec. ec.

IN MILANO.)(MDCCLXX.

Nella Stamperia di Giovanni Montani.

M.169 a CON LICENZA DE' SUPERIORI.

PERSONAGGI.

MITRIDATE, Re di Ponto, e d' altri
Regni, amante d' Aspasia.
*Sig. Cavaliere Guglielmo D' Ettore Virtuoso
di Camera di S. A. S. Elettorale di Baviera.*
ASPASIA, promessa sposa di Mitridate,
e già dichiarata Regina,
Signora Antonia Bernascon̄i.
SIFARE, figliuolo. di Mitridate, e di
Stratonica, amante d' Aspasia,
Sig. Pietro Benedetti, detto Sartorino.
FARNACE, primo figliuolo di Mitri-
date, amante della medesima,
Sig. Giuseppe Cicognani.
ISMENE, figlia del Re de' Parti, amante
di Farnace,
Signora Anna Francesca Varese.
MARZIO, Tribuno Romano, amico di
Farnace,
Sig Gaspare Bassano.
ARBATE, Governatore di Ninfea,
Sig. Pietro Muschietti.

Compositore della Musica.

Il Sig. Cavaliere Amadeo Wolfgango Mozart, Accademico Filarmonico di Bologna, e Maestro della Musica di Camera
di S. A. Rma il Principe, ed Arcivescovo
di Salisburgo.

ATTO

M.169 b.

ALTEZZA
SERENISSIMA.

Ccoci ossequiosamente
ad implorare da V. A. S. un
Clementissimo Patrocinio, ed
Aggradimento a favore della
presente Drammatica Rappresen-
tazione, che per Prima espo-
niamo sopra queste Ducali Regie
Scene, solito Carnovalesco Inter-

M.169 c.
3
te-

---

tenimento. La scelta di Canto,
e di Ballo, unita a quei decorosi
accompagnamenti, co' quali ab-
biamo diligentemente procurato
arricchirla, speriamo, che
meritar possa da questa Nobiltà
generosa una favorevole appro-
vazione, qualora però assistita
ella sia dal Superiore Compati-
mento di V. A. S., alla quale
con profondissima osservanza
presentiamo, protestandoci ris-
pettosissimamente
Di V. A. S.

Umil̄mi Divot̄mi Ser. Obl̄mi
Gli Associati.

M.169 d.

Four pages from the libretto of *Mitridate*, published in Milan, 1770.

M.178 a

M.178 b

M.178 c

M.178 d

Costume designs by Heinrich Lefler for a production of *Zaide*
in Vienna, 1902.

Apollo et Hyacinthus

'ON THE 18TH March, 1767 to little Mozartl, for the composition of the music to an oratorio, a gold medal of 12 ducats', we are told by the Register of the Salzburg Privy Purse,[1] and early the following month Mozart's part of *Die Schuldigkeit des ersten Gebots* was repeated. His next commission, which followed immediately, was to write the music for the Latin play which it was the custom for the students to perform at the University to mark the end of each term. The play was usually written by a member of the faculty, and was expected to treat of a religious or moral subject. Music was interspersed between the acts of the play, in the manner of the intermezzi or ballets which were played between the acts of operas in the secular, non-academic theatre. On 13 May, the play, performed by a cast largely drawn from the students of the Syntax class, was a tragedy, *Clementia Croesi*, by Father Rufinus Widl, Professor of Syntax at the University. The musical interludes were provided by a short opera, *Apollo et Hyacinthus*, its Latin libretto based on classical sources by the Reverend Professor, and its music composed by 'nobilis dominus Wolfgangus Mozart, undecennis, filius nobilis ac strenui domini Leopoldi Mozart, Capellae Magistri.'[2]

The ages of the cast ranged from twenty-three (Oebalus) to twelve (Hyacinthus), and the performance was accounted a great success. The Director of the Salzburg Gymnasium[3] noted that 'the music for it, composed by Wolfgang Mozart, a child of eleven, delighted everyone, and at night he gave us notable proofs of his musical art at the harpsichord.'

The full title of Father Widl's Latin comedy is *Apollo et Hyacinthus seu Hyacinthi Metamorphosis* (Apollo and Hyacinth, or The Metamorphosis of Hyacinth), and the Reverend Professor has cleaned up the myth considerably. Students of Ovid (or Robert Graves's *The Greek Myths*) will know that the Spartan prince Hyacinthus was a beautiful youth with

[1] In the Salzburg Provincial Archives.
[2] From the Libretto, a copy of which is in the Studienbibliothek, Salzburg.
[3] In the Minutes of the Gymnasium in the Salzburg Provincial Archives.

whom the god Apollo fell in love. But the West Wind was also in love
with Hyacinthus, and, one day when Apollo was teaching Hyacinthus
how to throw a discus, the insanely jealous West Wind (Zephyrus) caused
the discus to be arrested in flight and dashed against the boy's skull,
killing him. Apollo changed the dead youth into a flower, the hyacinth
on the base of whose petals his initials can still be seen. Father Widl,
however, must have felt that Greek bisexuality was somewhat
unedifying, for his characters are strictly heterosexual in their
behaviour. In his libretto, Hyacinthus and Zephyrus are friends.
Zephyrus is in love with Hyacinthus's sister Melia, who is also desired by
Apollo. The action begins with Zephyrus telling Hyacinthus of his love
for Melia and his jealousy of Apollo. Then Oebalus the King and his
daughter Melia appear, and make a sacrifice to Apollo. The sacrifice is
not accepted, and a thunderbolt scatters them all. Apollo appears,
having been banished by Jupiter, and seeks the protection of Oebalus.
(At this point the first two acts of the tragedy were performed.) Oebalus
informs Melia that Apollo demands her hand in marriage, and Melia
gives her delighted consent. Zephyrus now enters, announcing that
Hyacinthus has been slain by Apollo. Oebalus and Melia understandably turn against Apollo who, in a fury, causes Zephyrus to be
borne away by the winds. Melia reproaches Apollo. (Here, the final
two acts of the tragedy were performed.) Hyacinthus is now carried in,
dying, and declares that his murderer was not Apollo but Zephyrus.
Apollo changes Hyacinthus into a flower, and announces his own
betrothal to Melia.

Clearly, Ovid cannot be held responsible for Father Widl's libretto.
Indeed, the Preface in the *Neue Ausgabe* points out that Book 10 of Ovid's
Metamorphoses is clearly not the main source of the libretto, cites various
other classical versions of the myth, and suggests that Widl may have
used as an immediate source a *Lexikon Mythologicum* by Hederich
(Leipzig, 1741).

In his Preface in the *Neue Ausgabe*, the Viennese musicologist Alfred
Orel draws attention to the fact that *Clementia Croesi* and *Apollo et
Hyacinthus* together make an homogeneous whole, in an inner sense if
not in externals. There are parallels of motivation and incident in the
two libretti, but these need not concern us whose interest is only in
Mozart's work. *Apollo et Hyacinthus*, divorced from *Clementia Croesi*, makes
its own sense as an independent entity.

Mathias Stadler, who sang Oebalus, was a Scholar in Moral Theology
and Law; Felix Fuchs (Melia) was a Chorister and Student in the
Grammar Class; Christian Enzinger (Hyacinthus) was a Chorister and
Student in the Rudiments Class; Johann Ernst (Apollo) was a Chorister;
Joseph Vonderthon (Zephyrus) and Jakob Moser (Second Priest) were
Students in the Syntax Class; and Joseph Bründl (First Priest) was a
Student in the Poetry Class.

III

The Intrada or Overture to *Apollo et Hyacinthus*, a brief but well-constructed *allegro*, leads into a scene in recitative between Hyacinthus and Zephyrus, and later Oebalus and Melia. The Latin text appears not to have affected the young Mozart's natural skill in the setting of recitative, which sounds easy and uncontrived throughout the opera, though without reaching any heights of dramatic expression. The Chorus, 'Numen o Latonium', a stately *andante*, encloses a short solo in G major for Oebalus which possesses a touching dignity and simplicity reminiscent of Gluck (whose *Orfeo ed Euridice* had been produced in Vienna five years earlier, and who more recently had had two other operas staged there, at Schönbrunn and at the Burgtheater). After the thunderbolt – *Fulmen ignem et aram destruit* says the libretto – and more recitative, Hyacinthus has an aria, 'Saepe terrent Numina', an *allegro moderato* in B flat. Like most of the arias in *Apollo et Hyacinthus*, this is *da capo* in form; that is, it consists of two contrasting sections after which the first section is repeated. This seems to us today to be a form inhibitive of dramatic development, but really it is hardly more so than the aria and cabaletta which was soon to replace it in opera. The *da capo* aria reflects and conveys classical balance, while its successor portrays romantic unease: handled with dramatic skill, however, both types of aria can be made to represent much more complex states of feeling. Mozart does not achieve this kind of distinction anywhere in *Apollo et Hyacinthus* though he does frequently infuse a certain warmth into the atmosphere of stateliness contributed by the Latin verse.

In the recitative following Hyacinthus's aria, Apollo appears. His aria, 'Jam pastor Apollo' is not *da capo* in form, but a two-part piece whose initial calmly flowing *andantino* is followed by a brief *allegro*. Its orchestral postlude returns to the opening tempo, and brings the first act to an end.

At this point, the first two acts of the spoken tragedy, *Clementia Croesi*, were performed. The second act of *Apollo et Hyacinthus* begins with recitative for Oebalus and Melia in which Oebalus informs his daughter that Apollo seeks to marry her. The aria in which she (a boy soprano in the Salzburg performance) expresses her delight is a florid *allegro*, 'Laetari, iocari', formal rather than deeply felt. The ensuing recitative has to convey rather too much information, and does so somewhat clumsily and abruptly, but the aria for Zephyrus, 'En! duos conspicis', though slight, has a natural charm which we can now identify as Mozartian. Apollo has Zephyrus borne away by the winds in the recitative which follows, and then sings a duet with Melia, 'Discede crudelis!' in which the young Mozart reveals clearly that he is going to become a real composer of opera, for the duet is both lively and dramatic. It ends the second act, after which the third and fourth acts of the tragedy were performed.

After the recitative which opens Act III of *Apollo et Hyacinthus*, recitative which begins *secco* but into which the strings are introduced to fine effect, Oebalus has an aria, 'Ut navis in aequore luxuriante', a fierce *allegro* in which he expresses his rage at the murder of Hyacinthus. Recitative for Oebalus and Melia then leads to their duet, 'Natus cadit, atque Deus', perhaps the finest number in the score, expressive and imaginatively scored, its melody one of beauty and dignity [Ex. 2].

Ex. 2

After more recitative in which Apollo effects the transformation of Hyacinthus, the opera ends with a trio, 'Tandem post turbida fulmina', for Apollo, Melia and Oebalus, a joyous *allegro* in the young Wolfgang's most confident style.

Taken as a whole, *Apollo et Hyacinthus* is a firm step forward from *Die Schuldigkeit des ersten Gebots*; its libretto offered Mozart a little more opportunity for dramatic development, opportunity which he instinctively seized upon. One should not try to claim too much for the work, for it is basically no more than a pleasant piece of Salzburg baroque which has plenty of equals and indeed superiors among the works produced by local composers of the time. But there are occasional signs, or at least hints, of the mature Mozart, even if they are viewable only by hindsight.

There have been several revivals of *Apollo et Hyacinthus* in the twentieth century, the earliest at Rostock in 1922 in a German translation. During the Salzburg Festival of 1935 it was performed in a version for puppets. Though the work is not really suitable for professional presentation, schools might care to remember it when looking for an end-of-term opera.

III

La finta semplice

opera buffa in three acts

K. 51

Dramatis personae:

Fracasso, a Captain	(tenor)
Simone, his Lieutenant	(bass)
Don Cassandro, a rich gentleman	(bass)
Don Polidoro, his brother	(tenor)
Giacinta, their sister	(contralto)
Ninetta, chambermaid	(soprano)
Rosina, Fracasso's sister	(soprano)

LIBRETTO by Carlo Goldoni, revised by Marco Coltellini

TIME: mid-eighteenth century

PLACE: an estate near Cremona

FIRST PERFORMED at the Archbishop's Court, Salzburg, 1 May, 1769, with Joseph Meissner (Fracasso); Felix Winter (Simone); Joseph Hornung (Don Cassandro); Anton Franz Spitzeder (Don Polidoro); Maria Anna Braunhofer (Giacinta); Maria Anna Fesemayer (Ninetta); Magdalena Haydn (Rosina)

La finta semplice

AFTER BEING AT home in Salzburg attending to his duties at the Archbishop's Court for some months, Leopold Mozart became restless, and determined to embark upon another journey with his talented children. In September, 1767, the entire family set out for Vienna by coach, travelling via Lambach, Melk and St Pölten. In four days they reached Vienna where they took rooms in the Weihburggasse. Five weeks later they were giving concerts in Brünn and Olmütz (now Brno and Olomouc in Czechoslovakia). Both children became ill with smallpox, Wolfgang very seriously, but both recovered. By the following January they were back in Vienna where they were received at Court again by Maria Theresa and the new Emperor, her son Joseph II. In March the children performed for the Russian Ambassador in Vienna, Prince Galitsin, while in Salzburg the Prince-Archbishop Schrattenbach was giving instructions to his Pay Office that Leopold, unless he reported for duty in April, was to have his salary stopped.

According to Leopold, it was the Emperor Joseph II who first suggested that Wolfgang should write an opera for Vienna and who 'asked the boy twice whether he would like to compose an opera and conduct it himself'.[1] Wolfgang, Leopold tells us, said yes. But the Emperor may simply have been making polite conversation. In any case, the two leading Viennese theatres, the Burgtheater and the Theater am Kärntnertor, were under the control of an entrepreneur named Giuseppe Affligio (or Afflisio), one of those dubious Italian adventurers who seemed to do so well for themselves in eighteenth-century Vienna. A contract, stipulating a fee of one hundred ducats, was signed with Affligio, not for an *opera seria*, 'for no operas of that kind are being given now, and moreover people do not like them',[2] but for a comic opera or *opera buffa*. Wolfgang set to work composing a libretto provided by the Italian Marco Coltellini who had been the recognized court poet in Vienna since 1758. The title of the libretto, based on one by Carlo Goldoni, was *La finta semplice*. When Wolfgang had composed the first act, it was sent to be copied, and the parts were distributed to the singers who professed their delight and admiration. By the time the entire opera

[1] Leopold to Hagenauer, 3 February, 1768.
[2] Leopold to Hagenauer, 3 February, 1768.

was finished, however, various difficulties arose to hinder production. The impresario Affligio kept delaying the beginning of rehearsals, and instead put on other operas. Leopold was convinced that all the Viennese composers had schemed to prevent his son's opera being staged, but it seems more likely that Affligio was merely suffering from the malady of procrastination, not unknown to theatrical managers. It is true that a rumour was spread that it was not Wolfgang but his father who had composed the opera, and that Affligio claimed the singers had complained the work was unsingable. But Affligio was losing money on a company of French actors he had brought to Vienna and who were not drawing audiences, and he was not disposed to risk another failure.

These delays kept the Mozarts in Vienna throughout the summer of 1768. On 14 September, Leopold wrote to Hagenauer:

> Concerning Wolfgang's opera, all I can tell you is that an entire hell of musicians has risen up to prevent the proof of a child's ability. I cannot even insist on its performance, for if I do they have formed a conspiracy to stage it extremely badly and thus ruin it. I have been awaiting the return of the Emperor, otherwise I would have gone into battle long ago. Believe me I shall do everything that is necessary to protect the honour of my child.

A week later, Leopold presented a petition to the Emperor in which he set out all the facts of the case as he saw them, at considerable length. He claimed that the Italian singers thought the opera a marvel, that a first rehearsal had been held with full orchestra before the parts had been sufficiently studied, after which Affligio had suggested alterations which were subsequently made, that the opera was then passed over in favour of other works and that he had been unable to obtain a satisfactory explanation from Affligio, who had finally said to him that 'if I wanted to have the boy prostituted, he would ensure that the opera was ridiculed and hissed'.[1] The Emperor received Leopold graciously, and promised that justice would be done. But Emperors, even eighteenth-century Austrian ones, are no match for either civil servants or theatrical managers, and there was little that Joseph (the Emperor) could do, short of accepting entire financial responsibility for Affligio's theatrical affairs. This he was not willing to do. A year or two later Affligio became bankrupt and had to leave Vienna. In 1779 he was found guilty of forging bills of exchange in Florence and sentenced to the galleys for life.

The Mozarts remained in Vienna until the end of the year (see the following chapter), but La finta semplice did not reach the stage until the following year, and then not in Vienna but in Salzburg. The Archbishop of Salzburg, although he was not willing to pay Leopold for the months he was absent, was generous in another way. He commanded a

---

[1] The original of Leopold Mozart's petition is in the University Library, Glasgow. Printed in *Neue Mozartiana* (ed. H. G. Farmer and H. Smith: Glasgow, 1935).

performance of Wolfgang's *opera buffa* at his Court theatre on 1 May, 1769.

II

The libretto of *La finta semplice* ('The feigned idiot-girl' is an inelegant English equivalent) is by the Venetian playwright Carlo Goldoni (1707–1793). One of Goldoni's 'Drammi giocosi per musica', it had already been set to music by Salvatore Perillo, and staged during the carnival season of 1764 at the Theatro San Moisè in Venice. For Mozart it was slightly revised by Marco Coltellini, a playwright from Livorno who was at that time working in Vienna as Court poet. Coltellini contented himself with replacing some of the arias, and revising Goldoni's third act.

Act I: Fracasso, a Hungarian captain, and his lieutenant, Simone, have been billeted on the estate of two wealthy bachelors, Don Cassandro and Don Polidoro. Fracasso has fallen in love with Donna Giacinta, sister of the two brothers, while Simone has been flirting with Giacinta's maid Ninetta. Fracasso's sister, a Hungarian Baroness, is about to visit her brother, and the four lovers agree to a plan suggested by Ninetta, whereby the Baroness Rosina will pretend to be a simpleton which it is thought will intrigue the two brothers, one of whom is a pretended misogynist while the other is very much under the influence of his brother. This will divert the attention of the brothers from the activities of the two couples.

Ninetta leaves to meet Rosina and to instruct her. In due course the pretty simpleton arrives, and has little difficulty in enchanting Polidoro, who almost immediately makes a proposal of marriage to her. Rosina gives him no definite answer, but instead turns her attention to Cassandro, who does not melt quite so easily, though he is by no means unaffected by her charms. Rosina succeeds in extracting a valuable ring from Cassandro, who then invites everyone to a banquet in order to prevent Rosina from leaving with his ring still in her possession.

Act II: The banquet has not been a success. The two brothers, now both in love with Rosina, have quarrelled. While the somewhat drunken and befuddled Cassandro is asleep, Rosina replaces the ring on his finger. The brothers quarrel again over Rosina. Meanwhile, the four lovers have carried their plot a stage further. The two girls, mistress and maid, stage a joint disappearance, and the brothers are informed that Giacinta has taken the family jewellery. The brothers promise Fracasso and Simone they may marry the girls if only they will find them and bring them back.

Act III: The brothers continue to press their attentions upon Rosina, who eventually chooses Cassandro. The two soldiers return with the 'missing' girls, and all ends happily for everyone but Polidoro.

Goldoni's libretto is, of its kind, perfectly competent. It offered opportunities for Mozart to write a string of attractive, light-hearted arias. What it did not allow or encourage him to do, however, was to create a real comedy of character in musical terms. Whether the twelve-year-old Wolfgang would have been ready to respond to such encouragement is debatable, but he certainly worked miracles with the given material, and produced a number of arias which reveal remarkable individuality for one so young, and three finales of an excellence which suggests that he already found himself happier in the interplay of character than in the formal solo arias. It is interesting that *La finta semplice* and the two following pieces of juvenilia, *Bastien und Bastienne* and *Mitridate, Rè di Ponto*, preshadow the three forms of opera in which the mature Mozart was to become pre-eminent. *La finta semplice* is the beginning of a road which ends with *Figaro* and *Così fan tutte*; *Bastien und Bastienne* is a not unworthy forerunner of *Die Entführung aus dem Serail* and even *Die Zauberflöte*; while *Mitridate* leads to *Idomeneo* and *La clemenza di Tito*. These three early examples of Mozartian *opera buffa*, *Singspiel* and *opera seria* are, it is true, immature and lacking the complexities of the later works in each of those genres. They are nevertheless interesting in their own right, and not merely as foreshadowings of mature masterpieces.

For an Overture to *La finta semplice*, Mozart used a symphony (in D major, K. 45) which he had written some months earlier, merely making alterations to the instrumentation (omitting trumpets and drums, and adding flutes and bassoons), and also omitting the minuet. The three movements, *allegro*, *andante* and *molto allegro*, make a graceful introduction to the opera. The opening quartet for the two pairs of lovers, Giacinta and Fracasso, Ninetta and Simone, is a simple, joyous expression of well-being, and sets the mood for the entire opera, though individual arias move occasionally into gentler, more introspective moods. The first aria, 'Troppa briga a prender moglie' is for Fracasso's servant, Simone (bass). Like most of Simone's music, it is genial but colourless. He is no Leporello. Nor is Giacinta particularly striking. Her first aria, 'Marito il vorrei, ma senza fatica', has a quiet charm but is hardly memorable. The wealthy Don Cassandro, successful suitor of the 'finta semplice', is livelier. His music contains the usual *buffo* elements of rapid, staccato declamation, and comic repetition of phrases, but he nevertheless possesses some character of his own, though this is less evident in his first aria, 'Non c'è al mondo altro che donne', a lively, somewhat square *allegro*, than in his music in the second and third acts. Fracasso (tenor) is a pale adumbration of Ferrando in *Così fan tutte*. His first-act aria, 'Guarda la donna in viso', exists in two versions. Mozart's first setting, a graceful *andante*, is less apt though more appealing than his second choice. Rosina's first aria, 'Colla bocca e non col core' is one of the most successful in the opera, and would hardly sound out of place uttered by Fiordiligi or Dorabella in *Così fan tutte* which Mozart was to write more than twenty years later. It has a natural freshness which characterizes much of Rosina's music. Cassandro's brother Polidoro (tenor) now introduces himself in the aria 'Cosa ha mai la donna' in which Mozart's orchestration takes on a greater warmth and fullness as Polidoro describes the strength of his feeling for Rosina. This is a modified version of the aria 'Manches Übel will zuweilen' from *Die Schuldigkeit des ersten Gebots* of the previous year, in which, to very different words, it is sung by the Spirit of Christianity!

Cassandro's second aria, 'Ella vuole ed io torrei convenire non si può', is a conventional *buffo* piece, but with Rosina's 'Senti l'eco' [Ex. 3], a

Ex. 3

deeply-felt *andante* which looks forward to 'Dove Sono' sung by another Rosina in *Le nozze di Figaro*, Mozart suddenly transports us to a higher plane of experience than that which we have so far traversed in *La finta semplice*. Adding woodwind to his strings, he uses the oboe to present the echo of which Rosina sings. Ninetta's aria, 'Chi mi vuol bene presto mel dica', a graceful minuet, leads by way of a few bars of recitative into the first act finale in which, at first, the various characters are heard in exchanges of dialogue before uniting for a brief ensemble which brings down the curtain.

Act II opens with Ninetta's 'Un marito, donne care, ci bisogna ritrovare', a pleasant though conventional song for a conventional soubrette role. Simone fares better with 'Con certe persone' which, though not in itself especially memorable, is effective in context and is expertly in character. As much is true of Giacinta's 'Se a maritarmi arrivo', which has in addition a certain elegance to distinguish it from her first-act aria. Rosina's 'Amoretti che ascosi qui siete' [Ex. 4], though

Ex. 4

perhaps it looks back to Johann Christian Bach rather than forward to the mature Mozart, is a beautiful expression of tenderness and love, similar in mood to Susanna's 'Deh, vieni non tardar' in *Figaro*.

Cassandro's 'Ubriaco non son io' brings one down to earth again, though one must admire the manner in which the young Mozart's orchestra contradicts Cassandro's assertion that he is not drunk. Polidoro's 'Sposa cara, sposa bella', an affecting and dramatic piece which begins as a poignant lyrical *adagio* and then becomes dramatic in its anguish, is followed by Rosina's 'Ho sentito a dir di tutte le più belle'. The recitative preceding this aria is the only instance of accompanied recitative in the opera. The orchestra accompanies sympathetically as Cassandro falls into a drunken sleep. Rosina's aria is less interesting than her earlier three, and somewhat artificially pert. The comic duet for Fracasso and Cassandro, 'Cospetton, cospettonaccio', is virtually a solo for the bass, Cassandro, with Fracasso contributing no more than a few interjections. His aria which follows, 'In voi belle è leggiardria', is unremarkable, but the finale to the act is lively and well organized.

Simone's aria, 'Vieni, vieni, o mia Ninetta', which begins the third act, plods somewhat. Ninetta's response, 'Sono in amore, voglio marito', though livelier is no more striking. 'Che scompiglio, che flagello', sung by Giacinta before her pretended flight, is one of the more dramatic numbers in the score, and noticeably less formal than her earlier music, and a similar comment could be made on Fracasso's final aria, the lively 'Nelle guerre d'amore'. The last act finale is the most extended of the three.

One leaves *La finta semplice* wishing that it had been a more highly organized affair, for its three finales certainly hold one's interest, though the succession of solo arias tends to be a trifle enervating. A Salzburg performance in 1960, in the courtyard of the Residenz inside which the opera had been given its first performance, proved that it could still interest and entertain an audience whose expectations were informed and moderate, and that occasionally it could magically if momentarily raise itself to the level of Mozart's masterpieces of the 1780s.

IV

Bastien und Bastienne

Singspiel in one act

K. 50

Dramatis personae:
Bastienne, a shepherdess   (soprano)
Bastien, her beloved   (tenor)
Colas, a putative magician   (bass)

LIBRETTO by Friedrich Wilhelm Weiskern (additional verses by Johann Müller), after *Les Amours de Bastien et Bastienne* by Charles Simon Favart, Marie Justine Favart and Harny de Guerville

TIME: unspecified

PLACE: a village

FIRST PERFORMED, probably, at the house of Dr Anton Mesmer, Landstrasse, Vienna, in October, 1768, by amateurs. The first proven performance was in the Architektenhaus, Berlin, 2 October, 1890.

Bastien und Bastienne

I

ALTHOUGH LEOPOLD Mozart had failed in his attempts to get *La finta semplice* performed in Vienna in 1768, he was not keen to return to Salzburg while possibilities of other commissions for Wolfgang presented themselves. Two such commissions brightened the Mozarts' last months in Vienna. One emanated from a Jesuit priest, Father Ignaz Parhamer, who was very much in favour with the Court, and who ran an orphanage in the Landstrasse district. The Mozarts had met Father Parhamer, and were present when the Emperor laid the foundation stone for a new church at his orphanage. The church must have been built very quickly, for it was blessed on the Feastday of the Immaculate Conception, 7 December, on which occasion a Mass by Wolfgang was conducted by the young composer, in the presence of the secular and spiritual hierarchy of Vienna. Leopold wrote to Hagenauer that the Mass (K. 139) in C minor 'which little Wolfgang himself conducted has restored that reputation which our enemies, by preventing the performance of his opera, intended to destroy.'[1]

In Vienna, the Mozarts had also made the acquaintance of Dr Anton Mesmer, a young physician and ex-Jesuit from Baden who had become a figure of the Enlightenment, and who was later to discover the art or science of what we now know as mesmerism. Dr Mesmer had a large house in the suburb of Landstrasse, in the Rauchfangkehrergasse (now called Rasumovskygasse), and it is said to have been for a social occasion at his house that Wolfgang completed a short *Singspiel*, or opera with dialogue, *Bastien und Bastienne*, which he had probably begun to compose in Salzburg. It may have been performed *chez* Mesmer one evening in October, though not in a little theatre in Mesmer's garden, as one sometimes reads, for the theatre had not then been built. There is in fact no contemporary documentary evidence that this performance took place, for it is first mentioned in a biography of Mozart published thirty-seven years after his death.[2]

Bastien und Bastienne derives, at two removes, from a one-act opera *Le*

[1] 14 December, 1768.
[2] Von Nissen, G. N.: *Biographie W. A. Mozarts* (Leipzig, 1828).

Devin du Village, composed by the philosopher Jean Jacques Rousseau (1712–1778). In Book Eight of his *Confessions*, Rousseau gives his account of the creation of the work, and of its first performances. He wrote both libretto and music of this 'intermezzo in the Italian style' which was performed before Louis XIV at Fontainebleau in 1752, and publicly the following year at the Paris Opéra. The work's naturalness and simplicity charmed its hearers, and it remained popular for very many years. Six months after its first public performance, a parody of *Le Devin du Village* was produced in Paris, with the title *Les Amours de Bastien et Bastienne*. (Rousseau's village lovers had been called Colin and Colette.) The co-authors of the parody were Charles Simon Favart and Harny de Guerville. Favart's wife, Marie Justine Favart, a gifted singer and actress, who had also had a hand in the enterprise, appeared as Bastienne. *Les Amours de Bastien et Bastienne* enjoyed great success, not only in France but abroad, and was seen in Vienna as early as 1755. In 1764 it was produced again in Vienna, in a German translation and adaptation by a Viennese actor, Friedrich Wilhelm Weiskern. (Rousseau's original, *Le Devin du Village*, was staged in Vienna for the first time in 1760.)

The stages through which Rousseau's verses progressed can be seen by comparing the three versions of the heroine's first song, in which she bewails the loss of her beloved. Rousseau begins:

> J'ai perdu tout mon bonheur;
> J'ai perdu mon serviteur:
> Colin me délaisse.
> Hélas! il a pu changer!
> Je voudrois n'y plus songer:
> J'y songe sans cesse.

What Madame Favart sang in the parody, in a comic dialect, was

> J'nons pardu mon ami!
> Depis c'tems-là j'nons point dormi,
> Je n'vivons pü qu'à d'mi.
> J'nons pardu mon ami,
> J'en ons le coeur tout transi,
> Je m'meurs de souci.

Weiskern's Viennese version is hardly an improvement:

> Mein liebster Freund hat mich verlassen,
> Mit ihm ist Schlaf und Ruh' dahin;
> Ich weiss vor Leid mich nicht zu fassen,
> Der Kummer schwächt mir Aug' und Sinn.
> Vor Gram und Schmerz

Erstarrt das Herz,
Und diese Not
Bringt mir den Tod.

It is Weiskern's German translation of the Favart parody of Rousseau which Mozart set to music as *Bastien und Bastienne*, after the Salzburg trumpeter and poet Andreas Schachtner had made some alterations, and had turned Weiskern's prose text into verse.

In Rousseau's palely pleasant *opéra comique*, Colette, a shepherdess, consults a soothsayer, Colas, who tells her that her beloved Colin has temporarily deserted her for the lady of the manor, but that he really still loves her and is certain to return to her if she feigns indifference. The soothsayer then informs Colin that Colette loves someone else, but offers to help him regain her love. Eventually, the expected reconciliation takes place.

The soothsayer or magician retains his original name, Colas, in the Favart and Weiskern versions, only the names of the lovers being altered to Bastien and Bastienne. The scene is a village, with a distant prospect of open meadows. Bastienne laments that Bastien no longer loves her. Colas, the village soothsayer, enters, playing his bagpipes, and Bastienne seeks his aid. He assures her that Bastien is not really untrue to her, merely flattered by the attentions of a grand lady. Colas is willing to help Bastienne, if she will follow his instructions. To begin with she must conceal herself nearby. She does so. Bastien then appears, already more than willing to return to Bastienne. Colas informs him, however, that Bastienne has forsaken him. Reluctant to accept this, Bastien asks if Colas can return her to him by some spell or other. Colas produces his book of magic, from which he reads a spell. He then leaves, instructing Bastien not to move or look about him. Bastienne appears suddenly, as though by the magic of Colas, and, after the statutory amount of lovers' quarrelling, they admit their love for each other. Colas reappears, and is thanked by the happy couple.

The libretto, then, is undemanding. One might suppose it more suitable material for a twelve-year-old to set to music than the pieties of *Die Schuldigkeit des ersten Gebots*, the dull Latin verse used to disguise the nature of Apollo's feeling for Hyacinthus, or the complicated romantic farce of Goldoni. Let us see what Mozart made of it.

III

Bastien und Bastienne is not a work of extended forms, but an unambitious little one-act pastorale, interspersed with songs which are hardly grand enough to be called arias. The G major Overture, or Intrada as it is described in the score, is drawn to the appropriate scale, for it is over in a flash. Nevertheless, the motif on which it is based (Ex. 5)

Ex. 5

Violino I

p

quite clearly anticipates the opening of Beethoven's Eroica Symphony of thirty-five years later. Whether Mozart's little opera or its Overture was occasionally performed in the salons of Vienna that the young Beethoven might have frequented it is impossible to ascertain. Most likely it was not. As used by Mozart, the theme is probably meant to put us in mind of the bagpipes which Colas is playing when he first appears.

The simple, appealing character of the shepherdess Bastienne is established in her first song, 'Mein liebster Freund hat mich verlassen', a plaintive *andante* in 3/4 time, with a pair of oboes adding their characteristic colour to the otherwise purely string accompaniment. The song avoids Dresden daintiness by virtue of its youthful simplicity. This is more evidently the music of a child than any of the arias of *La finta semplice*, and it is impossible not to be as touched by its innocence as by its accomplishment. After a few lines of spoken soliloquy, Bastienne then sings 'Ich geh' jetzt auf die Weide', a cabaletta-like appendage to the first song, and a direct, unsubtle contrast to its mood. (The recitatives which are included in the *Neue Ausgabe* score are out of keeping with the *Singspiel* nature of the work. Mozart composed them to verses by Schachtner for a projected Salzburg performance which appears not to have taken place; the spoken dialogue is infinitely to be preferred.) For Bastienne's second song, the oboes of 'Mein liebster Freund' are replaced by horns. The orchestra is of modest proportions throughout the opera: strings with oboes and/or horns. Only in one of Bastien's songs ('Meiner Liebsten schöne Wangen') are flutes introduced.

For Colas's entrance, the strings imitate the sound of the bagpipes he is supposed to be playing, cleverly producing the effect of that instrument's notorious vagueness of pitch. Colas's song, 'Befraget mich ein zartes Kind', is suitably bucolic, not least in its curiously false emphases, with unstressed syllables set to strong downbeats. Bastienne's 'Wenn mein Bastien einst im Scherze' is in two sections, achieving contrast by changing its time instead of its tempo. The orchestra remains subservient, the first violins often in unison with the voice which in Bastienne's songs rises no further above the stave than G. (All three roles in the opera, though ostensibly for soprano, tenor and bass, could be managed comfortably by a baritone of only moderate range!) Bastienne's next song, 'Würd ich auch, wie manche Buhlerinnen', another exercise in the same vein of simple directness, is followed by one of the two duets in the opera, 'Auf den Rat, den ich gegeben', for Bastienne and Colas. In his first sketch Mozart wrote three bars of coloratura for both singers to conclude the duet, but on second thoughts deleted them, leaving the opera's mood of childlike simplicity undisturbed.

Bastien now enters, establishing himself immediately as a blustering young farmhand, and no Arcadian shepherd, with 'Grossen Dank dir abzustatten', a lusty and confident *allegro*, and his next song, 'Geh! du sagst mir eine Fabel'. Colas conjures up his magic powers in a dramatic C minor aria which parodies the high drama of *opera seria*, to nonsense words and scraps of Latin: 'Diggi, daggi, schurry, murry . . . fatto, matto, quid pro quo'. Flutes join the strings in Bastien's tender and charming love song, 'Meiner Liebsten schöne Wangen', which Mozart later arranged for voice and keyboard accompaniment for separate publication in a Viennese anthology of new songs. The reproachful words of Bastienne's gentle *andante*, 'Er war mir sonst treu und ergeben', are softened by the affectionate lilt of the music, but the following aria, first sung by Bastien ('Geh hin!'), then repeated by Bastienne ('Ich will') is dramatically more vivid. There next follows the only piece of accompanied recitative in the opera which, after three bars, broadens into *arioso* as Bastien threatens to kill himself, while his beloved merely interjects unfeeling exclamations of 'Viel Glück' (Good Luck). The duet, 'Geh, geh, geh, Herz von Flandern', in the course of which the lovers are reconciled, is the most extended number in the score, and the first one since the Overture to use both oboes and horns in the accompaniment. Both are used again in the finale, a happy though somewhat characterless trio for the lovers and Colas.

It is quite clear from the modest nature of the scoring and from the simplicity of the voice parts that Mozart wrote *Bastien und Bastienne* to be performed by amateurs; and the existence of Colas's recitatives in two versions, one for bass and one for alto, suggests that at some stage a performance by children may also have been contemplated. Though there is little that is memorable in the work, it does cohere in a way that the more ambitious *Finta semplice* does not, and it certainly confirms its young composer's natural gift for the stage.

V

Mitridate, Rè di Ponto

opera seria in three acts

K. 87

Dramatis personae:

Mitridate, King of Pontus and other kingdoms	(tenor)
Aspasia, betrothed to Mitridate and already proclaimed Queen	(soprano)
Sifare, son of Mitridate and Stratonica, in love with Aspasia	(soprano)
Farnace, elder son of Mitridate, also in love with Aspasia	(alto)
Ismene, daughter of the King of the Parthians, in love with Farnace	(soprano)
Marzio, Roman Tribune, friend of Farnace	(tenor)
Arbate, Governor of Nymphaea	(soprano)

LIBRETTO by Vittorio Amedeo Cigna-Santi, based on Giuseppe Parini's Italian translation of Racine's tragedy, *Mithridate*

TIME: 88 B.C.

PLACE: The Crimea

FIRST PERFORMED in Milan 26 December, 1770, at the Teatro Regio Ducal with Guglielmo D'Ettore (Mitridate), Antonia Bernasconi (Aspasia), Pietro Benedetti, known as Sartorino (Sifare), Giuseppe Cicognani (Farnace), Francesca Varese (Ismene), Gasparo Bassano (Marzio), Pietro Muschietti (Arbate)

Mitridate, Rè di Ponto

I

ON 5 JANUARY, 1769, the Mozarts arrived back in Salzburg. It was on 1 May, the Archbishop's name-day, that *La finta semplice* was performed for the first time. During the year, young Wolfgang continued to compose: his first Serenades date from these months, as well as the elegant Dominicus Mass (K. 66). (Dominicus was Wolfgang's boyhood friend, Father Dominicus Hagenauer, and the work was composed for Father Hagenauer's first Mass in St Peter's Church.) In November, the Archbishop conferred upon Wolfgang the title of Concertmaster of Salzburg, an honour which carried no immediate salary with it, for Leopold and Wolfgang were about to set out on their travels again, this time without the women of the family. They received permission to go to Italy, on the understanding that Wolfgang would draw no salary as Concertmaster until his return.

Father and son set out on 12 December, 1769, and three days later arrived in Innsbruck, where they stayed at the Weisses Kreuz. The Governor of the Tyrol, Count Johann Nepomuk Spaur, placed his carriage at their disposal, and they participated in a concert at the home of Count Leopold Künigl. By 20 December they were in Brixen in the South Tyrol (now Brissone, and part of the Italian Tyrol) and reached Bozen (Bolzano) on the 21st. On the various stages of their journey they encountered ex-Salzburg acquaintances or friends of Salzburg acquaintances eager to entertain them. In Rovereto a huge crowd gathered to hear Wolfgang play the church organ, and in Verona the Mozarts stayed at the Hotel Due Torri. Leopold made their presence known to the nobility and the musicians of the city, and Wolfgang wrote to his sister Nannerl in a mixture of German and Italian, describing an opera performance they attended. 'Ha una Schnoffelte voce e canta sempre um ein Viertel zu tardi, ò troppo à buon ora', he said of one of the singers.[1] On 5 January he performed at the Accademia Filarmonica, exciting, as usual, the wonder and admiration of his audience. His effect on the city of Verona during the few days he and his father were there was such that, the following year, Wolfgang received the unusual honour of being appointed titular Kapellmeister of the Accademia Filarmonica.

[1] 'She has a stuffed-up voice and always sings either a semi-quaver too late or too soon.'

From Verona the Mozarts continued on to Mantua, where they heard Hasse's opera, *Demetrio*, and Cremona, where they heard another opera by Hasse, *La clemenza di Tito*, which Wolfgang no doubt remembered twenty years later when he came to set the same subject. Eventually they reached Milan, where they found a number of eminent persons with Viennese connections, eager to welcome them. Wolfgang's letters to his sister Nannerl show him to be not at all fatigued by travel, and eager for work and play. 'I have no news,' he announces, 'except that Herr Gellert, the poet, has died at Leipzig, and since his death has ceased to write poetry.'[1] He describes in detail the singers and musicians he and his father have heard, and goes in for childish humour which seems rather more coarse to us today than it would have done in the eighteenth century which we like to think of as so elegant ('Every time the dancer leapt, he let off a fart').[2]

In Milan, Mozart met the famous composer Giovanni Battista Sammartini at a rehearsal of his *Cesare in Egitto*, gave a public concert which was followed by a huge reception at the palace of the Governor of Lombardy, Count Karl Joseph Firmian, and, through the good offices of Count Firmian, obtained a commission to compose the first opera of the following season in Milan. When the Mozarts left to continue their journey south, they were provided by their Milanese friends with letters of recommendation to influential people in Parma, Bologna and Florence. Wolfgang wrote several motets and arias at odd moments during their travels, and actually composed his first string quartet (K. 80) *en route* to Parma, at Lodi. In Parma they dined with the famous soprano Lucrezia Aguiari, known as La Bastardina or La Bastardella because of her illegitimacy. Wolfgang informed Nannerl that she had 'a beautiful voice, a wonderful throat and an incredible range',[3] and noted down several bars of fioriture he had heard her sing, ranging from middle C to the C three octaves above. In Bologna, the Mozarts met one of the most famous of living composers, the elderly Giovanni Battista Martini. The great composer and teacher greeted the fourteen-year-old Wolfgang warmly, tested his musical knowledge and ability and spoke of him with admiration. In Florence, the travellers were given an audience by the Grand Duke Leopold, the son of Maria Theresa, and Wolfgang gave a concert at the Duke's summer residence. An instant friendship sprang up between Wolfgang and an English boy of the same age, Thomas Linley. Linley's father was a composer of operas, many of which were staged at Drury Lane. The boy was studying the violin in Florence; when he and Wolfgang parted, both were in tears. (Linley was only twenty-two when he died by drowning in Lincolnshire.)

The Mozarts arrived in Rome shortly before Easter. One of the first things they did was attend a performance of Allegri's *Miserere* in the

---

[1] 26 January, 1770.   [2] 26 January, 1770.   [3] 24 March, 1770.

Sistine Chapel. This was the famous occasion when Wolfgang, immediately after the performance, wrote the music down from memory, and one of the papal choristers confirmed the accuracy of his transcription. At the usual receptions and concerts Wolfgang performed, and on two occasions encountered Charles, the Young Pretender to the English throne. On 8 May, Leopold and Wolfgang continued on to Naples, where they visited, amongst others, the British Ambassador Sir William Hamilton, 'whose wife plays the clavier with great feeling, and is very pleasant',[1] and at whose residence they met one or two of their old London acquaintances. After visits to several of the classical sites such as Pompeii and Herculaneum, and a very successful concert at the home of Count Kaunitz, they returned to Rome to find that Pope Clement XIV had awarded Wolfgang the highest class of the Order of the Golden Spur. The young Knight was given an audience by the Pope himself, and his letter to his sister the same day, signed 'Chevalier de Mozart', contained a postscript in Italian: 'Keep in good health, and make a mess in your bed by shitting in it.'[2]

The Mozarts left Rome on 10 July to make their way slowly home, and ten days later were in Bologna again. Here Wolfgang received the libretto of *Mitridate, Rè di Ponto*, the opera he had been commissioned to compose for Milan. They remained in Bologna until October, as the guests of Count Pallavicini who had invited them to stay at his country villa just outside the city. Wolfgang began to compose his opera, working mainly on the recitatives, for he would not complete the arias until he had made the acquaintance, in Milan, of the singers who had been engaged. In mid-October, he and his father arrived in Milan where an apartment had been found for them near the theatre. They met the singers, and Wolfgang was able to begin composing the twenty-two arias required. The rehearsal period was beset with the usual operatic intrigues. 'Thank God,' wrote Leopold to his wife, 'we have won the first battle and have routed an enemy who composed new arias for the prima donna, and tried to persuade her not to sing any of Wolfgang's.'[3] The first rehearsal with orchestra was held on 12 December, followed by three more (two of them in the theatre) on the 17th, 19th and 22nd. A successful dress rehearsal was held on 22 December; the first performance on 26 December, with Wolfgang directing from the cembalo, was a great triumph, with cries from the audience of 'Evviva il maestro!' and demands for encores. During the season *Mitridate* was performed twenty times. It appears not to have been performed again until it was revived in Salzburg in 1971.

---

[1] Leopold to his wife, 19 May, 1770. Lady Hamilton is not Nelson's Emma but Hamilton's first wife, who died in 1782.
[2] 7 July, 1770.
[3] 10 November, 1770.

II

The libretto of *Mitridate* was written by the Turin poet Vittorio Amedeo Cigna-Santi (1725–1785) for the composer Quirino Gasparini, whose *Mitridate* was staged in Turin in 1767. For Mozart, it was shortened somewhat, and altered in several places, but remains very close to the drama on which it was based, Racine's tragedy, *Mithridate* (1673). The plays of Racine, and this applies to *Mithridate* no less than to *Phèdre*, live by virtue of their poetry, not their plots. Racine's characters can hardly be considered apart from the poetry they utter. Each of them is almost a symbol of some aspect of passion, expressed in Racine's dramatic verse which not only fails to translate into another language but even loses its power when extracted from the context of its dramatic situation, in a way that the dramatic verse of Shakespeare, for example, does not. It would be idle, therefore, to expect to discover anything particularly Racinian in the fourteen-year-old Mozart's *Mitridate*. Something of Beaumarchais' sharpness of intellect can be found in *Le nozze di Figaro*, but to re-inject the individual poetry of Racine into the opera *Mitridate*, as Verdi was to succeed in transferring the essense of Shakespeare even into his early *Macbeth*, was something which young Wolfgang did not consider attempting.

Cigna-Santi's libretto made use of an Italian translation of Racine's play by Giuseppe Parini (1729–1799), one of the most estimable and engaging of Italian poets of his time, an elegant ironist who took Horace as his model. For operatic purposes the play's five acts were reduced to three, and two new characters were introduced: Ismene, daughter of the King of the Parthians, and in love with Farnace; and Marzio, a Roman Tribune and friend of Farnace. Cigna-Santi, nevertheless, made no secret of the fact that his libretto was closely based on Racine. 'Veggasi la tragedia del francese Racine, che si è in molte parti imitata,'[1] he advised readers of the libretto. Racine, in his preface to the play, justifies the liberties he has taken with historical fact, and claims 'I have put into [the play] everything that might help to explain the characteristics and the feelings of this prince, for instance his violent hatred of the Romans, his great courage, his shrewdness, his propensity to dissimilate, and finally that jealousy which was so much a part of him and which so often cost his mistresses their lives.'[2]

Mithridates, to give him his Anglicized name, was a king of Pontus in the second century B.C., who conquered several kingdoms in Asia Minor and Greece. In Racine's play, he is seen at the end of his career,

---

[1] 'See the tragedy by the Frenchman, Racine, which I have in part imitated'.

[2] J'y ai inséré tout ce qui pouvait mettre en jour les moeurs et les sentiments de ce prince, je veux dire sa haine violente contre les Romains, son grand courage, sa finesse, sa dissimulation, et enfin cette jalousie qui lui était si naturelle, et qui a tant de fois coûté la vie à ses maîtresses – Preface to *Mithridate* (1673).

attempting to deal with a new young wife who is loved by both of his sons, who are themselves step-brothers, and who is in love with one of them. The play ends with the death of Mithridates, the disgrace of one son, Pharnaces, who has sided with the Romans, and the betrothal of the Princess Monima to the other son, Xiphares:

Xipharès:	Moi, seigneur! que je fuie! / Que Pharnace impuni, les Romains triomphants, / N'éprouvent pas bientôt . . .
Mithridate:	Non, je vous le défends. / Tôt ou tard il faudra que Pharnace périsse: / Fiez-vous aux Romains du soin de son supplice. / Mais je sens affaiblir ma force et mes esprits; / Je sens que je me meurs. Approchez-vous, mon fils: / Dans cet embrassement dont la douceur me flatte, / Venez, et recevez l'âme de Mithridate.
Monime:	Il expire.
Xipharès:	Ah! madame, unissons nos douleurs, Et par tout l'univers cherchons-lui des vengeurs.

(*Xiphares:*	I, flee, my lord? With Pharnaces unpunished? The Romans shall not know triumph . . .
Mithridates:	No, I forbid you. Sooner or later, Pharnaces will perish. You may safely leave his punishment to Rome. But I feel my strength and my spirits weakening. I feel I am dying. Come close, my son. With this embrace whose sweetness comforts me, come and receive the spirit of Mithridates.
Monima:	He is dead.
Xiphares:	Ah, madame, let our sorrows unite, and throughout the universe let us seek to avenge him.)

The historical Mithridates the Great (Mithridates II) ruled in Pontus, a kingdom bordering the southern shore of the Black Sea and today part of Turkey, in the years 124 B.C. to 88 B.C. As a result of defeating several neighbouring rulers in battle, he became King of Armenia Major, and in 92 B.C. made a treaty with Rome. The action of Mozart's opera takes place in the last days of the King's life, in and around Nymphaeum, a seaport in the Crimea.

Act I, Scene 1. A square in Nymphaeum, with a distant view of the harbour. Arbate,[1] Governor of the Fort of Nymphaeum, and Sifare, son of Mitridate, have learned of the death of Mitridate in battle. Sifare considers himself the enemy of his half-brother Farnace, not only because of Farnace's treasonous ties with Rome, but also because they are both in love with Aspasia, whom Mitridate has taken as his fiancée and intended Queen. Aspasia, fearing the advances of Farnace now that his father is dead, asks Sifare for his protection, for it is he whom she really loves.

[1] In this synopsis, the characters are referred to by the Italian forms of their names, as used in the opera.

Scene II. A temple of Venus. Farnace presses his suit upon Aspasia. Arbate announces that Mitridate is not dead, and that his fleet is approaching the port. The news is received by the two sons and Aspasia with mixed feelings. Farnace plots with the Roman Tribune, Marzio.

Scene III. The seaport. Mitridate returns and explains that he has caused the news of his death to be reported, merely to confound his enemies. He announces that Farnace is to marry Ismene, a Parthian princess. Suspecting that both sons are in love with Aspasia, Mitridate consults Arbate and is told that Farnace has already declared himself, but that Sifare has given no indication that he, too, desires the lady. Highly jealous and suspicious by nature, Mitridate determines to discover the truth from Aspasia.

Act II, Scene I. The Royal apartments. Farnace informs Ismene that he no longer loves her. Mitridate suggests to her that she might find a more worthy husband in Sifare. He then questions Aspasia, and satisfies himself that Farnace has designs on both his wife and his throne. Calling Sifare to him, Mitridate instructs him to take good care of the Queen while he, Mitridate, deals with the traitorous Farnace. When they are left alone, Aspasia reveals to Sifare that it is he whom she loves. Sifare feels torn between his love for her and his loyalty to his father.

Scene II. Mitridate's camp. The King attempts to send Farnace on a military expedition, but in the ensuing argument the full truth is revealed. Mitridate, betrayed, as he thinks, by all those closest to him, condemns both sons and Aspasia to death.

Act III, Scene I. A garden. Ismene and Aspasia plead for the lives of the two brothers, but in vain. Aspasia determines to kill herself, but is prevented by Sifare.

Scene II. A prison tower. Farnace is visited in his cell by the Roman, Marzio, with whose aid he escapes. But he repents having plotted against his father, and helps him fight against the Romans, setting fire to the Roman fleet.

Scene III. The Royal courtyard. A distant view of the sea, and the Roman navy. Mitridate has been wounded in the battle. Before he dies, he is reconciled to both his sons. He unites Aspasia and Sifare, and pardons Farnace who is now reconciled with Ismene.

III

The Overture to *Mitridate* is a miniature three-movement symphony, *allegro-andante-presto*. Graceful and charming in itself, it makes no attempt to characterize or portray the mood or events of the opera. The opera is, not surprisingly, in the conventional *opera seria* form: in other words, it consists of a string of arias. We must seek the drama, then, not in complex ensembles of the kind we shall encounter later in *Figaro* and *Don Giovanni*, but within the individual arias and in the recitatives.

Mozart's *secco* recitatives in *Mitridate* are lively, sensitive, and responsive
to the requirements of the text. They are not, as so often in *opera seria*,
mere interludes between arias. Nevertheless, it is in the arias that we
shall best discover how successful Mozart has been in finding musical
equivalents to the dramatic verse of Racine.

Mozart's orchestra is the normal one for Italian opera of the period:
the usual strings plus two oboes and two horns. Trumpets are added for
the first aria, Aspasia's 'Al destin che la minaccia', whose excitingly
florid vocal line is certainly full of 'minaccia' (menace) for the soprano
with a less than perfect technique. 'Al destin che la minaccia' sets the
tone, or at any rate the method, for the entire opera, for one responds to
it as a virtuoso display piece, no doubt expertly tailored to the
requirements of Antonia Bernasconi, the first Aspasia. One is not,
however, immediately convinced, as one is with mature Mozart, that it is
in these and no other musical notes that the character would express
herself. Aria No. 2 reveals even more clearly that the young composer's
principal concern was to satisfy his singers rather than his librettist or
dramatist, for the words of Sifare's 'Soffre il mio cor con pace una beltà
tiranna' suggest music of deeper feeling than the flashily effective *allegro*
which Mozart provides. Sifare is one of three male roles in the opera
which Mozart composed for castrati. He and Arbate are sopranos, while
Farnace is an alto. In performance today, all three would have to be
made *travesti* roles and sung by two sopranos and a contralto. Male
singers of sufficient virtuosity do not exist, and Sifare's arias in
particular require the brightness of timbre of the soprano voice. Even
Aria No. 3, 'L'odio nel cor frenate', sung by Arbate, Governor of
Nymphaeum, is written as a coloratura display piece, with provision as
usual for the singer to improvise a cadenza in the final bars. The
cumulative effect of so many *allegro* arias, one after the other, is
somewhat wearisome, though individually each is certainly enjoyable.

With Aspasia's 'Nel sen mi palpita dolente il core' (No. 4), even
though it is another *allegro*, we find ourselves for the first time becoming
gripped by the drama, for in this G minor expression of Aspasia's
distress Mozart has communicated his heroine's feelings tersely and
directly. For once there is no long orchestral introduction or *ritornello*,
the agitated voice (Ex. 6) being preceded simply by a two-bar phrase.

There is no coloratura, and the vocal line is used dramatically rather
than purely musically. The character's hesitations, as well as her general

mood, are portrayed in the vocal line as well as in the choice of key. This is virtually the only aria in *Mitridate* which really gets to grips with the problem of composing an opera, whether *seria* or of any other style. In its expressive simplicity, it is worthy of the mature Mozart. Sifare's 'Parto: Nel gran cimento' (No. 5), too, is more individual an aria than most in *Mitridate*, an attractive a-b-a-b aria in which 'a' is an affecting *andante* which is all too brief, while 'b' is yet another piece of coloratura.

Sifare's first aria, 'Venga pur, minacci e frema' (No. 6) returns us with a vengeance to the world of pure virtuosity, the world in which all these characters meet, and lose their individuality. It is a long a-b-a piece, exploiting the male alto's low notes as well as his coloratura skill. No. 7 is a march to accompany the arrival of Mitridate and his troops. The Emperor's first aria is described in the score as a *cavata*, which is a word one rarely comes across. Grove defines it as a short *arioso*. (Its diminutive, *cavatina*, has come to mean a simple, legato melody, either vocal or instrumental.) Mitridate's 'Se di lauri il crine adorno', a simple, unaffected *andante*, is indicative more of his weariness after battle than of his more martial or regal qualities. No. 9, 'In faccia all' oggetto', is the first of Ismene's three arias. Ismene, of course, is a female soprano role, but it is not easy to detect any difference in style or manner between her arias and those of either the male soprano Sifare or the other female soprano Aspasia. Mozart composes gracefully, fluently and similarly for all three. Act I ends with Mitridate's aria, 'Quel ribelle e quell' ingrato', preceded by one of the relatively few sections of accompanied recitative in the opera. Where it does occur, before seven of the twenty-three arias, Mozart's accompanied recitative is always dramatically effective. He was, even at fourteen, capable of using his orchestra and voices in a dramatically meaningful way, when he was not otherwise occupied in keeping his singers happy in their arias. Mitridate's aria (No. 10), a martial flourish to end the act, adds trumpets to the normal orchestra again, and makes an effective contrast, albeit a conventionally heroic one, to the returning King's first aria.

After *recitativo secco*, Act II opens with No. 11, Farnace's 'Va, va, l'error mio palesa', yet another bravura piece, but one of the more individual of them, with a low tessitura exploiting what must have been the male alto's most effective register, from E above middle C to the A below. Mitridate's 'Tu, che fedel mi sei' (No. 12), a pleasant, gentle *adagio* with an *allegro* middle section, is followed by accompanied recitative for Sifare and Aspasia, leading into Sifare's, 'Lungi da te, mio bene' (No. 13), an exquisite *adagio* in which Sifare says farewell to Aspasia. This aria, with its melancholy horn obbligato, would not sound out of place if uttered by Fiordiligi in *Così fan tutte* twenty years later. It pays lip-service to the idea of the formal *da capo* aria by containing a second subject at a slightly faster tempo (*andante*) but its mood of tender resignation remains intact throughout. Aspasia's recitative and aria, 'Nel grave tormento' (No. 14) is in a-b-a-b form, a somewhat over-decorated *adagio* and an even more decorated *allegro*, with staccato runs up to a high C. In Ismene's second aria, 'So quanto a te dispiace', words and music seem at variance, the coloratura expressing nothing beyond the singer's virtuosity in producing it. The word 'pace' (peace) improbably stretches itself over seven bars of fioriture. Farnace's 'Son reo' (No. 16) is much more direct, dramatic and to the point, its changes of tempo and mood dictated by the words and the situation. No. 17, Mitridate's 'Già di pietà mi spoglio', while not especially remarkable out of context, is likewise at the service of the text and the drama, proving that the fourteen-year-old Mozart could have produced a much better opera had he not been obliged, not merely to consider the particular talents of the singers assigned to him in Milan, but also to be enslaved by them. Act II ends with the opera's only duet, 'Se viver non degg'io' (No. 18), sung by the unhappy lovers Aspasia and Sifare. This is one of the most beautiful numbers in the opera, its *adagio* opening as affecting as its *allegro* conclusion is dramatic and appropriate.[1]

Act III begins with Ismene's 'Tu sai per chi m'accese' (No. 19), a pleasing and relatively simple *allegro*. Mitridate contributes another of his martial arias, 'Vado incontro al fato estremo' (No. 20), an exciting and heroic *allegro* which asks for several high Cs from the tenor. Aspasia's recitative and cavatina, 'Pallid' ombre, che scorgete' (No. 21) moves with confident ease from agitated recitative to aria, an *andante* whose apparently serene vocal line is given added dimensions by the mood of the orchestra, then back, without a formal close, to accompanied recitative. Here the young Mozart is on the verge of anticipating Wagner's *durchkomponiert* music drama. Dramatic tension is sustained in the *allegro agitato* of Sifare's 'Se il rigor d'ingrata sorte', unhampered by any contrasting middle section. The Roman Marzio's single aria, 'Sei di regnar sei vago' (No. 23), characterizes him effectively with its crisp march rhythms, and Farnace's aria (preceded by accompanied recitative) 'Già dagli occhi il velo e tolto', in which he expresses his remorse, is both strong and brilliant. The opera ends with a quintet (No. 25) in which all five characters combine as a chorus: it makes a disappointingly perfunctory finale.

Listened to as a succession of arias sung in costume, *Mitridate* can be highly enjoyable. But one can hardly claim that in it Mozart has replaced Racine's poetry with music of equal power and resonance. For that kind of genius one must wait until *Idomeneo*.

---

[1] Leopold wrote to his wife that the two singers were enchanted with this duet and that 'the *primo uomo* has actually said that, if it does not please the audience, he will let himself be castrated all over again'. (15 December 1770)

VI

Ascanio in Alba

a pastoral opera in two acts

K. 111

Dramatis personae:

Venus	(soprano)
Ascanio, her grandson	(soprano)
Silvia, a nymph descended from Hercules	(soprano)
Aceste, a priest of Venus	(tenor)
Fauno, a shepherd	(soprano)

LIBRETTO by Giuseppe Parini

The action takes place in mythical times, in a part of the country, near Rome, where the city of Alba Longa was to be founded

FIRST PERFORMED in Milan, 17 October, 1771, at the Teatro Regio Ducal, with Geltrude Falchini (Venus), Giovanni Manzuoli (Ascanio), Maria Girelli-Aguilar (Silvia), Giuseppe Tibaldi (Aceste), Adamo Solzi (Fauno)

Ascanio in Alba

I

WOLFGANG AND HIS father spent several happy weeks in Milan after the première of *Mitridate*, attending concerts and receptions at several great houses, at one of which Wolfgang was delighted to be offered his favourite Austrian dish of *Leberknödel und Sauerkraut*. Early in February, 1771, they set out on the return journey to Salzburg, and, after a stay of several days in Venice, eventually arrived home on 28 March, 1771. Wolfgang was now fifteen years of age, pubescent, and a virtual Cherubino. He began to be extremely interested in the young ladies of Salzburg, but still managed to find time to compose. During the spring months he produced a number of works, including the oratorio *La Betulia Liberata* (K. 118) and several liturgical pieces for the Salzburg cathedral.

At this time, Wolfgang received his most important commission to date. The Archduke Ferdinand, third son of the Empress Maria Theresa, was to marry the Princess Maria Beatrice Ricciarda d'Este of Modena. The Archduke was Governor and Captain-General of Lombardy, and it was planned that his wedding would be celebrated in grand style in Milan, the capital of Lombardy. The Empress Maria Theresa commissioned an opera from the distinguished but quite elderly composer, Johann Adolph Hasse. As was the custom, a companion work, or *serenata* was required, and the Empress rather imaginatively, though doubtless on the advice of one of her courtiers, commissioned Wolfgang to provide this second piece. On 13 August Leopold and Wolfgang set out once again for Italy. Arriving in Milan, Wolfgang began work on the composition which has been variously described as *serenata, festa teatrale*, and *azione teatrale*. 'Dramatic serenade' or 'pastoral opera' are fairly accurate descriptions in English of *Ascanio in Alba*, the work which Wolfgang produced for the nuptial festivities. Usually on such occasions the principal opera and *serenata* were produced on the same evening, the lesser work acting as a prelude or curtain-raiser to the full-scale opera. This time, however, Hasse's *Ruggiero* and Mozart's *Ascanio in Alba* were performed on separate occasions. The royal wedding took place on 15 October, Hasse's opera was staged on the 16th, and *Ascanio in Alba* the following evening.

The letters of Leopold and Wolfgang from Milan to Frau Mozart in

Salzburg are full of information about the period during which Wolfgang's opera was composed. On 13 September Leopold was able to tell his wife that 'in twelve days, with God's help Wolfgang will have completely finished the *serenata*, which is really an *azione teatrale* in two parts'.[1] The leading role was to be sung by the famous castrato, Giovanni Manzuoli, whom Leopold and Wolfgang had already met in London, and Manzuoli often visited the young composer while the work was in progress. 'Everyone is extremely kind, and they all have the greatest respect for Wolfgang,' Leopold wrote to his wife. 'Indeed, we have not experienced the slightest unpleasantness, for all these famous singers are really splendid and sensible people.'[2]

Leopold went on to explain that the *serenata* was really a short opera, and described the elaborate preparations being made in Milan for the wedding festivities:

> The whole of Milan is busying itself, especially as most of the work has been left till the last moment. So now everyone is at work. Some people are preparing the theatre, as the whole building needs to be renovated and redecorated. Others are busy making preparations to receive His Royal Highness, engaging apartments, decorating the cathedral, procuring garments and liveries for the servants and engaging carriages and horses, and so on, for the balls.[3]

Wolfgang added a postscript to his sister: 'All praise and thanks to God, I am in good health, but I can't write much both because I have nothing to say and because my fingers ache from writing so much music.' He had by now completed the fifteen arias, eight choruses and three trios which make up the opera, and rehearsals were able to begin before the end of September. The wedding duly took place on 15 October, Hasse's opera was performed on the 16th, and *Ascanio in Alba* on the 17th. Leopold wrote home on the 19th to report that it had been 'such an extraordinary success that it is going to be repeated today. The Archduke has just ordered two copies. We are constantly stopped in the street by courtiers and others who want to congratulate the young composer. I'm sorry, but Wolfgang's *serenata* has so overwhelmed Hasse's opera that I simply can't tell you'.[4] A few days later, a third performance of *Ascanio in Alba* was given at which 'their Royal Highnesses the Archduke and Archduchess not only applauded so much that two arias had to be repeated, but both during the performance and afterwards they leaned over from their box towards Wolfgang and displayed their gracious approval by calling out "Bravissimo, maestro" and clapping their hands.'[5]

The elderly Hasse admitted some days later that his opera had totally

[1] 13 September, 1771.   [2] 21 September, 1771.   [3] 21 September, 1771.
[4] 19 October, 1771.   [5] Leopold to Frau Mozart, 26 October, 1771.

failed, but he was unenvious of Wolfgang's success and is even said to have remarked 'This boy will cause us all to be forgotten.'[1] It is no wonder that the Mozarts lingered on in Milan until early December, for Wolfgang's success had been so complete that it seemed possible some further commissions might accrue from it, if not permanent employment at the Archduke's court.

II

The libretto of *Ascanio in Alba* was written by Giuseppe Parini (1729–1799), the distinguished poet on whose translation of Racine's *Mithridate* the libretto of Mozart's *Mitridate* had been based. As was the custom on a royal occasion of this kind, the poet produced a masque-like entertainment whose characters were idealized impersonations of the royal personages to be honoured. Parini's story is related in conventional Arcadian verse: his Ascanio, descended from the goddess Venus, is the Austrian Archduke Ferdinand, while Venus herself is, of course, the Empress Maria Theresa. The nymph Silvia 'of the race of Hercules', to whom Venus gives Ascanio in marriage, is the Princess Maria Beatrice d'Este. Thus, at the first performance of *Ascanio in Alba*, the newly married royal couple had the agreeable experience of seeing themselves portrayed as beautiful and at least semi-divine, and hearing their virtues praised by a chorus of arcadian nymphs and genii.

The opera is in two parts; and, in view of its essentially static, masque-like nature, it is appropriate to refer to 'parts' rather than 'acts', a word which implies a higher content of dramatic tension. Part One begins with a chorus of genii and other amiable spirits, who sing the praises of the goddess Venus. Venus then informs her grandson Ascanio that the ground on which they stand is sacred, for these are shores which she and Aeneas, father of Ascanio, had visited together. The omens had suggested, she says, that this nation would become her favourite people. She, as a goddess, can hardly reign here locally, so Ascanio is to rule in her place. He is to be wedded to 'la più saggia ninfa che di sangue divin nascesse mai', the wisest nymph ever born of divine blood. (It was tactful of Parini to write 'saggia' rather than 'bella', for the Princess Beatrice was apparently no great beauty.) Venus assures Ascanio that this wise nymph Silvia already loves him, although she has never seen him, for Cupid had, at Venus's bidding, already involved himself in the affair. Ascanio says he will immediately seek out Silvia, and tell her that he, offspring of the gods, adores her. Venus, however, insists that he conceal his identity from Silvia for the time being, for she wishes to test the nymph's true feelings.

A band of shepherds appears, led by Fauno, to pay homage to Venus.

---

[1] 'Questo regazzo ci farà dimenticar tutti' (*Cenni storico-critici alla vita ed opera del G. A. Hasse* by Franz Kandler. Venice, 1820, p. 27).

Aceste, a priest of Venus, enters with Silvia, who is that day to become
the bride of Ascanio. Silvia is distressed because, though she piously
loves the husband chosen for her by the goddess, she is in love also with
the form of a handsome youth whom she has seen, though whether in a
vision or in reality she cannot tell. (This is, of course, Ascanio as revealed
to her by Cupid.) Aceste attempts to comfort her, assuring her that all
will be well, since all had been decreed by the goddess. Ascanio, who has
concealed himself nearby, begs Venus to allow him to reveal himself to
Silvia, but Venus tells him he must first be shown further proof of the
nymph's virtue.

In Part Two, Ascanio and Silvia meet, and Silvia is prevented by
Fauno from confessing too readily her love for the handsome youth.
Silvia resolves to put temptation from her by fleeing from Ascanio, and
placing herself under the protection of Aceste until her chosen
bridegroom should arrive to claim her. Venus reappears, however, to
present to the confused and delighted nymph the husband she has
chosen. Ascanio and Silvia express their relief and delight, and the
assembled company voice their gratitude to Venus, exhorting her to rule
the entire world, thus ensuring the happiness of everyone on earth.

III

The Overture of *Ascanio in Alba* is revealed to be a short, one-movement
allegro. Then Part One begins, and the first two numbers are an *andante
grazioso* 'che ballano le Grazie' (danced by the graces) and an *allegro*
chorus to be danced and sung by genii and graces. But Leopold
Mozart in one of his letters to Frau Mozart from Milan describes the
opening three movements, Overture, ballet and chorus, as a three-
movement symphony. 'The *andante* of the symphony,' he says, 'is danced
by eleven women: eight genii and three graces, or eight graces and three
goddesses. The final *allegro* of the symphony, which contains a chorus of
thirty-two voices, eight each of sopranos, contraltos, tenors and basses,
is also danced by eight men and eight women.'[1] That the many choruses,
largely homophonic, scattered throughout the work were danced as well
as sung is made clear by Leopold: 'The brief solos in the choruses,
sometimes for two sopranos, sometimes for soprano and alto, are
interspersed with solos for male and female dancers.'[2]

After a scene of somewhat plodding *recitativo secco* for Venus and
Ascanio, Venus's aria, 'L'ombra dei rami tuoi' (No. 3) makes a splendid
effect by its spaciousness and elegance, as well as its virtuosity. Mozart
varies his orchestra throughout the opera: some choruses are
accompanied only by wind, some arias only by strings. Venus's aria has

[1] Mozart subsequently used the first two movements with a new finale to make a
separate symphony (K. 120).
[2] 13 September, 1771.

strings, oboes and horns. No. 4 is a shortened reprise of the chorus, 'Di te più amabile', which was heard earlier as the opening chorus, after the ballet (or, as Leopold puts it, as the finale of the three-movement symphony).

The rôle of the eponymous hero was written for and sung in Milan by a soprano castrato, Giovanni Manzuoli, whom Wolfgang had met and had some singing lessons with in London six years earlier. Manzuoli was noted for the strength and firmness of his lower notes. He was also, at the time of the *Ascanio* première, in his forty-sixth year, so it is perhaps not surprising that the tessitura of his arias is kept low. In modern performance the role would most suitably be entrusted to a high mezzo-soprano. Ascanio's first aria, 'Cara, cara lontano ancora' (No. 5), is preceded by accompanied recitative in which the young hero rails against Venus's harsh decree that he keep his identity secret from Silvia. The recitative is disappointingly tame, the *allegro* aria agreeable, yet at the same time dauntingly formal. The shepherds' chorus, 'Venga, venga de' sommi eroi' (No. 6) follows; a simple, rather dull piece which will be heard several more times during the opera. Its first repetition is almost immediate, after a brief exchange of dialogue in recitative between Ascanio and Fauno. More recitative follows, leading to Fauno's fresh and lively *andante* aria 'Se il labbro più non dice' (No. 8), demonstrably written for a higher, more agile castrato than Manzuoli. The next chorus, 'Hai di Diana il core' (No. 9), an altogether more sprightly piece than the earlier ones, is preceded by twenty bars of orchestral introduction to which, doubtless, the nymphs danced.

After a succession of arias for soprano, whether male or female, it comes as a surprise to hear, in Aceste's recitative, a tenor voice. The chorus of shepherds is repeated again as No. 10 and, after further recitative by Aceste, as No. 11. Aceste's aria, 'Per la gioia in questo seno' (No. 12), is an appropriately joyous *allegro*, florid enough to suggest that Mozart's tenor in Milan must have had as flexible a voice as any of the castrati. In No. 13, a simple *andante* cavatina without orchestral introduction, the nymph Silvia sings with innocent feeling of the love she feels for the young stranger she has seen; here Mozart seems to have drawn on his own adolescent feelings of awakened sensuality. The vocal line is clear and unadorned, the orchestral comment warmly sympathetic. In the longer, more formal aria which follows, 'Come è felice stato' (No. 14), Silvia reverts to more conventional utterance, for this glittering *allegro*, although attractive as a piece of music, is hardly a proper equivalent to the words sung. The shepherds' chorus, 'Venga, venga de' sommi eroi', is heard for the penultimate time (No. 15), after which Ascanio appeals to Venus in an aria (No. 16) which, formally unsatisfactory, is dramatically one of the most effective pieces in the score, making use of three different tempi – *adagio, allegro* and *andante* – to portray three quite separate aspects of the youth's situation at that moment. He muses inwardly on the nobility of Silvia's soul ('Ah, di sì nobil alma') in a solemn *adagio*, externalizes his feelings in addressing Venus ('Se le virtù di lei') by quickening to an impassioned *allegro*, then pleads with the goddess to allow him to approach his beloved, delivering his plea ('Solo un momento') in an affecting *andante grazioso*. Venus's reply is delivered in a florid *allegro* aria, 'Al chiaror di que' bei rai' (No. 17), and Part One ends with a reprise of the chorus of genii and graces with which it began (No. 18).

Part Two opens with Silvia's (unaccompanied) recitative and aria, 'Spiega il desio le piume' (No. 19), another formal *da capo* aria full of opportunities for vocal display. The chorus of shepherdesses, 'Già l'ore sen volano' (No. 20) is suitably pastoral and yet quite lively. The *recitativo secco* which follows broadens for a time into *accompagnato*. Fauno's second aria 'Dal tuo gentil sembiante' (No. 21) is the longest and most glittering in the entire score, a fierce *allegro* with a short contrasting middle section rather quaintly marked 'andante ma adagio'. Fauno's aria is, in any case, an odd excrescence: he praises Ascanio's beauty of form and of soul. 'Happy the maiden,' he says, 'who is burned by so beautiful a flame, should you become a lover.' ('Se mai divieni amante / felice la donzella / che a fiamma così bella / allor s'accenderà') Fauno delivers these flattering sentiments in cascades of coloratura (Ex. 7).

Ex. 7

span-de qua - si adorar ti fa, a-do-rar ti fa.   Dal tuo gen - til sem -

bian

te ri

No. 22 is a comparatively brief aria for Ascanio, 'Al mio ben mi veggio avanti', which moves through too many tempi to be able to establish a mood in any of them. With Silvia's recitative and aria, 'Infelice affetti miei' (No. 23), we are suddenly transported ahead to the world of mature Mozart. The accompanied recitative preceding the aria, in which Silvia wrestles with the two images of love, chaste and erotic, which have revealed themselves to her, is written with the insight not of an adolescent but of the musical psychologist who was to bring similar but no greater gifts to the plight of Fiordiligi in *Così fan tutte*. The comment of the string accompaniment is as understanding, as consoling, as though we were listening to that opera, and not to a *sérénade d'occasion* at a royal court. (Ex. 8).

Ex. 8

The aria which follows is a sad and affecting *adagio* in which Silvia asks the gods to return her lost innocence to her: a touching but also astonishing piece to come from the pen of the fifteen-year-old Mozart. Its mood of sadness and disturbance is maintained in the brief muted *allegro* of the shepherdesses' chorus (No. 24). Ascanio's 'Torna, mio bene, ascolta' (No. 25) is disappointing, an *adagio* aria very respectably composed, but lacking any deep feeling. The shepherds' chorus, 'Venga, venga de' sommi eroi' is then heard for the last time (No. 26), and the tenor Aceste contributes his second and final aria, 'Sento che il cor mi dice che paventar non dêi' (No. 27), a lively but gentle *allegro* addressed to Silvia. No. 28 is a chorus in which the shepherds, shepherdesses and nymphs call upon Venus to descend. After further recitative, the chorus continues (now No. 29) at the same steady tempo. No. 30 is a repeat of No. 28. Finally, in more recitative, Venus unites the lovers, and the work ends with a trio (Nos. 31 and 32, separated by forty bars of *recitativo secco* for Venus) and a chorus in which all unite to praise the goddess. The trio is not unattractive, but the chorus is somewhat perfunctory.

Leopold informed Frau Mozart that Wolfgang's *serenata* was really a very short opera, lengthened only by 'the two grand ballets performed after each act, each of which should last three quarters of an hour'.[1] Dramatically simple, indeed static, *Ascanio in Alba* is nevertheless a work of considerable charm. In parts, it is more than that, for when the young Mozart found himself most touched by the situation of young love frustrated he produced music of deep feeling and humanity. Still a child, he is already at the threshold of maturity.

[1] 21 September, 1771.

VII

Il sogno di Scipione
a dramatic serenade in one act
K. 126

Dramatis personae:

Scipione (Scipio Africanus the Younger)	(tenor)
Constancy	(soprano)
Fortune	(soprano)
Publio (or Scipio Africanus the Elder) Scipione's uncle	(tenor)
Emilio, Scipione's father	(tenor)

LIBRETTO by Pietro Metastasio, based on Cicero's *Somnium Scipionis*

The action takes place in the north of Africa, *c.* 200 B.C., during the reign of Massinissa, King of eastern Numidia

FIRST PERFORMED at the Archiepiscopal Residence in Salzburg, either 29 April or 1 May, 1772

Il sogno di Scipione

LEOPOLD AND WOLFGANG lingered on in Milan, instead of returning home to Salzburg immediately after the performances of *Ascanio in Alba*, their reason for doing so being that Leopold thought it possible that the Archduke Ferdinand would offer Wolfgang a permanent position at his court. For several weeks the Archduke was absent from Milan with his new bride, and it was not until 30 November that he received the Mozarts. Meanwhile, father and son visited several Milanese friends and acquaintances, and young Wolfgang gave proof that, for all his humane genius, he was a son of his age, by writing to his mother and sister: 'I have seen four villains hanged here in the Piazza del Duomo. They hang them exactly as they do in Lyons.'[1] The Mozarts' interview with the Archduke was inconclusive, for after it Leopold could say no more in a letter to his wife than that the affair was not quite hopeless. But he could no longer delay returning to Salzburg, and early in December he and Wolfgang set out for home via Brixen (now Bressanone), arriving in Salzburg on 16 December. While they were travelling the Empress Maria Theresa had, on 12 December, 1771, written to her son the Archduke:

> . . . You ask me to take the young Salzburger into your service. I do not understand why, since I do not believe that you have need of composers or useless people . . . but if it would give you pleasure, I have no desire to hinder you. My remarks are intended only to prevent you from burdening yourself with people of no use to you and giving them titles. . . . If they were to be in your service, they would degrade that service if they continued to travel around the world like beggars. . . . What is more, [Mozart] has a large family.[2]

Probably as a result of his mother's cautionary remarks, the Archduke Ferdinand did not offer employment to Wolfgang, and the day after he and his father arrived back in Salzburg their employer Archbishop Schrattenbach died after a long illness. Leopold lost no time in applying to the Salzburg Cathedral Chapter to restore in full his salary, part of

---

[1] 30 November, 1771.

[2] In *Briefe der Kaiserin Maria Theresia an ihre Kinder und Freunde* (ed. Alfred Ritter von Arneth; Vienna, 1871). The original is in French.

which the late Archbishop had suspended due to his absence in Italy. His petition was granted. The election of a new Archbishop took three months, and it was not until the middle of March, 1772, that the name of Schrattenbach's successor was announced. He was Hieronymous Joseph Franz von Paula, Count of Colloredo, Prince-Bishop of Gurk. Colloredo was renowned for his worldliness in an age of especially worldly priests. He was known in Salzburg, where he spent winters at his country seat, for his lavish entertaining, and he was soon to become better known there for his enlightened, if autocratic ecclesiastical reforms. He was certainly to enliven the social and intellectual scene in Salzburg, though his relationship with the Mozarts was to be anything but smooth.

The new Archbishop made his solemn entry into his domain on 29 April, and the event was celebrated by the performance at the archiepiscopal residence of a *serenata drammatica* especially composed in his honour. Wolfgang was given the commission to compose the *serenata*, the subject chosen being *Il sogno di Scipione*, an already existing libretto by Metastasio. It was performed on either 29 April or 1 May.

II

Pietro Metastasio (1698–1782), one of the most famous Italian poets and librettists of his time, lived and worked from 1730 onwards in Vienna, where most of his thirty or more libretti were written. He became so popular that many of his libretti were set over and over again by several composers. He wrote graceful and fluent verses, usually upon classical subjects, and, although his characters were stiff and formal, they were perfectly adequate for the requirements of most eighteenth-century composers. His libretto, *Il sogno di Scipione* (Scipio's Dream), based on Cicero's *Somnium Scipionis*, was originally written in 1735 for Luc' Antonio Predieri (1688–1767), an Italian composer who was for some years Kapellmeister of the Hofkapelle in Vienna. Predieri's *Il sogno di Scipione* was produced at the imperial castle of Laxenburg, near Vienna, on 1 October, 1735, to celebrate the Empress Elisabeth's birthday. Metastasio, then the Imperial Court poet, had provided Predieri with a dull libretto liberally laced with references to the military defeats of a great general and his steadfastness and courage in adverse circumstances. The Emperor Charles VI had suffered defeats in Italy: hence these allusions, and the work's 1735 description, 'azione teatrale, allusiva alle sfortunate campagne delle armi austriache in Italia' (theatrical piece, with reference to the unfortunate campaign of the Austrian forces in Italy). The libretto was used a second time for the nameday of Francis I in 1743, when the composer was Giovanni Porta. Mozart took it over unchanged, including the *licenza* in which Charles VI was apostrophized. In his score he wrote hastily, copying direct from

Metastasio's original, 'Ma Scipio esalta il labbro e Carlo il cuore' (But Scipio extols the lip [i.e. pays lip-service to virtue] and Carlo the heart), and then crossed out 'Carlo', substituting 'Girolamo', the Latin form of Hieronymous, Christian name of the new Archbishop of Salzburg.

The plot of *Il sogno di Scipione* is extremely simple. The action takes place in North Africa, *c.* 200 B.C., during the reign of Massinissa, King of eastern Numidia. Scipione is not Publius Cornelius Scipio (known as Scipio Africanus the Elder, a distinguished Roman general in the second Punic War), but Scipio Africanus the Younger, his nephew whom he adopted as his heir. Scipio, asleep in Massinissa's palace, is visited in a dream by the goddesses of Fortune and Constancy, who invite him to decide which of them he will choose for his guide through life. Constancy tells him he is in that part of Paradise where his glorious ancestors dwell, and the ancestors, including his uncle who adopted him, and his real father, Aemilius Paulus, duly appear. Scipio Africanus the Elder lectures him on the immortality of the soul, while Aemilius Paulus stresses the transience and insignificance of earthly joys. Scipio wishes to become one of their blessed company, but is told he has first to save Rome. He chooses to follow Constancy rather than Fortune, whereupon Fortune invokes fierce thunder and lightning. Scipio awakens, and the moral of the tale is made explicit in the *licenza*, or final choral ode to the dedicatee.

III

A short, one-movement Overture at a moderately brisk tempo (which later became the first movement of the Symphony K. 163) leads straight into the opening recitative in which the sleeping Scipione is awakened by the haranguing of Fortune and Constancy. Scipione's aria, 'Risolver non osa' (No. 1), an elegant *andante*, is followed by Fortune's 'Lieve sono al par del vento' (No. 2), a fierce *allegro*. Constancy's 'Ciglio, che al sol si gira' (No. 3) is written for the same type of voice and virtuosity as Fortune. In fact, the two virtues which the librettist was so careful to distinguish from each other are made by Mozart to sound as one. The chorus, 'Germe di cento Eroi' (No. 4), sung by the spirits of blessed Roman heroes, is infinitely superior to the solo arias, solemnly beautiful music in which the composer's poetic imagination is apparent in every bar [Ex. 9]. Publio's 'Se vuoi che te raccolgano' (No. 5) is a dull piece containing some stiff coloratura passages, and Emilio's 'Voi collagiù ridete' (No. 6) is equally characterless: the three tenor voices in *Il sogno di Scipione*, those of Scipione, Publio and Emilio, appear not to have interested Mozart very greatly. In his second aria, 'Quercia annosa' (No. 7), Publio is given music of somewhat greater individuality to sing, but with Fortune's 'A chi serena io giro' (No. 8) we are back in the world of anonymous virtuosity. Constancy, like a rival prima donna, replies in

Ex. 9

similar terms (No. 9: 'Biancheggia in mar lo scoglio'). Scipione's 'Di che sei l'arbitra' is an oddly unsatisfactory aria, defeated by its too frequent changes of tempo. The *recitativo accompagnato* in which the conflict is resolved provides the only moments of real drama in the opera. There follows the *licenza,* or epilogue, in which all pretence that the hero of the occasion is Scipione is dropped, and a soprano, presumably Constancy, steps forward to apostrophize the new archbishop in glowing terms (No. 11: 'Ah perchè cercar degg'io'). Mozart has left two versions of this aria, the second composed later probably for a repeat performance of the opera, or perhaps simply as an alternative setting for the Archbishop to hear separately. The final chorus, 'Cento volte con lieto sembiante' (No. 12), is brief and conventional.

There is little that can positively be said now for *Il sogno di Scipione*, except perhaps to note that its arias are longer than those which Mozart was composing at that time in his operas for Milan. The score looks disappointing on the page, and a production at the Camden Festival in London in 1968 (sharing a double-bill with *Die Schuldigkeit des ersten Gebots*) merely confirmed that the young Mozart's heart was not in this particular chore. 'Formal and uninspired,' Dent called it,[1] an opinion from which it is difficult to dissent.

[1] *Mozart's Operas*, Edward J. Dent (London, 1913).

VIII

Lucio Silla

an *opera seria* in three acts

K. 135

Dramatis personae:

Lucio Silla, Dictator of Rome	(tenor)
Cecilio, a proscribed senator	(soprano)
Lucio Cinna, Roman patrician, friend of Cecilio and secret enemy of Silla	(soprano)
Celia, sister of Silla, and in love with Cinna	(soprano)
Giunia, wife of Cecilio	(soprano)
Aufidio, a tribune	(tenor)

LIBRETTO by Giovanni de Gamerra, revised by Pietro Metastasio

The action takes place in Rome, *c.* 80 B.C.

FIRST PERFORMED in Milan, 26 December, 1772, at the Teatro Regio Ducal, with Bassano Morgnoni (Silla), Venanzio Rauzzini (Cecilio), Felicità Suarti (Cinna), Daniella Mienci (Celia), Anna de Amicis (Giunia), Giuseppe Onofrio (Aufidio)

Lucio Silla

I

IN THE MONTHS after Archbishop Colloredo's accession, Mozart composed several symphonies (K. 128 to 130 and 132 to 134), minuets and other instrumental music, and a liturgical piece, *Regina coeli* (K. 127). Under the previous Archbishop he had received no salary, though he had the title of Konzertmeister. His new master was prepared to be more generous, and decreed that his Concert Master should be paid an annual sum of one hundred and fifty florins. Wolfgang and Leopold thanked the Archbishop by setting out on their travels again in the autumn, for Wolfgang had another opera to compose for the Milan Carnival season in December. They left Salzburg on 24 October, travelling via Innsbruck, where they stayed at the Goldener Adler for two nights (25th and 26th), continuing through Bozen (Bolzano), Trento and Rovereto to Verona, finally arriving in Milan on 4 November.

By mid-November the only one of the singers to have arrived in Milan was Signora Suarti who had been cast in the male soprano role of Cinna, which one would have expected to be performed by a castrato. The leading male soprano role of Cecilio was to be sung by the famous castrato Venanzio Rauzzini. The leading lady, Signora Anna Lucia de Amicis, was not expected until the beginning of December. While awaiting his singers, Wolfgang began work on the choruses of his opera which was to be *Lucio Silla*.

The librettist, Giovanni de Gamerra (1743–1803) had been in his time both abbot and soldier, and had also written a number of sentimental plays. (After Mozart's death, he was to translate *Die Zauberflöte* into Italian.) Gamerra had submitted his libretto of *Lucio Silla* to the leading librettist of the day, Metastasio, in Vienna, and Metastasio had made several changes to it and had even introduced an entirely new scene in the second act. Wolfgang had already composed some of the recitatives for the opera before leaving Salzburg, but these now needed to be redone because of Metastasio's alterations.

Gradually, the leading singers began to assemble. The first recitative and orchestral rehearsals were held on 12 December, but the tenor, Cordoni, who was to sing the title-role, was ill and unable to come to Milan. Another tenor was found, Bassano Morgnoni, a member of the church choir at Lodi, so Wolfgang postponed composing his arias until

Morgnoni's arrival a few days later. For the splendid Anna de Amicis, Wolfgang, so Leopold wrote to his wife, 'introduced into her main aria passages which are unusual, absolutely unique and extremely difficult, which she sings remarkably well'.[1] The first full orchestral rehearsal took place on 19 December, a second one the following day, a third on the 22nd, and a dress rehearsal on the 24th. The first performance was given at the Teatro Regio Ducal on 26 December. It began two hours late, as the Archduke was delayed on official business, and it lasted, with intervals between the acts, for six hours, ending at 2 a.m. According to Leopold, writing before the performance, the music was timed to last for four hours without the ballets. There are now no ballets included in the score of *Lucio Silla*, though Mozart certainly composed music for ballets to be danced between the acts, one of them being *Le gelosie del seraglio* (K. Anh. 109). For the performance to have taken four hours, the tempi must have been very leisurely: no doubt many of the arias were repeated. A vivid account of the first performance is given by Leopold in a letter to his wife:

> Picture to yourself the entire theatre which was so full by half past five that it would have been impossible to get one more person in. On a first night, the singers are always extremely nervous at having to perform before so distinguished an audience. But for three hours, singers, orchestra and audience, many of them standing, had to wait impatiently in an over-heated atmosphere for the opera to begin. Then the tenor, who was engaged as a substitute, is a church singer from Lodi who has never acted on a large stage before, in fact has only once or twice appeared as first tenor, and was called in only a week before the performance. At one point in the prima donna's first aria, where she was expecting an angry gesture from him, he did it in so exaggerated a manner that it looked as if he was about to strike her on the nose with his fist. The audience began to laugh, and De Amicis, caught up in her performance and not understanding why they were laughing, was put off and did not sing well for the remainder of the evening. What's more, she became jealous because the Archduchess began to applaud as soon as the leading man appeared on stage. This had been arranged by the castrato himself: he had seen to it that the Archduchess was informed he was so nervous that he might not be able to sing unless the court encouraged him by applause. To placate Signora de Amicis, she was summoned to court at noon the day after the performance, and had an audience with their Royal Highnesses for over an hour.[2]

The opera was an undoubted success, and was performed twenty-six times in Milan during the Carnival season, to full houses. However, Mozart was never again invited to compose an opera for Italy. *Lucio Silla* appears not to have been revived until 1929, when it was given in Prague in a German version. In an edition by Dr Bernhard Paumgartner it was

---

[1] 12 December, 1772.   [2] 2 January, 1773.

performed at the 1964 Salzburg Festival, and was first staged in Great Britain during the Camden Festival of 1967.

II

Mitridate, Scipio and now Lucio Silla, or Sulla to give him the name by which he is known in English: the young Mozart's librettists were keen on the classical world. And, of course, other heroes from ancient Greece and Rome were to follow, notably Idomeneo and Titus. Lucius Cornelius Sulla was a Roman soldier who distinguished himself in the wars between Rome and other Italian tribes. When civil war broke out in Rome in 88 B.C., Sulla, who had been about to take charge of the campaign against Mithridates in Asia Minor, marched on Rome with his troops. Appointing Cinna as Consul, Sulla then went to Asia Minor where he waged war successfully for some years, and returned to Rome only to find it necessary to defeat his enemies all over again. In 82 B.C. he became Dictator of Rome, killed most of his opponents, and proscribed forty senators and several hundred of the nobility. Gamerra's libretto deals not with these large events but with Sulla as a man in love with the wife of one of the senators he has proscribed. Gamerra's characters are the merest cardboard, their sentiments conventional, their actions ill-motivated and unconvincing. The conventions of eighteenth-century *opera seria* required that autocratic rulers be revealed ultimately, as, *au fond*, clement and benevolent creatures, however monstrous they may in real life have been. But Gamerra was not only a conventional librettist of his time, he was, on the evidence of *Lucio Silla*, a talentless and incompetent one.

The opera is in three acts. Act I, Scene I takes place on the banks of the Tiber, outside Rome, in a landscape of trees and ruins. In the distance the Quirinal Hill can be glimpsed. Cecilio, a senator proscribed by Silla, has illegally returned to Rome, and anxiously awaits his friend Cinna, a Roman patrician who has remained outwardly a friend of the Dictator, though secretly opposed to him. Cinna arrives, and Cecilio asks for news of his wife Giunia. Cinna tells him that Giunia mourns him, having been told by Silla that he is dead. She goes often to the graveyard which contains the tombs of her ancestors and the heroes of old, and if Cecilio takes the hidden path which leads there, he will be reunited with her.

Scene II. Giunia's apartment, decorated with statues of famous Roman heroines. Lucio Silla is there, with his sister Celia, the tribune Aufidio, and guards. Silla asks Celia to intercede for him with Giunia, whom he loves. Aufidio is opposed to Silla's pleading for the love of a woman who hates him, but Silla dismisses him as Giunia enters. Giunia makes it clear that she has nothing but contempt for the man who sent her husband into exile and is thus, at least indirectly, responsible for his death. She leaves, and Silla gives voice both to his fury that a woman should dare to speak to him so insultingly, and to his love for that same woman. Finally, he resolves that, since she has called him a tyrant, he will behave as one to her.

Scene III. The entrance to the underground burial chamber with monuments and tombs of Roman heroes. Cecilio hides as he hears Giunia approach with her entourage of maidens and nobles. Her followers pray to the spirits of the dead heroes to rise up against Silla, while Giunia prays to the spirit of her father to comfort and pity her, and to her dead husband to help her repulse Silla. Cecilio steps forward, and at first Giunia thinks it is his spirit which confronts her. At last she realizes he is alive, and the act ends with their joyful avowals of love.

Act II, Scene I. An archway in Silla's palace, decorated with military trophies. Silla considers putting Giunia to death, but Aufidio reminds him that she is popular, and the daughter of his dead enemy Caius Marius who is still fondly remembered by many. He advises Silla to take Giunia as his wife, before the populace and the Senate, an act which will be interpreted by them as one of reconciliation. As Silla and Aufidio leave, Cecilio rushes in with his sword drawn. He attempts to pursue Silla, but is restrained by Cinna who reminds him that Giunia's life depends on his acting prudently. Cecilio expresses his conflicting emotions, finally resolving either to free Giunia or to die with her. He leaves, and Silla's sister Celia enters. She and Cinna love each other, but each is inhibited from confessing this to the other, she because of embarrassment, and he because his hatred of her brother is even stronger than his love for her. Celia attempts to reveal her feelings to Cinna, but rushes out without having managed to do so. Giunia enters to tell Cinna that she has been bidden to appear before Silla in the presence of the Senate and the populace. Cinna tells her the tyrant intends to force her to marry him. He advises her to agree, and to murder him in the bridal bed. Horrified, Giunia refuses, and Cinna proposes to kill Silla himself.

Scene II. The Hanging Gardens. Silla tells Aufidio he will flood the streets with the blood of Roman citizens if they resist him. They depart, and Giunia, who has overheard their conversation, wonders at Silla's meaning. Cecilio enters to embrace his wife for what may well be the last time. When he has gone, Celia arrives. She is filled with sympathy for Giunia, and is happy because Silla has promised her she shall marry Cinna. Giunia resolves to plead with the Senate for her husband's life. If they should refuse, she will die with him rather than marry Silla.

Scene III. The Capitol. Silla enters with Aufidio, followed by senators. Citizens and soldiers are already present. Giunia enters. Silla asks the Senate to award him the hand of Giunia in a marriage that would end the feud between his supporters and those of Giunia's dead father. Giunia furiously rejects Silla, and at that moment Cecilio enters, again with his sword drawn. Silla orders both husband and wife arrested, and in the ensemble which concludes the act he expresses his fury at the example of their constant devotion to each other.

Act III. Scene I. A prison. Cecilio is in chains. He is visited by Cinna and Celia who promise to save both him and Giunia. Cecilio asks Celia to tell her brother that he will die abhorred by the gods and despised by Rome unless he returns to his senses. Celia undertakes this task, and Cinna tells Cecilio that, should she fail, he intends to kill Silla. Giunia is led in to say farewell to Cecilio, who is then taken out by Aufidio and the guards.

Scene II. The Capitol. Before the Senate and populace, Silla prepares to pass sentence on the senator who dared to make an attempt upon his life. His decree is that Cecilio and Giunia shall be set free, for he has learned that 'the soul prefers innocence and virtue to deceitful splendour'. Senators and populace unite in a final chorus in praise of Silla.

III

The Overture to *Lucio Silla* is one of Mozart's miniature three-movement symphonies in the Italian manner (i.e. without the Viennese minuet), a cheerful lightweight piece which no one in the Milan audience would have expected to relate in any way to the drama to follow. What they expected of the opera was, of course, a succession of arias, and this is what Mozart provided: eighteen solo arias, a duet, a trio and three choruses. Despite the unpromising libretto, the arias in general reveal a greater degree of dramatic relevance than one might have anticipated, and also range over a wider selection of shapes and forms. The first aria, Cinna's 'Vieni ov' amor t'invita', is a conventionally florid piece in strict *da capo* form, but a number of variations on this particular formal pattern are to be found later in the opera. Also, the accompanied recitative preceding several of the arias is more consistently expressive of the text than is the case in the earlier operas. This is not especially true of the recitative before Cecilio's 'Il tenero momento' (No. 2), which is itself no more than an attractive *aria di bravura*, but it does apply in particular to the music Mozart composed for Giunia, the *prima donna*. Before Giunia appears, however, the *seconda donna* has the first of her four arias, 'Se lusinghiera speme' (No. 3) a lively *grazioso* in a-b-a form, *b* being a mere twenty bars of *allegretto*.

From the first bars of the orchestral introduction to Giunia's 'Dalla sponda tenebrosa' (No. 4), it is obvious that Mozart is going to lavish his imaginative sympathy upon the unhappy heroine. The tone is warmer, more personal, and even the coloratura flights at 'la pena tua maggior', where Giunia rages against Silla in the style of the Queen of the Night hurling her hatred at Sarastro, are given an individuality of utterance. In its juxtaposition of tenderness and vitriolic abuse, Giunia's first aria is remarkable, and establishes her in rounder, more believable terms than those on which we have met Cinna, Cecilio or Celia. Not even the eponymous hero himself, in his first aria (and the first in which we hear a non-soprano male voice), is characterized so lovingly, for Silla's 'Il desìo di vendetta' (No. 5) is no more than a fierce *allegro* of not especially individual character. But the accompanied recitative for Cecilio, as he waits for Giunia at the entrance to the tombs, returns us unequivocally to the drama, with its terse ejaculations solemnly punctuated by the orchestral strings. The chorus 'Fuor di queste urne' (No. 6) encloses Giunia's grief-laden prayer and leads by way of further accompanied recitative to the duet for Giunia and Cecilio, 'D'Elisio in sen m'attendi' (No. 7) which closes the first act. This entire scene is one of great power, poetry and originality, and incidentally contains the first bars in the entire score in which Mozart moves momentarily into a minor key, for the majority of the arias and ensembles are in major keys, mainly in B flat, C and D. The duet for the lovers loses something of its sensuous quality in modern performance by being sung by two sopranos. It is more likely to remind the listener of the duets for Fiordiligi and Dorabella in the later *Così fan tutte*. But, sung by artists capable of projecting the drama as well as the music, it can sound both affecting and effective.

The first aria in Act II, 'Guerrier, che d'un acciaro' (No. 8), is an *allegro bravura* piece for the minor character of Aufidio (tenor). Cecilio's 'Quest' improvviso tremito' (No. 9) could be similarly described except that it is much more taut and dramatically to the point, and preceded by terse and forward-moving recitative. The juxtaposition of arias some of which sound like detached concert pieces while others exist only to move the drama forward is one of the most disturbing elements in *Lucio Silla*. For instance, Celia's 'Se il labbro timido' (No. 10) is a dull minuet, while Giunia's recitative and aria 'Ah se il crudel periglio' (No. 11), though a frankly virtuoso display piece, is both excitingly brilliant and an example of the bravura aria at its finest. Cinna's 'Nel fortunato instante' (No. 12) is, by comparison, workaday. This is not to gainsay that such arias can be highly enjoyable in first-rate performance. After all, second-rate Mozart is infinitely to be preferred to many other respected names at their best. But Mozart at his best is the enemy of Mozart at anything less than that.

Silla's aria 'D'ogni pietà mi spoglio' (No. 13), in two *allegro* sections, separated by a few bars of *arioso*, is followed by Cecilio's 'Ah se a morir mi chiama' (No. 14), a beautiful and tender *adagio*, in which Mozart makes especially imaginative use of oboes and horns as obbligato instruments. Although Celia's 'Quando sugl'arsi campi' (No. 15) is an attractive and graceful *allegro* aria, its voice part is conceived as though for violin, an instrument which could perform it far more expressively than the voice. It is followed by the highly expressive recitative which leads into Giunia's aria, 'Parto m'affretto' (No. 16). This aria is even more highly decorated than No. 15, but here the fioriture are more meaningfully used to project the heroine's distress. The entire aria is strikingly expressive. The chorus 'Se gloria il crin ti cinse' (No. 17) is a suitably ceremonial piece to accompany the dressing of the stage by Silla, the senators and populace as they arrive in the Capitol. The act ends with one of the finest numbers in the score, a trio in which Giunia and her husband Cecilio confront the tyrant Silla ('Quell' orgoglioso sdegno', No. 18). In the context of *opera seria*, so dramatic a confrontation within a set piece was highly unusual, for the action was usually advanced only in the *secco* recitatives, the arias expressing a character's reaction to events. The dramatic tension created in 'Quell' orgoglioso sdegno' must have seemed almost revolutionary in 1772.

The third act begins somewhat dully with another of Celia's featureless arias, 'Strider sento la procella' (No. 19), a sprightly *allegro* whose words speak of raging storms and horrors, but whose music remains determinedly, indeed mindlessly, cheerful. Similarly, No. 20, Cinna's 'De' più superbi il core', falls easily on the ear but can only be regarded as ineffectual, if intended as brave defiance of tyranny. Cecilio's 'Pupille amate' (No. 21), a touching and gentle minuet, may also seem inadequate as an expression of a husband's feelings towards his wife at what he thinks is his moment of death, but at least the music does not fight the words. The recitative, 'Sposo, mia vita', and aria, 'Fra i pensier' (No. 22) in which Giunia responds, are both the dramatic climax and musical peak of the opera. The long accompanied recitative, in its vivid projection of the drama, anticipates the Mozart of *Don Giovanni* while the aria, an *andante* in C minor, and the only minor key aria in the opera, possesses an emotional maturity and musical confidence which would be astonishing even if it were not composed by a youth of seventeen [Ex. 10]. The aria is not cast in the old *da capo* form,

Ex. 10 Andante

GIUNIA

Frà i pen-sier più fu ne-sti di mor-te ve - der par-mi l'e -

san - gue con - sor-te,

nor is it as long a piece as its preceding recitative would lead one to expect. The *andante* of the first section quickens to an *allegro*, yet it is not so much a quickening of tempo as an intensifying of feeling that the soprano should aim for. The end of the opera follows quickly. After Silla's clemency has been declared in *recitativo secco*, the populace praises him ('Il gran Silla', No. 23) in a joyous chorus in which Giunia, Cecilio and Cinna also join.

Lucio Silla, then, is an uneven but interesting work. As other writers have pointed out, Mozart composed it at a time when he was on the brink of manhood and when the romantic impulse which was making itself felt in the arts, especially in music, was awakening in him personally. It was unfortunate that he should have had to lavish his generous emotional responses upon such dull and incalcitrant material as Gamerra's libretto, and all the more remarkable that the finished opera should contain as much fine music as it does.

IX

La finta giardiniera

an *opera buffa* in three acts

K. 196

Dramatis personae:

Don Anchise, Mayor of Lagonero, in love with Sandrina   (tenor)

The Marchioness Violante Onesti, beloved of Count
  Belfiore; believed to be dead, she is now working in the
  service of the Mayor, disguised as a gardener's maid   (soprano)
  under the assumed name of Sandrina

Count Belfiore, lover of Arminda, but formerly the lover of
  Violante   (tenor)

Arminda, the Mayor's niece, a noblewoman from Milan,
  formerly in love with Ramiro, but now betrothed to
  Count Belfiore   (soprano)

Ramiro, Cavalier, in love with Arminda who has abandoned
  him   (soprano)

Serpetta, chamber-maid of the Mayor, with whom she is in
  love   (soprano)

Nardo, in reality Roberto, servant to Violante; now in the
  service of the Mayor as gardener; in love with Serpetta   (bass)

LIBRETTO by Raniero de' Calzabigi, revised by Marco Coltellini

The action takes place on the country estate of the Mayor, at Lagonero, near Milan. Time: mid-eighteenth century

FIRST PERFORMED at the Redoutensaal, Munich, 13 January, 1775, with Rosa Manservisi (Sandrina), Tommaso Consoli (Ramiro), Teresina Manservisi (Serpetta)

La finta giardiniera

I

AGAIN, LEOPOLD AND Wolfgang stayed on in Milan after the première of Wolfgang's opera. They no longer had expectations of permanent employment for Wolfgang from the Archduke Ferdinand, but Leopold had sent a petition to the Grand Duke of Tuscany, seeking to obtain a position for the young composer at his court in Florence. It was not until mid-January that he learned his request was being considered; by the end of February it was clear that no offer would be forthcoming from Florence, so the Mozarts made their way back to Salzburg, arriving home on 13 March, 1773. Neither father nor son was to set foot in Italy again.

Wolfgang had spent the waiting period in Milan busily composing: quartets, a divertimento, and the motet 'Esultate, jubilate' which he wrote for Rauzzini, the castrato who had sung the role of Cecilio in *Lucio Silla*. Back in Salzburg, the Mozarts moved from the Getreidegasse to a larger apartment on the other side of the river, in the Hannibalplatz, now called the Makartplatz. (One of its rooms, known as the Tanzmeister Saal or Dancing Master's Hall, is open to the public as a Mozart museum.) Mozart continued to compose vocal and instrumental pieces for church and social use. In the summer, the Archbishop went to Vienna on a visit to the Court, and Leopold seized the opportunity of taking Wolfgang to Vienna at the same time. He was secretive about his plans, though they were in general obviously directed towards seizing some advantage, real or imagined, for Wolfgang. Father and son arrived in Vienna on 16 July, and lodged with a family named Fischer at Number 18, Tiefer Graben. They also visited their friends Dr Mesmer and his family in their magnificent house in Landstrasse whose garden could now boast 'views and statues, a theatre, an aviary, a pigeon-loft, and a belvedere looking out over the Prater'.[1]

In August, Leopold and Wolfgang were granted an audience by the Empress Maria Theresa, and also by their employer, Archbishop Colloredo, who agreed to prolong their leave from Salzburg. Leopold kept up his efforts to secure engagements for Wolfgang, and the young

[1] Leopold to Frau Mozart, 21 July, 1773. The theatre, at least, was an addition since their 1768 visit when *Bastien und Bastienne* had probably been performed in the Mesmers' house.

composer busied himself with a number of compositions, including
several quartets. He also kept up his correspondence with his sister
Nannerl, sometimes in a variety of languages:

> Hodie nous avons begegnet per strada Dominus Edelbach, welcher uns di
> voi compliments ausgerichtet hat, et qui sich tibi et ta mère empfehlen lasst.
> Addio.[1]

During their months in Vienna, Leopold managed to secure for
Wolfgang a commission to provide music for a play, *König Thamos* by
Tobias von Gebler. The play, with two choruses by Wolfgang, was duly
performed the following year; but, since Mozart composed much more
music for *König Thamos* six years later, discussion of the work can be left
until a later chapter. At the end of September, 1773, father and son
returned to Salzburg. Their intention was to travel 'through St
Wolfgang, so that I can show our Wolfgang the pilgrimage church of his
patron saint, which he has not yet seen, and also St Gilgen, the famous
birthplace of his mother'.[2] Their financial situation, however, forced
Leopold to change his mind, and take the shortest route home, via St
Pölten, Linz and Lambach. Back in Salzburg, Wolfgang composed more
chamber music, symphonies, his first piano concerto and much
occasional music for the Salzburg court. In the second half of the year,
he produced several works for solo piano as well as music for the church.
    Wolfgang's next opera commission came from Maximilian III,
Kurfürst, or Elector, of Bavaria. He was to write an *opera buffa* for the
Munich carnival season of 1774–75. The libretto chosen was *La finta
giardiniera* (hardly translatable; literally 'The pretended garden-maid'),
which had been written by Raniero de' Calzabigi for the composer
Pasquale Anfossi, whose opera was produced in Milan the previous
carnival season. Wolfgang began to compose *La finta giardiniera* in
Salzburg, then set out for Munich with his father on 6 December, 1774,
to meet the singers and to complete the opera. His sister Nannerl
followed them three weeks later in order to attend the première which
took place at the Redoutensaal or Assembly Rooms in the Prannergasse,
on 13 January, 1775, a fortnight before Wolfgang's nineteenth
birthday.[3] During the period of composition, he suffered much from
toothache, though not seriously enough to delay his work.

---

[1] 12 August, 1773. 'Today we met Mr Edelbach in the street. He gave us your
compliments and sends his greetings to you and your mother. Farewell.'
[2] Leopold to his wife, 8 September, 1773.
[3] The comic operas, as opposed to the *opere serie* which were performed in Cuvilliés'
enchanting little Court Theatre, were usually performed on a stage rigged up in the
Redoutensaal which was otherwise in use as a ballroom. In Vienna to this day,
performances of such operas as *Le nozze di Figaro, Così fan tutte* and *Die Entführung aus dem
Serail* are occasionally given in that city's baroque Redoutensaal.

The first rehearsal of the opera was, according to Leopold, so well received that the date of the first performance was postponed in order to allow the singers to learn their parts more thoroughly and to act with greater confidence.

The morning after the première Wolfgang wrote to his mother:

Thank God! My opera was staged yesterday, the thirteenth, and was such a success that I cannot possibly describe to Mama the tumultuous applause. To begin with, the entire theatre was so packed that a great many people had to be turned away. After each aria there was great applause and shouts of 'Viva maestro'. Her Highness the Electress and the Dowager Electress (who were sitting opposite me) also called out 'Bravo' to me. At the end of the opera, during the pause when there is usually quiet until the ballet begins, people kept on shouting 'bravo' and clapping. No sooner did the applause die down than it would start up again. Afterwards I went with Papa to a certain room which the Elector and the entire court had to pass through, and I kissed the hands of the Elector and Electress and their Highnesses, all of whom were very gracious to me. Early this morning, His Grace the Prince-Bishop of Chiemsee sent me a message, congratulating me on the wonderful reception of my opera. I fear that we cannot return to Salzburg right away, and Mama must not wish that for she must know how good it is for me to be able to breathe freely. We shall return home in good time. One especially urgent and necessary reason for us to stay here is that my opera is being performed again next Friday, and it is vitally necessary that I should be present. Otherwise, my work would be quite unrecognizable, for very odd things happen here.[1]

Others, besides the young composer himself, praised the opera. J. F. Unger, Secretary of the Saxon Legation, wrote in his diary that 'the music was generally applauded',[2] and the poet Christian Schubart wrote that, in *La finta giardiniera*, 'flashes of genius appear here and there, though there is not yet that quiet altar fire that rises towards heaven in clouds of incense. If Mozart is not a forced hot-house plant, he is bound to grow into one of the greatest composers of music who ever lived.'[3] Mozart's employer, Archbishop Colloredo, came to Munich too late to witness the première, but in time to hear the praises of the young Salzburger sung by all. 'He was so embarrassed,' wrote Leopold to his wife, 'that he could only reply by bowing his head and shrugging his shoulders.'[4] A second performance of *La finta giardiniera* was given at the end of February, but with cuts because the *seconda donna*, who sang the role of Serpetta, was ill. (According to Leopold, she was absolutely

---

[1] 14 January, 1775.

[2] Dresden State Archives. Quoted in Jahn: *Life of Mozart* (Vol. 1, London, 1882). The original diary entry is in French, and continues: 'Elle est du jeune Mozart de Saltzbourg qui se trouve actuellement ici. C'est le même qui à l'âge de huit ans a été en Angleterre et ailleurs pour ce faire entendre sur le clavecin, qu'il touche supérieurement bien.'

[3] *Deutsche Chronik*, Augsburg, 27 April, 1775.

[4] 18 January, 1775.

wretched even when not ill.) A third and final performance followed on
3 March, at the end of the carnival season, after which the Mozarts
returned to Salzburg, though not before Wolfgang had competed in a
'clavier contest' with the composer and pianist Ignaz von Beecke, a
contest from which, according to the poet Schubart, Beecke emerged as
the victor.

II

The libretto foisted upon Mozart was by far the poorest he had yet had to
grapple with. It had served well enough the previous year as a peg for
Anfossi's music, for Anfossi's *Finta giardiniera* had proved to be
successful. After its Rome première, it was staged in Vienna in 1775 and
made its way to Paris in 1778. The author of the libretto, Ranieri de'
Calzabigi, was the librettist of three of Gluck's finest operas and his
partner in operatic reform, but his *Finta giardiniera* is a clumsily-written,
confused and confusing pot-boiler. He appears later to have disowned
it: it certainly does not appear in either the 1774 or 1793 editions of his
works. For Mozart, the libretto was revised by Marco Coltellini who had
earlier performed a similar service in connection with *La finta semplice*.

The Marchioness Violante Onesti has been wounded by her lover
Count Belfiore in a jealous quarrel. Thinking that he has killed her, the
Count flees. The Marchioness sets out on a journey in search of him,
accompanied by her servant Roberto. Arriving at the town of Lagonero,
they enter the service of the Mayor, Don Anchise, as gardeners. The
Marchioness assumes the name of Sandrina, and Roberto that of
Nardo.

At the beginning of Act I, several of the inhabitants of Lagonero are
busily decorating the Mayor's garden for the forthcoming reception in
honour of his niece Arminda who has become betrothed to Count
Belfiore. Ramiro, Arminda's former lover, is unhappy at having been
deserted by her, the Mayor is plotting to win the favour of his new
gardener's maid, while his chamber-maid Serpetta, to whom he has
previously addressed his attentions, sulks jealously, taking no comfort
from the fact that the gardener Nardo is infatuated with her. Sandrina
informs Nardo that she is weary of the attentions of the Mayor, and hints
that they may soon have to leave. Nardo is loath to leave Serpetta,
despite the fact that she appears to take no notice of him. Then Count
Belfiore arrives, greets his bride-to-be, and begins to boast to the Mayor
of his intellect, wealth and family distinction.

A brief scene follows in which Serpetta teases and flirts with Nardo.
Next, Sandrina and Arminda meet, and Arminda announces that she is
about to marry Count Belfiore, at which Sandrina faints. Rushing off to
seek help, Arminda asks Belfiore to stay with Sandrina until she returns.

When she does, Ramiro also enters, and the two pairs of ex-lovers recognize one another in some confusion and embarrassment. The Mayor enters, but is ignored by the others, who all leave. Serpetta enters to tell him that his beloved Sandrina and Belfiore are kissing and cuddling at the far end of the garden, and he rushes off. Belfiore and Sandrina enter. He is not certain if she is really Violante, and she at first refuses to enlighten him, but later gives the game away by reproaching him for his infidelity. Repentant, he kneels at her feet to seek forgiveness, whereupon Arminda, Ramiro and the others arrive on the scene, and the act ends in general reproaches and universal confusion. Serpetta is still jealous of Sandrina for having replaced her in the Mayor's affections, Arminda is understandably furious at the Count's fickle behaviour, and Ramiro is upset at the violence of Arminda's feelings towards Belfiore. The Mayor is dismayed at Sandrina's lack of interest in him, she is distraught, and Nardo is concerned that he can do nothing to help his mistress, while Belfiore is finally uncertain which of the two ladies to marry, since he loves them both.

Act II begins with Arminda in a fury over Belfiore's behaviour. Then Nardo enters, continuing his attempted courtship of Serpetta. Belfiore begs Violante (Sandrina) to return to him, but she still cannot bring herself to forgive him for his violent jealousy which had led to their original quarrel in which he had wounded her. The Mayor now makes a formal declaration of love to Sandrina, but she runs off in confusion. Ramiro enters with a message from Milan commanding the Mayor to arrest Belfiore for the murder of 'a certain Marchioness Violante'. The Mayor resolves at least to postpone the wedding, remarking that he cannot allow his niece to marry a murderer. Ramiro expresses to himself the hope that Arminda will now return to him.

The Mayor interrogates Belfiore who, in his confusion, incriminates himself. Sandrina comes to his defence by announcing that the Marchioness was wounded but not killed, and that she herself is the lady in question. 'I am the Marchioness Violante, and I forgive him,' she cries. But, left alone with Belfiore, she informs him that she merely passed herself off as Violante in order to save his life. She departs. Belfiore loses his senses in his confusion, and begins to rave.

Serpetta tells the Mayor that Sandrina has fled, but, when he and Ramiro have gone in search of her, she informs Nardo that Arminda has had her rival taken to the nearby forest 'where she may play the great lady among the wolves'. It is now night, and, in the forest, Sandrina wanders alone, exhausted, frightened and despairing. In quick succession there now enter Nardo and Belfiore, the Mayor, Arminda and Serpetta. In the darkness, the Mayor declares his love to Arminda, and Belfiore his to Serpetta, both under the impression that they are addressing Sandrina. Ramiro enters with torches, all are recognized by one another, and again confusion reigns. Sandrina and Belfiore, their minds unhinged, imagine themselves shepherds, and sing and dance together to the amazement of the others.

Act III begins with a mock-mad aria by Nardo, in an attempt to humour Belfiore and Sandrina. The Mayor has decided he would rather his niece married Ramiro, but she still prefers Belfiore. Belfiore and Sandrina now emerge from their temporary insanity, and are eventually reconciled. Arminda decides she had better make do with Ramiro, and Serpetta tells the Mayor she wants to marry Nardo whom she has only been putting to the test. The Mayor accepts the situation, and resolves to remain single. In a final chorus, all sing of the joys of true love.

It is possible to read into this farrago of nonsense various levels of significance. Indeed, one is almost driven to do so by the extreme superficiality of its treatment of romantic love, real or pretended madness, and jealousy leading to violence. But the temptation should be resisted, if one is to appreciate Mozart's opera for what it is, rather than for what it might have been. Apparently oblivious to the incoherence of his libretto, Mozart treated each aria separately, and set the words at their face value, without giving much thought to consistency of dramatic characterization. It is difficult to imagine what else he could have done. In the printed libretto, the listed roles are divided into two kinds: *parti serie* and *parti buffe*, serious parts and comic parts. The serious roles are those of Arminda and Ramiro, while the others are all comic, Violante-Sandrina and Belfiore as well as the more recognizably comic characters descended from *commedia dell' arte*, such as the Mayor, Serpetta and Nardo. The Mayor is surely none other than Pantalone on the way to becoming Doctor Bartolo, while Serpetta and Nardo derive from Columbine and Harlequin. But what is comic, to us, in the characters of Belfiore and Sandrina, in their tempestuous love with its violence and madness? To the eighteenth century, they were undoubtedly funny, simply as a matter of convention, and Mozart here unhesitatingly accepts the convention. At least, he intends to do so. As we shall see, in the heat of composition things occasionally worked out differently. But it is pointless to search in the libretto for traces of that ambivalence of mood, so curiously Mozartian, which have crept into the opera. Comparisons with Richardson's *Pamela*, with Goethe's *Werther*, and with late eighteenth-century literary trends are misleading, for the libretto of *La finta giardiniera* bears as close a resemblance to the literary and dramatic masterpieces of the century as manufactured television comedy today does to Beckett and Pinter.

A word of explanation is required as to why, although Mozart's opera is in Italian, it has come down to us in a performing version in German. In the winter of 1779, Mozart allowed the impresario Johann Böhm, who was then visiting Salzburg with his company, to perform *La finta giardiniera* in German as a *Singspiel*, with dialogue replacing the unaccompanied recitatives. The German translation was made by Franz Xaver Stierle, an actor in the company. This version was probably performed in Salzburg, and certainly in Augsburg (on 1 May, 1780) and elsewhere on Böhm's tour of South and West Germany, under the title *Die verstellte Gärtnerin* (The disguised gardener's maid). It was probably during this tour that the original Italian score of Act I was lost, for only its second and third acts are preserved today, and there is no known copy of the original Act I. Mozart's setting of the recitatives in Act I is therefore lost. The opera can be performed complete in Italian today only by re-composing the first act recitatives. As the German version is known to have had Mozart's blessing – the German text has been inserted in the original score by Leopold Mozart, with occasional slight musical alterations to make the notes fit the words – managements today usually perform the opera as a German Singspiel. It is known to have been produced in the eighteenth and nineteenth centuries under a number of titles, including that by which it is known in Austria and Germany today, *Die Gärtnerin aus Liebe* (The Gardener's Maid in Love).

III

The Overture to *La finta giardiniera* is a brief, two-movement piece, a crisp *allegro molto* followed by a somewhat limping *andantino grazioso*. (Mozart later added a finale, to make a little symphony, K. 121.) A problem arises immediately with the first number, an introduction consisting of a chorus within which five of the seven principal characters sing short solo passages. Modern productions (and perhaps the original production as well) tend to use the soloists as chorus, for the opera has no further need of a chorus, and it would be an extravagance to engage chorus singers for the first number only. But the chorus sing of their joy and well-being: 'Welches Vergnügen, welch' frohe Tage' in the German words which are all we have for Act I (What delight, what joyous days). The principals, however, are by no means all in a state of bliss. Ramiro's solo lines speak of despair, Sandrina is melancholy, Nardo anxious, and Serpetta jealous. Only the Mayor is happy, in anticipation that he will win Sandrina's love. Ideally, the chorus should consist of villagers cheerfully at work in the Mayor's garden. The music given to them is unexceptionable, but the way in which Mozart has contrived to insert the various characters' comments and feelings which differ widely from each other, while maintaining a basic tempo, is quite masterly.

The role of Ramiro was written for a castrato, and is nowadays usually given to a young mezzo. His first aria, 'Scheu ist das freie Vöglein' (No. 2) is a curiously light-hearted piece for someone who has been abandoned by his sweetheart, though Mozart's chirrupy accompaniment dutifully mirrors the poetic image of the (male) bird caught in a (female) net. The Mayor's aria, 'Zu meinem Ohr erschallet' (No. 3), apparently interpolated for the German version of the opera, is a lengthy *allegro*, with a spacious, formal orchestral introduction, in which, as the Mayor speaks of the 'delightful sounds of flute and oboe' which resound in his inner ear, we of course hear them in the accompaniment. When the more sombre tones of the violas and the fearful din of drums and trumpets assail him in the aria's *presto* finale, these too are heard, though quite mellifluously. The aria is a pleasant example of musical wit, though its relevance to the dramatic situation is slight. Sandrina's first aria, 'Wir Mädchen sind sehr übel dran' (No. 4), will be known to many who have never seen *La finta giardiniera*, for there used to be a delightful recording of it sung in English by Isobel Baillie: 'A maiden's is an evil plight.' A cheerful soubrettish rondo with an *allegro* coda, it is charming in itself, but gives no hint of the darker, more intense aspects of Sandrina's character. The role of Nardo, Sandrina's servant, is written for bass, and his music reflects a certain single-minded determination. His first song, 'Der Hammer zwingt das Eisen' (No. 5), with its mock-heroic martial air, makes its effect unsubtly, the hammer-strokes of which he sings being naively imitated in the orchestra. The song is an excellent piece of characterization of a kind one does not find in, for instance, Mozart's earlier *opera buffa, La finta semplice*. Although *La finta giardiniera* is, formally, little more than a string of arias, its composer is clearly thinking much more carefully and consistently in terms of dramatic characterization than previously. With a more imaginative libretto, *La finta giardiniera* might have become the first of the great comic operas of Mozart's maturity. Even as it is, its musical interest is considerable, though its dramatic interest remains slight.

Belfiore, the tenor hero of the opera, and Sandrina, its eponymous heroine, are potentially the most interesting characters in the work. A few short years later, and given more encouragement to do so by his librettist, Mozart would have found a way to reconcile their differing moods. Now, he can only present a different aspect of Sandrina's or Belfiore's character in each aria. In his entrance aria, 'Welch ein Reiz' (No. 6), Belfiore comes before us as a romantic young lover, a Belmonte or a Ferrando before his disillusionment. Yet this is a man who almost killed his mistress in a fit of jealous rage, and who is soon to be shown wavering indecisively between that same mistress and the new love whose beauty he apostrophizes so tenderly in 'Welch ein Reiz', as, like Tamino, he gazes upon a miniature portrait [Ex. 11].

Ex. 11

The Mayor's niece, Arminda, appears to change, if not her character, then at least her characteristics, from aria to aria. In No. 7, 'Wenn die Männer sich verlieben', the first sentiments we hear her address to her beloved are in the nature of a warning that, should he deceive her, she will be quick to take revenge. As things are to turn out, she reveals a certain perception in greeting Belfiore thus. What is disconcerting is that she does so in music which would come more suitably from the lips of a flirtatious lady's maid than from a member of the Milanese nobility. We next find Belfiore behaving like a comic oaf, and boasting of his splendid ancestry in a *buffo* aria whose musical interest is slight, and whose effect depends upon the singer's ability as a comedian (No. 8: 'Hier vom Osten bis zum Westen'). Serpetta's first solo is a simple little arietta, 'Das Vergnügen in dem Eh'stand' (No. 9). After she has sung one stanza, Nardo replies with a second, to the same music. Serpetta continues with No. 10, 'So bald sie mich sehen', a pert, soubrettish *allegro*, which slows down to an *andante* pace in its final section as she describes the shy modesty with which she responds to flattery. Serpetta's music in general fails to move away from a generalized soubrettish bustle and cheerfulness: by no means unattractive while one is hearing it, it does not linger in the memory. With the opening bars of the following number, Sandrina's 'Ferne von ihrem Neste' (No. 11), one is immediately transported to a quite different, much more sensitive world of feeling and experience [Ex. 12]. When her voice enters, sadly trailing

Ex. 12

along, as it were, a little behind the melody in the orchestra, the effect is oddly moving. Sandrina's tender little aria is in distinct contrast to her earlier, more spirited utterance (No. 4). One feels that here one is overhearing her real voice, just as later one experiences the same feeling in Act IV of *Le nozze di Figaro* when Susanna begins 'Deh, vieni non tardar.'

Perhaps the most interesting features of *La finta giardiniera* are the concertèd finales to Acts I and II which foreshadow the infinitely greater finales in *Le nozze di Figaro*. The first act finale begins with the first accompanied recitative to be heard in the opera, alternating with passages of *arioso* and eventually broadening into a piece of continuous music in which the several characters begin by singing the same melody, with individual variations, and later are set off against each other thematically. The orchestration is considerably richer than in the Italian *opere serie* with which Mozart had in recent years been occupying himself, and though the solo voices alternate with homophonic ensemble passages, the general effect is one of flexibility and ease. Act I of *La finta giardiniera* ends with much greater confidence of manner and variety of vocal and orchestral texture than it began.

I have used only the German titles of the arias in Act I since, although an Italian text has been re-constructed by consultation with Anfossi's opera which used the same libretto, Mozart's Italian *recitativo secco* is lost, and the opera, in any case, goes well in German, with dialogue instead of recitative. But, for the remaining acts, since Mozart's original score including recitatives is extant, I shall give both Italian and German titles of the separate numbers.

Arminda's aria at the beginning of Act II, 'Um deine Straf zu fühlen' (No. 13: 'Vorrei punirti, indegno'), raises the question of the work's style or genre in no uncertain terms. From a purely musical point of view, this is a grand aria in the manner of the *opera seria* of the time. It could easily have been sung by, say, Giunia in *Lucio Silla*. In the dramatic context of *La finta giardiniera*, however, it is no doubt meant to be performed in parody of a tragic heroine of *opera seria*. But it is by no means clear to what extent Mozart thought he was writing parody, or even setting a text which, in those particular verses, was meant to be comic. This is a question which will pursue us as far as Donna Elvira in *Don Giovanni*, and will still not be satisfactorily and finally answered. Heard out of context, Arminda's aria appears to be the same kind of utterance that Elvira pours forth in *Don Giovanni*, or Elektra in *Idomeneo*: an exciting and inventive vengeance aria. But listening to it at the beginning of Act II of *La finta giardiniera*, an *opera buffa*, did Mozart's audience in Munich in 1775 laugh at it, or at any rate assume it to be a caricature of the grand manner?

We are back in less ambivalent territory in Nardo's 'Nach der welschen Art' (No. 14: 'Con un vezzo all' Italiana'), an engaging rondo in which he attempts to pay court to Serpetta with phrases in Italian, French and English. But the Count's aria, 'Lass mich die Reize' (No. 15: 'Care pupille'), manages to be, in consecutive sections, both the meltingly ardent plea of a lover and the farcical outburst of a clown. Its first section is addressed to Sandrina-Violante, whose identity still confuses him, and its second to the Mayor who has surreptitiously taken her place at his side, and whose hand he finds himself kissing in error. Sandrina's 'Es ertönt und spricht ganz leise' (No. 16: 'Una voce sento al core') is a charming piece of dissimulation, and the Mayor's 'Wie? Was? ein Fräulein?' (No. 17: 'Una damina, una nipote') a typically self-important explosion of affronted dignity such as was expected at some point in the action from the stock Pantalone character. Ramiro, the only one of the four male would-be lovers to be conceived as a role for male soprano, is not one of Mozart's most individual characters. His love song, 'Ach, schmeichelhafte Hoffnung' (No. 18 'Dolce d'amor compagna'), is romantic in tone and properly exalted in sentiment, yet curiously unimpassioned.

The aria in which, having been accused by the Mayor of murder, and having again been confused by the identity of Sandrina, Belfiore becomes temporarily deranged, is preceded by accompanied recitative, and is, in fact, the first aria to have its stature increased in this way. Until now, Mozart has moved directly from *recitativo secco* to aria. Belfiore's recitative is obviously meant to be understood as parody, for here, and in the aria as well, Mozart's orchestra underlines to the point of over-emphasis every image in the verbal text. The aria itself, 'Schon erstarren meine Glieder' (No. 19: 'Gia di vento freddo'), is oddly ineffective as an expression of mental derangement, real or pretended, and the *menuetto* conclusion in which Belfiore is restored to his senses is especially feeble. Serpetta's 'Wer will die Welt geniessen' (No. 20: 'Chi vuol godere il mondo') is a more engaging aria, quaintly so in view of the crafty sentiments it expresses.

The action would seem to require a change of scene to the nearby forest in which Sandrina is wandering – and it is now her turn to be deranged – yet Serpetta's aria leads on without pause to Sandrina's, with only a few bars between Serpetta's voice in the Mayor's garden and Sandrina's in the forest. This is a problem for the scene designer, who may choose to solve it by interpreting Sandrina's 'grotta oscura' as being a dark place of the mind. The *allegro agitato* figure on the violins with which Sandrina's aria begins ('Ach haltet, Barbaren' or 'Crudeli, fermate': No. 21) [Ex. 13] persists throughout, and into the

Ex. 13

accompanied recitative which links the aria, the first part of a magnificent dramatic *scena*, with the second, a cavatina, 'Ach, vor Tränen' ('Ah, dal pianto': No. 22) in which the dramatic tension is sustained most remarkably. This scene, which leads by way of accompanied recitative into the second-act finale, is one of the finest in the score, and the one in which Mozart's future genius as a musical dramatist is most clearly adumbrated.

The finale proper begins with the arrival of the other characters in the forest: 'Hier in diesen Finsternissen' (No. 23: 'Fra quest' ombre e questo oscuro'), though it ought to be noted that it has really begun as far back as the beginning of Serpetta's 'Wer will die Welt geniessen', three arias earlier and in another scene, for the music has been continuous since then. This is an even more impressive finale than that to Act I. Mozart's ripening skill in vocal characterization is given full play, with the result that the *commedia dell' arte* puppets come to life, and the formality of the earlier succession of arias is superseded in a rich pattern of vocal and orchestral interplay.

The trio at the beginning of Act III, 'Seht dort, wie Mond und Sonne' (No. 24: 'Mirate, che contrasto'), is really a solo for Nardo, followed by a duet for Sandrina and Belfiore, a gaily innocuous piece in which Nardo attempts to distract the amorous attention of the mad pair from himself. The Mayor's *buffo* aria, 'Nun mein Herr' (No. 25: 'Mio padrone'), is of slight musical interest, but Ramiro's *allegro agitato*, 'Wenn du mich auch verlässest' (No. 26: 'Và pure ad altri in braccio'), is the most convincing of his expressions of deep feeling. The recitative and duet, 'Wo bin ich wohl?' (No. 27: 'Dove mai son?'), in which Sandrina and Belfiore awaken from sleep and from madness, is quite beautiful, from its opening bars in which the strings produce sweet sleep music, through the passing moods of the recitative and aria as the lovers tentatively rediscover the real depth of their feeling for each other, to its joyous conclusion as they reaffirm their love. In the recitative especially, Mozart's orchestral comment is masterly in its appropriateness and delicacy. After the plot has been rounded off in a short exchange in recitative (Italian) or dialogue (German), the opera ends speedily with a final chorus in which all express their joy, 'Lieb' und Treue hat gesieget' (No. 28: 'Viva pur la Giardiniera').

Unsatisfactory though it is in many ways, *La finta giardiniera* is a valuable work, not only because it contains some glorious music but also because in it we see Mozart taking his first, tentative steps along the path which was to lead to *Figaro* and *Così fan tutte*. He was, of course, to take other paths as well. One of them leads to *Die Zauberflöte* and another to *Idomeneo* and *La clemenza di Tito*. But if one feels that the way to *Figaro* was the most richly rewarding path to take, then one will cherish a special affection for the not quite real gardener's maid who does very little gardening, and also for her companions in this curious but engaging masquerade.

X

Il rè pastore

an opera in two acts

K. 208

Dramatis personae:

Aminta, a shepherd; legitimate heir to the throne of Sidon   (soprano)

Elisa, Phoenician shepherdess   (soprano)

Tamiri, daughter of the tyrant, Stratone   (soprano)

Agenore, a Sidonian nobleman   (tenor)

Alessandro (Alexander), King of Macedonia   (tenor)

LIBRETTO by Pietro Metastasio

The action takes place at Sidon, in Lebanon, at the time of Alexander the Great, *c.* 332 B.C.

FIRST PERFORMED at the Archiepiscopal Residence, Salzburg, 23 April, 1775, with Tommaso Consoli (Aminta)

Il rè pastore

I

THE MOZARTS RETURNED to Salzburg from Munich on 7 March, 1775, to find a new commission awaiting Wolfgang. The Archduke Maximilian, youngest son of the Empress Maria Theresa, on his way back from Paris where he had been visiting his sister Marie Antoinette, was to spend a few days in Salzburg at the end of April as the guest of Archbishop Colloredo who, understandably, wished to provide first-rate musical entertainment for the music-loving Habsburg. Mozart therefore had about six weeks in which to compose *Il rè pastore*, for it was this already often used libretto of Metastasio which had been chosen by the Archbishop or his advisers. There were musical entertainments for the Archduke on three evenings, April 22nd, 23rd and 24th. On the 22nd, a concert of music by Domenico Fischietti, second Kapellmeister of the Salzburg Court, was given, the soloists including two musicians from Munich, the castrato Tommaso Consoli who had sung Ramiro in *La finta giardiniera*, and the flautist Johann Becke. *Il rè pastore*, with Consoli as the young shepherd Aminta, was given on the 23rd, and another concert on the 24th at which several members of the local aristocracy performed, as did the Archduke himself. Also, 'at the end of the *musique*, the famous young Mozart was heard on the clavier and played various things by heart with as much art as pleasantness. Thus ended the day, and because of the Archduke's impending departure everyone retired early.'[1] From the Abbot Beda Seeauer's diary[2] we learn that the Archduke 'condescended to fiddle *violino secondo*' on this occasion.

The Archduke's Travel Journal refers to Mozart's opera as a cantata, and another Salzburg diarist, Joachim Ferdinand von Schiedenhofen, calls it a serenade.[3] It is just possible, therefore, that *Il rè pastore* (The Shepherd King) was not actually staged at the Archbishop's Residence, but given in concert performance.

[1] From the Archduke Maximilian's Travel Journal. MS in the Austrian State Archives, Vienna. The entry (for 24 April) was probably written by the Archduke's Chief Steward, Count Franz Xaver Rosenberg.

[2] Archive of St Peter's Church, Salzburg.

[3] The diary, privately owned, is on loan to the Salzburg Provincial Archives.

II

Metastasio's *Il rè pastore* was written in 1751 and set to music by the Viennese composer Giuseppe Bonno (1710–1788). (In 1781 when one of Mozart's symphonies was performed under Bonno's direction, the composer referred to him as 'der alte ehrliche brave Mann' [the sincere, worthy old man].[1] After Bonno, *Il rè pastore* was also set by at least twelve other composers before Mozart. Among them were Maria Teresa Agnesi, Galuppi, Felice Giardini, Gluck, Hasse, Arvid Hopken, Jommelli, Lampugnani, Christoph Nichelmann, Piccinni, Giuseppe Sarti and Uttini. An English composer, George Rush, set an English translation as *The Royal Shepherd*, which was produced at Drury Lane Theatre in 1764. After Mozart, a setting by Tommaso Giordani was produced in London in 1778 at the King's Theatre. Metastasio, Maria Theresa's Court Poet, was not only an elegant versifier but also a librettist of fine craftsmanship, some of whose libretti were set by as many as seventy different composers.

Mozart compressed the three acts of Metastasio's *Il rè pastore* into two. He may have been asked to keep the evening's entertainment to a reasonable length, or he may have been taking into consideration the forces available. The Archbishop did not maintain an opera company, so the singers would have to be drawn from a chorus whose formal function was to perform liturgical music. In a letter to Padre Martini, the following year, Mozart was to write: 'As far as the theatre is concerned, we are in a bad way here for lack of singers. We have no castrati, and we shall not get them easily because they insist on being well paid, and generosity is not one of our failings.'[2] Also, Metastasio's libretto is unusually static, even by the standards of *opera seria*, and although Mozart's opera is short, it is quite long enough given the nature of its subject, an actionless dissertation upon royal benevolence. Metastasio himself, however, considered *Il rè pastore* one of his finest libretti. 'Non ho mai scritto alcuna delle mie opere con facilità uguale e della quale io abbia meno arrossito' he wrote to a friend upon completing it in 1751. (I have not written any of my other works with such facility, and I feel much less ashamed of this one.)[3] It was Metastasio's second and third acts which were compressed into one by Mozart, several arias being thus omitted without much damage being done to the almost non-existent plot. A few slight additions were made, in order to compensate.

At the beginning of the opera, Sidon has been conquered by Alexander the Great (Alessandro) and his Macedonian army. Alexander has slain the tyrant Stratone, and is determined to place on the throne

---

[1] In a letter to his father, 11 April, 1781.   [2] Letter 205.

[3] Quoted by Einstein, op. cit., p. 402.

the son of the last rightful king, who has been hidden from the tyrant by a faithful retainer, and brought up as a shepherd, under the name of Aminta. The first act of the opera takes place in pleasant countryside near Sidon. A river, with a bridge across it, flows through the landscape, and in the distance can be seen the towers of the city. The young shepherd Aminta sits, a flute in his hand, in front of his cottage. He and the shepherdess Elisa are in love, and when she appears he expresses his fears for her safety, the country being overrun by Macedonian troops. Elisa reassures Aminta, reminding him that Alexander has liberated the country and has instituted a search for the legitimate heir to the throne, who is thought to be living among common people, unaware of his true identity. Aminta is unhappy that Elisa, who is of the pure blood of Cadmos, is forsaking her inheritance for him, but she swears that she loves him for himself and is unconcerned at his lowly calling. When she has left, Aminta expresses his contentment with the simple life, and his joy in loving and being loved by Elisa.

Alexander the Great now enters with his friend and adviser Agenore. The two men do not reveal their identities, but question Aminta about his life and background, testing the sincerity of his assertion that he scorns a life of pomp and riches. They are impressed with his replies and his demeanour, and are convinced that he is the lost heir to the throne whom Alexander has been seeking. Aminta leaves to water his flock, and Alexander also departs. Agenore is about to follow when Tamiri appears, dressed as a shepherdess. Daughter of the tyrant, she is in love with Agenore. After her father was conquered by Alexander, she had wandered about the countryside until given shelter by Elisa. Agenore attempts to persuade her to throw herself upon Alexander's mercy, but she is too proud to do so. They go off in separate directions, and Elisa reappears, searching for Aminta. When he enters, she informs him that her father has given permission for their marriage. They are interrupted by Agenore who reveals to Aminta that he is really the heir to the throne, and that he has only to present himself before Alexander to be crowned as king. Elisa is delighted, but Aminta is highly reluctant to change his state. She persuades him, however, to reveal himself to Alexander, and he agrees to do so, though with misgivings.

Act II consists of three scenes. The first takes place in Alexander's camp, where Aminta now lives. Elisa arrives, and attempts to see Aminta, but is turned away by Agenore, for Aminta is soon to be crowned King of Sidon and must now put duty before love. Sadly she leaves. Having heard that Elisa had come to see him, Aminta now emerges from Alexander's tent, but Agenore dissuades him from following her. When Alexander appears, Aminta again expresses his feeling that he will not make a good ruler. Alexander persuades him that heaven will turn him into an enlightened monarch, and insists that the time has come for him to dress himself in his royal garments in order to be presented to his subjects. Aminta leaves, and Agenore takes an opportunity to plead the cause of Tamiri with Alexander. Alexander wishes to find the missing princess, in order to assure her that he does not hold her responsible for her father's tyranny. Agenore informs Alexander that he knows Tamiri's whereabouts, and Alexander then reveals his desire that Aminta and Tamiri should marry, and rule jointly over Sidon. Agenore turns pale at this announcement, but remains silent.

The scene changes to a large cave some distance from the camp. Aminta and Agenore meet, and Agenore bitterly assures Aminta that he is sure to be happy, for he will have a worthy consort. Thinking that Agenore refers to Elisa, Aminta agrees. He leaves, and Elisa enters. She asks Agenore to confirm the truth of the rumour she has heard that Aminta will marry Tamiri. Agenore confirms it, to Elisa's anger and distress. When she has gone, Tamiri appears: She, too, feels bitter, and when Agenore reproaches her for being cruel to him, she in turn reproaches him for allowing her to be given in marriage to someone else.

The final scene takes place in the outer courtyard of the Temple of Hercules. Preparations for the coronation have been made, and Alexander arrives, accompanied by Macedonian and Sidonian nobles. Tamiri now enters, and throws herself upon Alexander's mercy, saying that she does not want to be Queen, as she is in love with Agenore. Elisa then implores Alexander's aid. She has loved Aminta since childhood, and lives only for him. At this point, Aminta enters, dressed as a shepherd again. He can be happy, he says, only with Elisa. Alexander is moved by the predicament of the four lovers. He decrees that Aminta and Elisa shall rule Sidon, and promises to establish another kingdom elsewhere for Agenore and Tamiri. The opera ends in general rejoicing, and the statutory chorus in praise of a wise and benevolent ruler. At the Salzburg performance, for 'Alexander the Great', the Archduke Maximilian no doubt understood 'Maximilian', or at least 'Maria Theresa'.

III

The Overture, a lively *molto allegro*, is a one-movement piece which leads directly into the first aria. As was his custom, Mozart made a symphony of it and the first aria, by adding a newly composed finale (K. 102). Aminta's 'Intendo, amico rio' (No. 1) is song rather than aria, a simple, gently scored pastoral song, the colours of flute and horn joining with the rippling vocal line and 6/8 rhythm to conjure up an agreeable atmosphere of peace and contentment. Aminta's role is written for male soprano; as Elisa is also a soprano role, this causes a problem in modern performance if both parts are sung by the same kind of lyric soprano voice. It is preferable, surely, to have some contrast of colour between the voices, and to give Aminta to the darker of the two.

Aminta's song, 'Intendo, amico rio', into which the overture has merged without coming to a close, now glides imperceptibly into *recitativo secco*. But Mozart does not keep up this pleasant impetus, for the recitative comes to an end on the usual cadence before Elisa begins her first aria, 'Alla selva, al prato, al fonte' (No. 2), a full-scale, formal *da capo* aria, complete with coloratura, and provision for a cadenza flourish at the end. An agreeable piece in itself, it glitters too much to be considered a suitable setting of its words which express a desire for the simple life, for woods, springs, fields and a 'rozzo augusto tetto' (rough, narrow roof). Aminta's 'Aer tranquillo' (No. 3), preceded by delicately scored *recitativo accompagnato*, is even more elaborate than Elisa's aria, though it, too, celebrates the tranquillity of green fields and flowing streams. An a-b-a *da capo* aria, its first section in B flat was used again by Mozart a few months later, to begin (this time in G major) his violin concerto K. 216 [Ex. 14].

Ex. 14

Violino I

Alessandro's arias are among the most conventionally conceived in the entire score, with their formal introductions, bravura passages and cadenzas. In the first of them, 'Si spande al sole in faccia' (No. 4), the monarch likens his own benevolence to the emergence of the sun after storms. Mozart makes a half-hearted attempt to offer the appropriate scene-painting in the orchestra, but his heart seems not to have been in the task. Agenore's first aria, 'Per me rispondete' (No. 5) is a tender *grazioso* of no great individuality except in its obvious contrast to the music given to the opera's other tenor, Alessandro. The third soprano voice, Tamiri's, is then heard in 'Di tante sue procelle' (No. 6), again a piece which, pleasing though it is, can hardly be said to make a strong effect. Before the duet for Elisa and Aminta which ends Act I, there is a long passage of accompanied recitative in which Aminta's plight is movingly portrayed. The *andante* orchestral figure which punctuates Aminta's words has something of the ambiguous bitter-sweet quality one associates with the *andantes* of the piano concerti of Mozart's Viennese years [Ex. 15]. The duet itself, 'Vanne, vanne a regnar' (No. 7),

Ex. 15 Andante

Violino I

is in two sections: a 3/4 *andante* followed by a 4/4 *allegro*, the subject of the *allegro* being related to that of the *andante*. It ends the act pleasantly, though its emotional temperature is rather cool when one considers the situation of the two lovers whom destiny is about to part.

Elisa's aria at the beginning of Act II, 'Barbaro! O dio' (No. 8) is much more aligned to the dramatic situation than was her bravura aria in Act I, even though it adapts itself to an a-b-a-b form, alternating *andante* and *allegro*. The *secco* recitative is rather lengthy for modern performance, although, as far as the plot is concerned, it contains very little padding. It just seems too long a time before the next aria, Alessandro's 'Se vicendo vi rendo felici' (No. 9), which, when it does come, is delightful, its pair of flutes competing happily with Alessandro's coloratura, its texture light and joyous. It is followed by the most famous aria in the score, one much performed as a concert aria by sopranos: Aminta's 'L'amerò, sarò costante' (No. 10). This is a rondo in five sections, an *andantino* of great beauty and tender feeling, and the emotional climax of the opera. That it was so intended by Mozart is attested to by his having scored it much more richly than any of the other arias (flutes, English and French horns, bassoons, and a solo violin obbligato). The criticism is sometimes made of 'L'amerò' that it is so determinedly undramatic as to be virtually a concert aria. But this is to misunderstand Aminta's mood of serene confidence in his love for Elisa. Tamiri's second aria, 'Se tu di me fai dono' (No. 11), is a simple yet affecting *andantino*, lightly scored for strings alone. It is followed swiftly by an aria in which Tamiri's lover Agenore expresses a depth of feeling similar to hers, but in an agitated *allegro* in C minor, the only minor key aria in the opera ('Sol può dir, come si trova', No. 12).

The final scene begins with Alessandro's 'Voi che fausti ognor donate' (No. 13), a somewhat stiffly formal *allegretto* which sounds perfectly correct and acceptable in context but lacks sufficient individuality to make any effect divorced from its placing in the opera.

The final chorus, 'Viva! Viva l'invitto duce!' (No. 14), is a livelier and more elaborate affair than some of Mozart's earlier closing ensembles have been: a four-part chorus sung by the five singers, with Elisa and Tamiri sharing the same vocal line, and several passages in which the voices are heard singly or in duet. It maintains the same tempo – *molto allegro* – throughout, allowing the opera to end on a brilliant, festive note, as befits the amiable social nature of the occasion on which it was first performed.

To speak of the occasion on which it was performed is to remind ourselves that Mozart composed *Il rè pastore*, like so many of his operas, for a single performance or series of performances, with no particular expectation that the work would ever be heard again. It is worth remembering this occasionally, as we examine Mozart's entire operatic *œuvre* two hundred years later, making use of criteria some of which the composer himself might well consider meaningless. The wonder is that this *pièce d'occasion* should have triumphed so completely over the circumstances of its composition; for, despite the fact that it is distinctly not held in any great esteem by Mozart commentators (even the perceptive Einstein dismisses it as 'one of his weakest'), *Il rè pastore* is more alive, and more likeable, than many of its predecessors. It is true that several of its arias are formal, and the point has often been made that the voice parts sound as though they were instrumentally conceived. That they do sound like the melodies which abound in the violin concertos Mozart was writing in this same year is incontestable. But the violin sings, too. My own experience with *Il rè pastore* is that, on paper, it looks as though it ought to be the most unsatisfactory of Mozart's early operas, whereas in performance its own special qualities of luminous orchestration, great variety of tone colour, and freshness of melodic inspiration, leap into prominence. There is much bravura writing, but the voice of humanity persistently breaks in, and this despite Metastasio's stiffly schematic libretto. *Il rè pastore* ought to be an uninteresting, old-fashioned work, but it is not. In it, Mozart contrives both to accept and to defy convention. He accepts the libretto and the form, finding his freedom in the ease and fluency of his orchestral writing, and in the depth of feeling with which he imbues several of the arias. The musical characterization may, in dramatic terms, be no more than rudimentary, but it is quite clearly the seed from which life-enhancing fruit was to emerge.

XI

Thamos, König in Aegypten

Choruses and *entr'actes* for a heroic drama
by Tobias Philipp von Gebler, the action
of which takes place in ancient Egypt.

K. 345

FIRST PERFORMED with Mozart's music in Salzburg, during the 1779–80 season, and then in Vienna, early in 1783. (The first two choruses were performed in a production of the play in Vienna on 4 April, 1774, and in Salzburg in 1776)

Thamos, König in Aegypten

I

WOLFGANG'S NEXT TWO years were spent quietly, and apparently not unhappily, in the Archbishop's service in Salzburg. From the spring of 1775 until the summer of the following year, he continued to compose the works required of him: church and chamber music, serenades and divertimenti for social occasions, charming *galant* pieces that were imbued with his own warmth and deep feeling. He was now twenty, and there is no reason to suppose he was indifferent to the charms of the young ladies of Salzburg. The music he composed reflected the ardour of his awakening manhood, his youthful energy, and his own curiously bitter-sweet sentiment. From the autumn of 1776, however, both Wolfgang and his father became increasingly dissatisfied with the conditions of their employment in Archbishop Colloredo's service, and began to think of planning another tour. Although the Archbishop appeared not to appreciate Wolfgang's unique genius, he still refused to allow him and Leopold to begin a concert tour in March, 1777. After a family conference, it was decided that, if Colloredo would agree to release Wolfgang alone, his mother should accompany him on a tour of Southern Germany, for Leopold was not willing for his son to travel by himself.

In August, Wolfgang petitioned for his release from the Archbishop's employment. After pointing out that a concert tour was necessary in order to improve the family's finances, and requesting a discharge for that purpose, he concluded:

I trust your Serene Highness will not take this most humble request amiss since, three years ago, when I asked permission to travel to Vienna, Your Highness graciously declared that I had nothing to hope for here and would do better to seek my fortune elsewhere. I humbly thank Your Serene Highness for all the favours I have received, and in the fond hope that I may serve Your Serene Highness more successfully in my years of manhood, I commend myself to your continuing grace and favour.[1]

The Archbishop's initial reaction was to declare that 'father and son, in accordance with the Gospel, have permission to seek their fortunes

[1] The petition is in the Provincial Archives at Salzburg.

elsewhere'.[1] Ultimately he relented, retained Leopold in his service, and allowed Wolfgang to go. On 23 September, Wolfgang and his mother set out for Germany, arriving in Munich the following day. The letter that Leopold sent after them reveals how sad and depressing the parting must have been for the entire family. 'After you had both left,' he wrote to his 'two dear ones', 'I walked wearily up our steps and flung myself into an armchair. While we were saying goodbye I had made a great effort to keep myself under control so as not to make our parting even more painful. In all the rush and confusion I forgot to give my son a father's blessing. I ran to the window and sent my blessing after you, but I missed seeing you drive out through the gate, and at last realized that you were gone, and that I had sat for a long time, unable to think at all. Nannerl wept bitterly, and I had a hard job consoling her.'[2] Little did poor Leopold realize that he was never to see his wife again.

The purpose of Mozart's latest journey was to seek not only specific commissions but also a possible appointment as composer at a court more sympathetic than that of Salzburg's Archbishop. 'Laugh heartily and be merry,' Wolfgang adjured his father in his first letter home, written only a few hours after his departure from Salzburg, 'and always remember as we do that our Mufti H. C. [his name for the Archbishop Hieronymous Colloredo] is a prick, but that God is compassionate, merciful and loving.'[3] ('I beg you not to make any more jokes about our Mufti,' was Leopold's reply. 'Remember that I am in Salzburg, and that one of your letters might get lost or find its way into other hands.'[4])

In Munich, Wolfgang called upon Count Seeau, supervisor of entertainments at the Bavarian Court, who advised him to seek an audience with His Highness the Elector, Maximilian III. A second visit to Seeau, however, found that gentleman less sanguine of Wolfgang's chances of success in Munich. The advice of Count Zeill, Bishop of Chiemsee, was sought. Zeill spoke to the Elector at dinner in the Nymphenburg, and discovered that the Elector thought Wolfgang ought first to make a bigger name for himself, in Italy or elsewhere, before seeking a permanent appointment at his court. When Wolfgang himself managed to speak to the Elector, it was not in formal audience. He simply managed, with the aid of the court cellist, to accost the Elector in his palace on his way to hear Mass before going off to hunt.

> When the Elector came up to me, I said, 'Allow me, Your Highness, to throw myself most humbly at your feet, and offer you my services.'
> 'So you have really left Salzburg for good?'
> 'Indeed, yes, Your Highness.'
> 'Why is that? Have you had a row with him?'
> 'Not at all, Your Highness. I merely asked him for permission to travel,

---

[1] Written on the verso of the petition.   [2] 25 September, 1777.
[3] From Wassenburg, 23 September, 1777.   [4] 27 September, 1777.

which he refused. So I was compelled to take this step, though for some time I'd had it in mind to leave, for Salzburg is no place for me, I can assure you.'

'Good Heavens, what a young fellow you are. But your father is still in Salzburg?'

'Yes, Your Highness. He too humbly begs to pay his respects to you,' and so on. 'I have already been to Italy three times, and I have written three operas, am a member of the Bologna Academy, for which I had to pass an examination over which many maestri have laboured and sweated for four or five hours, but which I completed in an hour. Surely that is evidence that I am competent to serve at any court. My sole wish, however, is to serve Your Highness who is himself so great a . . .'

'Yes, my dear boy, but there is no vacancy. I am sorry. If only there were a vacancy.'

'I assure Your Highness that I should not fail to be a credit to Munich.'

'Of course, but it's no use, there's no vacancy here.' He was walking away as he said this, whereupon I commended myself to his favour.[1]

Wolfgang considered one or two other possibilities while he was in Munich, among them a suggestion from the innkeeper and music-lover, Franz Albert, by which Albert and ten friends would club together to produce an annual salary to keep Mozart in Munich. But this scheme did not commend itself to Leopold. To him, the only respectable employment for a musician was in the service of royalty or, at least, nobility. Far more tempting was the possibility that the Bohemian composer, Josef Mysliweczek, ill with venereal disease in a Munich hospital, might obtain for Wolfgang a commission to write an opera for Naples the following year. Wolfgang visited Mysliweczek who, no more than forty, was already badly disfigured by his disease, and was assured that the commission was as good as his, and that he should go to Italy, 'where musicians are really appreciated and valued'.[2] Nothing, however, was to come of this. Eventually, convinced that nothing was to be gained by remaining in Munich, and urged by Leopold to continue his travels, Wolfgang and his mother left on the morning of 11 October, and arrived in Augsburg that evening.

They spent two weeks in Augsburg, visiting Leopold's relatives, and arranging concerts at which Wolfgang performed with local musicians. Wolfgang also made himself known at the Heiligkreuz monastery, where he spent a number of agreeable hours, although the standard of the monks' music-making apparently left much to be desired. The travellers' way next led through Hohen-Altheim, the country seat of Prince Kraft Ernst von Oettingen-Wallerstein, where they found the

---

[1] Mozart to his father: Munich, 30 September, 1777.

[2] Mozart to his father: Munich, 11 October, 1777. In the same letter he writes: 'I have an impossible longing to write another opera . . . I have only to hear an opera discussed, or sit in a theatre and hear the orchestra tuning up, to be quite beside myself.'

prince in mourning for his wife, and in no mood for music-making. On 28 October, they continued on to Mannheim.

This was not, of course, Wolfgang's first visit to Mannheim, whose court was famous for its orchestra which carried on the traditions of the seventeenth-century Viennese court orchestra and school of composition. He had last been in Mannheim at the age of seven. Now he was twenty-one, and there had been many changes. One development was of particular interest to him. Until now, opera had been dominated by Italy and the Italians. Poets invariably wrote their libretti in Italian. But during the sixties and seventies in Germany, opera in the vernacular was beginning to make its way. In Mannheim, there had been staged an *opera seria* in German – *Alceste* by Anton Schweitzer, with a libretto by Wieland – which had been successful enough to be followed by a second German-language opera, *Günther von Schwarzburg* by Holzbauer, a performance of which Wolfgang attended. He also involved himself, while in Mannheim, with rehearsals for a third German opera, *Rosamunde* by Schweitzer, substituting as leader of the orchestra for the composer who was indisposed. Among the singers he met were the tenor Anton Raaff for whom, three years later, he was to write the title-role of *Idomeneo*, and the bass Ludwig Fischer who would later create the role of Osmin in *Die Entführung aus dem Serail*.

On 6 November, Wolfgang played in the Academie or concert (*Schlakademie* as he called it) given in the presence of the Elector and Electress, who received him graciously, and whom Wolfgang reminded that he was perfectly capable of composing a German opera. He and his mother remained in Mannheim for four months in all, during which time the generally affectionate tone of the correspondence between Wolfgang and his father became somewhat strained. The expense of the journey was weighing heavily upon Leopold, who feared that Wolfgang was not taking his responsibilities seriously enough. Wolfgang's carefree attitude, his assertion that all was pre-determined by heaven so that one need not exert oneself unduly in attempting to improve one's fortunes, above all his almost contemptuous admonition to his father, 'Just don't crawl to people; I can't bear that',[1] all combined to disturb Leopold, who became really alarmed when he learned of Wolfgang's friendship with the Weber family in Mannheim, and in particular of his growing interest in Aloysia, the second of the Webers' four daughters. 'All of a sudden,' wrote Leopold, in answer to a wild suggestion of Wolfgang's, 'you strike up a new acquaintanceship with Herr Weber. Everything else is forgotten. Now this family is the most honourable, the most Christian family on earth, and the daughter is to play the leading role in a tragedy to be enacted between your own family and hers. . . . You think of taking her to Italy as a *prima donna*. Tell me, do you know of any *prima donna* who has stepped on to a stage in Italy without having first made a

[1] In a letter from Mannheim, 10 December, 1777.

number of appearances in Germany? . . . As to your proposal (I can hardly write when I think of it) to travel about with Herr Weber and, mark you, two of his daughters, it has nearly sent me out of my mind.'[1] The angry and distraught Leopold went on: 'Off to Paris with you! And be quick about it. Take your place among the great. *Aut Caesar aut nihil.* The mere thought of seeing Paris ought to have preserved you from all these flighty ideas.'

Leopold's long letter had an immediately sobering effect upon Wolfgang, who dismissed all thought of taking the Webers to Italy. Nevertheless, it was not until March that the Mozarts left Mannheim. On the evening of 13 March, sad farewells were said at the home of the Webers. The following morning the Mozart carriage rolled out of Mannheim, arriving nine days later in Paris, where Wolfgang and his mother took a room in the house of a tradesman called Mayer in the rue Bourg l'Abbé.

The day after their arrival Wolfgang called upon the flautist Johann Baptist Wendling, whom he had met in Mannheim and who had preceded him to Paris, and also upon Melchior Grimm who had befriended him and his father in Paris many years earlier. Since that time, Grimm had become a diplomat of some importance, and was able to procure several useful introductions for Wolfgang. Soon he met Joseph Le Gros, director of the *Concerts spirituels*, a series of concerts of instrumental and religious music, and Le Gros commissioned him to compose additional music for a Miserere by Holzbauer. François-Joseph Gossec, who was influential in Parisian musical life, and Jean Noverre, court ballet-master, whom Mozart had last encountered in Milan during the rehearsals of *Ascanio in Alba*, were also to prove useful. Through Noverre, Wolfgang obtained a commission to write an opera, *Alexandre et Roxane*.

We first hear of this commission in one of Wolfgang's letters to his father: 'I am not merely going to compose an act for an opera, but an entire opera *en deux actes*. The poet has already written the first act. Noverre, at whose house I lunch as often as I wish, arranged the entire thing. I think it is to be called *Alexandre et Roxane*.'[2] Leopold immediately gave his advice: 'I assume that, when you compose your opera, you will be guided by the French taste. As long as you can win applause and a decent amount of money, to hell with everything else. If your opera is a success, there will soon be something about it in the newspapers. I should be delighted to see that, if only to spite the Archbishop . . . I strongly advise you, before you write for the French stage, to listen to their operas and find out exactly what pleases them.'[3] But Wolfgang was not noticeably impressed by French music or musicians. He was willing to admit that the French had improved their taste sufficiently to be able at least to listen to good music as well as bad. 'But to expect them to

[1] 12 February, 1778.   [2] Paris, 5 April, 1778.   [3] Salzburg, 12 April, 1778.

realize that their own music is bad, or at least to notice the difference – Heaven help us! As for their singing! Good Lord, I hope I never hear a Frenchwoman singing Italian arias. I can forgive her when she screeches out her French trash, but not when she ruins good music. It's quite unbearable.'[1]

By the beginning of July, the opera project had not progressed any further; the librettist of *Alexandre et Roxane* was away in the country, at work on his second act. Meanwhile Wolfgang was contemplating another subject, a French translation of Metastasio's *Demofoönte*, 'interspersed with choruses and dances and completely adapted to French tastes'.[2] What, when first mentioned in April, had appeared to be a firm commission, became less and less firm as the weeks wore on. And Wolfgang was beginning to have doubts about his ability to set the French language which he thought detestable for singing. Even German, he said, was divine by comparison. At the end of July he told his father that, if he were to write an opera for France, it would have to be a grand opera. By September, the project had almost completely receded into the distance. Wolfgang by now wanted to leave Paris, and had given Noverre some kind of ultimatum. If a performance of the opera could be guaranteed as soon as it was composed, then he was willing to stay on for a further three months to write it. As this was not the way things were managed in Paris, Noverre was unable to agree, and that is the last we hear of *Alexandre et Roxane*; and, for that matter, *Demofoönte*, though Cherubini's first French opera, produced in Paris ten years later, was to be *Démophoon*, a French translation of Metastasio's libretto.

During these weeks, in which Wolfgang was thinking about opera, and at the same time actually composing music for a ballet by Noverre (*Les petits riens*, K. App. 10), tragedy struck the Mozart family in Paris. Wolfgang's mother, Maria Anna, became ill. She must have found life in Paris miserable, for she saw little of her son who went out every day to compose, there being no harpsichord or piano in their first lodgings. In one of her letters to Leopold she described how she sat at home all day as though she were in a prison cell. 'The room is so dark and looks out on such a small courtyard that, throughout the entire day, I never see the sun.'[3] Even when they moved to two rooms looking out on the street, she found them cold. In April she suffered from toothache, headache, a sore throat and earache. The following month she was in better health, but had herself bled, which Leopold had kept urging her to do. It was considered a good safeguard against ill-health in general, and she was accustomed to submitting herself to it in the spring. But a few days later she became ill again, with violent headaches, fever and diarrhoea. Melchior Grimm sent his doctor, but Maria Anna passed through stages of delirium and coma until, on 3 July at ten in the evening, in the presence of her son, she died, and was buried the following day in the cemetery of Saint-Eustache. She was fifty-seven years old.

The shock to the nervous system of her twenty-two-year-old son must have been immense, and a sensitive reading between the lines of the two letters in which he announced his mother's death to his father confirms this. On the surface, the letters reveal a coolness and calculation almost beyond comprehension, but what could the lad do? Indeed, who knows what he did do? An hour or two after his mother died, he sat down and wrote a letter to his father. Having considered how to break the news least brutally, he picked up his pen and began: 'Monsieur, mon très cher Père, I have very sad and distressing news for you, which in fact is why I have not replied sooner to your letter of June 11th. My dear mother is very ill . . .'[1] He went on to prepare his father for the worst. 'I do not mean to say that my mother will and must die, or that all hope is lost. She may recover her health and strength, but only if it is God's will.' He then described the symphony he had composed for the opening of the *Concerts spirituels*, and announced the death of 'that godless archrascal' Voltaire. But to his old friend the Abbé Bullinger in Salzburg, he wrote without reserve or artifice: 'Dearest of friends! For you alone. Mourn with me, my friend. This has been the saddest day of my life. I am writing this at two o'clock in the morning. I have to tell you that my mother, my dear mother, is no more. God has called her to Himself. It was His will to take her, I saw that clearly. And so I resigned myself to His will. He had given her to me, and only He could take her from me. You can imagine the anxiety, the fears and sorrows I have endured these past two weeks. . . .'[2] He described his mother's illness and death, and asked his friend to prepare his father to receive the news.

It was six days later that Wolfgang summoned up the courage to write again to Leopold, confessing that, when he had last written, his mother already lay dead. 'I hope that you and my dear sister will forgive me for this slight but very necessary deception, but I judged from my own grief and sorrow what yours would be, and could not bring myself to shock you suddenly with such dreadful news.'[3] The greater part of his long letter is about professional matters, and also contains much musical gossip.

When Leopold recovered from his initial distress, he began to realize that Wolfgang was not going to make his fortune in Paris. The Archbishop would have to be persuaded to take the young composer back into his service, and Wolfgang was going to have to be coaxed back into it. After a certain amount of intrigue in Salzburg, and much exchange of letters between father and son, it was agreed that Wolfgang should return to Salzburg as Kapellmeister and Court Organist. Leopold relaxed sufficiently to withdraw his objection to Wolfgang's

[1] Paris, 3 July, 1778.   [2] 3 July, 1778.   [3] 9 July, 1778.

correspondence with Aloysia Weber, and Wolfgang on his part began to turn his thoughts towards returning home – *via* Mannheim. He finally left Paris on 25 September, travelling by coach, reached Nancy on 3 October, and continued on to Strasbourg the following morning. After several days in Strasbourg where he gave three concerts which were poorly attended, he went on to Mannheim. Cannabich, the conductor of the Mannheim orchestra, was absent in Munich, but Wolfgang stayed with his wife and remained in Mannheim for more than a month. Leopold's letters to him became almost apoplectic, for Wolfgang's dawdling was costing money, and until he arrived home in Salzburg there was always the possibility that he would decide on a completely different course of action. 'Really, I don't know what to say to you,' Leopold wrote to Wolfgang in Mannheim. 'I shall either go mad or into a decline. It is impossible for me to recall, without going crazy, all the projects you have thought up and written about to me since your departure from Salzburg. In the end they were all mere proposals, empty words, and none of them came to anything. Did you draw eight *louis d'or* in Strasbourg merely in order to sit about in Mannheim? You hope to get an appointment there. An appointment? What does that mean? You cannot take an appointment at present in Mannheim or anywhere else in the world. I don't want to hear the word "appointment" again. . . . The most important thing now is for you to return to Salzburg. I don't want to hear any more about the forty *louis d'or* which you may or may not earn. Your entire aim seems to be to ruin me, simply so that you can go on building castles in the air.'[1]

While he was in Mannheim, Wolfgang toyed with two operatic projects, neither of which came to fruition. One was *Cora*, a drama about a Peruvian sun priestess, which two composers, one of them Gluck, had already declined to set to music. In a letter to the author of the libretto, Baron Heribert Wolfgang von Dalberg, who was also the manager of the Mannheim National Theatre, Wolfgang set out his terms but at the same time poured cold, or at least tepid, water on the project, and no more was heard of it.

The other project interested him more. A new genre of stagework, the melodrama, had become popular in Mannheim. These works contained no singing, merely declamation against a musical background. Melodramas constructed around one character were known as monodramas, and those involving two were duodramas. Wolfgang's friend and patron, Baron Otto Gemmingen, translator into German of Rousseau and Shakespeare, had written a duodrama called *Semiramis*, and was keen for Mozart to write the music for it. Mozart wrote to his father that Dalberg 'refuses to let me leave here until I have composed a duodrama for him, and in fact I did not hesistate for long for I have always wanted to write a drama of this kind. I can't remember whether I

[1] Salzburg, 19 November, 1778.

told you anything about this kind of drama when I was here before. On that occasion, I saw a piece of this kind performed twice, and was absolutely delighted. Indeed, nothing has ever surprised me more, for I had always imagined that this kind of piece would be quite ineffective. I expect you know that there is no singing in these works, only declamation with the music acting as a kind of *recitativo obbligato*. From time to time the actors speak while the music is being played, which creates the most wonderful effect.'[1] It is doubtful whether Mozart did, in fact, set *Semiramis*. There is no record of his or anyone else's setting of Gemmingen's text being performed, nor has any music Mozart may have written for it been traced. Nevertheless, he wrote to his father from Mannheim on 3 December that he was doing it without fee as a favour to Baron Gemmingen, and that he would bring the score back with him and finish it in Salzburg.

While Wolfgang and his mother had been in Mannheim earlier in the year *en route* to Paris, the Elector of Bavaria, Maximilian III, had died in Munich without issue, and Karl Theodor, the Palatinate Elector who was next in succession, had hurried from Mannheim to Munich to establish his claim. The headquarters of Karl Theodor's court were now in Munich, whither Wolfgang turned his steps.

When Wolfgang left Mannheim on 9 December, he made his way to Munich in fairly leisurely fashion, arrived on Christmas Day and stayed with the Weber family. Aloysia had procured an engagement with the Opera there, and had already begun to behave like a *prima donna*. She was no longer particularly interested in Wolfgang, and, when he formally declared his love for her, she lost no time in rejecting him. So, when Leopold tartly pointed out that four months had elapsed since Archbishop Colloredo had appointed Wolfgang Kapellmeister, and that people were beginning to say he was treating not only the Archbishop but also his own father as a fool, Wolfgang reluctantly embarked upon the short, final lap of his return journey, and, accompanied by his female cousin from Augsburg whom her uncle Leopold had invited to Salzburg, arrived home on 17 January, 1779.

The years 1779 and 1780 were, at least outwardly, relatively tranquil ones for Mozart. Though he must have continued to find the life of a provincial musician restrictive, and must have felt that his long tour had been, in one sense, a failure, since it had not brought him permanent rescue from what he thought of as the drudgery of his post in Colloredo's service, yet the music he composed during this time includes the serene E flat major Concerto for two pianos, K. 365, the beautiful 'Coronation' Mass, K. 317, written for the pilgrimage church of Maria Plain outside Salzburg, and the Sinfonia Concertante for violin and viola, K. 364.

During the 1779–80 season, Johann Böhm's theatre company played at the theatre in Salzburg. Böhm, the director of the company, was a

[1] Mannheim, 12 November, 1778.

sound musician, a violinist and conductor, and Mozart allowed him to use as Overture to one of the plays a symphony (in G minor, K. 183) which he had written six years earlier. Böhm's company performed not only plays but *Singspiele*, or plays with interspersed music, and included Mozart's *Finta giardiniera* during their Salzburg season, in German, as *Die verstellte Gärtnerin*, with dialogue replacing the recitatives. They must also have performed Gebler's play, *Thamos, King of Egypt*, for Mozart, who had composed two choruses for *Thamos* in 1773, now produced additional incidental music for *Thamos*.

II

Six years earlier, in the summer of 1773, when the then seventeen-year-old Wolfgang and his father spent several weeks in Vienna, Leopold had procured for his son a commission to write two choruses for the play, *Thamos, König in Aegypten*, by Tobias Philipp von Gebler. Gebler (1726–1786) was Privy Councillor, and Vice-Chancellor of the Imperial Bohemian Court Chancery. His play was published in Prague and Dresden in 1773, and was first performed on 11 December, 1773, in Pressburg (now Bratislava) by the Karl Wahr company. It was subsequently performed in Vienna on 4 April, 1774, at the Kärntnertor Theatre. Music for two choruses had been composed by Johann Tobias Sattler (who died in Vienna in December, 1774). According to the playwright, Sattler's choruses were 'not at all badly set, and have been revised by the Chevalier Gluck'.[1] It is not known whether Sattler's choruses were ever used: when Gebler was negotiating to have his play produced in Berlin, he wrote from Vienna on 13 December, 1773, enclosing the music for *Thamos* 'as set not long ago by a certain Sgr. Mozzart. It is his own original score, and the first chorus is very fine.'[2]

The play, with Mozart's two choruses, was performed in Vienna on 4 April, 1774, and the following notice appeared in a periodical called the *Historische-kritische Theaterchronik von Wien*:

> *Thamos*, a heroic drama in five acts, is by the well-known and well-favoured poet of *Der Minister* and *Clementine*. As in all the other plays by this author, his virtuous heart speaks through *Thamos*. The entire tragedy is full of warmth, of dignified heroic poetry, it is not as excessively long as other tragedies performed here, and for this reason it commends itself to our local poets, as well as for its equally pointed and thoughtful dialogue. It is no longer than five and a half folded pages.
>
> In his Preface, the author at once meets, with his own essential modesty, all the objections with which some wits might confront him, if they were determined to judge everything in a false light.

[1] In a letter to Christoph Friedrich Nicolai, Berlin, from Vienna, 31 May, 1773.
[2] To Nicolai (both letters quoted in *Aus dem Josephinischen Wien* by Richard Maria Werner (p. 51).

The apology made for the choruses in the first and fifth acts is no less praiseworthy, although in our opinion, unnecessary. They were effective, for the music by Herr Karl Mozzart is beautifully composed, and we imagine the author can have expected no more than that. It was a pity it was not better sung.[1]

In 1776, *Thamos, König in Aegypten* was performed in Salzburg. The critic of the *Theaterwochenblatt für Salzburg* explained that Gebler had attempted, in the manner of Klopstock, to 'bring the choruses of the ancient dramatists into heroic tragedy, and to link them up with the scenes in such a way as not to impair the interest of the action'. He thought the composer of the choruses had prolonged the fifth act unduly by repetitions, and added: 'The choruses ought to be sung straight through, and would be better interchanged. They could also be entirely omitted without harming the play, as was done in Vienna.' (He refers, presumably, not to the 1774 performances in Vienna, but to more recent ones.)

It was for performances of Gebler's play by the Böhm company in Salzburg during the season of 1779–80 that Mozart returned to his *Thamos* choruses, revised them, and composed additional music to accompany the play. Gebler was a Freemason. From the following synopsis of his play, which was derived, like Schikaneder's *Zauberflöte* a good ten years later, from the novel *Sethos* by the Abbé Jean Terrasson,[2] one can discern quite clearly that in this mish-mash of Masonry and Egyptology lies one of the seeds of Schikaneder's and Mozart's masterpiece of 1791:

Menes, King of Egypt, has been deposed by a usurper, Rameses, and, as it is thought, assassinated; but he is living under the name of Sethos as High Priest of the Temple of the Sun, the secret being known only to the priest Hammon and the General, Phanes. After the death of Rameses, his son Thamos is heir to the throne. The day arrives when Thamos attains majority, is to be invested with the diadem, and to select a bride. The friends of Menes seek in vain to persuade him to dispute the throne. He will not oppose the noble youth whom he loves and esteems. But Pheron, a prince and confidant of Thamos, has, in conjunction with Mirza, the chief of the virgins of the sun, organized a conspiracy against Thamos, and won over a portion of the army. Tharsis, daughter of Menes, who is believed by all, even her father, to be dead, has been brought up by Mirza under the name of Sais. It is arranged that she shall be proclaimed rightful heir to the throne, and, as she will then have the right to choose her consort, Mirza will secure her beforehand for Pheron. When she discovers that Sais loves Thamos, and he her, she induces Sais to believe that Thamos prefers her playmate Myris, and Sais is generous enough to sacrifice her love and her hopes of the throne to her friend. Equally nobly, Thamos rejects all suspicions against Pheron, and awards him

[1] Issue of 13 April, 1774. [2] Published in Paris in 1731.

supreme command. As the time for action draws near, Pheron discloses to Sethos, whom he takes for a devoted follower of Menes, and consequently for an enemy to Thamos, the secret of Sais' existence and his own plans. Sethos prepares secretly to save Thamos. Sais also, after being pledged to silence by an oath, is initiated into the secret by Mirza and Pheron, and directed to choose Pheron. She declines to give a decided answer, and Pheron announces to Mirza his determination to seize the throne by force in case of extremity. Sais, who believes herself not loved by Thamos, and will not therefore choose him as consort, but will not deprive him of the throne, takes the solemn and irrevocable oath as virgin of the sun. Thamos enters, and they discover to their sorrow their mutual love. Sethos, entering, enlightens Thamos as to the treachery of Pheron, without disclosing the parentage of Sais. Pheron, disturbed by the report that Menes is still living, comes to take council of Sethos, and adheres to his treacherous design. In solemn assembly, Thamos is about to be declared king, when Mirza reveals the fact that Sais is the lost Tharsis, and heiress to the throne. Thamos is the first to offer her his homage. When she is constrained to choose between Thamos and Pheron, she declares herself bound by her oath, and announces Thamos as the possessor of the throne. Then Pheron calls his followers to arms, but Sethos steps forward and discloses himself as Menes; whereupon all fall at his feet in joyful emotion. Pheron is disarmed and led off, Mirza stabs herself, Menes, as father and ruler, releases Sais from her oath, unites her with Thamos, and places the pair on the throne. A message arrives that Pheron has been struck with lightning by divine judgment, and the piece ends.[1]

For the Salzburg performances of Gebler's play, Mozart composed five orchestral pieces, revised the two choruses he had written in 1773, and added a third chorus, the text of which is not to be found in Gebler but was probably written by Salzburg's poet-musician, Johann Schachtner.

Gebler's five-act heroic drama is hardly likely to be revived on the modern stage, not even for the sake of Mozart's music which can be enjoyed fully without it. In its time, it was highly regarded, and translated into French and Italian, but it did not long survive. The poet and novelist Wieland liked it, but criticized the unreality of its virtuous characters and the exaggerated villainy of its villains. In 1783 Mozart, writing to his father from Vienna, thanked him for sending him certain scores and added: 'I am really sorry that I shall not be able to use the music of *Thamos*, but this piece, having failed here, is certain never to be performed again. If it were, it would be solely on account of the music, but that is hardly likely. It is certainly a pity.'[2]

III

Mozart's music for *Thamos, König in Aegypten* consists of three choruses, and five instrumental pieces, most of which were intended to be

---

[1] Jahn: *Mozart* (Vol. II, pp. 103–4).   [2] 15 February, 1783.

performed between the acts of the play. The opening chorus, 'Schon weichet dir, Sonne,' a solemn *maestoso*, immediately sets the mood of the play, and in so doing strikingly anticipates the tone of utterance of Sarastro's followers in *Die Zauberflöte*. A greeting to the rising sun, it apostrophizes sun or day as the benevolent ruling force and night as its evil counterpart. In its grandeur and evident high seriousness of purpose, this and the two later choruses in *Thamos* differ from any of the choruses in Mozart's operas composed up to this time. Flexible solo lines alternate with solemn four-part choral ritornellos. The orchestra is large, containing oboes, flutes, bassoons, horns, trumpets and timpani in addition to the usual strings, and the general effect is one of weight and grandeur, alleviated by the occasional division of the chorus into separate utterances by the male and female voices. The point has often been made that, in his music for the priests and Sarastro in *Die Zauberflöte*, Mozart strikes a deeper, certainly a more convincing religious note than in the baroque theatricality of most of his music written for the church. This depends, presumably, on how one defines the term 'religious'. Mozart's masses are, after all, musical counterparts of the joyousness of Austrian baroque as it is found not only in the Karlskirche of Vienna and other masterpieces of Fischer von Erlach but also in so many pilgrimage churches throughout Austria. But it is true that, in *Die Zauberflöte*, and indeed in the choruses from *Thamos*, Mozart has tapped in himself some more personal vein of devotion. By the time of *Die Zauberflöte* he was a Freemason; when he wrote the *Thamos* music he was not, though he could hardly fail to have been influenced by the Masonic symbolism of Gebler's play.

Each of the instrumental *entr'actes* was intended to be a musical summing-up of the preceding act, and each is prefaced in Mozart's score by a few words in his handwriting, noting the idea or theme he has attempted to portray. Above the movement which was played after Act I, he wrote: 'The first act ends with the decision arrived at by Pheron and Mirza to place Pheron on the throne.' As the final line is spoken by Mirza – 'Mirza ist ein Weib, und zittert nicht. Du ein Mann: herrsche oder stirb!' ('Mirza is a woman, and does not tremble. You are a Man. Conquer or die!') – three solemn C minor chords are played by the full orchestra, their effect underlined by pauses, again as in the Overture to *Die Zauberflöte*, and then a restlessly lively *allegro* follows, illustrative of the action which is being urged upon Pheron. The *entr'acte* between Acts II and III is meant to illustrate not action but character traits. 'Thamos' fine character,' says Mozart's note in the score, 'is shown at the end of the second act. The third act opens with Thamos and the traitor Pheron.' The music here is a graceful *andante* in E flat: although Mozart has written above specific phrases the words 'Pherons falscher Charakter' (Pheron's false character) and 'Thamos Ehrlichkeit' (Thamos' integrity), it cannot be claimed that he has succeeded in portraying these attributes musically [Ex. 16]. Nor, unless aided by sung words, is it within the power of music to describe character in this manner. No one hearing the attractive oboe solo in Ex. 16 would have connected it with Thamos' integrity unless asked to do so by the composer.

'The third act ends with the treacherous talk of Mirza and Pheron,' wrote Mozart above his next *entr'acte*, which begins with twenty-two bars of an agitated *allegro* obviously meant to illustrate treacherous conversation. Then the curtain rises and the music becomes an accompaniment to the stage action. Sais comes out of the house of the maidens of the sun, and looks out to see if she is observed. In order not

Ex. 16

to compel Thamos to renounce his throne, she swears her solemn oath to dedicate herself as a priestess of the sun. Phrases from her soliloquy are written above the notes, indicating that the soliloquy was to be spoken over the music. This is the only passage of melodrama in the score, but it reminds us that Mozart had recently, in Mannheim, been giving much thought to the subject of melodrama. The greater freedom it allowed him thematically, and in matters of phrasing, must have attracted him considerably.

'The fourth act ends in general confusion,' and the *entr'acte* which follows it portrays this confusion in an *allegro vivace assai* which begins violently in D minor. A later transition to D major presumably describes the eventual triumph of good over evil. The next musical piece is a chorus sung by the priests and maidens of the sun, a song of thanksgiving in which we again hear the composer of the great choruses of *Die Zauberflöte*. Above the music to be played after the fifth and last act, Mozart wrote 'Pheron's despair, blasphemy and death', and illustrates it with a musical thunderstorm. The remaining chorus, with which the Salzburg performances of the play must have concluded, was composed to words provided by Schachtner. A high priest (bass) exhorts the populace to fear the wrath of the gods, in an *arioso* solo which clearly anticipates the music of Sarastro, and the chorus then sings its reverent song of thanksgiving which ends in a joyous light-textured *allegro*.

The choruses for *Thamos* were later given Christian religious texts in Latin, and performed in Vienna. The music is of interest today for the light it throws on *Die Zauberflöte*, but it is also deserving of performance in its own right, though it is not easy to find a suitable context in which to present it, for it would hardly be satisfactory as a concert suite.

XII

Zaide

German *Singspiel* (incomplete)

K. 344

Dramatis personae:

Zaide	(soprano)
Gomatz	(tenor)
Allazim	(bass)
Sultan Soliman	(tenor)
Osmin	(bass)
Four slaves	(tenors)
Zaram, Head of the Sultan's Bodyguard	(speaking role)

LIBRETTO by Johann Andreas Schachtner

TIME: the past

PLACE: Turkey

FIRST PERFORMED in Frankfurt, 27 January, 1866. It was not performed during Mozart's lifetime

Zaide

I

IN ADDITION TO the *Thamos* music, and the church and chamber music which he was obliged to compose, Mozart began to work on another opera, or operetta as he called it, in Salzburg in the autumn of 1779. It is not known whether he was actually commissioned to do so, though he probably hoped or expected that his opera would be performed by Böhm's company during their Salzburg season. It was, however, not performed, nor did Mozart ever complete the second-act finale. (It may be that Mozart discontinued work on his 'operetta' when he received the commission to compose *Idomeneo* for Munich.) This operetta or *Singspiel* (a play with songs) is known to us as *Zaide*, though if Mozart ever had a title for it, it was probably *Das Serail* (The Harem).

Mozart was certainly still concerned to have *Zaide* performed when he was at work on *Idomeneo* in Munich in December, 1780, for his father wrote to him from Salzburg: 'As for Schachtner's drama, it is impossible to do anything *at the moment* as the theatres are closed, and there is nothing to be got out of the Emperor, who usually is so interested in everything concerned with the stage. It is better to let things be, as the music is not finished. Besides, who knows, this opera may later give you an opportunity of getting to Vienna.'[1]

The closure of the theatres, and the Emperor's temporary lack of interest in entertainment, were because the Empress Maria Theresa had died on 29 November. But several weeks later Mozart wrote from Munich to his father who was planning to attend the first performance of *Idomeneo*, reminding him to 'bring Schachtner's operetta. There are some people who come to the Cannabichs who might just as well hear something of this kind.'[2] We hear no more of *Zaide* until Mozart writes to Leopold from Vienna some months later, referring obliquely to *Zaide*, about which 'there is nothing to be done, for the same reason I have often mentioned',[3] and adding that Gottlieb Stephanie had promised him a new libretto. Mozart's final reference to *Zaide*, which is in the same letter, is that he has said to Stephanie that 'except for the long dialogue, which could easily be altered, the piece was very good, but not suitable for Vienna where people prefer comic pieces'.[4] Stephanie's new libretto

---

[1] 11 December, 1780. [2] 18 January, 1781.
[3] 18 April, 1781. [4] 18 April, 1781.

was for *Die Entführung aus dem Serail*, whose plot has much in common with that of *Zaide*.

II

Johann Andreas Schachtner (1731–1795), who provided Mozart with the libretto for the work we know as *Zaide*, has been mentioned earlier in this volume. He was the musician and family friend who, in a letter to Mozart's sister after the composer's death, wrote his reminiscences of Mozart as a child. As a poet, he was involved in the preparation of the libretto of *Bastien und Bastienne*, and provided words for a chorus which Mozart added to the music for *Thamos*. He also wrote plays for performance in Salzburg, and was later to translate the libretto of *Idomeneo* into German. By profession he was Court Trumpeter to the Archbishop of Salzburg, and also played the violin and the cello. He remained a friend of the Mozart family for life.

Schachtner based his libretto on that of a *Singspiel* called *Das Serail, oder Die unvermuthete Zusammenkunft in der Sclaverey zwischen Vater, Tochter und Sohn* (The Harem, or The Unexpected Encounter in Slavery of Father, Daughter and Son), written by one Franz Joseph Sebastiani for a *Singspiel* which was produced in Bozen (now Bolzano) in 1779 with music by Joseph von Friebert, an Austrian singer and composer. Michael Levey[1] has suggested that both Schachtner's and the Bozen libretto derive from Voltaire's play, *Zaïre*, which had been performed in Salzburg in 1778. Certainly the similarity of the heroines' names is striking, and the sub-title of the Bozen *Singspiel* sums up the dramatic situation in Voltaire. But both the Bozen and Salzburg libretti are lost, and it is not possible to reconstruct a plot from the words of the arias in sufficient detail to settle the question. The autograph score of the work, lacking only an Overture and probably a final ensemble, was discovered amongst Mozart's papers after his death. In 1799 Mozart's widow sold to the publisher Johann Anton André all of Mozart's work in her possession; André published the untitled *Singspiel* in 1838, as *Zaide*, adding an Overture and final chorus to complete the work, with Schachtner's text reconstructed and rewritten by Karl Gollmick. It was in this version that *Zaide* received its first performance, in Frankfurt on 27 January, 1866. Its first major revival was in Vienna, on 4 October, 1902, revised by R. Hirschfeld, who made further alterations to the libretto and removed André's additions, substituting parts of Mozart's *Thamos* music. There have been many revivals during the twentieth century, in editions by Rudolph, Meckbach, Paumgartner and others, among them a performance by puppets in Zürich in 1918. *Zaide* was performed in London at the Toynbee Hall in 1955.

Voltaire's *Zaïre* dates from 1732. A French composer, Joseph Royer (*c.*

[1] Michael Levey: *The Life and Death of Mozart* (London, 1971), p. 120.

1700–1755), produced an opera named *Zaide* in 1739. I have been unable to discover if it is based on *Zaïre*; the same composer's *Pandore* is a setting of Voltaire's play of that name.

To invent dialogue for the plot suggested by the words of the arias and ensembles, and by the occasional word cues written in Mozart's autograph score, is not a difficult task, and in the following section of this chapter I suggest music which could be used for an Overture and a final chorus. A synopsis of the plot might run thus: Gomatz has been taken prisoner by the Sultan Soliman. At the beginning of the opera he is seen working with a group of slaves. When the others move off, he remains, wringing his hands and bewailing his fate. Eventually, he seeks refuge from his cares in sleep. While he is sleeping, Zaide, the Sultan's favourite, enters and declares her love for Gomatz. She leaves her miniature portrait by his side. He awakens, finds it, and in turn expresses his love for her. Zaide reappears and they sing a love duet. Allazim, the overseer of the Sultan's slaves, offers to help them both escape. The first act ends with a trio in which all three anticipate a happy future.

Act II begins with the Sultan enraged to find his favourite Zaide missing, enticed away 'von einem Christenhunde, von einem Sklaven' (by a Christian dog, a slave). Zaram, chief of the Sultan's bodyguard, has discovered that the lovers had escaped disguised in Turkish clothing procured for them by Allazim, and assures the Sultan that they will be brought back before they can reach the frontiers of his domain. The Sultan threatens a cruel vengeance. At this point, a character named Osmin, apparently the Sultan's Harem overseer, sings a song which hardly advances the plot, and can only have been inserted for what is known in the parlance of modern show-business as 'comic relief'. The lovers are brought back, and the Sultan is moved neither by Zaide's pleading nor by her defiance. Allazim attempts to appeal to the Sultan's finer feelings, but in vain. The last number composed by Mozart is a quartet in which Zaide, Gomatz, Allazim and the Sultan Soliman express their feelings, and the others beg the Sultan to be merciful. Presumably, in the ensuing dialogue it was revealed that Gomatz and Zaide were in fact the son and daughter of Allazim, and all were pardoned and set free by the Sultan. How the incestuous feelings between brother and sister were dealt with, alas, we do not know. A final ensemble of reconciliation would have ended the opera.

III

Alfred Einstein[1] is of the opinion that a symphony composed by Mozart in Salzburg in April, 1779, K. 318 in G major, is the missing Overture to *Zaide*. He even claims to hear, in the contrasting themes of the

[1] *Mozart, His Character, His Work*, p. 228.

symphony's opening section, tone-portraits of the stern, unbending Sultan and the pleading Zaide, and, in the *andante*, an expression of the love that exists between Zaide and Gomatz. He considers the matter clinched by the 'Turkish' character of the final bars of the symphony. Friedrich-Heinrich Neumann, in his Foreword to *Zaide* in the *Neue Ausgabe*[1] is unconvinced by Einstein's argument. He points out that the Symphony was known to have been finished on 26 April, before Mozart had completed the opera (if, indeed, he had even begun it), and that it was contrary to Mozart's practice to write his Overture before he had completed the rest of the opera. A stronger argument against Einstein's assumption, he says, is to be found in the orchestration of the symphony, in which Mozart writes parts for four horns, whereas nowhere in *Zaide* does he ask for more than two.

I find myself in agreement with Neumann rather than with Einstein. Several other Mozart symphonic movements will yield up contrasting themes, masculine aggression alternating with feminine compliance, and 'Turkish' music was often introduced by Mozart into instrumental works without the excuse of dramatic relevance, e.g. the *Rondo alla Turca* of the A major piano sonata, K. 331. Neumann's two points are more convincing. Certainly it is unlikely that Mozart, a practical musician, would have scored for four horns in the overture of an opera while refraining from using more than two throughout the rest of the work. That said, however, I must admit that the symphony in question, even though it was probably never intended as such, does make an excellent Overture to *Zaide*. It is exactly contemporary with the rest of the score, and bears no less close a relationship to it stylistically or in general dramatic terms than do Mozart's earlier overtures to their own operas. Also if one wants to think of its themes as representing characters in the opera, the themes themselves are sufficiently accommodating to lend themselves to such an exercise. The opening *allegro* could, indeed, refer to the Sultan and Zaide, and the *andante*, though it is really not tender enough for love music, will, at a pinch, suffice. The martial, quasi-Turkish sound of the finale makes an appropriate prelude to the *allegro* opening chorus of slaves. After all, if the opera is to be performed, it needs an overture: *pace* Michael Levey,[2] Mozart would never have considered it complete without one.

The first number in the opera is a song, sung by one of the four slaves (all tenors), 'Brüder, lasst uns lustig sein', with an eight-bar unison refrain for all four. This is the only appearance of the chorus, such as it is, in the entire work. Still, they can hardly be dispensed with, for Slave Number One cannot be expected to address his exhortation, 'Brothers, let's be merry and bravely defiant of adversity', to himself. This tenor slave does not appear again in the opera, so a producer could conceivably decide to dispense with him, and give his song to the tenor

[1] Barenreiter Verlag, Cassel, 1957.   [2] *The Life and Death of Mozart*, p. 121.

Gomatz who must, in any case, be one of the slaves. If one were to attempt this economy, however, a difficulty would arise in that, immediately after his merry song, Gomatz's next utterance is bitter and despairing. Perhaps it is better to have the song sung by an anonymous slave: it is a banal little piece.

The second number is the first of the two long passages of melodrama in *Zaide*, in which the words are not sung, but spoken either in the pauses between musical phrases or to the accompaniment of the music. This was the new path of musical drama which Mozart had discovered in Mannheim the previous year and about which he had written enthusiastically to his father. At the time, he felt that this was the best method of treating recitative. The accompanied monologue which Gomatz declaims as he bewails his fate and seeks temporary release in sleep is a striking and highly effective use of the technique which is best known to us today from the example in Beethoven's *Fidelio*, in which Leonore and Rocco descend to Florestan's cell to dig his grave. The advantage of this technique lies in the greater freedom it gives to the composer; its disadvantage is that the marriage of spoken word with 'sung' music, even though the music may be sung by instruments instead of human voices, is an uneasy and unbalanced one. The use of melodrama at certain moments in a lyrical score can be highly effective, as it is in *Zaide*. But the freedom gained by the composer at such moments needs to be offset by a more consciously formal arrangement of his music at other moments: again, as it is in *Zaide*. If the role of Gomatz is given to a competent actor (the music he has to sing later does not call for a singer of exceptional range or flexibility), then this, his opening scene [Ex. 17], can be immensely affecting, as much for the expressive quality of Mozart's isolated phrases as for the dramatic force of the interspersed verbal phrases.

The aria (No. 3: 'Ruhe sanft, mein holdes Leben') which Zaide sings over the sleeping Gomatz is a gentle lullaby, quite different in the character of its melody from the *andante* arias of Mozart's earlier Italian operas. For one thing, it is less formal, more song than aria; for another, the German words have encouraged a domestic, intimate tone which emphasizes the music's links with the Bachs, Johann Sebastian as much as Johann Christian.

Gomatz's first aria (No. 4: 'Rase, Schicksal, wüte immer') is an eccentric piece, though effective in its context. Its childish text, which simply alternates phrases of defiance against the Sultan with expressions of rapture at the sight of Zaide's portrait ('dieses Bild macht alles gut'), has a somewhat inhibiting effect on the tempo and temper of the music. But, even in its crudity of form, as well as its naivety of expression, Gomatz's aria, like Zaide's, reveals links with the world of the Viennese domestic *Zauberoper*, the genre which was to give to the world a bewildering variety of masterpieces, from Mozart's own *Zauberflöte* in

Ex. 17

1791 to the plays of Nestroy and Raimund, with music by various theatre composers, in the nineteenth century. The simple little love duet (No. 5: 'Meine Seele hüpft vor Freuden') looks forward to Raimund's *Der Bauer als Millionär* as much as to the more immediate future and *Die Entführung aus dem Serail*. Throughout the Italian operas Mozart had been composing since childhood, we have seen a sure line of development towards artistic maturity, but it is in the vernacular simplicity of utterance and style in *Zaide* that we discover the composer suddenly on the verge of finding his own individual voice; the voice of *Die Entführung* and *Die Zauberflöte*, but equally of *Le nozze di Figaro*, *Don Giovanni* and *Così fan tutte*, for it is from this confident base of newly found *Innigkeit* that Mozart was able to create the musical language for Susanna's most heartfelt expressions of feeling, for Fiordiligi's 'Fra gli amplessi' and for Donna Elvira's 'Mi tradi quell' alma ingrata'.

There is a danger, in performance, of Gomatz being made to seem quite unheroically comic, due to the ineptitude of Schachtner's libretto, for in his first two arias he is of divided mind. In 'Rase, Schicksal', he continually alternates between expressions of defiance and love, while in 'Herr und Freund, wie dank' ich dir' (No. 6) he is torn between a desire to thank his protector Allazim and an even greater desire to hasten to his beloved Zaide. But the coda in which, having rushed off stage, Gomatz comes back to sing a final, tender 'Herr und Freund, wie dank' ich dir' is both unusual and touching, rather like Mozart's addition of his own verbal comment to Goethe's poem in his setting of 'Das Veilchen' five years later.

Allazim's first aria (No. 7: 'Nur mutig, mein Herze') is a conventional *da capo* aria of no great character, though again it gains from its un-Italianate simplicity, and from not being overladen with passages designed merely to display the voice. It may have been written with a particular singer in mind, for it presents its own kind of difficulty to the average bass, asking him to produce his high F several times. The first act ends with a trio (No. 8: 'O selige Wonne') in two sections: an *andante* which becomes agitated towards the end as Zaide fears she perceives threatening storm clouds on the horizon, and a delightful *allegro* in which optimism returns, as 'Gottes Schirm' (God's umbrella), a rainbow, appears in the sky.

The second section of melodrama in *Zaide* is that which begins Act II. This time it does not constitute a *scena* in itself, but is used instead of sung recitative to precede the Sultan's aria, 'Der stolze Löw' lässt sich zwar zähmen' (No. 9). In his aria, the Sultan sees himself as a proud lion goaded into fury: his rage is vividly portrayed in the orchestra, which includes trumpets and kettle drums not used elsewhere in the opera, and is indicated in the voice part both by wide leaps and the urgent tempo, an *allegro* quickening to *presto*. The preceding melodrama is an even finer example of the genre than the passage in Act I. For the most part, brief orchestral passages, sometimes no more than a single chord, alternate with phrases of spoken dialogue, though at one point the orchestra steals in under the Sultan's words, rising to a crescendo at 'so schlecht gewähren kannst'.

Osmin, keeper of the harem, but presumably no eunuch since he sings bass, has only one song, 'Wer hungrig bei der Tafel sitzt' (No. 10), an *allegro buffa* aria, and the only comic song in the entire *Singspiel*. If *Zaide* is to be regarded as a first attempt at the kind of work which finally reached the stage as *Die Entführung aus dem Serail*, then it is probably true that the character of Osmin was given a larger part to play in the latter work merely to pander to the Viennese preference for comedy. *Zaide*, by comparison with *Die Entführung*, is a very serious opera: a romance rather than a romantic comedy. The Sultan's second aria (No. 11: 'Ich bin so bös' als gut') merely repeats the sentiments of the first, and in the same manner though at greater length.

The next two numbers in the score are arias for Zaide. In the first, a charming A major *andantino* in rondo form (No. 12: 'Trostlos schluchzet Philomele'), she compares herself to a caged nightingale seeking freedom. The following aria (No. 13: 'Tiger! wetze nur die Klauen'), despite its formal *da capo*, paints a vivid picture of Zaide's rage against the Sultan, and her despair. The *allegro assai* is launched with no more orchestral introduction than two bars. 'Tiger!' is the epithet she proudly flings at the Sultan. The last time she does so is in the final bar, when the first syllable is heard with the orchestra's last chord, the second syllable thrown down unaccompanied: a brilliant and original stroke. The *larghetto* section of the aria, as Zaide thinks of Gomatz and his fate, makes a touching contrast. There is an odd coincidence to be found, in that the opening *allegro* contains a musical phrase, to the words 'straf' ein törichtes Vertrauen', which occurs again in Schubert's *Winterreise*, in the song 'Der Wegweiser', to a very similar verbal phrase: 'Welch ein törichtes Verlangen'. It is hardly likely that Schubert saw a score of *Zaide*: nor, in its context, is Mozart's use of the phrase as memorable as Schubert's, nearly half a century later.

Allazim's aria, 'Ihr Mächtigen seht ungerührt' (No. 14) is disappointingly characterless, its several changes of tempo seeming contrived and thus unconvincing. But the final number in the score as it has come down to us, the quartet 'Freundin, stille deine Tränen' (No. 15), is a most felicitous piece, ravishingly scored and most persuasively laid out for the voices of the four characters, whose conflicting emotions are conveyed with feeling and clarity. It comes to a quiet end, leaving the dramatic conflict unresolved. For stage performance today with a reconstructed libretto, a final chorus should be added. One possible solution would be to use part of the *Thamos* music; another would be to adapt a chorus from one of Mozart's liturgical works composed in Salzburg in 1779 or 1780.

Despite Schachtner's naive and clumsy libretto, *Zaide* is an opera which is decidedly more than simply a rough first draft of *Die Entführung*. It is Mozart's first real attempt at opera in the vernacular, or *Singspiel*; and from the naturalness and ease of its music, as well as from its humanity and warmth, one can discern how enthusiastically the composer took to the genre. This sentimental romantic play with music ought not to be pushed into the shade by the admittedly much more accomplished *Entführung* of two years later.

XIII

Idomeneo, Rè di Creta

opera seria in three acts

K. 366

Dramatis personae:

Idomeneo, King of Crete	(tenor)
Idamante, his son	(soprano; later rewritten as tenor)
Arbace, confidant of the King	(tenor)
Ilia, daughter of King Priam of Troy	(soprano)
Elettra, daughter of King Agamemnon of Argos	(soprano)
High Priest of Neptune	(tenor)
Voice of Neptune	(bass)

LIBRETTO by Giambattista Varesco, based on an earlier libretto by Antoine Danchet

TIME: Shortly after the end of the Trojan wars

PLACE: Sidon (now Khania), in Crete

FIRST PERFORMED in Munich, 29 January, 1781, at the Court Theatre (now Cuvilliés Theatre, with Anton Raaff (Idomeneo), Vincenzo dal Prato (Idamante), Dorothea Wendling (Ilia), Elisabeth Wendling (Elettra), Domenico de' Panzacchi (Arbace), Giovanni Valesi (High Priest)

Idomeneo, Rè di Creta

I

IN SEPTEMBER 1780, a new theatrical manager arrived in Salzburg with his company. His name was Emanuel Schikaneder. Thus began the Mozart family's connection with the man who, years later in Vienna, was to collaborate in the creation of *Die Zauberflöte*. Wolfgang, Leopold and Nannerl were enthusiastic theatregoers, and saw most of the plays staged by Schikaneder and his troupe: *Singspiele*, comedies, mono-dramas, ballets, plays such as Beaumarchais' *Barbier de Séville*, and German adaptations of Gozzi's *Le due notte affanose* and Shakespeare's *Hamlet*. Schikaneder himself soon became a friend of the Mozart family, joined in their social activities, and gave them permanent passes to his theatre. After a few weeks, however, the family party was reduced from three to two, for on 5 November, having secured six weeks' leave of absence from the Archbishop, Wolfgang departed for Munich. He had been commissioned by Karl Theodor, now both Elector Palatine and Elector of Bavaria, to compose the *opera seria* for the Munich carnival season at the beginning of 1781. The librettist was Giambattista Varesco, Chaplain to the Court of the Prince Archbishop of Salzburg, and the opera told the story of Idomeneo, King of Crete at the time immediately following the Trojan wars.

Mozart, having received the Abbé Varesco's libretto, had begun work on the opera in Salzburg in October, but, as was customary, he expected to write most of the arias after he had become acquainted with the singers. In Munich, he met again many of his old friends in the Mannheim Orchestra, and attended a number of performances mounted in honour of the Bavarian Elector. Consequently, the composition of *Idomeneo* proceeded rather slowly. Mozart required a number of alterations and adjustments to be made to the libretto, and his usual method of communicating with Varesco in Salzburg was not direct but through Leopold. Almost immediately after his arrival in Munich, he had written to his father with a request that Varesco change the words in Ilia's aria in Act II, Scene II: '"Se il padre perdei, in te lo ritrovo": this verse could not be better. But now comes something that always seems unnatural in an aria to me, and that is an aside. In dialogue, these things are quite natural, for a few words can be said quickly as an aside. But in an aria, where individual words have to be repeated, it has an adverse effect. Even if this were not the case, I should prefer an aria that flows without interruption.'[1]

Not all the singers pleased Mozart. 'I shall have to teach my molto amato castrato dal Prato [Idamante] the entire opera, for he has no notion how to sing a cadenza effectively, and his voice is so uneven,' he wrote to Leopold.[2] But he was respectful about Anton Raaff, the tenor who was to sing Idomeneo, and whom he had come to know on a previous visit to Munich. Raaff, at sixty-six, was obviously past his best, and Wolfgang thought that 'some courtesy ought to be shown him on account of his grey hair. He was here with me yesterday, I played over his first aria for him and he was very pleased with it. Of course he is old, and can no longer show off in such an aria as that in Act II, "Fuor del mar ho un mar nel seno". So, since he has no aria in Act III and since, because of the sense of the words, his Act I aria cannot be as cantabile as he would like, he wants an attractive aria to sing after his last speech, "O Creta fortunata", instead of the quartet. Thus, I can discard an unnecessary piece, and Act III will be much more effective.'[3]

The exchange of letters continued for two months, instructions regarding the libretto alternating with gossip or with Leopold's advice on how to get rid of a cold ('Footbaths are an excellent remedy').[4] On 29 November, Mozart wrote: 'The aria for Raaff which you have sent me does not please either him or me at all. I shall make no comment on *era*, for in an aria of this kind that is always wrong. Metastasio makes that mistake sometimes, but only rarely, and in any case those particular arias are not his best, and is there any necessity for it? Besides, the aria is not at all what we expected it to be. It ought to portray only peace and contentment, whereas it does so only in the second part. After all, we have seen, heard and felt sufficiently throughout the entire opera all the misfortune Idomeneo has had to endure! Tell me, don't you think the speech of the subterranean voice is too long? Give it careful thought. Imagine to yourself the theatre, and remember that the voice must be terrifying, that it must penetrate, and that the audience must believe in it completely. How can it achieve that effect if the speech is too long, and if, because of its length, the listener becomes convinced that it means nothing at all? If the speech of the Ghost in *Hamlet* were not so long, it would be much more effective.'[5]

Wolfgang had apparently promised to write an aria for Schikaneder, to be inserted in one of the plays he was to produce in Salzburg, for Leopold had occasion in mid-November to admonish his son: 'What on earth are you thinking of? The way you are treating Mr Schikaneder is quite shameful. On my name-day, when we went shooting, I said to him "The aria is sure to be here tomorrow." Knowing what I did, what else

[1] 8 November, 1780.   [2] On 15 November, 1780.
[3] 15 November, 1780.   [4] Leopold to Wolfgang, 25 November, 1780.
[5] Wolfgang to Leopold, 29 November, 1780.

could I say to him? A week earlier, I had had to tell him that you had not yet finished it. . . . I really do not know what story I can tell him when he comes to shoot with us tomorrow. As you know, I am not much good at telling lies. All that I can say is that the aria simply missed the mail coach, that the extra postage was too much for you, and that it is sure to come by the next coach. But I refuse to tell any more lies. And it is very kind of him to give us three free passes to any seat in the theatre over such a long period.'[1]

In his letters home to Salzburg, Mozart gave his opinion of the singers' capabilities and characters (Raaff is a 'worthy and thoroughly decent fellow'; dal Prato a rascal 'rotten to the core'), wrote of his social activities with musicians and courtiers, and described the Bavarians as, in general, boorish. When his father's letters threatened to become self-pitying and sentimental, Wolfgang responded: 'Please do not write any more melancholy letters to me, for what I need most of all just now are cheerful spirits, a clear head, and an inclination to work, and one cannot have these when one is depressed.'[2] Here the artist speaks: at other times, the voice of the dutiful and affectionate son makes itself heard, in gossip about plays in Salzburg, mutual acquaintances, and requests for 'the recipe for cooking sago'. The death of the Empress Maria Theresa was, not surprisingly, felt less deeply in Munich than in Salzburg, and none of the theatres were closed. Nevertheless, the Bavarian court went into mourning for the relatively short period of six weeks, and Mozart asked Leopold to have his black suit sent from Salzburg, 'for I, too, must weep with the others'. His postscript adds a reminder about the black suit: 'I must have it, or I shall be laughed at, which is never very pleasant.'[3]

Leopold advised his son 'when composing to consider not only the musical but also the unmusical public. You must remember,' he added, 'that for every ten real connoisseurs, there are a hundred ignoramuses; so don't neglect the so-called popular style.'[4] Wolfgang's reply was that 'there is music in my opera for all sorts of people'. In the same letter, he mentions that he has now been away from Salzburg for six weeks, and adds that he remains in Archbishop Colloredo's service only for the sake of his father. 'If I had followed my own inclination before leaving the other day, I would have wiped my arse with my contract with the Archbishop, for I swear to you on my honour that it is not Salzburg itself but the Prince-Archbishop and his conceited court who every day become more intolerable to me.'[5]

All of these letters contain details concerning changes required by Mozart to Varesco's libretto. Mozart complained that both the scene between Idomeneo and his son Idamante in Act I and the first scene in Act II between Idomeneo and Arbace were too long. 'They are sure to

---

[1] Leopold to Wolfgang, 18 November, 1780. [2] 24 November, 1780.
[3] 5 December, 1780.   [4] 11 December, 1780.   [5] 16 December, 1780.

bore the audience, especially as in the first scene both singers are bad
actors, and, in the second, one of them is. Besides, the dialogue consists
merely of narrative describing what the audience have already seen
themselves. These scenes will be included in the printed libretto as they
stand, but I should like the Abbate to indicate how they may be
shortened as drastically as possible, otherwise I shall have to shorten
them myself.'[1]

Leopold's reply contains so much of interest concerning the libretto
that it must be quoted at length:

I sent for Varesco immediately, for I received your letter only at five this
evening, and the mail coach leaves tomorrow morning. We have considered
the first recitative from every point of view, and we both see no way to shorten
it. It is a direct translation from the French, according to the agreed draft.
What is more, if you consult the draft, you will find it was suggested that this
recitative should be lengthened somewhat, so that father and son should not
recognize each other too quickly. But now you will make it ridiculous if you
have them recognize each other after they have exchanged only a few words.
Let me explain what I mean. Surely Idamante must explain why he is there.
Then he sees the stranger, and offers his services. Idomeneo must at least then
mention his own sufferings, and must also return his greetings. Then
Idamante can tell him how he sympathizes with the stranger, for he too has
experienced misfortune. Idomeneo's reply must be a question. Idamante can
then describe the king's misfortune, and with his mysterious words 'Uom più
di questo', Idomeneo gives Idamante a ray of hope. Idamante then asks
eagerly, 'Dimmi, amico, dimmi dov'è?' This in turn makes Idomeneo ask
'Ma d'onde . . .' Surely, at this point, Idamante must speak in such a manner
that he is revealed as a son worthy of his father, and thus awaken in Idomeneo
admiration and respect, and a desire to know who he is. Also, when he does
recognize his son, how much more interesting the situation becomes. But if it
is absolutely necessary to make a cut, I have come to the conclusion that it
should be after Idamante's recitative 'Che favelli? Vive egli ancor? . . .'
which ends with 'Dove quel dolce aspetto vita mi renderà.' Idomeneo: 'Ma
d'onde nasce questa, che per lui nutri tenerezza d'amor?' From here, you
could cut to 'Perchè quel tuo parlar sì mi conturba?' Idamante: 'E qual mi
sento anch' io', and then continue. At page 32 in Varesco's copy, one and a
half pages will thus be omitted. I mean the beautiful description of
Idamante's heroic act, where he begins 'Poressi almeno io . . .' Thus the
recitative will be shortened by one minute, yes indeed, an entire minute.
What a great gain! Or do you want to have father and son rush up and
recognize each other in the way that Harlequin and Brigella, when they are
disguised as servants in a foreign country, meet, recognize and embrace each
other immediately? Remember that this is one of the finest scenes in the
entire opera; in fact it's the principal scene, on which the entire remainder of
the plot depends. Furthermore, the audience can hardly be bored by this
scene, since it is in the first act.

You can't cut anything more in Act II, except a little of Idomeneo's second

[1] 19 December, 1780.

speech. Idomeneo: 'Un sol consiglio or mi fa d'uopo. Ascolta. Tu sai quanto a' Troiani fu il mio brando fatal.' Arbace: 'Tutto m' è noto . . .' Then the dialogue continues, and you can't cut a single word without destroying the sense. Besides, the entire recitative can't last long, for several passages have to be spoken eagerly and quickly. And if you were to cut it, you'd gain no more than half a minute. What a gain! Nor can this recitative weary any one of the audience, for it's the opening scene in Act II. What you could perhaps cut is a passage after Arbace's recitative, 'male s'usurpa un rè . . .', when Idomeneo immediately replies, 'Il voto è ingiusto.' Then you could omit Idomeneo: 'Intendo, Arbace . . .', and Arbace: 'Medica mano . . .' The question is whether it is worth while to make an alteration which will gain you two and a half minutes at the most. I am by no means certain, especially as these recitatives are so placed that they cannot weary the audience. Everyone is attentive during the first act of an opera, and the very first recitative of the second act can never weary anyone. The whole question seems rather ridiculous to me. It is true that, in rehearsal, where there is nothing to interest the eye, a recitative can be thought tedious. But, in the theatre, where between the stage and the audience there is so much to attract one's interest, a recitative like this is over almost before it is noticed. You can tell everybody that from me. However, if despite all this something has to be cut, I insist that the passages must still be printed in full. Varesco knows nothing of what I have written to you.[1]

Mozart explained to his father that it was not his wish to shorten those two scenes, but that he had consented to it because Raaff and dal Prato ('the most wretched actors that ever appeared on any stage'[2]) spoilt the recitative by delivering it without the slightest enthusiasm or spirit.

The Elector himself attended an orchestral rehearsal which took place in a large room in his palace, and heard Ilia's Act II aria, 'Se il padre perdei', remarking to the composer 'Who would have thought so much could come out of such a little head?' But Mozart continued to have difficulties with his leading tenor. 'Raaff is the best and most faithful fellow in the world,' he told his father, 'but he is so set in his old routines that it would make your blood boil. Consequently, it's very difficult to compose for him, though it's easy if you're willing to write conventional arias, as for instance his first one, "Vedrommi intorno". You will like it when you hear it, but if I had written it for Zonca[3] it would have fitted the text much better. Raaff is too fond of chopped noodles[4] and pays no attention to expression.'[5]

Mozart had a particularly bad time with Raaff over the very beautiful quartet he had composed for Idomeneo, Idamante, Ilia and Elettra. His tenor would have preferred at this point in the opera an aria for himself.

---

[1] 22 December, 1780.   [2] 27 December, 1780.

[3] Giovanni Battista Zonca (1728–1809), an Italian bass, was one of the Mannheim court musicians.

[4] Mozart's way of describing extended coloratura passages for the voice.

[5] 27 December, 1780.

'Non c' e da spianar la voce' (There's no opportunity to display the voice), he complained of the quartet. Mozart's comment to Leopold in recounting Raaff's remark was that in a quartet of this kind, the words had to be spoken rather than sung, which was something Raaff would never understand. To Raaff, he merely said: 'My dearest friend, if I knew of one single note which could be changed in this quartet, I'd change it straight away. But there is nothing in my opera which I'm more content with than this quartet. When you have sung it through once with the others, you are sure to change your mind. I have taken very great care to meet your requirements in your two arias so far, and I shall do the same with the third one, and I hope successfully. But where trios and quartets are concerned, the composer must be allowed a free hand.'[1]

Raaff was reasonable enough to accept Mozart's defence and explanation of his method of composition, but Mozart had by no means come to the end of his problems with his tenor, who next took objection to some of the words of his final aria, on the grounds that the vowel sounds were such as to make the vocalization difficult. He suggested instead that Mozart write music to fit some words he had come across in a libretto by Metastasio. Mozart appealed for help to his father, who persuaded an angry Varesco to provide new words. Mozart also raised with the librettist, through his father, some more points concerning the troublesome Act III:

> My head and my hands are so full of the third act that it would be no surprise if I were to turn into a third act myself . . . In scene 6, after Arbace's aria, I notice that Varesco has Idomeneo and Arbace on stage. But how can the latter reappear immediately? Fortunately, there is no need for him to be on at all. But, to be safe, I have composed a somewhat longer introduction to the High Priest's recitative. After the chorus of mourning, the king and the entire populace depart, and in the next scene the stage direction is 'Idomeneo in ginocchione nel tempio.' That is quite impossible. He must enter with his entire suite. We need a march here, so I have composed a very simple one for two violins, viola, cello and two oboes, to be played *mezza voce*. While it is being played, the King appears, and the priests prepare for the sacrifice. Then the King kneels and begins his prayer.
>
> In Elettra's recitative, after the subterranean voice has uttered, there should be a stage direction: 'Partono'. I forgot to look at the copy which has been prepared for the printer to see whether it is there, and if so, where it occurs. It seems to me very silly that everyone should hurry away for no other reason than to allow Madame Elettra to be alone.[2]

It was intended that the opera should have its first performance early in January, but there were two postponements, and Mozart told his father that 'the dress rehearsal will not take place until the 27th – N.B. my birthday – and the first performance will be on the 29th.'[3] He added

---

[1] 27 December, 1780.   [2] 3 January, 1781.   [3] 10 January, 1781.

that this delighted him, as it gave him an opportunity for further rehearsal. Later, he wrote: 'The rehearsal of Act III went off splendidly. It was thought to be much superior to the first two acts. But the libretto is too long, and consequently the music too (as I have said all along). Therefore Idamante's aria, "No, la morte io non pavento" is to be omitted. It is, in any case, out of place where it is, but those who have heard the music regret that it has to go. The omission of Raaff's last aria is regretted even more, but one must make a virtue of necessity. The speech of the Oracle is still far too long, and so I have shortened it. Varesco need not know anything of this, as it will be printed in full as he wrote it.'[1]

Varesco, it appears, was concerned not only about the treatment his libretto was receiving, but also about his fee. He had done a great deal of extra work, he claimed, and therefore expected to receive more money. But 'tell Varesco from me,' wrote Mozart to Leopold, 'that he will not get a farthing more out of Count Seeau[2] than was agreed upon, for all his alterations were made, not at the Count's request but at mine.'[3] 'Varesco has just now been to see me,' replied Leopold. 'The greedy, avaricious fool simply can't wait for his money. . . . In spite of his decent income, the fellow is hopelessly in debt.'[4]

As late as 18 January, Mozart was still working on the music for what he referred to as the confounded ballet – a divertissement and not an integral part of the opera. But all was ready in time for the dress rehearsal. Leopold and Nannerl came to Munich for the first performance of *Idomeneo* on 29 January, 1781. The performance was applauded and the work generally liked. The notice in the *Münchner Staatsgelehrten und vermischten Nachrichten* on 1 February read as follows: 'On the 29th of last month, the first performance of the opera *Idomeneo* was given in the new opera house here. Libretto, music and German translation are all by natives of Salzburg. The sets, among which those of the harbour and of the temple of Neptune are particularly striking, were masterpieces by our famous local stage designer, Court Counsellor Herr Lorenz Quaglio, and attracted the admiration of all.' The name of the Salzburg native who composed the music was not given. Incidentally, it is perhaps somewhat confusing to find the theatre referred to as 'new', both in this newspaper report and on the title-page of the libretto where it is called the 'Teatro nuovo di Corte', for Cuvilliés' beautiful little rococo theatre had been open since 1753. Presumably, however, the description 'new' merely lingered on, perhaps to distinguish the court theatre from an older, seventeenth-century theatre.

Idomeneo was repeated on 3 February, and again on 3 March. Several months later, in Vienna, Mozart briefly considered making alterations

---

[1] 18 January, 1781.
[2] The supervisor of entertainments at the Bavarian Court.
[3] 18, January, 1781. [4] 22 January, 1781.

to the opera and attempting to have it performed there. He would, he told his father, have rewritten the role of Idomeneo for bass, and offered it to his friend Ludwig Fischer, a magnificent singer who was later to create the role of Osmin in *Die Entführung aus dem Serail*. He would also have 'made several other alterations, and done it more in the French style'.[1] However, nothing came of this. It was not until March 1786 that *Idomeneo* was performed in Vienna, and that was a private performance at Prince Auersperg's town palace, by and for the nobility. For this occasion, Mozart made extensive alterations, including the recasting of the role of Idamante for tenor. As it was Lent, the opera cannot have been staged, but must have been given in concert form. The singers included Giuseppe Antonio Bridi as Idomeneo, Baron Pulini as the tenor Idamante, Anna von Pufendorf as Ilia and the Countess Hatzfeld as Elettra. Of this performance, the short-lived periodical *Pfeffer und Salz* wrote: 'His opera, too much filled up with accompaniments, which was given by the nobility at Prince Auersperg's, did not receive the approbation that is usually vouchsafed to his art when he is heard on the pianoforte.'[2]

Although *Idomeneo* was produced several times during the nineteenth century in Germany and Austria, almost invariably sung in German, it was not until 1931, when a number of productions were mounted to commemorate the one hundred and fiftieth anniversary of its first performance, that the opera began to be considered as the earliest of Mozart's operatic masterpieces, in quality the equal of, if in style different from, *Le nozze di Figaro, Don Giovanni* and *Die Zauberflöte*. Some of its music had been used in an English *pasticcio, The Casket*, by Michael Rophino Lacy, produced at Drury Lane in 1829, but the first British performance of *Idomeneo* did not take place until 1934, in Glasgow. The opera is now well established in the international repertory.

II

Varesco's libretto was derived from one written by Antoine Danchet for the French composer André Campra, whose *Idoménée* was produced at the Paris Opéra in 1712. What Varesco did was to turn Danchet's five-act French libretto into a three-act Italian *opera seria*, but with choruses to be treated in the manner of Gluck's French operas, and to make various changes, especially to the ending of the original. He seems to have taken Metastasio as his model, for his libretto reads like a somewhat inexpert imitation of that master. Danchet's and Varesco's characters are legendary personages, and the plot in which they find themselves involved derives ultimately from the biblical story of Jepthah and his

[1] Vienna, 12 September, 1781.
[2] Copies in the City Library, Vienna, and the Studienbibliothek, Salzburg. Quoted in Deutsch.

daughter. The version of the story which comes to us through Homer and Greek legend has it that King Idomeneus of Crete ('Idomeneo' is the Italian form of his name), returning home at the end of the Trojan war, was caught in a tempest. He vowed that, if he should be saved, he would sacrifice the first person he met on dry land to Poseidon, god of the sea. This turned out to be his own son. The gods therefore punished Crete with pestilence, and Idomeneus was exiled to Calabria. (Whether or not there was an historical Idomeneus depends upon whether Homer wrote history or fiction.)

The first scene of Act I takes place in the apartments of Ilia in the royal palace at Sidon, on the island of Crete. Ilia, the daugher of King Priam of Troy, has been taken as hostage by Idomeneo, and sent, along with other Trojans, to Crete. She bewails her fate, and that of her father and brothers, and the city of Troy. Part of the Greek fleet which conveyed her to Crete has been destroyed by a tempest, and it is most probable that Idomeneo has been drowned. She herself was rescued by Idomeneo's son, Idamante, with whom she has fallen in love. She fears, however, that Idamante loves Elettra, who has sought refuge on the island after the murder of her mother Clytemnestra by her brother Orestes, and who also loves Idamante. Idamante enters to say that some ships of Idomeneo's fleet have been sighted, and that to celebrate the King's safe return he has decreed that the Trojan prisoners shall be set free. He then declares his love for Ilia. The Trojans are brought in and Idamante gives them their freedom. Elettra now enters, and reproaches Idamante for favouring the Trojans, but he replies that the Greeks can afford to be generous in victory. They are interrupted by the arrival of Arbace, adviser and confidant to Idomeneo, who informs them that Idomeneo has not survived. Ilia, still mourning the loss of her native Troy, also feels pity for Idomeneo. Elettra is distressed for a more selfish reason. She fears that, should Idamante now become King of Crete, he will immediately make Ilia his Queen. She expresses her jealousy and envy of Ilia, and swears vengeance on them both.

The scene changes to the seashore. The voices of Idomeneo's crew can be heard, calling on the gods to save them from the sea. At last, a small group, consisting of the King himself and a few of his followers, struggles on to the beach. Idomeneo asks his followers to leave him alone to confide his sufferings to his native skies. In soliloquy, he reveals the vow he made to Neptune[1] that he would sacrifice the first person he met after his safe landing. Already he regrets his cruel vow. Always he will see before his eyes the spectre of his victim, proclaiming his innocence. He looks up to see a man approaching, his eyes red with tears. Torn with guilt at the sight of his victim, Idomeneo curses the gods for their savage barbarism. The stranger offers his assistance to

[1] The librettist uses the Roman name of the god, instead of the Greek Poseidon, presumably because the opera is in Italian.

Idomeneo, and tells him that he is mourning the death of the heroic king who had been absent for many years fighting the Trojans. Soon, father and son are made aware of each other's identity. When Idamante attempts to embrace him, however, Idomeneo turns away in despair, ordering his son not to follow him, and to beware of seeing him again. Idamante is horrified, and wonders what he can have done to offend his father. The act ends with a march, and a chorus celebrating the King's return and honouring the gods.

In Act II, Scene I, in his royal apartments in the palace, Idomeneo reveals to his friend and adviser Arbace the vow he has made to Neptune, a vow he can fulfil only by sacrificing his own son. Arbace advises him to send Idamante abroad, where some other god can protect him, and to find another victim for Neptune. Idomeneo resolves to send Idamante to accompany Elettra back to her father's court at Argos. Arbace leaves to inform Idamante and Elettra, and to make preparations for their journey. Ilia now enters to congratulate Idomeneo on his safe return. He in turn expresses the hope that she will be able to forget her sorrows and find peace, and she replies that she has found a new homeland in Crete, and a new father in Idomeneo. After she has left him, Idomeneo realizes that she is in love with Idamante, and is forced to acknowledge to himself that Neptune will gain three victims, one killed by the sword, and two by sorrow. Though he is freed from one tempest, another rages within him.

Elettra now enters, happy that she is to be escorted to her own country by Idamante. She is confident that, when he is away from Ilia's side, Idamante will come to love her instead. In the distance, a march is heard, summoning the travellers to depart.

The second scene of Act II takes place at the port of Sidon. The travellers sing of the calm, tranquil sea which awaits them. Idomeneo bids farewell to Elettra and to Idamante who departs with extreme reluctance. Suddenly, a violent thunderstorm breaks out. The crowd is convinced that it denotes the anger of Neptune: they ask who can be responsible for offending the god. Idomeneo admits that he is the guilty one. He asks Neptune to punish him alone, for he refuses to sacrifice an innocent victim. The crowd rushes away in terror from a huge monster which Neptune has summoned up from the depths of the sea.

The first scene of Act III is set in a garden of the royal palace. Ilia sings of her love for Idamante, who arrives to tell her that he is going to fight Neptune's monster which is ravaging the country. He expects to die, and thus end his suffering. Ilia confesses that she loves him. They swear their love and fidelity to each other, and are suddenly interrupted by the arrival of Idomeneo and Elettra. Idamante asks his father once again to reveal why he continually avoids him, but Idomeneo cannot bring himself to confess the truth to his son, and instead commands him to leave the country and seek his fortune abroad. Ilia declares that she will leave with him, but Idamante insists she should remain safely in Crete. Arbace enters, to implore Idomeneo to address and calm the populace. When the King has gone, Arbace prays to the gods for mercy.

The scene changes to a public square in front of the palace. Before the assembled people, the High Priest of Neptune demands of the King the name of the sacrificial victim whose blood will appease the wrath of Neptune. Idomeneo is forced to reveal that it is his own son, Idamante. The people express their horror, and even the High Priest condemns Idomeneo's vow as inhuman.

The next scene takes place in the Temple of Neptune. Priests are preparing for the sacrifice, when Idomeneo enters with his retinue and several citizens. He prays to Neptune for mercy and clemency, but when shouts of victory are heard outside, and Arbace rushes in to announce that Idamante has slain the monster, the King realizes that nothing now will assuage the god's wrath but the blood of the promised victim. Idamante, who has been told of his father's vow, enters clothed in sacrificial white, but with a victor's garland on his head. He offers himself for sacrifice, to redeem his father's vow. Idomeneo falters, but Idamante assures him he does not fear death. Ilia attempts to offer herself in Idamante's place, when suddenly the subterranean voice of Neptune is heard, pronouncing that love has triumphed, and that Idomeneo should abdicate in favour of Idamante and his bride, Ilia. All are content with the god's judgment except Elettra who, left alone, expresses her despair and jealous fury.

In the final scene, again in the public square, Idomeneo addresses his people for the last time. Neptune and all the gods now look with favour on Crete, and he is happy to stand down in favour of Idamante and Ilia. At last, he says, peace has returned to his heart. The opera ends with a chorus of homage to the new royal couple.

III

In its combination of majesty and drama, the splendid D major Overture conveys perfectly the unique quality of this, not only Mozart's finest *opera seria* but also his last until *La clemenza di Tito* which he composed during the final months of his life. The correspondence between overture and opera, which would have been fortuitous in any of Mozart's earlier works for the stage, is deliberately contrived, for with *Idomeneo* the twenty-five-year-old composer suddenly leaps into greatness. The confidence with which he spreads his orchestral tone-colours, the masterly transitions from an assertive D major, through the gentle second subject in A minor, to the quietly tense final bars which are not a musical close but a leading on and into the drama, all these assure us, before the curtain has risen, that the young Mozart is now a fully-fledged master. When the curtain does rise, it is on Ilia alone, whose character, gentle and feminine, is projected in her first two bars of unaccompanied recitative. The upper strings then steal in, and we are immediately seized by the dramatic situation as set forth in Mozart's most expressive *recitativo accompagnato*. One of the many glories of *Idomeneo* is its accompanied recitative in which Mozart reveals a new mastery. Nothing is dramatically irrelevant, neither the orchestral colouring nor the occasional anticipation of themes from the aria which is to follow, nor the sudden changes from *accompagnato* to *secco* and back, nor the flexibility of procedure which frequently allows arias to rise or fall into recitative without formal orchestral introductions or codas. Ilia's aria (No. 1: 'Padre, germani, addio') is marked *andante con moto* but its passionate forward movement gives it an urgency usually only achieved by a faster tempo. Particularly remarkable is the manner in which, without sacrifice of melodic interest, Mozart is able to ensure that the declamation is clear and pointed. Ilia's exclamations of 'Grecia', the shape of several key phrases, the punctuation of the words by means of rests and melodic intervals, all these reveal how important and significant to Mozart were the operas he had seen in Paris and Mannheim. No longer is he to the slightest extent following a plan laid down by composers of the past. From the Italians he has learned the importance of melody, from Gluck and Piccinni how to involve the chorus in the drama, and from the Germans the value of expressive recitative. But he is no longer a pupil. He has become a master.

Ilia's aria moves, with not even a bar's rest to encourage applause, straight into *secco* recitative, as Idamante enters with his followers.

The rôle of Idamante was written by Mozart for the young castrato, Vincenzo dal Prato, whose vocal range appears to have been closer to that of a mezzo-soprano than to a soprano. At the private performance five years later in Vienna, the Idamante was a tenor, for whom Mozart made changes in the ensembles in which he took part, i.e. the trio and the quartet, and of course the duet with Ilia which he completely re-wrote. He also provided a new aria for Idamante. Whether he made these changes because, by 1786, he believed the role should be sung by a really masculine voice instead of a castrato, or whether they were forced upon him because Baron Pulini, the nobleman who wished to sing Idamante, was a tenor, is not known. Most stage performances now use a tenor Idamante, though occasionally the role is sung at the original pitch by a female soprano or mezzo-soprano. Those who favour a female voice argue that it is closest in sound to the timbre for which Mozart wrote, and that, since we accept female singers as Cherubino and Octavian, to prefer a male Idamante on the grounds of dramatic verisimilitude is irrelevant and inconsistent. But Mozart wrote Cherubino for a female soprano, not a castrato, and that particular 'farfallone amoroso' is a pubescent youngster. Strauss's Octavian is clearly modelled on Cherubino, and, of course, is also written for the female voice. We do not have on our stages today the type of voice for which Mozart originally composed the rôle of Idamante, and since he did re-write the rôle for tenor (the rôle, incidentally, not of an adolescent but of a young man, mature enough to marry and to replace his father as King), my own preference is for the 1786 changes and for a tenor Idamante.

Whether the rôle is sung by tenor or soprano, it should include the three arias composed for Mozart's 'molto amato castrato dal Prato', the first of which (No. 2: 'Non ho colpa') is a virile, passionate declaration of love. It is not over-decorated, unlike most arias for male castrato in Mozart's earlier *opere serie*, though whether this can be taken as proof of the composer's greater maturity and independence of fashion, or as a further indication that dal Prato was, as Mozart said plainly enough in his letters to Leopold, an incompetent singer, is by no means certain. What is certain is that, in this aria, and indeed throughout the opera, Mozart has written with an even greater originality and imagination for his orchestra. There can be no doubt that he was inspired by the high standard of the Mannheim Orchestra, a group of players of whom Dr Burney had written, several years earlier: 'There are more solo players in this, than perhaps in any other orchestra in Europe; it is an army of generals, equally fit to plan a battle as to fight it.'[1] It has even been claimed by commentators that, in *Idomeneo*, Mozart's orchestra is richer and more dazzling than in any of his later operas. The brilliance of his orchestral colouring is certainly remarkable in *Idomeneo*, as is the manner in which he suits his instrumentation to the demands of the dramatic situation.

The chorus (No. 3: 'Godiam la pace') in which Trojans and Cretans celebrate peace and the return of Idomeneo is a bright, joyous piece, with short duet sections, the first for two Cretan maidens, the second for two Trojan soldiers. The recitative which follows begins as *secco* recitative, becomes accompanied for Idamante's desperate exclamations of sorrow when he learns of the probable death of his father, reverts briefly to *recitativo secco* and thus to a lessening of the emotional temperature for Ilia's sympathetic comment after he has left, and then broadens again into the *recitativo accompagnato* which leads into the aria in which, after Ilia in her turn has departed, Elettra expresses her jealous fury. The fierce dramatic attack of Elettra's aria (No. 4: 'Tutte nel cor vi sento') must have astonished the Munich audience in 1781: it sounds startling even today, for in it Mozart sacrificed all the conventional virtues to dramatic effect. Elettra's rage erupts in snarling bursts of energy. Her phrases are closer to declamation than to melody, and her entire scene builds in ferocity and intensity, from the very beginning of her recitative to the aria, whose orchestral beginning is no mere formal prelude and whose vehement chromaticism is much more

[1] Burney: *The Present State of Music in Germany* (1773).

effective than conventional passages of coloratura, through to its
desperate final climax [Ex. 18].

Ex. 18

- tà, ven - det-ta e cru - del - tà, ven-det-ta e cru - del - tà.

The aria comes to no formal end, but is interrupted by a distant
chorus of shipwrecked sailors, though at this point somehow a scene-
change has quickly to be effected during a few bars of music, and a few
seconds of time. In Munich, Quaglio's baroque scenery probably
consisted of backdrops which were flown and wings which could be
moved by machinery, so that the process of changing was a fairly simple
one. Nowadays, we manage things less simply and more inelegantly.

It is with the double chorus of Idomeneo's shipwrecked company that
Mozart, for the first time in *Idomeneo*, uses his chorus in the Gluckian
manner as an integral part of the drama, for the earlier chorus of praise
and joy was purely formal in its function. 'Pietà, Numi, pietà!' (No. 5)
consists of two choruses, one in the distance, presumably out at sea, and
one closer: 'coro lontano' and 'coro vicino'. The distant chorus is
divided into four parts, the nearer one into two; and, except at the
beginning and end where their cries for help resound antiphonally, their
vocal lines are sharply contrasted. Like Elettra's aria, the chorus does
not draw to a close but merges into the first words sung by Idomeneo,
after he and a few other survivors have managed to struggle ashore.
Thus the usual division into separate numbers is obscured by the
continuing music, as the storm within Elettra is externalized in the
tempest which has wrecked Idomeneo's fleet and which now spews him
up to the apparent safety of dry land. This flexibility of form, which
recurs in the second act, renders *Idomeneo* unique amongst the operas of
Mozart. So too does the way in which the chorus is used. In Mozart's
earlier *opere serie*, and in Italian eighteenth-century opera in general,
very little use is made of the chorus. Even the formal opening and closing
choruses frequently turn out on close inspection to be no more than
ensembles of the four or five principal characters. In Gluck and in
French opera, however, the chorus played an important part in the
dramatic structure of the work, and it is from what he saw and heard in
Paris that Mozart derived his ideas for the choruses in *Idomeneo*.

It is important to remember that, along with Mozart's concern for the
dramatic viability of his music, there co-existed his continued
compliance with the requirement that he write arias to suit the
capabilities of the available singers. As we have already seen from his
correspondence with his father, the choice of Anton Raaff for the rôle of
Idomeneo presented Mozart with certain problems. He respected the
achievements of the elderly, old-fashioned singer, but found himself

having to compromise over the kind of music he wrote for him. This, of course, was not his first encounter with Raaff whom he had heard sing in Mannheim and whom he had come to know well in Paris three years earlier. At that time he had written to his father from Paris:

I must now say something about our Raaff. You will doubtless remember my writing somewhat unfavourably of him from Mannheim and not being very impressed with his singing – in short that I didn't like him at all. But the reason for that is that I really didn't hear him properly in Mannheim. I have now just heard him at a rehearsal of Holzbauer's *Günther*, dressed in his everyday clothes, with his hat on and a stick in his hand. When he was not singing he stood about like an awkward child; when he began to sing his first recitative, it went reasonably well, though every now and then he was given to shouting, which I couldn't bear. He sang the arias in so obviously offhand a manner, and some notes with far too much emphasis, that I didn't care for it at all. This is his habitual way of singing, and it may be a characteristic of the Bernacchi school, for he was a pupil of Bernacchi. Also, at Court, he always sang arias which, in my opinion, didn't suit his voice at all, so I simply didn't like him. But when he made his début here at a Concert Spirituel, he sang J. C. Bach's scena 'Non so d'onde viene' which, by the way, is a favourite of mine. Then I really heard him sing for the first time, and I liked him – in his particular style of singing, that is, although the style itself, the Bernacchi method, is not to my taste. Raaff is too much given to dropping into a *cantabile* style. I'm sure that when he was young and in his prime this must have been very effective and have taken people by surprise. And indeed I like it, but he overdoes it and so, in my view, it becomes ridiculous. I do like him singing short pieces, such as andantinos, and he also has a few arias which he gives in his individual style. Well, each to his own method. I imagine that his forte was bravura singing, and you can tell this from his style, as far as his age permits. He had good lungs and long breathing, and then those andantinos. His voice is beautiful and very pleasing. If I shut my eyes and listen to him, he reminds me of Meisner, except that Raaff's voice is even more pleasing. I am talking about their voices as they are at present, for I have never heard them in their prime. So I can only discuss their style or method of singing, which a singer always retains. Meisner, as you know, has the bad habit of exaggerating his vibrato at times, turning a note that should be sustained into distinct crotchets or even quavers, and I could never stand this. It really is a detestable habit, and one quite contrary to nature. The human voice vibrates naturally, but in its own way, and only to a certain extent, so that the effect is beautiful. That is the nature of the human voice, and people imitate it not only on wind instruments but also on strings, and even on the clavier. But the moment one oversteps the natural limit, it is no longer beautiful because it is contrary to nature. Then it reminds me of an organ when the bellows are puffing. Now Raaff never does this, in fact he can't bear it. So far as a real cantabile is concerned, there I prefer Meisner to Raaff (though by no means unconditionally, for he too has his mannerisms). But in bravura singing, in long passages and roulades, Raaff is an absolute master, and, what is more, his diction is perfectly clear, and thus beautiful. Also, as I said, his andantinos or little songs are charming. He has composed four German songs which are absolutely beautiful.[1]

Mozart, then, understood his leading tenor's strengths and weaknesses, and composed for him accordingly. The recitative preceding his first aria is expressive of Idomeneo's anguish, and the aria itself (No. 6: 'Vedrommi intorno l'ombra dolente') is set forth clearly in two sections, an *andantino sostenuto* followed by an *allegro molto*. The vocal style is less individual, less modern, than in Elettra's aria, but the orchestra continues to be used with a freedom which must at the time have seemed completely novel.

The correspondence quoted on pp.145–148 revealed a difference of opinion between composer and librettist concerning the recitative scene between Idomeneo and Idamante which culminates in their recognition of each other as father and son. Varesco was right to point out that the scene needed to be long enough to allow the recognition to occur naturally, but Mozart, practical man of the theatre as well as great composer, knew that, with two singers who were ineffective actors, a long scene in recitative would be boring. And like Verdi, who said 'The boring is the worst of all styles',[2] but unlike certain more recent composers who seem to consider it the most effective, Mozart was concerned to avoid boring his audiences. The scene in question was cut in Munich, but ought to be performed in full whenever singer-actors of sufficient merit are available. *Opera seria* does not call for singers who do not possess acting ability; on the contrary it requires especially gifted actors.

Idamante's aria (No. 7: 'Il padre adorato') is considerably more effective than his earlier aria in this act: direct and human in its expression of feeling, again unadorned and gaining dramatically thereby, and defining Idamante more clearly as a character than did his earlier love song. The act ends in festivity to celebrate the safe return of the King. A brilliant march (No. 8) with sections displaying the woodwind to advantage is followed by a magnificent chorus, marked 'Ciaccona' (Chaconne), alternating the full chorus with sections for two pairs of duettists, male and female, who also sing as a quartet.

At the beginning of Act II, Arbace's aria (No. 10: 'Se il tuo duol') in which he attempts to console Idomeneo, though in words far too arcane to have been of much comfort, is a dashing *allegro*, brilliantly written for the voice, though conventional in form even to the provision for a final improvised cadenza. The aria is hardly called for by the dramatic situation, and was composed merely for the sake of the singer, Domenico de' Panzacchi, an accomplished artist but of the old school, and one who would have expected to be given at least one bravura *da capo* aria. It is, however, surely preferable to include this aria, rather than

---

[1] Paris, 12 June, 1778.   [2] Osborne: *The Complete Operas of Verdi*, p. 80.

the *scena* which Mozart composed in Vienna on 10 March, 1786, for the private performance at the Palais Auersperg later that month. At that performance, Arbace's aria and his scene with Idomeneo which preceded it were replaced by accompanied recitative for Ilia and the tenor Idamante, leading to an aria, 'Non temer, amato bene' for Idamante (K. 490). The words may have been provided by Da Ponte, with whom Mozart was then collaborating on *Le nozze di Figaro*: the composer is not likely to have asked Varesco to provide a text, as their relationship had by that time come to an end. The new aria is beautiful, but essentially undramatic, with a splendid violin obbligato which was played by Count Hatzfeld, a close friend of Mozart, and the husband of the Elettra of that performance.

In one of his letters to his father from Munich, Mozart mentioned his intention to include at this point in Act II an *andantino* aria for Ilia, with obbligato parts for four wind instruments, flute, oboe, horn and bassoon. The aria, 'Se il padre perdei' (No. 11), is a gentle, lyrical piece, perhaps no more dramatic than Mozart's 1786 interpolation for his tenor Idamante, but somehow perfectly in place, as well as in character, the sweet, loving character of Ilia. The four concertante instruments are given prominent parts to play, and their soothing colours add greatly to the beauty of this serene E flat major aria in which Ilia sings to Idomeneo of her love and gratitude. It is clear that Mozart enjoyed writing for his friends in the Mannheim orchestra as much as for Dorothea Wendling, his capable and musicianly Ilia. The fourth, fifth and sixth bars of the voice part ('la patria il riposo, tu padre mi sei') have been thought closely to resemble Tamino's 'ich fühl es, ich fühl' es' in his *Bildnisarie* in *Die Zauberflöte*. The resemblance is, however, fleeting and hardly significant.

As though there were to be no disrupting applause at the end of Ilia's aria, Mozart has followed it immediately with the phrase which we have heard in the aria played by the wind instruments, but now given to the strings and marked to be played in the tempo of the preceding aria, to usher in Idomeneo's recitative. Its harmony is now more menacing, and a sense of brooding unease spreads throughout the recitative in which the King reflects bitterly on the outcome of his cruel and cowardly vow. His aria, 'Fuor del mar' (No. 12), is the one which Mozart thought the most successful in the entire opera, and which Raaff was so pleased with that he used to sing it night and morning during the rehearsal period [Ex. 19]. It is an old-fashioned bravura aria in a-b-a form, because that was the kind of aria the old tenor was used to, but within the conventional framework Mozart has composed a magnificent outburst of emotion in which, while the words speak of the turbulence of the sea, the music projects the King's inner conflict. The aria exists in two versions, the second being merely the first somewhat simplified and made easier for the singer by the omission of passages of fioritura which

Ex. 19

Mozart referred to as 'chopped noodles'. It is probable that the second version was composed when it became evident that the elderly Anton Raaff was no longer capable of managing the 'chopped noodles'. But the passages of heroic coloratura are an essential facet of the aria. The eminent Austrian Mozart scholar Bernhard Paumgartner contended that Mozart composed the simplified version later, probably for the Vienna performance, and as part of his own progressive desire to move away from archaic forms rather than out of consideration for a particular singer. I do not think this likely. There are no valid grounds for considering the simplified version musically superior to the original; it was most likely composed before the Munich première and sung by Raaff. Only if the Idomeneo is unable to handle the long passages of coloratura should the second version be used in present-day performances. Of his original Munich version of the aria, Mozart wrote to his father: 'The aria is excellently adapted to the words. You hear the *mare* [sea] and the *mare funesto* [baleful sea], and the musical passages are suited to *minacciar* [threatening].'[1]

The aria for Elettra which follows (No. 13: 'Idol mio') presents her in a gentler light than most of her other scenes in the opera, for she happily anticipates her journey to her homeland with Idamante. This gentle *andante* is accompanied by strings alone in such a way that its mood of contentment and peace remains unbroken from beginning to end. Like so many numbers in *Idomeneo*, it has no formal end: Elettra's final note coincides with the opening chord of a C major March (No. 14) at first heard in the distance but gradually rising to a crescendo during the change of scene to the port from which Elettra and Idamante are to sail. As soon as she hears the march, its horns and trumpets at first muted, Elettra announces in five bars of recitative that it is calling her to board the vessel, and she leaves to do so just as the scene is quickly being changed and the orchestra, mutes removed, rises to its fortissimo. From the beginning of Elettra's aria (or from the beginning of 'Fuor del mar', if the simplified version is sung, for it is linked to the following recitative) through to the end of Act II, the music now continues without formal pause; even when a march or a chorus is followed by a few bars of *recitativo secco*, it is linked so as to prevent the dramatic tension being broken by applause.

The serene calm of the sea is mirrored in the E major chorus 'Placido

[1] Munich, 27 December, 1780.

è il mar' (No. 15), between whose first and second statements of its warm and comforting melody lies Elettra's solo, which is the still centre of the entire opera, a timeless moment of sheer beauty [Ex. 20].

Ex. 20

So a - vi Zef-fi-ri so-li spi-ra - te, del fred-do ho - re a —— li-ra cal ma-te.

The chorus runs without a break into a few bars of recitative in which Idomeneo bids his son depart, and then Idamante launches the great trio ('Pria di partir, o Dio': No. 16) in which the conflicting emotions, none of them joyful, of the three characters are clearly delineated, and their depression wells up to become desperation, and finally to find outward form in the terrifying storm and appearance of the monster, a projection of the hatred, fury and misery in the hearts of the protagonists. The last bars of the trio become the beginning of the tempest, amd then the terrified onlookers burst into their chorus (No. 17), 'Qual nuovo terrore', as the tempest worsens and the monster appears. 'Who is the guilty one?' cry the citizens, their cry echoed three times by the wind instruments. They are answered by Idomeneo's tortured *recitativo accompagnato*, after which they burst into their terrified D minor chorus, 'Corriamo, fuggiamo' (No. 18). As the people disperse in fear, their cries can still be heard in the distance, and both chorus and act end in an ominous quietness as Idomeneo is left standing alone to face not only the angry god but also his own conscience, if indeed they are separate entities.

Act III begins with an aria which has become well-known in concert performance, Ilia's 'Zeffiretti lusinghieri' (No. 19), a gentle expression of love, in the key of E major which Mozart used for the serenity of the chorus 'Placido è il mar' in Act II. Ilia's aria is preceded by accompanied recitative which anticipates the aria's opening theme, a theme expressive not only of love and tenderness but also of a warmth and maturity which are not so apparent in her arias in the earlier acts [Ex. 21]. Other

Ex. 21

Zef - fi - ret - ti lu - sin - ghie-ri, deh vo - la - - -
- - - - - - te al mio te - so - ro,

commentators have drawn attention to the moment of poetry in the concluding phrase of the second theme where, with the repetition of the phrase, the moving chromatic harmonies deepen and emphasize the expressiveness of the melody. And, as so often in this opera, Mozart moves the drama on at the conclusion of the aria by continuing the music without pause into the recitative, allowing it to progress from aria to accompanied recitative to *recitativo secco*, thus bringing the emotional temperature down through smooth gear-changes to the dialogue between Idamante and Ilia, and then causing it to rise again in their duet (No. 20: 'S'io non moro a questi accenti'), in whose accompaniment we hear a variant of a theme from the Overture, which has already made its way into the opera more than once. The duet is light and pleasing, but hardly one of the more memorable numbers in the score. For the Vienna performance of 1786, Mozart provided a new duet for tenor and soprano, 'Spiegarti non poss'io', which I find musically preferable to the original one but, on balance, less suitable dramatically, for it comes to a full close whereas the earlier duet is not separated in this manner from the following scene. The means by which Mozart created longer units, entire scenes instead of separate numbers, and even sometimes linked scenes, seem to me one of the most interesting features of *Idomeneo*. There can be no doubt that it was Mozart's conscious intention in Munich to create a unified work of art. Presumably, by the time of the single performance in Vienna five years later, he thought of that unified work of art as something which had been created, had existed, in its Munich performances, and not something which need necessarily be recreated in Vienna. It is otherwise difficult to explain the decidedly patchwork nature of his additions, even when they are musically equal or superior to his first thoughts.

Although the original duet was written for male and female sopranos, it presents no difficulties to a tenor Idamante, and for dramatic reasons is to be preferred to the Vienna replacement. The *recitativo accompagnato* which precedes both versions is intensely dramatic. Idamante's happiness at discovering that Ilia loves him is expressed in breathless phrases, while Ilia's confidence is commented upon by an orchestra that knows better the difficulties yet to be overcome. Her expression of love is no more than two bars long, yet how melting her two phrases, how warm and consoling the strings of the accompaniment. At the end of the duet Mozart moves us inexorably forward to the great quartet (No. 21: 'Andrò ramingo e solo') by again merging duet, accompanied recitative, unaccompanied recitative, accompanied recitative and quartet into one another. I used earlier the simile of the smooth gear-change in describing this process, but it is really more like automatic transmission. This is the quartet which Raaff grew to like after Mozart had explained it to him, the quartet of which Mozart said he did not know how to change a single note. It begins and ends with the same low-lying phrase for Idamante; at the end Idamante leaves sadly to go into exile, as the orchestra completes his phrase for him.

Mozart also referred to this quartet as one in which the characters talk more than they sing, and it is true that, at its conclusion, one feels one has experienced an ensemble of rare dramatic intensity, as well as one of equally rare beauty. The four characters, Idomeneo, Idamante, Ilia and Elettra, have reached a moment of deep significance in their lives, and the manner in which, within the formal framework of the quartet, Mozart has conveyed their despair, fury, resignation and love, is almost unique in opera. Not until the trios and quartets of Verdi (there is a famous example in *Rigoletto*) does one find a parallel to this quartet, not even in the later operas of Mozart himself. Years later, Mozart's wife was to relate that 'once, when singing in this quartet, he was so deeply affected that he was obliged to desist, and for a long time would not look at the composition again.'[1] This, too, is Idamante's feeling when, unable to complete his final phrase, he departs slowly, while the orchestra falteringly, sadly, completes it for him and then fades into silence.

I have said that, in *Idomeneo*, Mozart was more concerned with the aesthetic viability of the work than with pandering to his singers, and I believe that the evidence of the opera itself supports that assertion. But circumstances forced Mozart to compromise. The character of Arbace is really superfluous, and certainly does not need the two arias he is given. His second, which follows the quartet, holds up the dramatic action for no good purpose: simply to allow a minor character to voice his forebodings, or, to be more accurate, to allow a first-rate singer another opportunity to show off his voice. Arbace's 'Se colà ne' fati è scritto' is a conventional three-part *da capo* aria, an *andante* both stately and gracious, though hardly an apt musical setting of the words, which are more intelligently treated in the elaborate accompanied recitative preceding the aria. The recitative, in fact, develops from a motif in the quartet which it follows, suggesting that musico-dramatic requirements were still in Mozart's mind when he made provision for the aria. It is a pity that the aria itself should be so static and even placid, for it occupies a key position between the climactic quartet and the great public scene in which a victim is to be sacrificed to Neptune, and it cannot fail to sound decidedly anticlimactic in performance.

The next scene contains musical riches, but is laid out in a rather unusual manner. Something of the melodrama which Mozart had toyed with in *Zaide* must have remained in his mind as he composed the scene for Idomeneo and the High Priest (No. 23), for the music and its disposition at this point put one in mind of the earlier work. The orchestra begins with a *maestoso* flourish, to which presumably the King and his followers entered. Two bars, marked *largo*, probably sufficed for the entrance of the priests, and then there follows an agitated *allegro* passage for the violins, which must have been the point at which the populace rushed on to the stage to beg Idomeneo to save them. The dignified recitative, in which the High Priest urges Idomeneo to the temple to perform the sacrifice, and asks who is to be the victim, to which

[1] Jahn, op. cit., Vol. II, p. 153.

the King replies that it is his own son, leads to the horrified reaction of
the populace in the chorus 'O voto tremendo' (No. 24), a powerfully
expressive cry of woe. The effect of the unison passage at the words 'già
regna la morte' is tremendous. The other-worldly beauty of the High
Priest's solo is followed by the return of 'O voto tremendo' and, most
shattering moment of all, the orchestral conclusion in which, after the
overbearing sadness of Mozart's choral music, the sudden consolation
of C major momentarily lightens the gloom. But only momentarily,
though it is a glimpse of the eventual happy ending, for a slow and
solemn march (No. 25) in F major now covers the change of scene to the
sacrificial altar of the temple. This is the march which Mozart described
to his father in one of his letters from Munich, quoted earlier (p. 148).

The next scene opens with Idomeneo's prayer (No. 26: 'Accogli, o rè
del mar'), a beautiful piece in which the singer's smoothly flowing *legato*
must, one feels, surely affect any gods who may be listening. Idomeneo
is supported by the chorus of priests in a virtually monotone chant.
Suddenly a D major flourish of trumpets, an exclamation from an off-
stage chorus, and the arrival on-stage of Arbace reveal that Idamante
has slain the monster. But, when Idamante himself enters, he is already
dressed in the robes of the sacrificial victim, and in a long and masterly
passage of dialogue with his father in accompanied recitative he
announces his readiness to die. It is in Idamante's self-control and
courage, revealed in this recitative, that one glimpses the future ruler of
the island, and a wiser man than his unhappy father. The librettist
Varesco gave him an aria to sing, at the moment of death, and Mozart
dutifully set it. But 'No, la morte io non pavento' (No. 27), an agreeable
enough *allegro-larghetto-allegro da capo* aria in itself, holds up the action
unforgivably, and, as we have seen from his correspondence, Mozart
himself agreed to its excision before the first performance. The aria is, in
any case, a shade too long, and is probably best omitted from stage
performance. It ends in what we have by now come to think of as typical
Idomeneo-fashion: that is, with a transition into accompanied recitative,
in this case an exchange of farewells between father and son. The scene
continues in accompanied recitative with the intervention of Ilia, the
orchestra here at its richest and most inventive. Suddenly a subterranean
rumbling is heard, and the statue of Neptune is seen to move. The voice
of the god is heard (No. 28), to the accompaniment of solemn chords on
three trombones and two horns. The tone colour of the trombones was
unusual in the orchestra of Mozart's day, and was reserved for unusual
effects, such as the accompaniment to a god's utterance, or some other
supernatural occurrence, like the Commendatore's invitation to
supper in *Don Giovanni*. Mozart's letters to Leopold have revealed to us
how important he considered the voice of Neptune in *Idomeneo*. He
composed the god's speech at least three times, the third and most
concise version being, surely, the most effective.

The exclamations of relief uttered by most of the other characters are interrupted by the violent fury of Elettra. It was here that Mozart, as we have already noted, asked for the insertion of a direction to get everyone else off-stage, on the grounds that they would hardly have loitered to listen to her ravings, though equally it seemed odd to him that they should depart for no other apparent purpose than to allow her to sing without interruption! Elettra's recitative and C minor aria (No. 29: 'D'Oreste, d'Ajace ho in seno i tormenti') present a problem to the director of the opera, for they are musically and dramatically superb and cannot possibly be omitted, though Mozart reluctantly omitted the aria at the première, nor can they easily be fitted in elsewhere; yet Varesco's libretto is so clumsily constructed that the aria is awkwardly placed in its present position. But what a superb outburst it is, a sustained scream of frustrated rage, expressing itself not in the conventional bravura of the old *opera seria* but in the fierce declamation of its phrasing and the cutting edge of its harmonies. Even the violins' trills are used to convey and to emphasize Elettra's agitation.

The opera's final scene opens with Idomeneo's recitative (No. 30: 'Popoli!') and aria (No. 31: 'Torna la pace al core'). A string figure played by the first violins, and related to that figure in the Overture which has occurred throughout the opera, is repeated canonically by second violins, then violas, then cellos and basses [Ex. 22], and

Ex. 22

introduces the dignified recitative in which the King abdicates in favour of his son. The aria was omitted from the Munich première, as the third act was thought to be too long, but it should always be included in performance. Not only is it an attractive, though conventional, a-b-a *adagio* aria, it is also the only aria in the opera in which Idomeneo is seen to be at peace with himself. In addition, it performs a quasi-symbolic function, representing the return to order and peace of the island kingdom, after the terrors occasioned by Idomeneo's vow and Neptune's displeasure. It is fitting, too, that we should take our leave of the old King with due deference, and allow him to express, with a stately, old-fashioned dignity, his relief and his return to inner peace and serenity. The festive chorus (No. 32: 'Scenda Amor') which concludes the opera contains a short orchestral interlude to which the ballet dancers no doubt contributed.

It is probably here, at the end of the opera, that the ballet (catalogued separately as K. 367) was performed at the première. In eighteenth-century *opera seria*, the music for the ballet, which was rarely considered an integral part of the opera itself, was as often as not provided by another composer. Writing to his father from Munich during the gestation period of *Idomeneo*, Mozart informed him that 'as there is no extra ballet, but merely an appropriate divertissement in the opera, I have the honour of composing the music for that as well. I am glad of this, however, for now all the music will be by the same composer.'[1] The ballet music consists of five movements, the first of which, a powerful Chaconne in D major, opens with a phrase similar to the beginning of the final chorus, 'Scenda Amor, scenda Imeneo'. After a *larghetto* section in B flat, there is a restatement of the Chaconne. The D major *Pas seul* begins with a largo of great pomp, then quickens to *allegretto* and *più allegro*. The Passepied in B flat is graceful, the delicate G major Gavotte pleased its composer sufficiently for him to make use of it in the last movement of his Piano Concerto K. 503 five years later, and the Passacaille is a pleasant rondo, less grand than the Chaconne and more simply scored.

It is with *Idomeneo* that the series of great operas by Mozart begins in earnest. Janus-headed, *Idomeneo* looks to the future with its sense of drama, its power and originality, and its newly-found freedom of form, though it also says an affectionate farewell to the past, to the old *opera seria*, to the kind of aria which Mozart's Idomeneo, Anton Raaff, preferred to sing. 'To write operas now is my one burning ambition,' Mozart had written to his father from Mannheim three years before *Idomeneo*. 'I envy everybody who is composing one.'[2] And it is true that, in most of the great works of his maturity, his symphonies, quartets and, above all, his piano concerti, he writes as though for the theatre. There is as much dramatic interplay in the exchanges between piano and orchestra in the concerti as there is in the Act II finale of *Le nozze di Figaro*. The earliest stage work in which real dramatic conflict plays a more than passing and fragmentary rôle is *Idomeneo*. It comes as no surprise to learn that, when the English organist and composer Vincent Novello and his daughter Mary visited Mozart's widow in 1829, she told them that the happiest time of her husband's life was when he was composing *Idomeneo*. Constanze must have been told this by Mozart: she could not have observed it, for their courtship did not begin until some months later in Vienna.

[1] 30 December, 1780.   [2] 4 February, 1778.

XIV

Die Entführung aus dem Serail

Singspiel in three acts

K. 384

Dramatis personae:

Constanze	(soprano)
Blonde, her maid	(soprano)
Belmonte	(tenor)
Pedrillo, his servant	(tenor)
Pasha Selim	(speaking role)
Osmin, Overseer of the Pasha's Estate	(bass)
Klaas, a sailor	(speaking role)

LIBRETTO by Gottlieb Stephanie Jr., based on Christoph Friedrich Bretzner's *Belmonte und Constanze*

TIME: Mid-sixteenth century

PLACE: The Pasha Selim's Palace, on the coast of Turkey

FIRST PERFORMED in Vienna, 16 July, 1782, at the Burgtheater, with Caterina Cavalieri (Constanze), Therese Teiber (Blonde), Johann Valentin Adamberger (Belmonte), Johann Ernst Dauer (Pedrillo), Karl Ludwig Fischer (Osmin), Dominik Jautz (Pasha Selim)

Die Entführung aus dem Serail

I

MOZART CAN HARDLY have expected, when he left Salzburg to make the short journey to Munich for *Idomeneo*, that he would never again live in the town of his birth. Yet it was to be so: he was to spend the ten years of life left to him as a resident of Vienna. He and his father and sister remained in Munich for some weeks after the première of *Idomeneo*, and the younger Mozarts enjoyed the social life of the carnival. At the beginning of March, 1781, they paid a visit to nearby Augsburg for a few days. On 12 March, Wolfgang left Munich, having been summoned to Vienna by his employer the Archbishop who was visiting his ailing father, the Imperial Vice-Chancellor. Mozart arrived in Vienna at 9 a.m. on 16 March, was given accommodation in the Deutsches Ordenshaus (House of the Teutonic Order) in Singerstrasse where the Archbishop had his headquarters, and by 4 p.m. the same day was participating in a concert.

Life as part of the entourage of Archbishop Colloredo must have been particularly humiliating for the young composer after his weeks of freedom and success in Munich. 'We lunch about twelve o'clock, which unfortunately is a little too early for me,' he wrote to his father the day after his arrival. 'Our party consists of the two valets, that is, the body and soul attendants of His Lordship, the auditor Herr Zetti, the confectioner, the two cooks, Ceccarelli,[1] Brunetti[2] – and my insignificant self. Please note that the two valets sit at the head of the table, but at least I have the honour of being seated above the cooks. Well, I merely imagine that I'm back in Salzburg. A lot of stupid, coarse jokes are exchanged at table, but no one jokes with me for I never say a word, or if I have to speak I always do so with the utmost gravity. As soon as I have finished my lunch, I get up and leave. We do not eat together in the evening, but are each given three ducats, which goes a long way!'[3]

The Archbishop's musicians were required to accompany him to the homes of the nobility, and to wait in an ante-chamber until required to perform. This was especially galling to Mozart who had been received in

---

[1] Francesco Ceccarelli, castrato.

[2] Antonio Brunetti, violinist and leader of the Archbishop's orchestra, for whom Mozart wrote several compositions.

[3] 17 March, 1781.

more liberal style by the nobility of Rome, Milan, Paris, London and, indeed, Vienna. He made it clear that he did not intend to submit to being treated as a lackey. When the Archbishop's musicians were required to appear at the house of Prince Galitzin, the Russian Ambassador, Mozart made his way there alone, because he felt ashamed to be seen in the company of his colleagues. Arriving at the Ambassador's residence, he 'took no notice either of the valet or the lackey, but walked straight on through the rooms into the music room, for all the doors were open, went straight up to the Prince, paid him my respects and stood there talking to him. I had completely forgotten my colleagues Ceccarelli and Brunetti, for they were not to be seen. They were hiding by the wall behind the orchestra, not daring to take a step forward.'[1]

Mozart attempted to lead an independent social life in Vienna, renewing his contacts with old friends and patrons among the aristocracy, and also endeavouring to supplement his meagre income by accepting engagements to perform outside the Archbishop's service. In April he took part in a charity concert at the Kärntnertor Theater and was received with greater applause, both as composer and as pianist. He was enraptured with the size of the orchestra, its string section based on forty violins, and its wind instruments including six bassoons, and thrilled at the reception he received. Vienna, he told his father, was the best place in the world. Simply to be there was sufficient for him. When, suddenly, he was informed that, within a few days, the Archbishop and his household would be returning to Salzburg, Wolfgang wrote to his father for advice. He wanted nothing better than to be allowed to stay in Vienna and take a few pupils, but Leopold cautioned him against acting rashly. Matters, however, soon came to a head, and some weeks later Mozart wrote again to his father:

Mon très cher Père,
    I am still boiling with rage. And you, my dearest and most beloved father, will doubtless feel with me. My patience has been tried for so long that at last it has given out. I am no longer so unfortunate as to be in the Salzburg service. Today has been a happy day for me. Just listen to this. Twice already, that – I don't know what to call him – has uttered to my face the greatest *sottises* and impertinences. As I wanted to spare your feelings, I have not repeated these to you, and if I refrained from taking my revenge on the spot it was only because I always had you, my beloved father, before my eyes. He called me a rascal and a dissolute fellow, and told me to go, and I endured it all even though I felt that not only my honour but also yours was being attacked. I remained silent, because you wished it so. Now listen to this. A week ago, the footman came up to my room unexpectedly, and told me I was to move out immediately. All the others had been told in advance of the day of departure, but not I. So I hastily packed everything into my trunk, and old

____
[1] Mozart to his father, 24 March, 1781.

Madame Weber was kind enough to offer to put me up. I have an attractive room in her house, and what's more I am living with people who are obliging and who supply me with all the things I sometimes need in a hurry, and which are not easily obtainable when you are living alone.

I arranged to travel home by the mail coach today, that is Wednesday May 9th. But in that short time I was not able to collect the money owing to me, so I postponed my departure until Saturday. When I showed up today, the valets told me that the Archbishop wanted to give me a parcel to take to Salzburg. I asked whether it was urgent. They said yes, it was of the greatest importance. 'Then I am sorry,' said I, 'that I cannot have the honour of obliging His Grace, for I cannot leave before Saturday' – for the reason I've already stated. 'I have left this house and am living at my own expense. So it is only natural that I cannot leave Vienna until I am in a position to do so, for surely no one will expect me to lose money.' Kleinmayr, Moll, Bönike and the two valets all agreed that I was perfectly right. When I went in to the Archbishop – by the way, I must tell you first that Schlauka, one of the valets, advised me to say that the mail coach was already full, since the Archbishop would regard this as a better reason than the true one – well, when I went in to see him, his first words were: *Archbishop:* 'Well, young fellow, when are you off?' *I:* 'I wanted to go tonight, but all the seats were taken.' Then he rushed ahead in one breath. I was the most dissolute fellow he knew, no one else served him as badly as I did, and I had better leave today or he would write home and have my salary stopped. I couldn't get a word in edgeways, for he blazed away like a fire. I listened to it all very calmly. He lied to my face that my salary was five hundred gulden, and called me a rascal, a scoundrel and a conceited ass. Oh, I can't tell you everything he said. Finally my blood began to boil, and I couldn't stop myself from saying 'Then Your Grace is not satisfied with me?' 'What, do you dare to threaten me, you scoundrel? There is the door! I shall have nothing more to do with such a miserable wretch.' Finally I said, 'Nor shall I have anything to do with you.' 'Be off, then!' As I left the room, I said 'So be it. You shall have it in writing tomorrow.' Now tell me, most beloved father, did I not say that too late rather than too soon? Listen to me now. My honour means more to me than anything else, and I know that you feel the same way. Do not worry about me in the slightest. I am so sure of my prospects in Vienna that I would have resigned even if I had had no cause. As I now have a cause, three times over, it would not have been to my credit to stay. On the contrary, twice I acted in a cowardly fashion, and I could not do so a third time.

As long as the Archbishop remains in town I shall not give a concert here. You are completely mistaken if you imagine I shall be thought badly of by the Emperor and the nobility, for the Archbishop is detested here, and most of all by the Emperor. In fact, he is furious because the Emperor did not invite him to Laxenburg. By the next post I shall send you a little money, just to prove to you that I am not starving here.

Now please be cheerful about this, for my good luck is just beginning, and I hope that mine will also be yours. Write to me, in code, that you are pleased, as indeed you ought to be. In public, however, you should condemn me so that no one will think you are to blame. But if, in spite of this, the Archbishop should offer you the slightest indignity, come at once to Vienna and bring my sister, for I give you my word all three of us can earn our living here. It would be better, however, if you could put up with it there for another year. Do not send any more letters to the Deutsches Haus, nor enclose them in packages to the Archbishop. I want to hear no more about Salzburg. I hate the Archbishop to the point of madness.

Adieu. I kiss your hands a thousand times and embrace my dear sister with all my heart, and remain for ever your obedient son

W. A. Mozart

Just address your letters to me: Auf dem Peter, im Auge Gottes, 2nd floor. Please let me know soon that you approve, for that is all that is lacking in my present happiness. Adieu.[1]

'Old Madame Weber', into whose house Wolfgang had moved, was the mother of Aloysia, his Mannheim love. Aloysia was now married and as Aloysia Lange had become a leading sopano with the German Opera in the Burgtheater. Her father had died, and Frau Weber supplemented the family income by letting rooms in the house in which she and her other daughters lived. Remembering his son's past entanglements with the Weber family, Leopold was furious at Wolfgang's move, and also highly displeased that he should have left Archbishop Colloredo's service so precipitately. He simply failed to understand his son's temperament or to sense that the old social order in Europe had already entered upon its last phase. The American Revolution was five years past, the French Revolution was already brewing, and though Wolfgang was no revolutionary he was someone who knew his own worth both as man and as artist. He bore no animosity towards the aristocracy while it befriended him, though he was careful not to pay too high a price for its patronage. He would never sacrifice his self-respect or, as he called it, his honour.

To Count Arco, who was in charge of the Archbishop's household staff, Mozart asserted that the Archbishop was at fault. 'If he knew how to deal with people of talent, this would never have happened. I am the most amiable fellow in the world, Count Arco, provided that people are the same with me.' 'Well,' Arco replied, 'the Archbishop considers you an insufferably conceited fellow.' 'I imagine he does,' said Mozart, 'for I certainly am towards him. I treat others as they treat me. When I see that someone despises and belittles me, I can be as proud as a peacock.' When Arco asked, 'Do you not think that I too have frequently to swallow unpleasant words?' Wolfgang's reply was, 'You no doubt have your reasons for putting up with it, and I have my reasons for refusing to do so.'[2]

On 8 June, Mozart went to the Deutsches Haus to present a memorandum to the Archbishop, but was received instead by Count Arco who literally kicked him out of the Archbishop's ante-chamber:

[1] 9 May, 1781.   [2] From Mozart's letter to his father, 2 June, 1781.

'How easy it would have been to persuade me to remain – by kindness rather than insolence and rudeness. I had sent a message to Count Arco that I had nothing further to say to him, for he attacked me so rudely when I first spoke to him, and treated me like a rogue which he had no right to do. Heavens above, as I've already said, I wouldn't have gone to him the last time if he had not added in his message that he had received a letter from you. . . . If he was really so well disposed towards me, he ought to have reasoned quietly with me, or have let things take their course, instead of using words like "clown" and "scoundrel" and booting a fellow out of the room with a kick in the arse. But I am forgetting that he was probably ordered to do so by our worthy Prince Archbishop.'[1]

The Webers took good care of Mozart, allowing him to concentrate on composing, seek pianoforte pupils, and keep up his contacts with the court and the nobility who could be of use to him. He wrote piano sonatas for his pupils and himself to play, as well as sonatas for piano and violin, and other chamber music much of which was published by the famous Viennese firm of Artaria & Co. The greater part of July he spent at the country house of the Austrian Vice-Chancellor and Chancellor of State, Johann Philipp, Count Cobenzl, on one of the beautiful wooded slopes of the Kahlenberg, overlooking Vienna. (The hill is now named Cobenzl, after the Count.) Cobenzl and his friends, like most of the Viennese aristocrats, treated Mozart as an equal. Their attitude to him, and to artists in general, especially musicians, was decidedly liberal for the period. Count Cobenzl himself took letters to the post for Mozart, and drove him to and from the city when necessary. At the end of July, Mozart was back in Vienna, and quickly began to work on a new opera, *Die Entführung aus dem Serail* (The Abduction from the Harem).

The seeds of *Die Entführung* had been sown some months earlier, when Gottlieb Stephanie, Stage Director of the German Opera in Vienna, expressed his high opinion of *Zaide* and promised to provide Mozart with a new libretto. Stephanie (1741–1800) had begun adult life in the army, before going on the stage and eventually becoming, in 1769, a producer and dramatist at the Burgtheater. His elder brother, Christian Gottlob Stephanie, was an actor in Vienna. On 30 July, Gottlieb Stephanie gave Mozart a libretto. Writing to his father two days later, Wolfgang claimed already to have composed three numbers:

> The libretto is quite good. The subject is Turkish, and the title is *Belmonte und Constanze* or *Die Verführung* [sic] *aus dem Serail*.[2] I shall write the Overture, the chorus in Act I and the final chorus in Turkish style. Mlle Cavalieri, Mlle

[1] 9 June, 1781.
[2] Mozart wrote '*Verführung*' (seduction) for '*Entführung*' (abduction). His biographers generally comment that he was no doubt thinking of his own Constanze (Weber)!

Teiber, M. Fischer, M. Adamberger, M. Dauer and M. Walter are to sing in it. I am so delighted to be composing this opera that I have already finished Cavalieri's aria, and Adamberger's, and the trio at the end of Act I. I am pressed for time, it is true, for it is to be performed by the middle of September, but the circumstances connected with the date of performance and, in general, all my other prospects stimulate me to such an extent that I rush to my desk with the greatest eagerness and stay there in absolute delight.[1]

It was the hope of Mozart and Stephanie that the opera would be staged in honour of the visit of the Grand Duke Paul of Russia (the future Tsar Paul I) and his consort, Maria Feodorovna. However, the Grand Duke's visit was postponed until November, and, when he did finally arrive, the operas performed for him were two by Gluck, *Iphigénie en Tauride* in the German translation by Alzinger, and a revival of *Alceste*. Mozart and Stephanie therefore gave themselves more time to work on *Die Entführung* which was not performed until July of the following year.

Meanwhile, life with the Webers was becoming complicated. Mozart had begun to court Constanze, the third of the four Weber girls, and there was already a certain amount of gossip in Vienna about this. Frau Weber and the guardian of her daughters, one Johann Thorwart, were concerned that he should either undertake eventually to marry or refrain from seeing Constanze, so Mozart found it expedient to move from the Weber household early in September to a room on the third floor of a house in the Graben. He assured his father that, although the voice of nature spoke as strongly in him as in other young men, yet he had never been to bed with a woman because 'in the first place I have too much religion, in the second place too great a love of my neighbour and too firm principles of honour to seduce an innocent girl, and in the third place too much horror and disgust, too much dread and fear of disease and too much care for my health to go about with whores'. He then went on to reveal that he had now come to the conclusion that 'a bachelor is only half alive', and that he had fallen in love.

> But who is the object of my love? Do not be horrified again, I implore you. Surely not one of the Weber girls? Yes, one of the Webers – but not Josefa, not Sophie. Constanze, the middle one. In no other family have I ever come across such differences of character. The eldest is lazy, fat and treacherous, and as cunning as a fox. Madame Lange is a false, malicious woman, and a flirt. The youngest is still too young to be anything in particular but a good-natured scatterbrain. May God protect her from seduction! But the middle one, my good, dear Constanze, is the martyr of the family and, perhaps for that very reason, the most kind-hearted, the cleverest, in short the best of them all. She looks after the entire household, and yet they blame her for doing nothing right . . . She is not ugly, though by no means beautiful. Her whole beauty consists in two little black eyes and an attractive figure. She is

[1] 1 August, 1781.

not witty, but she has enough common sense to enable her to fulfil her duties as a wife and mother.[1]

At the persuasion of Constanze's mother and her guardian, Mozart signed a document agreeing to marry Constanze within three years or to make financial compensation. When the document had been signed and her guardian had left the house, Constanze took the contract from her mother and tore it up, with the words 'Dear Mozart, I need no written assurance from you. I believe what you say.'[2]

On Christmas Eve, a pianoforte contest was held at the Hofburg, in the presence of the music-loving Emperor, Joseph II, between Mozart and the Italian pianist and composer Muzio Clementi. The Emperor composed a theme which the two composers were required to vary, accompanying each other alternately. For this, Mozart received a fee which was the equal of half his old annual salary from the Archbishop of Salzburg. In the spring he gave concerts in the Burgtheater and in private houses, and at the end of May took part in the first concert to be given in the refreshment pavilion in the Augarten. The *Wiener Zeitung*, a newspaper which still exists in Vienna, wrote favourably of the event. (The Augarten concerts were to become among Vienna's most popular musical entertainments: nowadays the pavilion houses the Austrian national porcelain factory.)

On three separate evenings during May, Mozart had played the three acts, now completed, of *Die Entführung aus dem Serail*, at the house of his friend and patroness Countess Thun. At the beginning of June, rehearsals for its production at the Burgtheater began at the theatre, and on 16 July, 1782, the opera was given its first performance. Mozart's report to his father on the première is lost, but of the second performance, three nights later, he wrote:

I hope that you received safely my last letter informing you of the favourable reception of my opera. It was given yesterday for the second time. You will hardly believe it, but yesterday the cabal against it was even stronger than on the first night. The whole of the first act was hissed. But still they could not prevent the loud shouts of 'bravo' during the arias. I was counting on the final trio [of Act I], but as ill-luck would have it, Fischer made a mistake, which made Dauer (Pedrillo) go wrong too, and Adamberger alone could not save the trio. The result was that its whole effect was lost and this time it was not encored. I was in such a rage, and so was Adamberger, that I said immediately that I would not let the opera be performed again without a short rehearsal for the singers. In the second act, both duets were encored as on the first night, and also Belmonte's rondo, 'Wenn der Freude Tränen fliessen'. The theatre was almost more crowded than on the first night, and by the day before there were no reserved seats left either in the stalls or in the

[1] 15 December, 1781.
[2] From Mozart's letter to his father of 22 December, 1781.

third circle. All the boxes were gone, too. The opera has brought in 1200 gulden in these two performances.[1]

Mozart's mention of the cabal reminds one that the habits of Viennese theatre audiences have changed hardly at all in the last two hundred years. The fact is that *Die Entführung* was a huge success. It was given several more performances during the season of 1782–83 in the Burgtheater, and a great many more in subsequent seasons at the Kärntnertor Theater. During Mozart's lifetime, it was also his greatest stage success outside Vienna. Within the following five years it was produced in Prague, Warsaw, Bonn, Frankfurt, Leipzig, Mannheim, Karlsruhe, Cologne, Salzburg, Dresden, Riga, Munich, Weimar, Aachen, Cassel, Pressburg (now Bratislava), Augsburg, Nuremberg, Mainz, Rostock, Altona, Hanover, Hamburg, Breslau, and Coblenz. During Mozart's lifetime there were also productions in Graz, Berlin, Lübeck, Amsterdam, and Budapest. After the third Viennese performance, Mozart told his father: 'People are absolutely crazy about this opera. It does one good to hear such applause.'[2] By the end of the month he had arranged a suite of music from the opera for wind instruments ('for if I don't someone will anticipate me and secure the profits'[3]). When Mozart lunched with Gluck, the elderly composer expressed his admiration of *Die Entführung*.

The Viennese critics praised not only the opera but also the singers, complimenting them in singing from their hearts and also for articulating clearly. Count Zinzendorf's was one of the very few dissenting voices. In his diary, he noted on 30 July: 'Tonight at the theatre *Die Entführung aus dem Serail*, an opera the music of which is pilfered from various others. Fischer acted well. Adamberger is a statue.'[4] Mozart was certainly fortunate in his cast, who were fine singers and in their prime. Karl Ludwig Fischer (Osmin), one of the finest basses of his day, was thirty-seven; Valentin Joseph Adamberger (Belmonte), a famous tenor and later a successful teacher, was thirty-nine; Caterina Cavalieri (Constanze), Viennese despite her Italian-sounding name, was a cultivated musician though only twenty-two.

The Russian royal couple for whose entertainment the opera was originally commissioned finally heard it three months after the première. 'I thought it advisable to resume my place at the clavier and conduct it,' Mozart told his father. 'I did so partly in order to rouse the orchestra who had gone to sleep, and partly, since I am in Vienna, in order to appear before the royal guests as the father of my child.'[5]

Even Goethe had words of praise, though reluctant ones, for *Die*

[1] 20 July, 1782.   [2] 27 July, 1782.
[3] Mozart to his father, 20 July, 1782.
[4] The diaries of Count Karl von Zinzendorf are preserved in the Vienna State Archives.
[5] 19 October, 1782.

Entführung. Describing his own attempt to write a *Singspiel* called *Scherz, List und Rache* with the composer Philipp Christoph Kayser, he confessed that 'all our endeavours to limit ourselves to economy and simplicity were lost the moment Mozart appeared on the scene. *Die Entführung aus dem Serail* put an end to all our hopes, and the piece we had worked on so hard was never heard of again in the theatre.'[1] But when *Die Entführung* was performed in Weimar in the autumn of 1785, Goethe attended three performances, after which his comment to his collaborator Kayser was distinctly cool:

> *Die Entführung aus dem Serail*, composed by Mozart, was given recently. Everyone declared himself in favour of the music. The first time they played it tolerably well, but the text is very bad and the music too did not appeal to me. The second time it was badly performed, and I even left the theatre. But the piece survived, and everyone praised the music. When they gave it for the fifth time, I went to it again. They acted and sang better than previously. I ignored the text, and I can now understand the difference between my judgment and the work's impact on the public. So I know where I stand.[2]

The Emperor's comment on the opera after its première was somewhat equivocal. 'Too beautiful for our ears, and an enormous number of notes, my dear Mozart,' he said. With quiet confidence, Mozart replied, 'Only as many as are needed, Your Majesty.'[3]

II

The libretto which Stephanie gave Mozart in July, 1781, was not his own original work, but an adaptation of a libretto by Christoph Friedrich Bretzner which had already been set to music by Johann André and performed at the Döbbelin Theater in Berlin in May of the same year. Bretzner was a Leipzig merchant who had written a number of libretti, but *Belmonte und Constanze, oder Die Entführung aus dem Serail* was not even his original conception. Several libretti dealing with escape from a Turkish harem had been written in the 1760s and 1770s; indeed, as we have seen, Mozart's *Zaide* in 1779 was a setting of one of them; the English composer Charles Dibdin's *The Seraglio* (1776) was another. *Die Entführung* is said by some Mozart commentators to derive from Isaac Bickerstaffe's play *The Captive*. But *The Captive*, though it shares a Turkish setting with *Die Entführung*, is dissimilar in plot. Bickerstaffe's *The Sultan, or A Peep into the Seraglio*, produced at Drury Lane in 1775, is closer to Bretzner in that it contains two characters who are clearly

[1] Goethe: *Italian Journey* (London, 1962, p. 418).

[2] From the Weimar Sophien Edition of Goethe's Works, section IV, Vol. 7, p. 143.

[3] This story, recounted by several writers on Mozart, first occurs in the *Leben des K. K. Kapellmeisters Wolfgang Gottlieb Mozart* (Prague, 1798) by Mozart's friend and admirer, Franz X. Niemetschek (1766–1849).

prototypes of Osmin and Blonde. They are 'Osmyn, Chief of the Eunuchs' and 'Roxalana, an English slave'.

Coincidences, if that is what they were, appear to have abounded at the time. Bretzner published a letter in the Berlin *Litteratur- und Theater-Zeitung* in 1780 in which he expressed his astonishment that another librettist, Gustav Friedrich Wilhelm Grossman, had been working on almost identical lines. Bretzner had written to his composer, André, drawing his attention to the fact that Grossman's libretto for Christian Gottlieb Neefe's *Adelheit von Veltheim* resembled his, since both were concerned with a harem, and both contained an elopement. Neefe's opera reached the stage first, at Frankfurt in September, 1780. Bretzner is said to have published the following protest, after Mozart and Stephanie's opera had been staged: 'A certain individual, Mozart by name, in Vienna has had the audacity to misuse my drama *Belmonte und Constanze* for an opera text. I herewith protest most solemnly against this infringement of my rights, and reserve the right to take the matter further.'[1] However, Bretzner must later have come to know more about the certain individual, Mozart, for in 1787 he published, anonymously, a novel *Das Leben eines Lüderchen*, in which *Le Nozze di Figaro* is frequently mentioned, and in 1794 he translated *Così fan tutte* for performance in Leipzig.

Presumably, Stephanie had adapted Bretzner's libretto without informing him. Nevertheless, the playbill for the first performance of *Die Entführung aus dem Serail* at the Burgtheater describes the work as 'A play with music, in three acts, freely adapted from Bretzner for the Imperial and Royal National Theatre, and set to music by Herr Mozart, Kapellmeister'. Stephanie's name is not mentioned.

Another possible source, for Bickerstaffe, as well as for Bretzner and Grossman, is *Soliman second, ou les Trois Sultanes*, a *pasticcio* with words by Favart, also known as *Roxelane*, which was produced in Paris in 1761. Favart's libretto was based on an earlier one by the librettist and dramatist, Jean François Marmontel.[2]

While he was at work on the opera in the autumn of 1781, Mozart kept his father informed of its progress. His letter of 26 September is especially fascinating for the light it throws on the nature of his collaboration with Stephanie and indeed his method of operatic composition in general:

As the original text began with a monologue, I asked Herr Stephanie to make

---

[1] Quoted in Deutsch, p. 211. However, this protest did not appear in the *Leipzigen Zeitungen* in 1782, when it was supposed to have appeared, and there is a possibility that, in this form, it is spurious. It was first quoted in C. von Wurzbach's *Biographisches Lexicon des Kaisertums Österreich*, published in Vienna in 1868. But see pp. 182–184.

[2] A note in the second edition of Bickerstaffe's *The Sultan* says it 'is taken from Marmontel'.

a little arietta out of it, and then to put in a duet instead of making the two men chatter together after Osmin's short song. As we have given the role of Osmin to Herr Fischer, who certainly has an excellent bass voice (though the Archbishop told me he sang too low for a bass, so I assured him he would sing higher in future!), we ought to take advantage of it, especially as he has the entire Viennese public on his side. But in the original libretto Osmin has only this short song and nothing else to sing, except in the trio and the finale; so we have given him an aria in Act I, and he will have another in Act II. I have explained to Stephanie the kind of words I need for this aria: indeed I had finished composing most of the music for it before Stephanie knew anything about it. I enclose only the beginning and the end, which is bound to be effective. Osmin's rage is made comical by the accompaniment of the Turkish music. In working out the aria I have given full scope to Fischer's beautiful low notes (in spite of our Salzburg Midas). The passage 'Drum beim Barte des Propheten' is indeed in the same tempo, but with quick notes. But as Osmin's rage gradually increases, just when the aria seems to have finished, there is an *allegro assai*, in a totally different tempo and in a different key. This is bound to be very effective, for, just as a man in a towering rage oversteps all the bounds of order, moderation and propriety, and completely forgets himself, so too must the music forget itself. But as passions, whether violent or not, must never be expressed in such a way as to excite disgust, and as music, even in the most terrible situations, must never offend the ear, but must please the hearer, or in other words must never cease to be music, I have gone from F (the key in which the aria is written) not into a remote key but into a related one: not its nearest relative, D minor, however, but into the more remote A minor.

Let me now turn to Belmonte's aria in A major, 'O wie ängstlich, o wie feurig'. Would you like to know how I have expressed it, and even indicated the throbbing of his heart-beats? By the two violins playing octaves. This is the favourite aria of all who have heard it, and it is mine too. I wrote it specially to suit Adamberger's voice. You feel the trembling – the faltering – you see how his throbbing breast begins to swell: this I have expressed by a crescendo. You hear the whispering and the sighing, which I have indicated by the first violins with mutes and a flute playing in unison.

The Janissary chorus is, as such, all that can be desired: in other words, short and lively and written to please the Viennese. I have sacrificed Constanze's aria a little to the flexible throat of Mlle Cavalieri: 'Trennung war mein banges Los, und nun schwimmt mein Aug' in Tränen.' I have tried to express her feelings, as far as an Italian bravura aria will allow it. I have changed the 'Hui' to 'schnell', so that it now runs thus: 'Doch wie schnell schwand meine Freude.' I really don't know what our German-language poets are thinking of. Even if they do not understand the theatre, they ought not to make their characters talk as if they were addressing a herd of swine. 'Hui, sow!'

Now for the trio at the end of Act I. Pedrillo has passed his master off as an architect, to give him an opportunity to meet his Constanze in the garden. Pasha Selim has taken him into his service, but Osmin, the steward, knows nothing of this, and, being an ill-mannered boor and a sworn foe to all strangers, is impertinent and refuses to let them into the garden. It begins quite abruptly, and, since the words lend themselves to it, I have made it quite a respectable piece of real three-part writing. Then suddenly the major key begins pianissimo – it has to be very quick – and it winds up with a great deal of noise, which is always appropriate at the end of an act. The more noise the better, and the shorter the better, so that the audience doesn't have time to cool down, and their applause is lively.

I have sent you only fourteen bars of the Overture, which is very short with alternate fortes and pianos, the Turkish music always coming in at the fortes. The Overture modulates through several keys, and I doubt whether anyone, even if his previous night had been restless, could possibly fall asleep over it. But here's the rub: I finished the first Act more than three weeks ago, as well as one aria in Act II and the drunken duet (especially for the Viennese gentry) which consists entirely of my Turkish tattoo. But I cannot compose any more, because the whole plot is being altered – to tell the truth, this is at my own request. At the beginning of Act III there is a charming quintet, really a finale ensemble, which I should prefer to have at the end of Act II. In order to make this practicable, great changes must be made: in fact an entirely new plot must be introduced. But Stephanie is up to the eyes in other work, so we must be patient. Everyone abuses Stephanie. It may be that, with me, he is friendly only to my face, but, after all, he is arranging the libretto for me, and, what is more, doing so exactly the way I want it, so I can't, in all honesty, ask more of him than that.[1]

The alterations involved enlarging the role of Osmin, and also altering the plot so that Belmonte is revealed not as the Pasha's son, but as the son of his old enemy, thus rendering the Pasha's clemency all the more remarkable. Less than three weeks later, Mozart was able to give his father further news of the progress of *Die Entführung*:

Now as to the libretto of the opera, you are quite right as far as Stephanie's work is concerned. Still, the poetry is perfectly in keeping with the character of the stupid, surly, malicious Osmin. I am well aware that the verse is not exactly first-rate, but it fitted in and agreed so well with the musical ideas which were already buzzing about in my head that it could hardly fail to please me. I'd like to bet that, when it is performed no one will find any fault with the verse. As for the verse in the original libretto, I have really nothing against it. Belmonte's aria, 'O wie ängstlich', could hardly be better written for setting to music. Except for that 'Hui' and 'Kummer ruht in meinem Schoss' [Sorrow rests in my bosom] – for sorrow cannot be said to rest – the aria is not too bad, particularly the first part. Besides, in my view, in an opera the poetry must be completely the obedient daughter of the music. Why do Italian comic operas please people everywhere, despite their miserable libretti, even in Paris where I myself witnessed their success? Precisely because in them the music reigns supreme, and when one listens to it one forgets everything else. An opera is certain of success if the plot is well worked out, the words written to suit the music and not shoved in here and there for the sake of some miserable rhyme – which, God knows, never enhances the

---

[1] Mozart to his father. Vienna, 26 September, 1781.

value of any theatrical performance, whatever it is, but rather detracts from it. I am talking about words, or even entire verses, which ruin the composer's whole idea. Verses are certainly the most indispensable element for music, but rhymes solely for the sake of rhyming are the most detrimental. Those high and mighty people who set to work in such a pedantic fashion will always come to grief, both they and their music. The best thing of all is when a good composer, who understands the theatre and is talented enough to make useful suggestions, meets that true phoenix, an able poet. When that happens, no fears need be entertained as to the applause even of the ignorant. Poets rather remind me of trumpeters with their professional tricks! If we composers were always to stick so faithfully to our rules, simply because they were very sound at that time and no one knew any better, we should be concocting music as unpalatable as their libretti.[1]

On the Burgtheater poster, *Die Entführung aus dem Serail* was announced as a 'new *Singspiel*' or play with songs. The enlightened liberal Emperor Joseph II had lately been attempting to encourage the production of German-language operas, but with no great success, for Viennese audiences continued to show that they much preferred the musically sophisticated Italian opera to the usually crudely conducted German plays whose dialogue was interspersed with simple little songs. Adamberger, Mozart's first Belmonte, called the North German style of singing 'Lutheran'. Mozart had already made two contributions to the *Singspiel* genre, the one-act *Bastien und Bastienne* when he was a child of twelve, and the abortive *Zaide* a mere two years before *Die Entführung*. *Zaide*, its plot so similar to that of *Die Entführung*, was in one sense a first draft of the latter work, for in it Mozart found the style and the approach he was to adopt in *Die Entführung*, for which, however, he composed completely new music. The *Singspiel*, until this time, had remained essentially North German in style, which did not commend it to the Viennese. The nobility much preferred Italian opera, while the lower Viennese social orders were devoted to their peculiar local type of popular play with songs interspersed. Joseph II's new National Theatre, brought into being to alter this state of affairs, had opened in 1778 with a work called *Bergknappen* by Umlauf, but it was only with the production of *Die Entführung* that the *Singspiel* found itself raised to the status of opera. Nine years later, *Die Zauberflöte* was to prove the genre capable of producing great opera.

A fascinating notice of the Vienna production of *Die Entführung* was published in Johann Friedrich Schink's *Dramaturgische Fragmente*,[2] as the prelude to more general remarks on operas and their libretti:

. . . [Bretzner's] *Entführung aus dem Serail* happens to be the most inept of his lyric pieces, and greatly inferior to Grossman's opera on a similar subject [*Adelheit von Veltheim*], although Grossman's too is not worth a quarter of the

---

[1] 13 October, 1781. [2] Published in Graz, 1782.

fanfares with which its author has, with much exemplary modesty, been announcing it. Bretzner has, in my opinion, unnecessarily stretched his plot to last for three acts. In addition, his characters are deficient in both charm and vitality. . . . The improvements which have now been made are also rather unsatisfactory. What I like least is the alteration of Bretzner's dénouement. In Bretzner, the Pasha forgives Belmonte because he recognizes him to be his own son. In the Viennese improvement he does so because he considers it a far greater act to forgive an enemy than to revenge oneself upon him : a motive which is indeed more noble, but also, as is invariably the case with such exalted motives, much more unlikely. The worst of it is that, with this improvement, Bretzner's reason for making the Pasha a renegade is entirely removed, and the alteration is thus rendered all the more absurd.

These eternal magnanimities are an abomination, and no longer the fashion anywhere except on our stages. Yet one may count almost with certainty on a raging success for a piece in which there is enough of this magnanimous reconciliation and forgiveness, however unlikely the means by which they are arrived at. This taste is of benefit to the author's pocket, but less so to art and not at all to the education of the people. The theatre has clearly the greatest influence on such education. Tastes wrongly formed in this manner are thereby vitiated, so that the work of the finest authors goes for nothing. The drama is a greater living influence than any book, and those who come to literature with a taste already corrupted will receive no impression from even the most tasteful of books. This is quite understandable: how is one to recognize truth and nature if one has no feeling for truth and nature?

. . . Die Entführung aus dem Serail has been received with great applause in Vienna. But it owes this applause to the excellent music of Herr Mozart and to the excellent performance of the singers of the National Theatre. I am no real connoisseur of music. I have no understanding of the aesthetic rules of composition, nor can I read music. I judge it merely by the general principles of all the fine arts, by the principles of truth and nature. Music which affects the human heart, and the human passions, which stirs up joy, sorrow, and in short every kind of sentiment, which is something more than mere ear-tickling, but real nourishment for the soul: this is the kind of music I pronounce excellent, and the real product of musical genius. Judged by these principles, Herr Mozart's music has my entire approval, and I admit with pleasure that only Benda and Gluck are capable of touching and moving my heart more strongly than Herr Mozart has done with his beautiful music.

Bretzner's protest against the unauthorized use of, and improvement o, his text by Stephanie has been mentioned earlier. Whether he did, in act, protest in 1782 in the words quoted is uncertain. He did, however, nsert a notice the following year, in the 21 June, 1783, issue of the Berlin Litteratur- und Theater-Zeitung:

An anonymous person in Vienna has been pleased to adapt my opera Belmont und Constanze for the Imperial and Royal National Theatre, and to have the piece printed in this altered shape. I ignore the changes in dialogue, as they are inconsiderable; however, the adapter has, at the same time, interpolated a vast number of songs the words of which are in many cases most edifying and touching. I should not like to deprive the improver of the glory deserved by his work, and I therefore take this opportunity of specifying these songs interpolated by him as belonging to the Viennese edition and Mozart's composition.

The following are the interpolations:
Belmont's first aria: Hier soll ich dich denn sehen, etc.
The duet for Belmont and Osmin: Verwünscht seist du, etc.
Osmin's aria: Solche hergelaufene Laffen, etc.
Osmin's duet: Ich gehe, doch rate ich dir, etc.
Osmin's recitative, up to the beginning of his aria
Constanze's aria: Martern aller Arten, etc.
Blonde's aria: Welche Wonne, welche Lust, etc.
Belmont's aria: Wenn der Freude, etc.
The quartet and finale
Belmont's aria: Ich baue ganz, etc.
Osmin's aria: O wie will ich triumphieren
The recitative and duet: Welch Geschick, etc.
The whole finale

I end with a sample of the improver's work, from the quartet:

PEDRILLO: But Blonde, alas, the ladder –
              Will you be worth as much? (*Reveals that he will risk being hanged*)
BLONDE: Jack Pudding! Are you mad?
              Indeed, you would have done better
              To turn the question round.
PEDRILLO: But Sir Osmin –
BLONDE: Let's hear it.
CONSTANZE: Will you not then explain it?

BELMONT: (*simultaneously*)	PEDRILLO:
I shall, but do not grieve.	Did not Osmin perchance
A rumour some believe;	(It's easy to believe)
Trembling, I ask is it true	Exert a master's will
The Pasha's loved by you?	And make you do his drill?
His favours you receive?	Such a bargain I'd not make.
CONSTANZE (*weeping*):	BLONDE (*boxing his ears*):
Oh, how you make me grieve.	To that, my answer take.

PEDRILLO: Now I know how we stand.
BELMONT: Constanze, O forgive.
BLONDE: You are not worth my hand
CONSTANZE: I live for you alone
BLONDE: The rascal dares to ask
              If I've been true to him
CONSTANZE: Belmonte thought that I / Had responded to the Pasha's
              advances.

PEDRILLO: My Blonde's honesty / I'll swear to, without doubt.
BELMONT: Constanze's true to me / Of that there is no doubt. Etc.

That is what I call improvement!

C. F. Bretzner,
Leipzig, 27 April, 1783.

III

The action of *Die Entführung aus dem Serail* takes place in and around the palace of the Pasha Selim, in Turkey, somewhere by the sea. The time is mid-sixteenth century. Act I is set in a forecourt outside the palace. Belmonte, a young Spanish nobleman, has come in search of his betrothed, Constanze, who, together with her maid Blonde, and Belmonte's servant Pedrillo, had been captured by pirates and sold into slavery. Pedrillo had somehow managed to get a message to Belmonte, informing him of their whereabouts. As he is wondering how to effect an entrance into the palace, Belmonte hears someone approaching. It is the Pasha's steward or overseer, Osmin, who has come outdoors to pick figs. Belmonte asks Osmin if this is, in fact, the Pasha Selim's palace, but Osmin's replies are surly, and when Belmonte asks for Pedrillo, Osmin flies into a rage and chases him off.

Pedrillo now appears, exciting a fresh outburst of fury from Osmin who is clearly jealous of Blonde's affection for him. Pedrillo, he says, is a worthless rogue interested in nothing but chasing women. He deserves to be 'first beheaded, then hanged, then impaled on red-hot spikes'. Finally, Osmin disappears into the palace, and Belmonte reappears. He and Pedrillo greet each other warmly, and Belmonte learns that all three captives were bought by the Pasha Selim who has treated them with consideration. The Pasha is enamoured of Constanze, but will not force his attentions upon her. Pedrillo assures Belmonte that his Constanze is still faithful. He is not so sure of Blonde, for the Pasha gave her to the hateful Osmin who guards her jealously. Belmonte explains that he has a ship waiting just outside the harbour, ready to take them all aboard at a moment's notice. But first he must speak with Constanze. Pedrillo informs him that the Pasha will very shortly be returning from a journey, and that Constanze will be with him. Since the Pasha is especially interested in architecture, Pedrillo will introduce Belmonte as a talented architect from Italy, and thus gain him entrance to the palace. Belmonte and Pedrillo withdraw as the Pasha and his entourage are heard to approach.

Preceded by a chorus of Janissaries singing his praises, the Pasha arrives with Constanze. When their attendants have departed, the Pasha pleads, obviously not for the first time, for his captive's love. He reminds her that he could use force, but he wants her to give her heart freely. Constanze tells him she has pledged her love to Belmonte from whom she has been cruelly separated. The Pasha gives her one more day to consider her answer, and Constanze sadly enters the palace. Pedrillo now approaches the Pasha and presents Belmonte who offers to place his talents as an architect at the Pasha's disposal. Selim receives him graciously, agrees to test his ability the following day, and asks Pedrillo meanwhile to attend to Belmonte's needs. Belmonte and Pedrillo are about to follow Selim indoors when their way is blocked by Osmin who, suspicious of Belmonte, refuses to accept that he is a guest of the Pasha, and attempts to chase him away again. At last, Belmonte and Pedrillo succeed in pushing their way past him into the palace.

Act II is set in the palace garden, to one side of which stands a small kiosk. Osmin and Blonde emerge from the kiosk in the middle of a quarrel. She makes it clear to him that, though bullying may be the Turkish way to a woman's heart, she is an Englishwoman and therefore used to her freedom. She requires to be coaxed. Osmin observes that Englishmen must be mad to allow such a state of affairs, but he beats a hasty retreat when Blonde threatens to scratch his eyes out.

Constanze now appears, still lamenting her separation from Belmonte, and is soon followed by Selim who demands to know her final answer. When she remains steadfast in her refusal, he reminds her that he could order her to be tortured. She scornfully defies his threats, and returns indoors. After the Pasha has left the garden, Pedrillo and Blonde meet, and Pedrillo tells her of Belmonte's arrival. He explains that, later in the evening, he and Belmonte will help the two women to escape to the waiting ship, after Osmin has been put out of action with drugged wine. Blonde rushes off to give Constanze the joyful news. Osmin enters the garden, and Pedrillo persuades him to break the laws of Mahomet and enjoy a delicious wine. Osmin is soon tempted, and in due course falls drunkenly asleep.

Belmonte now enters, and is joined by Constanze and the others. After their first happy moments of reunion, Belmonte utters his fear that Constanze may have responded to the advances of the Pasha, and Pedrillo takes the opportunity to voice similar doubts about Blonde and Osmin. The ladies are hurt and insulted by the jealous suspicion of their lovers, and the men are made to apologize. When peace has been restored, and tribute has been paid to the virtues of true love, the four lovers part to await midnight and their escape.

Act III begins outside the palace. To one side are the palace walls and the windows of Constanze's rooms. Opposite is Osmin's apartment, while in the background there is a view of the sea. It is midnight. Pedrillo enters with Klaas, a sailor from Belmonte's ship, who carries two ladders which he places against the appropriate windows. Klaas then returns to the ship to prepare for an immediate sailing, Belmonte arrives, and Pedrillo sings his serenade first under Constanze's and then under Blonde's window, the agreed signal for the two women to appear.

Constanze and Blonde duly climb down their ladders. At this moment, a still sleepy Osmin is dragged out by a black mute servant who, in a dumb show, indicates the escaping foursome. Osmin rouses the palace guard and all four are captured. Osmin is exultant at the thought of the dreadful tortures to which they will be subjected.

The final scene takes place in a hall in the palace. The captives are brought before Selim who is furious at what he regards as Constanze's duplicity. Belmonte reveals that he is not a student of architecture but a wealthy Spanish nobleman, and asks the Pasha to set a ransom which, however high it is, will be paid by his father. Unfortunately, however, mention of his father's name only increases the Pasha's fury, for it appears that Belmonte's father, when he was Governor of Oran, had been responsible for driving Selim (who was, originally, himself a Spanish nobleman) into exile, robbing him of his beloved and of all his possessions. Belmonte is forced by the Pasha to admit that, in this situation, his father would exact full vengeance upon the son of an old enemy. Selim and Osmin withdraw, to consider what punishment would be suitable for the son of Selim's old enemy. Left alone, the lovers bewail their certain fate, but Constanze and Belmonte find some consolation in the thought that they will die together. Pasha Selim returns, and announces that he despises Belmonte's father too greatly to emulate his behaviour. He sets all four captives free. When Osmin protests at the loss of Blonde, Selim remarks that, if one cannot win a woman by kindness, it is better to give her up. All, except the still grumbling Osmin, unite in singing the praises of the merciful Pasha.

IV

The Overture, *presto-andante-presto*, contrasts a brisk C major *presto*, whose fortes introduce Mozart's 'Turkish music', with a tender *andante* in C minor. The *presto*, when it returns, does not come to a full close but flows into Belmonte's opening number, which is the *andante* of the Overture again, this time in C major. The 'Turkish' colouring in the Overture is achieved by exotic orchestration, with piccolo, triangle, cymbals, kettle- and bass-drums very much in evidence in the forte passages. One's attention is caught by the sheer high spirits and exhilaration of the music, though it seems to promise a jollier, less complex work than it, in fact, prefaces. In Belmonte's aria, 'Hier soll ich dich denn sehen' (No. 1), we hear the charming tune first heard in the Overture, now sounding less plaintive in A major. Indeed, it throbs with a fervent expectation as Belmonte prepares to see his beloved Constanze once again. Belmonte may not be the most individual of Mozart's tenor heroes (they are not particularly memorable as characters, with the arguable exceptions of Tamino in *Die Zauberflöte* and Ferrando in *Così fan tutte*) but he announces himself as an ardent lover with his very first aria, and in the single-mindedness of his devotion to Constanze he achieves an almost heroic status; heroic of voice, also, for his music postulates a more ringing sound than is produced by the average lyric tenor who is cast in the role.

Osmin introduces himself with a strophic song, 'Wer ein Liebchen hat gefunden' (No. 2), which Belmonte attempts unsuccessfully to interrupt with a spoken question after each stanza, after which he and Osmin finally converse in a *buffo* duet. Virtually every number in *Die Entführung*, unlike those of the old *opera seria*, advances the dramatic action, and this song with duet does so quite skilfully. By his choice of key, G minor, and the way in which he varies the accompaniment from stanza to stanza, Mozart characterizes Osmin much more clearly than the words of his solo song contrived to do. Osmin, incidentally, is often, even usually, portrayed as having a figure, if not the sexual incapacity, of a eunuch. Clearly, he is no eunuch. He is not the Pasha's harem-keeper, who would doubtless have been a eunuch; he is the Pasha's steward and overseer, to whom one of the Christian slaves, Blonde, has been given. Osmin himself makes it perfectly clear that he is a man of sexual passions. The duet with Belmonte which follows Osmin's strangely melancholy little song is simple but effective, conveying Belmonte's desperate determination and Osmin's cruel and bullying intransigence, while at the same time remaining an enjoyable comic duet.

Osmin's aria, 'Solche hergelauf'ne Laffen' (No. 3) is the one which, as he informed his father, Mozart had virtually finished composing before the words had been written. An explosive *allegro con brio*, its opening bars, hammering away on and around one note, characterize Osmin's malignant and dogged stupidity [Ex. 23]. Mozart's own description of

Ex. 23

Sol - che her-ge- lauf-ne Laf - - - - fen,

the aria is accurate: Fischer's beautiful low notes are certainly exploited, and the character's rage is made more comical by the Turkish element in the accompaniment. 'Ich hab' auch Verstand' (I've got brains, too) boasts Osmin, and when he repeats the phrase it lies an octave lower, for emphasis. This, one might think, is the end of the aria; but no, there is a coda, 'Drum beim Barte des Propheten' (By the beard of the Prophet) which, as Mozart says, 'is indeed in the same tempo, but with quick notes'. The note-values are shorter, which makes the music quicker, though the basic tempo remains. The effect is of a quickening of Osmin's rage. Then, again as described by Mozart,[1] there comes a second coda – though separated from the first by two short lines of dialogue. This time, both key and tempo change, as Osmin works

[1] In his letter of 26 September, 1781.

himself into a paroxysm of frustrated rage with 'Erst geköpft, dann gehangen' (First beheaded, then hanged). Mozart was aware that 'passions, whether violent or not, must never be expressed in such a way as to excite disgust . . . in other words, music must never cease to be music', so, as he pointed out, he moves from the F major of the aria proper, 'not into a remote key, but into a related one: not its nearest relative D minor, however, but into a more remote A minor'. But his A minor explosion, with the Turkish colouring of cymbals and drums at full blast, must have sounded decidedly wild to his audiences, especially the final bars in which the music skids to a halt which is positively Beethovenian. Osmin is revealed in this aria as more than, and different from, a comically harmless, if bad-tempered old eunuch. His rages are comic, but they are dangerous too, for he certainly means it when he threatens Pedrillo that he will be 'Erst geköpft, dann gehangen, dann gespiesst auf heisse Stangen' (First beheaded, then hanged, then impaled on red-hot spikes). And, in this second coda, Mozart's music takes Osmin's words seriously. Throughout the opera, too, Mozart uses his orchestra to comment on the situation and on the characters' motivations. Osmin's 'Ich hab' auch Verstand' is mocked by a cheeky little oboe figure [Ex. 24], and the Turkish clamour is often used ironically.

Ex. 24

Belmonte's A major aria 'O wie ängstlich, o wie feurig' (No. 4), preceded by its ineffably tender four bars of recitative (Ex. 25], was its

Ex. 25

Con-stan - ze!   Con-stan - ze!   dich wie - der - zu - se - hen,   dich!

composer's favourite aria in the entire opera. Again, his own description of it to his father is accurate: 'You feel the trembling – the faltering – you see how his throbbing breast begins to swell. . . . You hear the whispering and the sighing, which I have indicated by the first violins with mutes and a flute playing in unison', though the mutes appear not to have survived into the printed score. (The present whereabouts of the autograph score of Act I, formerly in the Staatsbibliothek, Berlin, are unknown.) Not only is the aria a beautiful piece of tone-painting, it is also melodically and harmonically an expression of deeply felt emotion, pervaded throughout by the lover's ardent feeling for his beloved. Mozart's expressive means are many and varied. He makes imaginative use of his woodwind instruments to support Belmonte's expression of sentiment; he also produces a crescendo of feeling with the repetitions of the phrase 'Es hebt sich die schwellende Brust' (My bosom swells to bursting), rising up the scale by augmented seconds [Ex. 26]. Even the six

Ex. 26

es hebt sich die schwel-len-de Brust, es hebt sich die schwel-len-de Brust, es hebt sich die schwel - len-de Brust.

bars of orchestral postlude exude their own tender charm as their sighing diminishes from forte to pianissimo.

The Janissaries' Chorus, 'Singt dem grossen Bassa Lieder' (No. 5) is, as Mozart described it, 'all that can be desired, in other words short and lively, and written to please the Viennese'. No one has asked exactly what he meant by this. Was he referrring to the superficiality of Viennese, as opposed to serious German taste, or did he think the Viennese were all Turks? The answer, though not obvious, is quite simple. Almost exactly one hundred years earlier, in 1683, the Turks had advanced to the very walls of Vienna, thus threatening not only the city of Vienna but the whole of Western civilization. The battles fought then were still vividly alive in the folk memory – memorials to them are to be found all over Vienna to this day – and at the time of *Die Entführung* in 1782 there was a real fear that the Turks might return to the attack. Russia and Turkey were at war, the Austrian Emperor had formed an alliance with Catherine the Great, and the Grand Duke Paul of Russia was expected to visit Vienna. (Initially, as we have seen, it was for his visit that *Die Entführung* was commissioned.) But it was not Mozart's intention to give his Viennese audiences a slight *frisson* with his Turkish military music. The Janissaries, in any case, were not Turks but Christians captured in the Balkans and elsewhere, converted by force to Islam, and made to form part of the standing army, especially the Sultan's guard. 'Janissary music', therefore, was Turkish military music, with the emphasis on 'military'. It had become the fashion in Vienna for the royal household to keep a military band which played Janissary music. Maria Theresa did so, and her son the Emperor Joseph kept up the custom. Mozart's Viennese were used to hearing and enjoying Janissary music in the parks and the Prater: this was why he knew it would appeal to them in a manner in which it would be less likely to appeal in Salzburg, Innsbruck, Linz, or Prague. The Turks had left behind them in Vienna a taste for Turkish music as well as for

Turkish coffee. Not that Mozart's Turkish music is necessarily Turkish: a nineteenth-century Russian biographer of Mozart, Alexander Ulibicheff,[1] noticed in the Janissaries' Chorus many points of resemblance to Russian national melodies, among them the alternation of relative major and minor keys. Mozart could easily have come to know Russian songs and melodies at the palace of Prince Galitzin, the Russian Ambassador in Vienna. Whether it is Russian, Turkish, or simply Mozart's idea of Turkish, the tune the chorus sings is odd by the standards of Viennese classicism. An opening seven-bar phrase is followed by one of four bars; in the next passage, a seven-bar phrase is answered by one of nine. This begins and ends the chorus. A contrasting central section is sung by a solo quartet.

It is to the strains of the music singing his praises that Pasha Selim makes his first entrance. His is a non-singing role, which is unusual in opera, though not entirely without precedence. Mozart's letter to his father on 1 August, 1781, two days after he had received the libretto to compose, mentions four male singers whom he expected would sing in the opera: Fischer, Adamberger, Dauer and Walter. The first three sang the roles of Osmin, Belmonte and Pedrillo respectively at the première, but the Pasha was portrayed by an actor, Dominik Jautz. It would seem that Herr Walter was intended to sing the Pasha Selim, but that plans fell through because for some reason or other he became unobtainable and Mozart considered no other available singer suitable. This is pure conjecture, but what is reasonably certain is that it was not Mozart's intention from the very beginning that the Pasha should be only a speaking part. Presumably, had the role been sung, it would have been developed and given a greater importance in the working-out of the drama.

We have learned from Mozart's letter that he to some extent sacrificed Constanze's aria, 'Ach, ich liebte' (No. 6) 'to the flexible throat of Mlle Cavalieri'. (Mozart's delightful phrase for 'flexible throat' is 'geläufige Gurgel'.) But the aria, admittedly an *allegro* bravura piece after its nine bars of *adagio* introduction, sensitively delineates the character's situation. The coloratura sounds desperate rather than high-spirited, just as Violetta's 'Sempre libera' in *La traviata* does, at a moment of equal emotional stress. Constanze's mood at the beginning of the aria is regretful and nostalgic, though later, as she unfolds her feelings to the Pasha, the music expresses an angry frustration. Mozart makes much use of solo instruments in the orchestra. This aria is a superb piece of musical characterization: it does, however, call for a singer with a very flexible throat and an immense vocal range. A later aria, 'Martern aller Arten', will make demands on the soprano's range at both ends of her

[1] In his *Nouvelle Biographie de Mozart, suivie d'un aperçu sur l'histoire générale de la musique, et de l'analyse des principales œuvres de Mozart* (Moscow, 1843).

voice. 'Ach, ich liebte' asks her to sing, with agility, passages containing high Cs and Ds [Ex. 27]. Act I ends with the exhilarating trio in which

Ex. 27

Osmin tries in vain to prevent Belmonte and Pedrillo from entering the palace. Mozart's description of the trio in his letter quoted in full earlier in this chapter can hardly be bettered. The trio certainly makes a lively, applause-inducing finale to the act.

Since *Die Entführung* is a *Singspiel*, or play with songs, there is not a great deal of recitative (and, of course, what there is is accompanied recitative), the action being advanced by the dialogue which separates the musical numbers. Producers of the opera today tend to cut the dialogue to the minimum necessary to convey the plot: this seems to me to be misguided, for it spoils the balance and shape of the work. The same problem is encountered, of course, with *Die Zauberflöte*. Whoever has been fortunate enough to encounter a production of *Die Zauberflöte*, Mozart's great apotheosis of the *Singspiel*, with its dialogue performed in full, will know what a great difference is made not only to the formal relationships within the work but also, somehow, to the fundamental nature of the opera. *Die Entführung* is a lesser work than *Die Zauberflöte*, but it, too, deserves to be treated with respect. Especially in Act II, where there is a certain amount of plot to be expounded, the dialogue should be retained intact.

'Durch Zärtlichkeit und Smeicheln' (No. 8), the charming and rather stately little song in which Blonde tells Osmin how women are treated in the western world, contains three flourishes written smoothly into the vocal line, the first of which takes the soprano up to B, the second to her high C sharp, and the third to the E above. The first Blonde, Therese Teiber, whose father was a violinist in the orchestra, was obviously proud of her high range. Mozart accompanies her song with strings only, their warmth emphasized by the violas which sometimes double the tune an octave below the first violins. Blonde, the composer seems to be telling us, is a warm-hearted, though quite strong-willed young lady. The music he has written for her throughout the opera characterizes her as the first of that long line of Viennese soubrettes – his own Zerlina, Susanna, Despina, Papagena, Weber's Ännchen, through to the *seconde donne* of Viennese operetta – who somehow contrive to combine charm

with managerial instinct. Blonde's character is more fully revealed, and
the action advanced a stage further, in her duet with Osmin, 'Ich gehe,
doch rate ich dir' (No. 9). In the preceding dialogue, she has boasted
'Ich bin eine Engländerin, zur Freiheit geboren, und trotze jedem, der
mich zu etwas zwingen will!' (I am an Englishwoman, born in freedom,
and I defy anyone who attempts to coerce me), though I have heard
performances, in Germany, in which Blonde's nationality has been
suppressed! In the duet, she shows herself to be more than a match for
Osmin. His stupidity and her supremacy are conveyed musically: he
hammers away with his simple sequences and triads, and then tries to
impress her with his bass voice, going down to his low E flat and then up
to his high F at the phrase 'bis du zu gehorchen mir schwörst' (until you
swear to obey me), only to be mocked by Blonde who imitates his low
notes in a soprano growl of her own, down to her A flat below middle C
[Ex. 28], to the words 'und wenn du der Grossmogul wärst' (even if you

Ex. 28

were the Grand Mogul). In the central *andante* of the duet, Osmin
exclaims 'O, Engländer, seid ihr nicht Toren' (O Englishmen, what
fools you are), again in his somewhat lumpish triads, while Blonde's
carefree roulades soar above him in easy contrast to his dim-wittedness.
The battle of the sexes is fought and won during this duet. In the
opening *allegro*, Osmin sets the pace. He loses ground in the *andante*, and
is routed in the final *allegro* by Blonde who threatens him physically, and
who also asserts her musical superiority, forcing him to imitate her
melody.

There are no sacrifices made to Mlle Cavalieri's flexible throat in
Constanze's second aria, 'Traurigkeit ward mir zum Loose' (No. 10),
though there certainly are in the aria which follows it, which could
perhaps be described as the most elaborate cabaletta ever composed
(No. 11: 'Martern aller Arten'). 'Traurigkeit' is preceded by a poignant
adagio recitative passage, beginning 'Welcher Kummer herrscht in
meiner Seele', accompanied only by strings. A chromatic falling phrase
[Ex. 29] expressive of Constanze's deep sorrow persists throughout the

Ex. 29

A page of the manuscript of *Die Entführung aus dem Serail*: part of the final *allegro* of Osmin's aria, 'Solche hergelauf' ne Laffen'.

Title-page from an early piano score of *Die Entführung aus dem Serail*.

Costume designs by Franz Gaul for a production of *Der Schauspieldirektor* in Vienna, 1880.

above: Title-page from an early piano score of *Le nozze di Figaro.*
below: Silhouettes of Ann Storace and Francesco Benucci,
the first Susanna and Figaro.

Costume designs by Alfred Roller for Gustav Mahler's production of
Le nozze di Figaro in Vienna, 1902.

Engravings of scenes from *Le nozze di Figaro* by J. H. Ramberg, 1827.

Costume designs by Heinrich Lefler for Gustav Mahler's production of *Così fan tutte* in Vienna, 1900.

Così fan tutte

o sia

la fcuola degli amanti,

per il Cembalo

dal

Sign. Volfgango Amadeo Mozart.

Raccolta I.

Weibertreue

oder

die Mädchen ſind von Flandern,

ein komiſches Singſpiel in zwey Acten

vom

Herrn Wolfgang Amadeus Mozart.

Im Klavierauszuge

von

Siegfried Schmiedt.

Erſtes Heft.

Leipzig, in der Breitkopfiſchen Muſikhandlung.

M.58b.

Title-page from an early piano score of *Così fan tutte*.

Title-page from an early piano score of *La clemenza di Tito*.

La Clemenza di Tito

Opera feria

Del Sign. W. A. Mozart

Aggiustata per il Piano Forte

Del Sign. A. E. Müller

M.57a

In Hamburgo presso Günther e Böhme

Costume designs by Franz Gaul for a production of *La clemenza di Tito*
in Vienna, 1888.

recitative, which leads into an aria of elegiac sadness, in G minor, Mozart's preferred key for moods of lament: the key of Pamina's 'Ach, ich fühl's' in *Die Zauberflöte* to which 'Traurigkeit' is not dissimilar in character. The dark notes of a pair of basset-horns are brought in to make the grief-laden accompaniment even heavier, almost dragging, in its hopeless resignation.

Constanze's next aria, 'Martern aller Arten' (No. 11), presents certain problems in performance. It is an exacting coloratura display piece, and follows hard upon the heels of 'Traurigkeit', giving the soprano no chance to rest. It is also burdened, if that is the word for such entrancing music, with an orchestral prelude of 60 bars which lasts more than two minutes in performance. (The entire aria takes nine minutes to perform.) It is true that there is a page of dialogue separating the two arias which, if spoken in full, takes between two and a half and three minutes. Usually, however, the first part of the dialogue, a short scene for Constanze and Blonde, is omitted, leaving only a shortened four or five lines between Constanze and Pasha Selim. Directors staging the opera find it difficult to invent 'business' for Constanze and Selim during the prelude; I have even seen the curtain brought down at the conclusion of 'Traurigkeit', enabling the prelude to 'Martern aller Arten' to be played as an *entr'acte* or overture while the scene is changed, with the curtain going up again only a few bars before Constanze sings the opening lines of her aria. In his autobiography, that eccentric Mozartian Sir Thomas Beecham put forward his own solution: 'I have taken upon myself to solve the problem of this absurd bug-a-boo by transferring the air to the beginning of the second scene of Act III. In the first, Constanze together with Belmonte has been captured while endeavouring to escape from the Seraglio, and while the scene is being changed the orchestra will play the opening section of "Martern aller Arten" which is purely instrumental. The curtain goes up again as she is dragged before the Pasha, and it is here that she hurls defiance at him. Neither the time nor place, it seems to me, is unfitting for this incident.'[1] This seems to me to be an eminently sensible suggestion. Wherever it is placed in the opera, 'Martern aller Arten' will sound like the formal defiance aria from *opera seria* that it is; it is rather strange that Mozart should have produced for *Die Entführung* so expansive an aria with so elaborate an introduction. But what a splendid outburst it is, this defiant C major explosion with its momentary plea for pity overridden by the proud scorn of its vocal display, and the brave supporting argument of solo flute, oboe, violin and cello. Fierce coloratura in the voice's highest range alternates with descents to regions well below those in which the soprano voice is comfortable. At the conclusion of the aria, Constanze leaves the Pasha to soliloquize. He is astonished at the courage she has summoned up, and concludes, 'Also, was Drohen und

[1] Beecham: *A Mingled Chime* (London, 1944).

Bitten nicht vermögen, soll die List zuwege bringen' (So, what neither my threats nor my pleas can accomplish must be brought about by cunning). We do not, however, discover what form Selim's cunning might have taken, for whatever plans he may have formulated are overtaken by events.

Despite the fact that Mozart lifted its tune [Ex. 30] from the finale of

Ex. 30

Wel - che Won - ne, wel - che Lust regt sich nun in mei - ner Brust, wel - che Won-ne, wel-che Lust regt sich nun in mei - ner Brust!

his D major Flute Concerto (K. 314) of four years earlier, Blonde's swift and joyous expression of excitement at her imminent escape, 'Welche Wonne, welche Lust' (No. 12), is an enchanting example of Mozart's genius in expressing character traits in musical terms. The bustling extroversion of Blonde's little song is perfectly in character, both in its direct simplicity and its boisterously plebeian high spirits. In 'Frisch zum Kampfe!' (No. 13), Pedrillo has his turn to anticipate a change in the situation, singing noisily of the battle in which he is about to engage. Bold confidence and a certain caution alternate in his words as well as in the musical phrases to which Mozart has set them. Valour, however, finally wins out over timidity. Then Pedrillo's duet with Osmin, 'Vivat Bacchus!' (No. 14), dances merrily past in a flash, as the Christian and the Muslim settle down to their drinking session. Mozart's 'Turkish' orchestration is very much to the fore in this duet which, as he told his father, was written to please 'i signori viennesi'.

Belmonte is now, at last, about to meet his beloved Constanze again, and he contemplates the moment in 'Wenn der Freude Tränen fliessen' (No. 15), a warm and tender expression of love whose tone becomes more urgent as it progresses. It has long been the practice to transfer this aria to the beginning of Act III to replace 'Ich baue ganz auf deine Stärke', the aria which ought to be sung there. The reasons put forward are that the aria awkwardly holds up the action where it is placed in Act II, delaying the reunion of the two lovers, and that the aria put by Mozart at the beginning of Act III is not one of his best. Perhaps it is not: we shall consider it in due course. But one does not improve a Shakespeare sonnet by omitting the weaker lines from one's reading of it. 'Wenn der Freude Tränen fliessen' should stay where it is, immediately preceding the Quartet which ends Act II. The Quartet, 'Ach, Belmonte! Ach, mein Leben!' (No. 16), begins as a duet for Belmonte and Constanze. The second pair of lovers, the servants Pedrillo and Blonde, then have their few bars of duet which they use to discuss the plans for their escape, after which the quartet proper begins. This is one of Mozart's great operatic ensembles, like the Quartet in *Idomeneo*, or the magnificent act finales in *Così fan tutte*, *Le nozze di Figaro* and *Don Giovanni*. Mozart delineates his four characters with remarkable psychological insight, and the central section of the Quartet, a grave C minor, in which the men hesitantly voice their suspicions that the women may have succumbed to the advances of their Turkish captors, encloses the still and serious centre of a work which for the most part has moved briskly from incident to incident. The style of utterance given to Belmonte and Constanze, both in their moment of doubt and in their subsequent reconciliation, is different from that of the servants, whose phrases are sprightlier, more staccato. When all doubts have been resolved, the music moves into quicker tempi and brighter keys, to end the act on a happy, optimistic note.

We come now to Act III and its opening aria, the much maligned 'Ich baue ganz auf deine Stärke' (No. 17), only to find that it is one of Mozart's most charming tenor love songs. Surely the only possible excuse for omitting it would be the singer's inability to negotiate its several florid passages which are certainly difficult. In its combination of elegance and warmth, this aria is almost the equal of Don Ottavio's 'Il mio tesoro' in *Don Giovanni*. Pedrillo's enchanting little serenade, 'Im Mohrenland gefängen war ein Mädchen hübsch und fein' (No. 18), contrives to sound quite Moorish, as well as oddly dangerous in its veering between major and minor. Its hushed pizzicato string accompaniment conjures up a warm, quiet Middle-Eastern night: its four short verses serve as a signal to the women to be ready for their escape. But the escape is foiled, and Osmin now has his great song of triumph and revenge, 'O wie will ich triumphieren' (No. 19). With the aid of a lively piccolo part in the accompaniment, he loses himself in a riotous orgy of anticipated sadistic lust, his bass voice ranging over a wide compass, showing off its lowest notes, and at one point sustaining a low D for eight bars. Fischer, the first Osmin, must have been a prodigious singer. A pupil of the tenor Anton Raaff, Mozart's Idomeneo, he was renowned both for the range and flexibility of his voice.

The penultimate number of the opera, consisting of the recitative 'Welch' ein Geschick' and duet 'Ha! du solltest für mich sterben' (No. 20), opens promisingly. The *adagio* recitative, one of the rare passages of recitative in *Die Entführung*, is really a piece of *arioso* and a deeply moving one, as the lovers speak what they think to be their final words of love and farewell before going to their death together. Their phrases are bound into formal shape by a persistent motif in the orchestra and the *sforzati* in the violins, with a syncopated accompaniment in the lower strings. The opening *andante* of the duet retains the affecting quality of the recitative or *arioso*, but when, in the final *allegro*, the lovers have conquered their fear of death and sing of their joy in leaving the world together, Mozart's music, perhaps because the composer cannot share their faith in eternal life, comes perilously close to sounding facile. Exaltation was certainly within Mozart's range, but perhaps not in these circumstances and at this moment.

In the dialogue following the duet, Selim reveals himself to be a man of the liberal enlightenment, and sets the lovers free. The Finale (No. 21) is an expanded form of the *vaudeville*, an ending to a play in which each character sings a verse to the same tune, followed by a chorus refrain. Many French plays with music ended thus: Beaumarchais' *Le Mariage de Figaro*, for instance. (Originally, *vaudeville* was the name of a popular satirical song; then it came to mean the kind of play in which these songs were inserted; the word finally came to rest in the first half of the twentieth century, by which time it had come to denote the American and British Commonwealth equivalent of English Music Hall.) Mozart's *vaudeville* is interrupted by Osmin who, defeated and frustrated, reverts to his Act I threats of beheading and hanging, before rushing away in a fury. There follows a quiet *andante sostenuto* in which the four principals, in block harmony, underline the moral of the story, before the Janissaries burst in with a final lively chorus of praise for their noble Pasha, a chorus in which Mozart's 'Turkish tattoo' comes to the fore again, to end the opera noisily and happily.

Despite its somewhat primitive structure, and the fact that it occasionally misplaces an aria or misjudges its length, *Die Entführung aus dem Serail* is, together with *Idomeneo,* musically one of the richest of Mozart's pre-*Figaro* operas. It is hardly surprising that its first audiences enjoyed the work so enormously, and that even Mozart's ex-employer, Archbishop Colloredo, remarked after its first Salzburg performance, 'Es wäre wirklich nicht übl' (It's really rather unusual).[1] Also, although it is easy and perhaps chic to sneer at the benevolence of the Pasha Selim, and to see in it nothing more than the eighteenth-century artist's kow-towing to the constitutional monarchy by portraying absolute rulers of all kinds and all ages as essentially wise and clement, the fact nevertheless remains that *Die Entführung*'s message of forgiveness and the returning of evil by good is one that is just as important and relevant to the world today as it was in 1782. Carl Maria von Weber revealed his under-standing of the real worth of the opera when he wrote that 'in *Die Entführung* Mozart's artistic experience reached its maturity; it was only his worldly experience which was to develop later. The world was justified in expecting from him more operas like *Figaro* or *Don Giovanni*, but with the best will in the world he could not have written another *Entführung*. I believe I perceive in this opera every man's happy, youthful years, whose bloom is never to return, and in eradicating whose defects one irrevocably loses a certain charm.'[2]

[1] Quoted in Leopold's letter to his daughter, of 19 November, 1784.
[2] Quoted in Max Maria von Weber's *Carl Maria von Weber: ein Lebensbild* (Berlin, 1912).

XV

L'Oca del Cairo

K. 422

and

Lo sposo deluso

K. 430

(unfinished works)

L'Oca del Cairo

A FEW DAYS after the first performance of *Die Entführung aus dem Serail*, Mozart wrote urgently to his father, requesting parental consent to his marriage. On 4 August, 1782, no consent having been received, Wolfgang and Constanze were married in St Stephen's Cathedral, Vienna; Leopold's letter, attempting to dissuade Wolfgang from so serious a step, arrived the following day. The newly wedded couple took lodgings at No. 25, Wipplingerstrasse, and a few months later moved a few doors to No. 17, 'on the third floor of the small Herberstein house which belongs to Baron von Wetzlar, a rich Jew'.[1] Wolfgang's letters to his father remain those of a dutiful and loving son, but into his father's correspondence there creeps a note of bitterness and disappointment. Wolfgang writes of his success in finding pupils among the nobility, conveys Viennese gossip, and occasionally reveals that he is aware of what is going on outside Vienna and Salzburg: 'I have heard about England's victories[2] and am greatly delighted, for as you know I am a thorough Englishman.'[3] He had been taking English lessons, as well as practising his French, and expected soon to be able to read English as easily as French and the Italian he spoke fluently.

During the carnival season of 1783, Mozart and a company consisting mainly of his in-laws performed a little pantomime at the Redoutensaal, lasting a half-hour, to fill the interval between dances.[4] An actor called Müller provided the verses, and Mozart composed the music. The introduction, one *scena* and a few fragments are all that have survived of this naive and charming little work (K. 446). During the season, the Mozarts also gave a ball. 'We began at six in the evening and stopped at seven. What, only one hour? No, no. Seven in the morning.'[5] In the spring, there were Sunday excursions to the Prater, the huge Viennese entertainment park which Mozart loved, the company usually consisting only of 'my pregnant little wife and her not pregnant but fat and healthy little husband.'[6]

[1] Mozart to his father, 22 January, 1783.
[2] The relief of Gibraltar and the defeat of the French navy.   [3] 19 October, 1782.
[4] The Redoutensaal is a ballroom in the Hofburg, still used for social occasions and musical performances.
[5] Mozart to his father, 22 January, 1783.
[6] Mozart to his father, written in the Prater, 3 May, 1783.

A son was born to the Mozarts on 17 June, baptized the same day in the church in the square Am Hof, and named Raimund, after their landlord Baron Raimund Wetzlar von Plankenstern who had proved a good friend to the Mozarts, though they were by this time no longer living in his Wipplingerstrasse house, but in the Judenplatz. Mozart was achieving a reasonable success as composer, performer and teacher. His concertos and other instrumental works were beginning to be published, and he was acclaimed as a pianist, appearing at concerts before the Emperor and in the private houses of the nobility. Among his pupils was the Countess Josepha Pálffy, a niece of Archbishop Colloredo. At this time, Mozart wrote a number of piano concerti which are among his loveliest compositions, and many arias for his friends and colleagues. When Count Rosenberg, who was in charge of all Viennese theatres, urged Mozart to write an Italian opera, the vogue for German-language works having subsided again, the composer replied that he would be delighted to do so, but that so far he had not found a libretto which sufficiently attracted him. To his father, however, he confided that he now preferred German-language opera. 'Is not German as singable as French and English? Is it not more so than Russian? Very well then! I am now writing a German opera for myself. I have chosen Goldoni's comedy, *Il servitore di due padroni*, and the whole of the first act has now been translated. Baron Binder is the translator. But we are keeping it a secret until it is completely finished.'[1]

Baron Binder was Johann Nepomuk Friedrich, Baron Binder von Kriegelstein. His translation of Goldoni's *Servant of Two Masters* was probably never completed, for no more is heard of this project. It is possible, however, that the songs 'Warnung' ('Männer suchen stets zu naschen') K. 433 for bass, and 'Müsst ich auch durch tausend Drachen' K. 435 for tenor, composed at this time, were intended for the opera. They were certainly intended to be sung by characters named Carl (tenor) and Wahrmond (bass). But Mozart must in due course have convinced himself that the star of Italian opera was in the ascendancy, for he finally began to make serious moves in the direction of procuring an Italian libretto. He wrote to Leopold:

The Italian opera buffa has started up again, and is very popular. The buffo bass is particularly good: his name is Benucci.[2] I have looked through more than a hundred libretti but I have hardly found a single one which satisfies me. That is to say, there are so many alterations which would have to be made that any poet, even if he were to undertake to make them, would find it easier to write a completely new text – which indeed it is always best to do. Our poet here now is a certain Abbate da Ponte. He has an enormous amount to do in

[1] 5 February, 1783.
[2] Francesco Benucci (*c.* 1745–1824), for whom Mozart was to write the rôles of Figaro in *Le nozze di Figaro* and Guglielmo in *Così fan tutte*.

revising plays for the theatre, and he is at present writing an entirely new libretto for Salieri, which will take him two months. He has then promised to write a new libretto for me. But who knows whether he will be able to keep his word, or whether he will want to? As you know, these Italians are very civil to one's face. Well, we know them. If he is in league with Salieri, I shall never get anything out of him. But I should certainly love to show that I can write an Italian opera. So I've been thinking that, unless Varesco is still very annoyed with us over the Munich opera,[1] perhaps he would write me a new libretto for seven characters. Enough! You will know best whether this is likely. Perhaps he could jot down a few ideas so that when I come to Salzburg we could work them out together. The most essential thing is that, for the most part, the plot should be a comic one. If possible. he should provide two equally good female parts, one of them *seria*, the other *mezzo carattere*, both of them to be equally important and excellent. The third female character could be entirely comic, so could all the males be, if necessary. If you think that Varesco may be interested, please discuss it with him soon. But you mustn't tell him I'm coming to Salzburg in July, or he will do no work, for I should very much like to have some of it while I am here in Vienna. Tell him too that his share will amount to at least 400 or 500 gulden, for the custom here is that the librettist gets the takings of the third performance.[2]

In Da Ponte, Mozart was to discover his finest librettist. The composer Antonio Salieri (1750–1825) was composer to the court, and was to become court Kapellmeister. Jealous of Mozart, Salieri certainly did nothing to help advance his career, though he could easily have done so. Mozart was soon to begin his partnership with Da Ponte, but in the meantime he was content to work once again with his old Salzburg colleague, Varesco. By 21 June, he had received from Varesco the draft of an original libretto, *L'Oca del Cairo* (The Goose of Cairo), and thought it satisfactory for his purpose. 'I must speak to Count Rosenberg at once,' he told his father who had forwarded Varesco's draft, 'in order to ensure that the poet will get his reward. But I consider it a great insult to myself that Herr Varesco doubts that the opera will be successful. He can be certain of one thing: his libretto will not be successful if my music is no good, for in an opera the chief thing is the music. So, if the opera is to be a success and Varesco is to be rewarded, he must alter and recast his libretto as much and as often as I want him to, and not follow his own inclinations, for he has not the slightest knowledge or experience of the theatre. You may even let him know that it doesn't matter to me whether he writes the libretto or not. I know the plot now, so anyone can write it as well as he can.'[3]

Mozart spent about six months working on the composition of Act I of *L'Oca del Cairo*, amongst other things, but one hears no more of it or of Varesco after February, 1784, by which time Mozart had become involved in his next abortive opera project. Of *L'Oca del Cairo* he then told his father: 'At present I have not the slightest thought of proceeding

<hr>

[1] *Idomeneo.*   [2] 7 May, 1783.   [3] 21 June, 1783.

with it. I have works to compose which will bring me in immediate money, but may not do so later. The opera will always bring in some; and, besides, the more time I take the better it will be. As it is, the impression I have gained from Varesco's text is that he has written it too quickly, and I hope that in time he will realize this himself. That is why I still want to see his libretto as a whole: he need only jot it down roughly. Then we can make drastic alterations. But there is certainly no need to hurry. . . . What I have composed has been tucked away safely.'[1]

II

Among Mozart's papers after his death were found the first act of the text of *L'Oca del Cairo* and a detailed synopsis of the second and third acts, all in Varesco's handwriting. It would seem, then, that the plot really was Varesco's own work, and not an adaptation of some earlier libretto, play or novel. The dramatis personae are:

Don Pippo, Marchese di Ripasecca	(bass)
Donna Pantea, his wife (living under an assumed name)	(? soprano: no music for her exists)
Celidora, his daughter	(soprano)
Biondello, a wealthy gentleman	(tenor)
Calandrino, Donna Pantea's nephew	(tenor)
Lavina, Celidora's companion	(soprano)
Chichibio, Don Pippo's steward	(bass)
Auretta, Donna Pantea's maid	(soprano)

The action of the opera takes place at Ripasecca, on the Spanish coast, and the plot is as follows: Don Pippo, Marchese di Ripasecca, a vain and haughty fool, has by his ill-treatment forced his wife, Donna Pantea, to leave him; he believes her dead, but in fact she is living, concealed, somewhere abroad. Biondello, hated by Don Pippo, loves his daughter Celidora, whom Don Pippo intends shall marry Count Lionetto di Casavuota; he himself has fallen in love with her companion Lavina, who has come to an understanding with Calandrino, Biondello's friend and Pantea's nephew. The two girls are confined in a fortified tower and closely guarded. Don Pippo has been induced to promise Biondello that, if he succeeds in gaining access to Celidora within the year, her hand shall be his reward. Calandrino, a skilful mechanic, has constructed an artificial goose large enough to contain a man, and with machinery capable of motion. This is conveyed to Donna Pantea who, disguised in Moorish costume, is to display it as a kind of carnival sideshow. It is hoped that Don Pippo may consent to its exhibition

[1] 10 February, 1784.

before the two girls, and that Biondello may thus be conveyed into the tower. As a condition, Calandrino exacts from his friend a promise of Lavina's hand.

The opera begins on the anniversary of the wager. Don Pippo is about to marry Lavina, and awaits the arrival of Count Lionetto to marry Celidora; his house is filled with preparations for festivity. The curtain rises as the whole household, including the coquettish maid Auretta and her lover, the house-steward Chichibio, are having their hair dressed. Calandrino enters in great perturbation. Donna Pantea has not arrived, and a violent storm gives rise to the fear that she may fail to appear. Some other device must therefore be hit upon. Calandrino promises marriage to Chichibio and Auretta, if they can succeed in abstracting Don Pippo's clothes, and thus prevent his leaving the castle. This they undertake to do. The scene changes: Celidora and Lavina are conversing on a terrace on the fourth storey of the tower, to which they have obtained access in secret. The lovers appear below on the other side of the moat, and a tender quartet ensues. The new plan is to throw a bridge across the moat, and scale the tower. Workmen arrive, and the task is eagerly commenced; but Chichibio and Auretta, chattering about their marriage, have failed to keep watch, and now announce that Don Pippo has gone outside. He himself speedily appears, summons the watch, stops the work, and drives the lovers away.

In the second act, Pantea lands with the goose in a violent storm. It is a carnival day, and the assembled crowd is full of amazement at the natural and rational movements of the goose, which is supposed to have come from Cairo. Auretta and Chichibio inform Don Pippo of the wonderful sight. He causes Pantea to come forward, and she informs him that the goose, having lost its speech from fright during the storm, can only be restored by the use of a certain herb which grows in a lonely garden. Don Pippo, delighted, commissions Calandrino to take Pantea and the goose into the pleasure garden, so that the two girls may enjoy the spectacle. The finale represents the carnival ground, close to the tower, the two ladies looking on from their window. A dispute arises, in which Biondello takes part. Don Pippo, as magistrate, is called on to dispense justice. Some ridiculous action is carried on, ending in a general tumult. Pantea then puts Biondello into the goose, and enters the garden. Meanwhile, Calandrino informs Don Pippo that Biondello, in despair, has set out to sea in a small boat, and his story is confirmed by the weeping Auretta. Don Pippo, in high delight, forms a ludicrous wedding procession, and proceeds to the tower, where Celidora and Lavina stand at the window while the goose performs various antics for the amusement of the crowd. Finally, Don Pippo appears in the great hall of the tower, accompanied by the two ladies and the goose, in full confidence of his triumph, and only needing the arrival of Count Lionetto to celebrate the wedding. Chichibio enters with a discourteous refusal from the Count. As Don Pippo is in the act of giving his hand to Lavina, Pantea advances in her true person, the goose begins to speak, opens, and Biondello steps out. Don Pippo is beside himself, and is ridiculed by them all. He ends by promising to amend his ways, and the three couples are made happy.[1]

At the beginning of their work on *L'Oca del Cairo*, Mozart had asked his father to remind Varesco of the need to stress the comic element in the plot, 'for I know the taste of the Viennese'.[2] He and his wife spent the months of August, September and October in Salzburg, where he no doubt had several meetings with Varesco. What further information we have about progress on the opera comes from three of Mozart's letters to Leopold, written from Vienna in December, 1783. In the first, he informed his father that

I have only three more arias to compose, then the first act of my opera is finished. With the aria buffa, the quartet and the finale I can safely say I am perfectly satisfied – in fact quite delighted. I should be sorry, therefore, to have written so much good music in vain, which must be the case unless some absolutely necessary alterations are made. Neither you nor the Abbate Varesco nor I reflected that it will have a very bad effect, indeed it would completely ruin the opera, if neither of the two principal female characters were to appear on the stage until the last moment, but were to be always wandering about on the ramparts or terraces of the tower. One act of this might pass muster, but I am sure the audience would not stand a second. This objection first occurred to me at Linz, and I see no way out of it but to contrive that some scenes of the second act shall take place in a room in the fortress. The scene where Don Pippo gives orders for the goose to be brought in could be the room in which Celidora and Lavina are confined. Pantea comes in with the goose and Biondello pops out. They hear Don Pippo coming, and Biondello pops into the goose again. This would provide an opening for a good quintet, which would be all the more comic because the goose would be singing too.

I must confess to you, however, that my only reason for not objecting to the whole of the goose business is that two men of greater penetration and judgment than I, by whom I mean yourself and Varesco, have not disapproved of it. But there would still be time to think of something else. Biondello has only undertaken to make his way into the tower: whether he does it as a sham goose or by some other trick, makes no difference at all. I cannot help thinking that many more comic and more natural effects might be produced if Biondello were to remain in human form. For instance, the news that, in despair at not being able to make his way into the fortress, he has thrown himself into the sea could be brought in right at the beginning of the second act. He might then disguise himself as a Turk, or something of the kind, and bring Pantea with him as a slave-girl (a Moorish one, of course). Don Pippo is anxious to purchase the slave for his bride, so the slave-dealer and his slave-girl must be admitted into the fortress in order for her to be

---

[1] Jahn, Vol. II, pp. 53–54.   [2] 21 May, 1783.

inspected. This could give Pantea an opportunity for mocking and bullying her husband, which would greatly improve her part, for the more comic the opera is, the better. I hope you will expound my views fully to the Abbate Varesco, and tell him that I beg him to get seriously to work. I have worked hard enough in this short time. Indeed, I should have finished the first act, if I did not require some alterations made to the words in a few of the arias. But don't tell him that at present.[1]

A few days later, Mozart wrote again about the problem of bringing the two women down from the bastions of the fortress earlier in the opera: 'Do your very best to make my libretto a success. I wish that in Act I the ladies could be brought down from the ramparts when they sing their arias, in which case I would willingly allow them to sing the whole finale up above.'[2] Varesco was apparently quite willing to make the change, for an altered version of this scene exists, as well as the original text. But then Mozart made further demands. Again, he wrote to his father:

I have received your last letter of the 19th, enclosing a portion of the opera. Let me deal with this first, as it is most urgent. The Abbate Varesco has written beside Lavina's cavatina: 'a cui servera la musica della cavatina antecedente,'[3] that is, Celidora's cavatina. But that is out of the question, for the words of Celidora's cavatina are despairing and inconsolable, whereas those of Lavina's are full of hope and comfort. Besides, for one singer to repeat the song of another is a practice quite outmoded now, and it was never popular. At best it is only suitable for a soubrette and her lover if they are subsidiary characters.[4] My idea would be to begin the scene with a good duet, which could well begin with the same words, with a short addition for the coda. After the duet, the conversation could proceed as before: 'E quando s'ode il campanello della custode.'[5] Mlle Lavina will have the goodness to depart, not Celidora, so that the latter, as prima donna, may have an opportunity to sing a fine bravura aria. This, I think, would be a gain for the composer, the singers and the audience, and the entire scene would gain in interest. Besides, it is scarcely likely that the audience would tolerate the same aria from the second singer, after having heard it sung by the first.

I do not know what either of you mean by the following direction: At the end of the newly-interpolated scene between the two women in Act I, the Abbate has written: 'Segue la scena VIII che prima era la VII e così cangiansi di mano in mano i numeri.'[6] This leads me to suppose that he intends the scene after the quartet, where the two ladies sing their little songs from the window, one after the other, to remain. But that is impossible. The act would

[1] 6 December, 1783.   [2] 10 December, 1783.
[3] 'for which the music of the preceding cavatina will serve'.
[4] Mozart had made use of this device in *La finta giardiniera*, where Serpetta and Nardo each sing a stanza to the same music, in the arietta 'Das Vergnügen in dem Eh'stand'.
[5] 'And when the custodian's bell is heard'.
[6] 'Scene VIII, formerly Scene VII, follows, and thus the numbers are correspondingly altered.'

be lengthened out of all proportion, and quite ruined. I always thought it rather ludicrous to read:

Celidora: Tu qui m'attendi, amica. Alla custode farmi veder vogl'io; ci andrai tu poi.

Lavina: Si, dolce amica, addio (Celidora parte).[1]

Lavina sings her song. Celidora enters again and says: 'Eccomi, or vanne' etc.[2] Then out goes Lavina, and Celidora sings her song, as though they were soldiers on guard, relieving each other. It is surely much more natural that, since they are all together for the quartet in which they plan their attack, the men should then go to collect the necessary assistance, leaving the two women to retreat quietly to their apartments. The most that can be allowed them is a few lines of recitative. I cannot imagine that it was intended to retain the scene; Varesco must simply have forgotten to indicate that it was to be omitted. I am very curious to hear your excellent idea for bringing Biondello into the tower: provided it is amusing enough, I'd be prepared to overlook the fact that it may appear unnatural. I am not at all alarmed by the idea of fireworks, for the arrangements of the Viennese fire brigade are so good that there is not the slightest danger. *Medea* has been performed here repeatedly, at the end of which half the palace collapses in ruins while the other half goes up in flames.[3]

Six weeks later, Mozart laid the music of *L'Oca del Cairo* aside, intending to come back to it after the libretto had been got absolutely right. But there was no urgency attached to its composition, nor a firm commission with a date of performance to be met, so it is hardly surprising that the opera was never completed.

III

Apart from some rough sketches, the music extant for *L'Oca del Cairo* consists of two duéts, three arias, some recitative, a quartet and the first act finale, none of which was fully orchestrated by Mozart. For the most part, they are simply the voice parts and a bass line, with an occasional indication of intended scoring or texture. What exists can be, and has been, edited for performance without great difficulty, and it is clear even from these fragments that the opera would have been a considerably more mature work than Mozart's most recent Italian *opera buffa, La finta giardiniera*. The opening duet, 'Così si fa', for the two servants Auretta and Chichibio, in which they quarrel and make up, would not be unworthy of Susanna and Figaro. Curiously it contains an anticipation [Ex. 31] of a phrase in the duet 'Crudel, perchè finora' (sung in Act III of *Le nozze di Figaro* by Susanna and the Count). Auretta's pert *andante* aria, 'Se fosse qui nascoso', shades off into recitative, of which Mozart had composed no more than the first couple of bars before skipping into the

[1] Celidora: Wait for me here, my friend. I wish to see the custodian; you may go later. Lavina: Yes, sweet friend, good-bye (Celidora leaves).

[2] 'Here I am, you may go now' etc.   [3] 24 December, 1783.

Ex. 31

next number, 'Ogni momento', a C major *presto* aria of great vitality for Chichibio, a typical *buffo* piece yet not without individuality. Two pages of *recitativo secco* exist, leading to Don Pippo's aria. Until recently, it was thought that Mozart had merely sketched out the voice part of the aria, 'Siamo pronte alle gran nozze', until a copy made by the Bergamo composer Johannes Simon Mayr (1763–1845) was found in the Mayr archives in the Bergamo Civic Library. Mayr had met Mozart's widow in Vienna, and had presumably been shown the *Oca del Cairo* manuscripts. Mayr's copy reveals that the aria is scored for oboes, bassoons and horns as well as the usual strings, and that it ends as a trio, for Mozart had gone on to set the remainder of the scene as a trio in which Don Pippo is joined by Auretta and Chichibio, the trio growing naturally out of Don Pippo's lively *allegro* aria. The quartet, 'S'oggi, o Dei', for Celidora, Lavina, Biondello and Calandrino advances the action in lively fashion and also cleverly distinguishes and characterizes the two pairs of lovers, while the Act I finale, a septet ('Su via, putti, presto, presto'), lasting a good twelve minutes or more, and ranging over a variety of moods and changes of tempo, is Mozart's first great comic opera finale, a firm step on the road to the Act II finale of *Figaro*, with its clearly defined musical delineation of the characters, and a final *presto* section which is positively Rossinian in its high spirits. The remaining number composed by Mozart is another duet for Auretta and Chichibio, 'Ho un pensiero'. It is not certain where this was intended to be sung, as no words for it appear in the manuscript of Varesco's libretto. The wind instruments play an important part in the orchestral colouring of this attractive and sprightly piece.

The *Oca del Cairo* fragments were first published in 1855 by André, who had purchased them from Constanze Mozart many years earlier, along with other Mozart manuscripts. They were given a concert performance in Frankfurt, in April, 1860. A stage production of the opera was mounted in Paris at the Fantaisies-Parisiennes on 6 June, 1867, in which numbers from another unfinished Mozart opera, *Lo sposo deluso* (discussed later in this chapter), were included, as well as arias Mozart composed for insertion into Bianchi's *La Villanella rapita* (also discussed later: see p. 215). The opera was arranged by Titus Charles Constantin, to a new French libretto by the Belgian poet and music critic, Victor van Wilder. Wilder's French version was subsequently translated into German and produced in Berlin, Vienna, Leipzig and elsewhere. In Italian, it was staged in London at the Theatre Royal, Drury Lane, in 1870. There have been productions in the present century, not only of Wilder's version but of several others. In 1936, a new version, in one act, with the libretto amended by Giovanni Cavicchioli and the score reconstructed by Virgilio Mortari, was staged in Salzburg. An Overture was provided (the finale of the Serenade, K. 320) and the concert aria, 'Bella mia fiamma' K. 528, was also called into service. Another adaptation, by Hans Redlich, was performed in Italian at Sadler's Wells Theatre, London, in 1940. The Salzburg 1936 version has occasionally been revived and was performed in Japan in 1971, while the Redlich was given again by the Royal College of Music, London, in 1960, this time in English as *The Cairo Goose*. It shared a double-bill with Gluck's *Orpheus*. In Gotha, in 1929, the musical fragments of *L'Oca del Cairo* and *Lo sposo deluso* were adapted to fit a German version of the libretto of the latter opera, under the title *Der betrogene Bräutigam*. In 1975, *L'Oca del Cairo* was staged at the Schloss Charlottenberg in Berlin.

Lo sposo deluso

IV

Mozart had hesitated to visit Salzburg in the summer of 1783, fearing that the Archbishop might have him arrested, as he had not yet obtained his formal dismissal. But, summoning up his courage, he informed his father that 'I care very little for Salzburg and not at all for the Archbishop: I shit on both of them'.[1] He and Constanze spent three summer months in Salzburg, where Wolfgang, unmolested by Archbishop Colloredo, discussed *L'Oca del Cairo* with Varesco. Little Raimund Leopold Mozart, left behind in Vienna in the care of a foster mother, died on 19 August of intestinal cramp at the age of eight weeks. It is not certain whether Wolfgang and Constanze learned of his death before their return to Vienna in the autumn.

Early in July, while still in Vienna, Mozart had warned his father he did not intend to rush *L'Oca del Cairo*, as he preferred to work slowly and deliberately. He added that, in any case, 'an Italian poet here' had brought him a libretto, and that, if it were trimmed and adjusted to his taste, he might make use of it. The Italian poet could only have been Lorenzo da Ponte. There was no other Italian poet of repute in Vienna at the time: Metastasio had died the previous year, and Casti did not arrive in Vienna until the following year. Mozart, we know, had already met Da

[1] 12 July, 1783.

Ponte two months earlier (according to Da Ponte's *Memoirs*[1] the meeting
had taken place in the house of Baron Wetzlar, Mozart's friend, admirer
and ex-landlord), and the poet had promised to write a libretto for him,
once he had got rid of his obligation to Salieri which was expected to
take two months (see p. 201). Probably at the beginning of 1784, Mozart,
having had Da Ponte's libretto for several months, began to compose
the opera which was to be called *Lo sposo deluso*. He completed the
overture, two arias, a trio and a quartet, and then abandoned the work.

V

Mozart composed so little of *Lo sposo deluso o sia La Rivalita di tre Donne per
un solo amante* (The deluded bridegroom, or The rivalry of three women
for one lover), which was to have been an *opera buffa* in two acts, that
there is no possibility of it being performed as an opera, though the four
extant numbers have been made use of in stage performance. Mention
has already been made (p. 208) of the German production, *Der betrogene
Bräutigam*, which included both the *Oca del Cairo* and *Sposo deluso*
fragments. The characters in *Lo sposo deluso* are listed in the libretto thus:

First buffo caricato[2]: Bocconio, a rich and stupid man, betrothed to Eugenia
(to be sung by Signor Benucci)
First buffa: Eugenia, a young Roman woman of noble birth, somewhat
capricious, engaged to Bocconio, but really in love with Don Asdrubale
(Signora Fischer)
First mezzo character role: Don Asdrubale, a Tuscan officer, very
courageous, and in love with Eugenia (Signor Mandini)
Second buffa: Bettina, niece of Bocconio, a vain girl, in love with Don
Asdrubale (Signora Cavalieri)
Second buffo caricato: Pulcherio, scornful of women, and a friend of
Bocconio (Signor Bussani)
Second comic character role: Gervasio, tutor of Eugenia, who then falls in
love with Metilde (Signor Pugnetti)
Third buffa: Metilde, virtuoso singer and dancer, false friend of Bettina, and
in love with Don Asdrubale

The action takes place in and around Livorno. Acquaintance with the
complicated detail of the plot is hardly necessary to an appreciation of
Mozart's music. Eugenia and Don Asdrubale, who really love each
other, have been separated by a misunderstanding. Believing Asdrubale
to be dead, Eugenia agrees unwillingly to become the bride of the
elderly fop, Bocconio. When she encounters Asdrubale again, he is
being pursued by two other women, Bettina and Metilde. The opera
ends with the fop Bocconio deceived and disillusioned, as the title had
promised, and with Asdrubale choosing his true love Eugenia from

[1] Lorenzo da Ponte: *Memoirs* (translated: New York, 1929).
[2] Or exaggerated comic role.

among the three women interested in him. Bettina is paired off with Pulcherio, and Metilde with Gervasio.

The Overture to *Lo sposo deluso* begins with a flourish of trumpets and drums and a cheerful, bustling *allegro*, followed by a tender *andante*. The opening flourish returns, not to bring a reprise of the *allegro*, but to introduce the opening number, a quartet, 'Ah, che ridere!' in which Bettina, Asdrubale and Pulcherio make fun of the elderly bachelor's forthcoming marriage, as he attempts to complete his toilet. The light-hearted quartet makes good use of music from the *allegro* of the Overture, and could be thought as fine a beginning of an opera as the opening trio of *Così fan tutte*, were it not that it tends to outstay its welcome. But, though fully scored, the music in its present state represents Mozart's first thoughts only, and might well have been pruned in a final draft.

Eugenia enters to a bravura aria, 'Nacqui all'aura trionfale', for which Mozart completed the voice part, the bass line of the accompaniment, and the first violins' part in the orchestral introduction [Ex. 32]. Had the aria been completed, it would have been a fine mock-

Ex. 32

heroic piece in the manner of Fiordiligi's 'Come scoglio' in *Così fan tutte*. Pulcherio's 'Dove mai trovar quel ciglio?' is also no more than a voice part and an occasional indication of instrumentation: however, one can tell that, if it were elegantly scored, it would make an engaging and witty aria for the tenor misogynist. The trio for Eugenia, Asdrubale and Bocconio, 'Che accidenti! Che tragedia!' is fully scored. Eugenia and Asdrubale are astounded to meet each other again, while Bocconio is in a state of confusion. Mozart is clearly by now a master of the art of expressing a complex of emotions in ensemble, for the deep feeling of Eugenia and Asdrubale is reflected in this music just as strongly as the comedy of the situation. Had *Lo sposo deluso* been completed and staged, it might easily have become the first of Mozart's great Italian comic operas. His proposed cast was a fine one. Benucci, who was to have sung Bocconio, became Mozart's first Figaro, and the Signor Fischer who was cast as Eugenia was Nancy Storace, his first Susanna.[1] Signora Cavalieri (Bettina) is she to whose flexible throat Mozart sacrificed his artistic scruples in *Die Entführung aus dem Serail*. The quality of the music he wrote for both *L'Oca del Cairo* and *Lo sposo deluso* reveals him as now absolutely ready for the challenge of *Figaro*, which was still, however, two years away.

[1] It is because Nancy Storace, who married an English violinist John Abraham Fisher in Vienna in 1784, is described as Signora Fischer [*sic*] that *Lo sposo deluso* is thought to have been composed in that year. Her husband ill-treated her and was banished from Vienna by the Emperor, after which Miss Storace reverted to her maiden name. Presumably, however, Mozart could have begun *Lo sposo deluso* in the summer of 1783, and put it aside with the intention of working on it again at a later date. It may still have been considered an active project when, in 1784, a cast list was drawn up including the name of Signora Fischer, and was perhaps finally abandoned some months later.

XVI

Der Schauspieldirektor

Comedy with music, in one act

K. 486

Dramatis personae:

Frank, an impresario	(speaking part)
Eiler, a banker	(speaking part)
Buff, an actor	(bass)
Herz, an actor	(speaking part)
Madame Pfeil, actress	(speaking part)
Madame Krone, actress	(speaking part)
Madame Vogelsang, actress	(speaking part)
Herr Vogelsang, singer	(tenor)
Madame Herz, singer	(soprano)
Mademoiselle Silberklang, singer	(soprano)

LIBRETTO by Gottlieb Stephanie Jr.

TIME: 1786

PLACE: Salzburg

FIRST PERFORMED in Vienna, 7 February, 1786, in the Orangery at the palace of Schönbrunn, with Aloysia Lange (Madame Herz), Caterina Cavalieri (Mademoiselle Silberklang), Johann Valentin Adamberger (Vogelsang), Joseph Lange (Buff). The non-singing roles were performed by Gottlieb Stephanie (Frank); Franz Karl Brockmann (Eiler); Joseph Weidmann (Herz); Johanna Sacco (Madame Pfeil); Maria Anna Adamberger (Madame Krone); Anna Maria Stephanie (Madame Vogelsang)

Der Schauspieldirektor

I

1784 WAS PROFESSIONALLY a successful year for Mozart, a year in which he composed such important works as the E flat piano concerto K. 449 and a further five piano concerti, the Quintet for piano and wind instruments K. 452, and two string quartets. In the summer he fell ill: shortly after his recovery a second son, Karl Thomas, was born to Constanze on 21 September.

In addition to the two fragmentary works discussed in the preceding chapter, Mozart contemplated at least one other project at this period of his life in Vienna, but did not get very far with it. Shortly after abandoning *Lo sposo deluso*, he began to set a libretto, *Il regno delle Amazoni* by Giuseppe Petrosellini, which had already been used by the composer Agostino Accorimboni for an opera staged in Parma in 1783. Mozart composed only one trio (K. 434), before apparently realizing how poor the libretto was. Among his occasional arias and ensembles written to be sung in the operas of other composers, two pieces which he composed in November, 1785, for insertion in Francesco Bianchi's *La villanella rapita* are worthy of mention. The opera was staged at the Burgtheater on 28 November, and Mozart's interpolations are the quartet, 'Dite almeno, in che mancai' (K. 479) and the trio 'Mandina amabile' (K. 480). The singers for whom they were written were Celesta Coltellini (whose father had written the libretto of Mozart's *La finta semplice*), Stefano Mandini, who was to sing the role of the Count at the première of *Le Nozze di Figaro*, Vincenzio Calvesi and Francesco Bussani. Both the quartet and the trio are pieces which would not have disgraced *Figaro* or *Don Giovanni*. In their witty vocal characterization and their masterly orchestral accompaniment, they must have stood out boldly from their context. Count Zinzendorf, that Viennese Pepys, attended a performance of the opera, and noted in his diary: 'To the opera . . . *La villanella rapita*. The quartet is fine.'[1]

Professor Anton Klein, a lecturer on philosophy and aesthetics who had written several popular plays as well as the libretto of the opera *Günther von Schwarzburg* by Ignaz Holzbauer, sent Mozart a libretto, *Rudolf von Habsburg*, with the request that he set it to music. Mozart acknowledged receipt of the libretto in a long letter in which he spoke

[1] Quoted in Deutsch, p. 257.

pessimistically of the future of German-language opera, but promised to give Klein's libretto serious consideration. 'In case I should feel inclined to set it to music,' he wrote, 'I should like to know beforehand whether a production has been arranged for any particular place. For a work such as this, from the point of view of both poetry and music, deserves better than to be left to chance. I shall hope for an explanation on this point from you.'[1] Presumably Klein had no plans for the work's production, for the project was not taken any further.

Mozart's sister Nannerl had married and moved from Salzburg to St Gilgen on the Wolfgangsee. Though she was only ten miles away, life must have become lonelier for Leopold in Salzburg, so he was delighted when Wolfgang invited him to visit Vienna. Leopold arrived in mid-February, 1785, and stayed with his son and daughter-in-law. The Mozarts had now moved to an apartment in a house in the Schulerstrasse, close to St Stephen's Cathedral. On his first evening in Vienna Leopold was taken to a concert at which Wolfgang's magnificent, fiercely turbulent D minor piano concerto (K. 466) was performed for the first time. The following day he met the great composer Joseph Haydn at a performance in Mozart's apartment of three new string quartets which Mozart was to dedicate to Haydn. Leopold wrote proudly to Nannerl of this meeting: 'Haydn said to me, "As an honest man, I tell you before God that your son is the greatest composer I know, either in person or by name. He has taste and, moreover, the most profound knowledge of composition." '[2]

The fifty-three-year-old Haydn had, the previous day, become a Freemason. It was only within recent years that Freemasonry had become fashionable in Vienna, but now a number of the most prominent people in the arts and sciences and in society were joining the fraternity. The Masonic emphasis on brotherhood and friendship appealed to Mozart who himself became a Mason early in 1785. He had already composed his first Masonic composition, the cantata 'Dir, Seele des Weltalls' (K. 429), and was to compose other music for Masonic ceremonies after being initiated into membership of the lodge *Zur wahren Eintracht* (True Concord) whose temple was located in a house near the Hoher Markt.

Leopold Mozart found life with Wolfgang an exhausting round of concerts, dinners and other social engagements. When he attended the Burgtheater concert at which Wolfgang played his B flat major piano concerto (K. 456), he was 'only two boxes away from the very beautiful Princess of Württemberg, from which position all the interplay of the instruments came to me so clearly that, in sheer delight, tears came into my eyes. When your brother left the platform, the Emperor waved his hat and called "Bravo, Mozart!" And when he came out to play, there

---

[1] Letter of 21 May, 1785.   [2] Letter of 16 February, 1785.

was a great deal of applause.'[1] Leopold left Vienna at the end of April to return to Salzburg and to his duties in the employ of the Archbishop. Wolfgang and Constanze accompanied him out of Vienna as far as Purkersdorf in the Vienna Woods, where father and son said farewell. They had no reason to suspect it was to be farewell for ever.

After Leopold's departure, Mozart plunged back into his life of composing and performing. One of his pupils at this time was the English composer, Thomas Attwood, then in his twentieth year. A note to Attwood exists in Mozart's hand, in English, postponing a lesson: 'This after noon I am not at home, therefore I pray you to come to morrow at three & a half.'[2] In the autumn of 1785, Mozart began work on *Le nozze di Figaro*, but broke off when he received a commission from the Court to compose a one-act *Singspiel* for a special occasion at Schönbrunn. The Governor-General of the Austrian Netherlands, Duke Albert of Sachsen-Teschen, and his wife the Archduchess Marie Christine, a sister of the Emperor, were visiting Vienna. At the same time, Prince Stanislas Poniatowski, nephew of the King of Poland, was also in Vienna. Joseph II gave a reception for his distinguished guests in the long Orangery at Schönbrunn, apparently the only large hall in the palace which could be properly heated. The reception was given on 7 February, 1786, and the musical entertainment consisted of two short operas, one German and one Italian. Mozart's commission was to write the music for the German *Singspiel*. The Orangery at Schönbrunn, only part of which is still standing, was directly opposite the Schlosstheater. In Mozart's day it was a structure some 625 feet long, 36 feet wide and 25 feet high. The *Wiener Zeitung* of 8 February, 1786, gives this account of the occasion:

On Tuesday, His Majesty the Emperor gave a festival at Schönbrunn, for Their Excellencies the Governors-General of the Imperial and Royal Netherlands, and a gathering of the local nobility. Forty courtiers as well as Prince Poniatowski being invited, these escorted their own ladies, and at three o'clock set out from the Hofburg in pairs, travelling by both open and closed carriages. His Imperial Majesty accompanied Her Serene Highness the Archduchess Christine. The party alighted at the Orangery, which had been prepared most lavishly and attractively for luncheon for the guests. The table, beneath the orange trees, was most prettily decorated with both local and exotic flowers, blossoms and fruits. While His Majesty, the distinguished visitors and the guests partook of their meal, the Imperial and Royal Chamber Musicians performed on wind instruments. After the banquet, a new play with arias, called *Der Schauspieldirektor* [The Impresario] was performed by actors of the Imperial and Royal National Theatre on a stage especially erected at one end of the Orangery. At its conclusion, an opera buffa, likewise newly composed for this occasion, and entitled *Prima la musica e poi le parole* [First the music and then the words], was given by the company

---

[1] Letter to Nannerl, 16 February, 1785.   [2] Quoted in Deutsch, p. 249.

of the Court Opera, on the Italian stage erected at the other end of the Orangery. All this time, the Orangery was most gloriously illuminated with numerous lights from candelabra and wall-brackets. After nine o'clock, the entire company returned to town in the same order, each coach being accompanied by two grooms with links.

The Emperor instructed his Director of Entertainments, Count Orsini-Rosenberg, to pay one hundred ducats to Salieri, who had composed the music of *Prima la musica e poi le parole*, and fifty ducats to Mozart for *Der Schauspieldirektor*. This was not unfair, for *Der Schauspiel-direktor* is a one-act play by Gottlieb Stephanie, the librettist of *Die Entführung aus dem Serail*, to which Mozart contributed the musical numbers consisting merely of an Overture, two arias and two ensembles.

Both Mozart's and Salieri's operas were performed together again a few days later at the Kärntnertor Theater. Apparently two further performances were given there, 'with extraordinary success and attendance'.[1]

II

The idea for the plot of *Der Schauspieldirektor* is said to have been given to Gottlieb Stephanie by the Emperor himself. It is hardly an original idea, for various librettists had produced amusing back-stage skits of this kind, among them Goldoni and Metastasio. Stephanie's comedy is set in Salzburg, where a theatre impresario is attempting to gather together a new company. Several actors and singers present themselves to him for audition, the rival *prime donne* behaving especially badly as they compete for his attention. The actors and actresses perform in interpolated scenes from *Der aufgehetzte Ehemann* (a translation of Vanbrugh's *The Provoked Husband*), *Bianca Cappello* by August Gottlieb Meissner, and *Die galante Bäuerin*. The chief interest in the play must have been in its *risqué* dialogue and in its several topical allusions. Mozart's music is utilized when the rival *prime donne* sing their audition arias, and when a quarrel breaks out between them, with the tenor attempting to act as peacemaker. In a vaudeville finale, the singers agree rather ambiguously that 'Jeder Künstler strebt nach Ehre, wünscht der einzige zu sein' (Every artist strives for glory, and wants to be the only one). Stephanie himself played the Impresario, Herr Frank; the singers, who were given such appropriate names as Vogelsang (Birdsong), Herz (Heart) and Silberklang (Silver Sound), were the tenor Adamberger who had been Belmonte in *Die Entführung*, and two *prime donne* who were real-life

---

[1] According to the *Ephemeriden der Litteratur und des Theaters*, Berlin, 1786. Vol. III, p. 189.

rivals, Aloysia Lange (Mozart's sister-in-law) and Caterina Cavalieri for whose 'flexible throat' the role of Constanze in *Die Entführung* had been written.

Even during Mozart's lifetime, *Der Schauspieldirektor* was performed in several new arrangements, and the nineteenth century produced many more. At Weimar in 1791, Goethe produced a version which, under the title *Theatralische Abenteuer* (Theatrical Adventure), combined Cimarosa's intermezzo *L'Impresario in angustie* with Mozart's music for *Der Schauspieldirektor*. Among the nineteenth-century versions was one by Louis Schneider (1845), sub-titled *Mozart und Schikaneder*, in which Stephanie's fictitious characters were turned into Mozart, Schikaneder (the actor-manager, and librettist of *Die Zauberflöte*) and Aloysia Lange (Mozart's sister-in-law), and Mozart is seen to be composing *Die Zauberflöte* with the aid of Schikaneder. Most modern productions resort to re-writing Stephanie's text which is both too mediocre and too localized to be of interest now. The structure of the plot, however, is worth preserving, if only as an excuse for Mozart's music for *Der Schauspieldirektor* to be heard on the stage. The music itself takes no more than twenty-five minutes to perform, so that a modern version of the opera with a revised text makes a suitable curtain-raiser to an evening of one-act operas, or to a performance of Mozart's other one-act *Singspiel, Bastien und Bastienne*. The practice of padding it out with other Mozart arias or concerted pieces has little to recommend it. The Overture and four numbers are quite sufficient for a compact one-act piece, and are in fact written 'in character' for the situation outlined by Stephanie. It is rare for modern productions of *Der Schauspieldirektor* to utilize Stephanie's complete text. Generally, new dialogue sufficient to provide a setting or context for the musical numbers is written for the characters of the Impresario, his rival sopranos and Herr Buff, and the other characters all dispensed with.

III

Mozart composed his music for *Der Schauspieldirektor* between 18 January and 3 February, 1786, taking time off from *Le nozze di Figaro* to do so. The Overture, a compact and fast-moving *presto*, is full of such warmth and gaiety, and its themes so graceful, that it could as suitably precede a performance of the masterpiece *Le nozze di Figaro*. The ariette, 'Da schlägt die Abschiedsstunde' (No. 1) which serves to introduce the soprano, Madame Herz, begins poignantly as a *larghetto* in G minor, but ends with an *allegro* bravura section which gives the singer an opportunity to show off her coloratura agility and her range, for she is twice asked to touch a high D. Mademoiselle Silberklang's 'Bester Jüngling' (No. 2) has perhaps less sensibility, and more directness of style, though it follows the same pattern as Madame Herz's aria, its sweet *andante* contrasting with an *allegretto* in which Mademoiselle Silberklang demonstrates that her coloratura is the equal of her rival's; though not her range, for she rises no higher than B flat.

The trio (No. 3) in which the rival sopranos each assert 'Ich bin die erste Sängerin' (I am the prima donna), while the tenor, Herr Vogelsang, tries vainly to keep the peace between them, is Mozart the opera composer at his most inventive. How brilliantly he characterizes the two rivals and the ineffective moralizing of the tenor. This is the art of the musical dramatist at its finest. Madame Herz still has the edge over her rival as far as her high notes are concerned, for, though Mademoiselle Silberklang reaches a high D in the trio, Madame Herz is at that moment singing the F a third above her [Ex. 33]. And it is Madame Herz

Ex. 33

who, asked to caricature a heart-felt *adagio* by singing the single word 'adagio', does so to a tune which has all the depth of feeling of one of Mozart's violin concerto slow movements [Ex. 34].

Ex. 34

The *Schlussgesang* or final ensemble, 'Jeder Künstler strebt nach Ehre' (No. 4), is a vaudeville in which the three voices (and a fourth, for the actor playing Buff now reveals himself to possess a baritone or bass voice of moderate range which enables him to contribute a solo passage) combine to point the moral of the tale, insofar as it has one. It makes a somewhat flat and disappointing finale, after the sparkle of the preceding arias and trio.

XVII

Le nozze di Figaro

comic opera in four acts

K. 492

Dramatis personae:

Figaro, servant to Count Almaviva	(bass)
Susanna, maid to Countess Almaviva	(soprano)
Dr Bartolo	(bass)
Marcellina, his former housekeeper	(soprano)
Cherubino, page to Count Almaviva	(soprano)
Count Almaviva	(baritone)
Don Basilio, a music teacher	(tenor)
Countess Almaviva	(soprano)
Antonio, gardener to Count Almaviva	(bass)
Barbarina, his daughter	(mezzo-soprano)
Don Curzio, a notary	(tenor)

LIBRETTO by Lorenzo da Ponte, based on the play *Le Mariage de Figaro* by Beaumarchais

TIME: Mid-eighteenth century

PLACE: Count Almaviva's castle of Aguas-Frescas, not far from Seville

FIRST PERFORMED in Vienna, 1 May, 1786, at the Burgtheater with Luisa Laschi (Countess), Ann [Nancy] Storace (Susanna), Dorotea Bussani (Cherubino), Maria Mandini (Marcellina), Anna Gottlieb (Barbarina), Stefano Mandini (Count), Francesco Benucci (Figaro), Francesco Bussani (Bartolo and Antonio), Michael Kelly (Don Basilio and Don Curzio).

Le nozze di Figaro

I

A FEW MONTHS after Leopold Mozart returned to Salzburg from his stay in Vienna, he began to grumble in letters to his daughter that her brother had not written to him for some time. In November, however, he was able to tell Nannerl that 'At last I have received a letter of twelve lines from your brother, dated November 2nd. He asks forgiveness because he is up to the eyes in work on his opera *Le nozze di Figaro*.' Leopold continues: 'I know the piece. It is a most tiresome play, and the translation from the French will certainly have to be altered a great deal if it is to be effective as an opera. God grant that the libretto may be a success. I have no doubt about the music. But there will be a great deal of running about and discussing things before he gets the libretto exactly the way he wants it. No doubt he has gone on postponing matters, as is his charming habit, and has let time slip by. He must now get down to serious work, for Count Rosenberg is prodding him.'[1]

The librettist was Lorenzo da Ponte, whom Mozart had met through Baron Wetzlar two years earlier. At that time, Da Ponte had indicated that he would be happy to write a libretto for Mozart. But it was Mozart who suggested Beaumarchais' play *Le Mariage de Figaro* as a subject, as Da Ponte makes clear in his *Memoirs*, written many years later:

> I could see that the sweep of [Mozart's] genius demanded a subject of great scope, something multiform, sublime. In conversation with me one day in this connection, he asked me whether I could easily make an opera from a comedy by Beaumarchais, *Le Mariage de Figaro*. I liked the suggestion very much, and promised to write him one. A few days previous, the Emperor had forbidden the company at the German theatre to perform that same comedy, which was too licentiously written, he thought, for a self-respecting audience: how then propose it to him for an opera? Baron Wetzlar offered, with noble generosity, to pay me a handsome price for the words, and then, should we fail of production in Vienna, to have the opera presented in London, or in France. But I refused this offer, and proposed writing the words and the music secretly, and awaiting then a favourable opportunity to show them to the Directors, or to the Emperor himself, for which step I

---

[1] Letter of 11 November, 1785.

confidently volunteered to assume the responsibility. Martini[1] was the only one who learned of the beautiful secret from me, and he, with laudable high-mindedness, and because of his esteem for Mozart, agreed that I should delay working for him until I should have finished the libretto for *Figaro*.

I set to work accordingly, and as fast as I wrote the words, Mozart set them to music. In six weeks everything was in order. Mozart's lucky star ordained that the Opera should fail of scores at just that moment. Seizing that opportunity, I went, without saying a word to a living person, to offer *Figaro* to the Emperor.

'What?' he said. 'Don't you know that Mozart, though a wonder at instrumental music, has written only one opera, and nothing remarkable at that?'

'Yes, Sire,' I replied quietly, 'but without Your Majesty's clemency I would have written but one drama in Vienna!'

'That may be true,' he answered, 'but this *Mariage de Figaro* – I have just forbidden the German troupe to use it!'

'Yes, Sire,' I rejoined, 'but I was writing an opera, not a comedy. I had to omit many scenes and cut others quite considerably. I have omitted or cut anything that might offend good taste or public decency at a performance over which the Sovereign Majesty might preside. The music, I may add, as far as I may judge of it, seems to me marvellously beautiful.'

'Good! If that be the case, I will rely on your good taste as to the music and on your wisdom as to the morality. Send the score to the copyist.'

I ran straight to Mozart, but I had not yet finished imparting the good news when a page of the Emperor's came and handed him a note, wherein he was commanded to present himself at once at the Palace, bringing his score. He obeyed the royal order, allowed the Emperor to hear various selections, which pleased him immensely, or, to tell the truth without exaggeration, astounded him. Joseph had an exquisite taste in music, as indeed he had in all the arts. The great success this opera had throughout the civilized world was soon to show that he had not been mistaken in his judgment.[2]

There is no reason to imagine Da Ponte's *Memoirs* more reliable than anyone else's. He was, after all, writing in America at least twenty years later, and he had a greater than normal propensity to exaggerate. But, allowing that his account of conversations with the Emperor may be highly coloured, his story is no doubt true in outline, and does reveal to us that the choice of subject was Mozart's and not Da Ponte's. His claim that the opera took only six weeks to write and compose is less likely to be true. We know that Mozart was already at work on *Figaro* at the beginning of November, 1785, and that he interrupted it to compose the music for *Der Schauspieldirektor* in the second half of January, 1786. Mozart's own catalogue states that he finished the opera on 29 April,

---

[1] The Spanish composer Vincente Martin y Soler (1754–1806), three of whose operas were written and produced in Vienna between 1785 and 1787 with libretti by Da Ponte (see p. 232).

[2] *Memoirs* of Lorenzo da Ponte.

1786, but this must mean simply that he completed the Overture at this late date, for the first performance of *Figaro* was given on 1 May.

It is unlikely that the Emperor thought Mozart had composed only one opera (presumably *Die Entführung aus dem Serail*). He would surely have known of *Idomeneo*, even if he had forgotten the *Finta semplice* imbroglio of seventeen years earlier.

Joseph II had, as Da Ponte relates, forbidden the National Theatre to perform Beaumarchais' *Le Mariage de Figaro*. Mozart's old friend, Emanuel Schikaneder, had brought his company to the Kärntnertor Theater and announced a performance of *Die Hochzeit des Figaro*, a translation by Johann Rautenstrauch of Beaumarchais' play, on 3 February, 1785. Three days before the performance, Joseph II sent the following note to Count Johann Anton Pergen, President of the Government of Lower Austria: 'I hear that the well-known comedy *Le Mariage de Figaro* is said to have been proposed for the Kärntnertor Theater in a German translation. Since this piece contains a great deal that is objectionable, I shall expect the Censor either to reject it altogether or at least require such alterations to be made that he can be held responsible for the performance of the play and the impression it may make.'[1]

The performance did not take place, but the play was published in Vienna later in the year, the translator dedicating the printed work to the memory of the two hundred ducats he had lost through the Emperor's ban!

Mozart's work on Da Ponte's libretto, *Le nozze di Figaro*, was interrupted not only by *Der Schauspieldirektor* but also by the composition of two more piano concertos, the A major K. 488 and C minor K. 491, both of them masterpieces, and the performance by aristocratic amateurs of *Idomeneo*, for which he provided additional music (see p. 150). Finally (and, according to Da Ponte, despite the intrigues of his rival the librettist Casti),[2] *Figaro* was staged on 1 May, 1786, at the Burgtheater. Da Ponte in his *Memoirs* describes how at the last moment he thwarted Count Rosenberg's attempt to deprive the opera of its ballet:

There was a certain Bussani,[3] who had a post as inspector of costumes and stage properties, and was jack-at-all-trades save at that of an honest man. Having heard that I had woven a ballet into my *Figaro*, he ran forthwith to the Count [Rosenberg] and in a tone of amazed disapprobation cried:

[1] The Emperor's note is preserved in the State Archives, Vienna.
[2] In a letter to Nannerl, dated 28 April, 1786, Leopold asserted that 'there has been a surprisingly strong cabal against [the opera]'. He continued: 'Salieri and all his adherents will move heaven and earth against it. Herr and Madame Duschek told me recently that my son met with such violent opposition because of his extraordinary talent and ability.'
[3] It seems hardly likely that this could be Francesco Bussani who sang both Bartolo and Antonio in the first performance of *Figaro*, but he is otherwise unidentifiable.

'Excellency, the *signor poeta* has put a ballet in his opera!'

The Count sent for me at once and, frowning darkly, launched into this dialogue, a fine counterpart of the one I had with his Barnabotic Excellency:

'So, the *signor poeta* has used a ballet in *Figaro*?'

'Yes, Excellency.'

'The *signor poeta* does not know that the Emperor has forbidden dancing in his theatre?'

'No, Excellency.'

'In that case, *signor poeta*, I will tell you so now.'

'Yes, Excellency.'

'And I will tell you further, *signor poeta*, that you must take it out!'

His '*signor poeta*' had a significant tone of its own which gave the phrase the meaning of 'Signor Jack-ass' or something of the sort. But my 'Yes, Excellency' and 'No, Excellency,' had their innuendo too.

'No, Excellency.'

'Have you the libretto with you?'

'Yes, Excellency.'

'Where is the scene with the dance?'

'Here it is, Excellency.'

'This is the way we do it.'

Saying which he took two sheets of my manuscript, laid them carefully on the fire and returned the libretto me:

'You see, *signor poeta*, that I can do anything!'

And he honoured me with a second *Vade*.

I hurried to meet Mozart. On hearing such a story from me, he was desperate – he suggested going to the Count, giving Bussani a beating, appealing to Caesar, withdrawing the score. It was a task for me to calm him. But at length I begged him to allow me just two days' time, and to leave everything to me.

The dress rehearsal of the opera was to be held that day. I went in person to invite the Sovereign, and he promised to attend at the hour set. And in fact he came, and with him half the aristocracy of Vienna. The Abbé Casti likewise was in the royal party.

The first act went off amid general applause, but at the end of it[1] there comes a pantomimic scene between the Count and Susanna, during which the orchestra plays and the dance takes place. But the way His Excellency Can-All had adapted the scene, all one could see was the Count and Susanna gesticulating and, there being no music, it all looked like a puppet show.

'What's all this?' proclaimed the Emperor to Casti, who was sitting behind him.

'You must ask the poet that!' replied the Abbé, with a significant smile.

His Majesty, therefore, sent for me; but instead of replying to the question put to me, I handed him my manuscript, in which I had restored the scene. The Sovereign glanced through it, and asked why the dancers had not appeared. My silence gave him to understand there was some intrigue behind it all. He turned to the Count, asked him to explain; and he, spluttering, said that the ballet had been left out because the opera had no dancers.

'But can't they be procured at some other theatre?' asked His Majesty.

[1] Da Ponte must mean the end of Act III.

Rosenberg answered that they could.

'Very well, let Da Ponte have as many as he needs.'

In less than half an hour twenty-four dancers, what with supers, had come in. By the end of the second act the scene which had been suppressed was in shape to be tried; and the Emperor cried:

'Oh, now it's all right!'[1]

The two minor tenor roles of Basilio and Don Curzio were doubled at the première by a twenty-three-year-old Irish singer, Michael Kelly, who was engaged at the Italian Opera in Vienna from 1783 to 1786 under the name of Michele Ochelli. His *Reminiscences*, published in London in 1826, and written by Theodore Hook largely at Kelly's dictation, contain the tenor's account of the rehearsals and première of *Figaro*:

Of all the performers in this opera at that time, but one survives – myself. It was allowed that never was opera stronger cast. I have seen it performed at different periods in other countries, and well too, but no more to compare with its original performance than light is to darkness. All the original performers had the advantage of the instruction of the composer, who transfused into their minds his inspired meaning. I shall never forget his little animated countenance when lighted up with the glowing rays of genius: it is as impossible to describe it as it would be to paint sunbeams.

I called on him one evening; he said to me, 'I have just finished a little duet for my opera; you shall hear it.' He sat down to the piano, and we sang it. I was delighted with it, and the musical world will give me credit for being so, when I mention the duet, 'Crudele perchè finora farmi languire così.' A more delicious *morceau* never was penned by man, and it has often been a source of pleasure to me to have been the first to have heard it, and to have sung it with its greatly gifted composer.

I remember at the first rehearsal of the full band, Mozart was on the stage with his crimson pelisse and gold-laced cocked-hat, giving the time of the music to the orchestra. Figaro's song, 'Non più andrai, farfallone amoroso,' Benucci gave with the greatest animation and power of voice. I was standing close to Mozart, who, *sotto voce*, was repeating, 'Bravo! Bravo! Benucci'; and when Benucci came to the fine passage, 'Cherubino, alla vittoria, alla gloria militar,' which he gave out with stentorian lungs, the effect was electricity itself, for the whole of the performers on the stage, and those in the orchestra, as if actuated by one feeling of delight, vociferated 'Bravo! Bravo! Maestro! Viva, viva, grande Mozart.' Those in the orchestra I thought would never have ceased applauding, by beating the bows of their violins against the music-desks. The little man acknowledged, by repeated obeisances, his thanks for the distinguished mark of enthusiastic applause bestowed upon him.

The same meed of approbation was given to the finale at the end of the first act; that piece of music alone, in my humble opinion, if he had never composed anything else good, would have stamped him as the greatest

[1] Da Ponte: *Memoirs.*

master of his art. In the *sestetto*, in the second act, which was Mozart's favourite piece of the whole opera, I had a very conspicuous part as the Stuttering Judge.[1] All through the piece I was to stutter; but in the *sestetto* Mozart requested I would not, for, if I did, I should spoil his music. I told him that, although it might appear very presumptuous in a lad like me to differ with him on this point, I *did*, and was sure the way in which I intended to introduce the stuttering would not interfere with the other parts, but produce an effect; besides, it certainly was not in nature that I should stutter all through the part, and when I came to the *sestetto* speak plain; and, after that piece of music was over, return to stuttering; and I added (apologizing, at the same time, for my apparent want of deference and respect in placing my opinion in opposition to that of the great Mozart) that unless I was allowed to perform the part as I wished, I would not perform it at all.

Mozart at last consented that I should have my own way, but doubted the success of the experiment. Crowded houses proved that nothing ever on the stage produced a more powerful effect; the audience were convulsed with laughter, in which Mozart himself joined. The Emperor repeatedly cried out 'Bravo!' and the piece was loudly applauded and encored. When the opera was over, Mozart came on the stage to me, and, shaking me by both hands, said, 'Bravo! young man; I feel obliged to you; and acknowledge you to have been in the right, and myself in the wrong.' There was certainly a risk run, but I felt within myself I could give the effect I wished, and the event proved that I was not mistaken.

I have seen the opera in London and elsewhere, and never saw the judge portrayed as a stutterer, and the scene was often totally omitted. I played it as a stupid old man, though at the time I was a beardless stripling. At the end of the opera, I thought the audience would never have done applauding and calling for Mozart; almost every piece was encored, which prolonged it to nearly the length of two operas, and induced the Emperor to issue an order on the second representation that no piece of music should be encored. Never was anything more complete than the triumph of Mozart, and his *Nozze di Figaro*, to which numerous overflowing audiences bore witness.[2]

The performance on 1 May was received with great enthusiasm by a crowded house, and many numbers had to be encored. At the second performance on 3 May, five pieces were encored, and at the third on 8 May there were seven encores, and one duet had to be sung three times. The opera, it seemed, was an immense success. Mozart had conducted the first two performances from the harpsichord, after which the conductor and composer, Joseph Weigl, who was then only twenty, took over for the remaining seven of the season. The day after the third performance, the Emperor addressed a memorandum to Count Rosenberg: 'To prevent the excessive duration of the operas, without

[1] This is not entirely accurate. The finale Kelly refers to is that of Act II, and the sextet is in Act III. Perhaps the opera was first performed in two acts (four scenes), with only one interval.
[2] From Michael Kelly's *Reminiscences* (London, 1826).

however prejudicing the fame often sought by opera singers from the repetition of vocal pieces, I deem the enclosed notice to the public [that no piece for more than single voice is to be repeated] to be the most reasonable expedient. You will therefore have some posters printed to this effect. The same ruling is to be observed forthwith by the German *Singspiel* company, and notice to this effect to be given.'[1]

It is thought that the Emperor was persuaded to issue this edict by persons who were jealous of Mozart's success, and this may well be so. But it is difficult to give credence to Michael Kelly's story, which implies that the Emperor had banned encores of solo arias, which he had clearly not done:

> One morning, while we were rehearsing in the grand salon of the palace, His Majesty accompanied by Prince Rosenberg entered the salon, and addressing himself to Storace, Mandini and Benucci, said: 'I dare say you are all pleased that I have desired there shall be no more encores; to have your songs so often repeated must be a great fatigue, and very distressing to you.' Storace replied: 'It is indeed, Sire, very distressing, very much so.' The other two bowed, as if they were of the same opinion. I was close to His Majesty, and said boldly to him: 'Do not believe them, Sire, they all like to be encored. At least, I am sure I always do.' His Majesty laughed, and I believe he thought there was more truth in my assertion than in theirs.[2]

However popular *Figaro* may initially have been, its success appears to have been decidedly eclipsed by Martin y Soler's *Una cosa rara* which, upon its production in November, was so wildly acclaimed that *Figaro* was immediately forgotten. There were no further performances of Mozart's opera in Vienna for the next two years.

Two days after the première of *Figaro*, the publisher Torricella inserted an advertisement in the *Wiener Zeitung*:

> *Le Nozze di Figaro. Die Hochzeit des Figaro.*
> Since I am so fortunate as to be able already to supply the highly estimable public with this beautiful as well as ingenious work by the celebrated Kapellmeister Mozart, I wished not to withhold from the respected lovers of music any longer the news that the score of the entire opera can be obtained to order from my establishment at the cheapest possible price.
> Acquainted with the estimable public's excellent taste, I have engaged experienced musicians to make a pianoforte score as well as one for a quartet of two violins, viola and bass. Amateurs of music will be able to acquire these also very shortly. Those who wish to purchase the opera in one form or another are therefore requested to enter their names in good time, so that they may be served as expeditiously as possible with this opera which is already greatly in demand in the neighbouring Imperial and Royal states as well as abroad.

[1] Vienna, State Archives.   [2] Kelly: *Reminiscences*.

Christoph Torricella. Purveyor and publisher of Art, Engravings and Music, in the Kohlmarkt next to Milani's Coffee House.

The two arrangements mentioned did not appear, but an arrangement of several numbers from the opera for wind ensemble was made by Johann Wendt, the second oboist in the orchestra. This was probably played by the Octet drawn from the Court orchestra, which formed the Emperor's chamber music ensemble. Wendt's arrangement of the Overture and fourteen numbers from the opera was not published until 1791.

An interesting review of the opera appeared in the *Wiener Realzeitung*, not immediately after the première, but in July, after several performances had been given:

> On Monday, 1 May, was performed at the Imperial and Royal National Court Theatre (for the first time) *Le Nozze di Figaro. Die Hochzeit des Figaro*. An Italian Singspiel in four acts. The music is by Herr Kapellmeister Mozart.
>
> 'What is *not allowed* to be said these days, is sung' one may say with *Figaro*.[1] This piece, which was *prohibited* in Paris and not allowed to be performed here as a *comedy* either in a bad or in a good translation, we have at last had the felicity to see represented as an *opera*. It will be seen that we are doing better than the French.
>
> Herr Mozart's music was generally admired by connoissuers already at the first performance, if I except only those whose self-love and conceit will not allow them to find merit in anything not written by themselves.
>
> The *public*, however (and this often happens to the public), did not really know on the first day where it stood. It heard many a *bravo* from unbiased connoisseurs, but obstreperous louts in the uppermost storey exerted their hired lungs with all their might to deafen singers and audience alike with their St! and Pst!; and consequently opinions were divided at the end of the piece.
>
> Apart from that, it is true that the first performance was none of the best, owing to the difficulty of the composition.
>
> But now, after several performances, one would be subscribing either to the *cabal* or to *tastelessness* if one were to maintain that Herr *Mozart*'s music is anything but a masterpiece of art.
>
> It contains so many beauties, and such a wealth of ideas, as can be drawn only from the source of innate genius.
>
> Some journalists liked to tell that Herr Mozart's opera had not pleased at all. It may be guessed what sort of correspondents they must be who recklessly publish such obvious lies. I believe it to be sufficiently well known that it was precisely the third performance and the frequent demand for encores to which it gave rise that led to the imperial *decree* which a few days later publicly announced *that it would in future be forbidden to repeat* in an opera any piece written for more than a single voice.[2]

---

[1] The quotation is from Act I of Beaumarchais' *Le Barbier de Séville*.

[2] *Wiener Realzeitung*, 11 July, 1786.

In addition to Francesco Benucci as Figaro, with whom Mozart was impressed, and who was to be Guglielmo in *Così fan tutte* and Leporello in the first Viennese performances of *Don Giovanni*, the cast included several of the finest Italian singers in Vienna as well as the English soprano Ann (Nancy) Storace as Susanna and the twelve-year-old Anna Gottlieb as Barbarina. Fräulein Gottlieb was to be the first Pamina in *Die Zauberflöte* five years later. That assiduous Viennese opera-goer Count Zinzendorf thought 'Mozart's music singular, hands without head',[1] and confided to his diary after the first performance: 'the opera bored me.'[2] But a Hungarian poet, Franz Kazinczy, wrote that 'the joy which this music causes is so far removed from all sensuality that one cannot speak of it. Where could words be found that are worthy to describe it?'[3]

In the winter of 1786, *Le nozze di Figaro* was produced in Prague; according to the press, no other opera had ever caused such a sensation. Hearing of its great success, Mozart went to Prague in January, 1787, attended one performance of *Figaro* and conducted another, and also gave a concert which included his Symphony in D major K. 504, later known as the Prague Symphony. The city took Mozart to its heart, and entertained him royally. He wrote to his pupil Baron Gottfried von Jacquin that, at one of the balls he attended,

> I looked on with the greatest pleasure while all these people flew about in sheer delight to the music of my *Figaro*, arranged for quadrilles and waltzes. For here they talk of nothing but *Figaro*. Nothing is played, sung or whistled but *Figaro*. No opera is drawing audiences like *Figaro*. Nothing, nothing but *Figaro*. Certainly a great honour for me.[4]

It is no wonder that Mozart responded as warmly to Prague as Prague to him. He was to return there twice to stage new operas.

II

By birth Lorenzo da Ponte was Jewish: his real name was Emmanuele Conogliano. His father was a leather merchant in Ceneda (now the town of Vittorio Veneto) who, when he was a widower of forty, fell in love again with a Christian girl of sixteen. So that he could marry her he had himself and his three sons received into the Roman Catholic Church, and as was the custom the family took its new name from the bishop who performed the ceremony.

Lorenzo da Ponte, as he became, was then only fourteen, but he already displayed a precocious appetite for literature and for amorous adventure. Despite these inclinations his father decided he should study for the priesthood. Ten years later, as the Abbe da Ponte, he went to

---

[1] Zinzendorf's Diary, 4 July, 1786.   [2] Ibid., 1 May, 1786.
[3] From the *Autobiography of Franz Kazinczy* (2nd edition, Budapest, 1879).
[4] Letter of 15 January, 1787.

Venice and embarked on a career of debauchery. One beautiful woman succeeded another, escapade followed escapade. Da Ponte became a friend of the famous adventurer Casanova, survived various scandals, but eventually found himself facing a serious charge of seducing a married woman, living with her outside the sacraments, and procreating illegitimate children with her. To avoid arrest Da Ponte fled across the border into Austria. Arriving in the then Austrian town of Gorizia he put up at the first inn he found and immediately, if we are to believe him, captivated the proprietress.

Da Ponte stayed on in Gorizia long enough to become the leading figure in its literary and artistic life. But the assorted charms of this small Austrian provincial town were too few for him. When he heard there was a chance of obtaining a post at the Court Theatre in Dresden he left. But Dresden did not suit him either, and in 1782, armed with a letter of introduction to the celebrated composer Antonio Salieri, Da Ponte arrived in Vienna.

Salieri was a composer with great influence in the circles in Vienna where it mattered. When Da Ponte presented himself Salieri passed him on to Count von Rosenberg, Grand Chamberlain of the Court and Director of the Imperial Theatres, and through him Da Ponte eventually gained an audience with Joseph II.

The Emperor made Da Ponte Court Poet and Librettist to the Imperial Theatre. Fortunately for him, he had arrived in Vienna at a time when Italian opera had become the fashion. But his first attempt to write a libretto, for Salieri, was a humiliating failure. His second attempt, however, this time for the Spanish composer Martini (or Martin y Soler), was more successful. As librettist and translator, Da Ponte was in considerable demand, though it was largely for hackwork. Da Ponte himself claimed later that

> There were only two composers in Vienna deserving of my esteem: Martini, at the time the composer most favoured by Joseph II, and Mozart. Though gifted with talents superior perhaps to those of any other composer in the world, past, present or future, Mozart had, thanks to the intrigues of his rivals, never been able to exercise his divine genius in Vienna, and was living there unknown and obscure, like a priceless jewel buried in the bowels of the earth and hiding the refulgent excellence of its splendours. I can never remember without exultation and complacency that it was to my perseverance and firmness alone that Europe and the world in great part owe the exquisite vocal compositions of that admirable genius.

Though Da Ponte's claim is manifestly untrue, he certainly was largely instrumental in persuading Joseph II to accept Le Mariage de Figaro as an operatic subject. He further collaborated with Mozart on Don Giovanni and Così fan tutte. One of Da Ponte's mistresses in Vienna was the Italian soprano Adriana del Bene, usually known as 'La Ferrarese', since she came from Ferrara.[1] Her moral reputation was dubious, and no one appears to have thought very highly of her as singer and actress. Yet the rôle of Fiordiligi in *Così fan tutte* was written for her.

Da Ponte's eventual fall from grace in Vienna was due very largely to his championship of 'La Ferrarese'. Infatuated with her and unable to accept that she was simply not a good enough singer, he importuned everyone on her behalf. He is even said to have gone so far as to write anonymous letters to the new singers engaged for the opera, discouraging them from coming to Vienna.

The Emperor Joseph II died and was succeeded on the throne by his brother Leopold. Da Ponte who could now no longer count on royal protection began to look for work elsewhere. After a few months in Trieste, where he renewed his friendship with Casanova, Da Ponte made his way to London with Nancy Grabe, a girl he had met in Trieste, and whom he may have married, though there is no proof that he did.

For a time, Da Ponte flourished as a librettist, translator, and poet in London, and after four years he was sent on a tour of Italy to engage new singers for the opera. On his arrival back in London, Da Ponte's luck changed, and he fell into debt. It was the year 1800 and he was fifty-one. He began a new career as a London bookseller and publisher. But five years later he was again close to bankruptcy. His wife Nancy had taken their four children to America to visit relatives, and some months later Da Ponte made a sudden decision to join them there. He was never to see Europe again.

When he arrived in Philadelphia after an unpleasant two months at sea, he realized there was no prospect of resuming his career as an operatic librettist, because there was as yet no opera at all in America. Da Ponte went into business, first as a grocer, then as a teacher of Italian and Latin, later as a grocer again. His trade extended: he became distiller, milliner, and transport agent in the small town of Sunbury in Pennsylvania.

After seven years, he went to New York as a teacher; he and his wife added to their income by running a boarding-house for his students. He acquired a new local fame as a disseminator of Italian literature and culture in the New World. In his old age, he became the first Professor of Italian Literature at Columbia College. The appointment was unpaid: Da Ponte's only earnings were the fees paid by the students attending his lectures. But in November, 1825, when he was seventy-six, something happened which gave him immense delight – the very first season of Italian opera in America opened in New York with some of the finest European singers of the day, including Manuel Vicente Garcia and his

---

[1] 'La Ferrarese's' real name was Adriana Gabrielli (*c.* 1755–*c.* 1799). She sang in Vienna between 1788 and 1791, and subsequently in Warsaw and Venice, where she is thought to have ended her days.

daughter Madame Malibran. Among the operas performed was *Don Giovanni.*

Eight years later, now in his mid-eighties, the indefatigable Da Ponte managed to persuade the people of New York to build their own opera house, raised one hundred and fifty thousand dollars for the purpose, and in November, 1833, opened the New York Opera House, under his own management. It was not only the first New York opera house, but probably the first ever to be built in North America. Da Ponte lived on for another four years, publishing the occasional poem or pamphlet, but still, now without success, seeking pupils as well.

On 16 August, 1838, his doctor informed Da Ponte's friends and family that the old man's life was drawing to a close, and many of them assembled to pay their last respects. One of his pupils who was present wrote:

> It was one of those afternoons of waning summer, when the mellow sunset foretells approaching autumn. The old poet's magnificent head lay upon a sea of pillows, and the conscious eye still shed its beam of regard upon all around him. Besides several of his countrymen there were assembled some members of the Italian opera company, who knelt for a farewell blessing at the bedside of their expiring bard. All wept as the patriarch bade them farewell and implored a blessing on their common country.

The following evening, 17 August, 1838, Lorenzo da Ponte died at the age of eighty-nine.

III

Pierre Augustin Caron de Beaumarchais was born, the son of a master watchmaker, in Paris in 1732. Though largely self-educated, he read widely in French and English literature. It was his intention to go into his father's business, and indeed he did so with such success that by the age of twenty-two he had become watchmaker to the King. Purchasing an office in the Royal Household, he married the widow of his predecessor in that office, and acquired the right to add 'de Beaumarchais' to his family name of Caron because of some property belonging to his wife. The marriage did not last; nor, apparently, did Beaumarchais' vocation as a watchmaker, for by the age of twenty-seven he is to be found teaching the harp to the daughters of Louis XV. An astute speculator, he managed to acquire sufficient wealth to purchase a secretaryship in the Royal Household, while still in his twenties.

In 1764, now aged thirty-two, Beaumarchais travelled to Spain. His ostensible purpose was to defend the honour of his sister who had been jilted by a writer named Clavijo in Madrid (a curious incident, around which Goethe was to write his play, *Clavigo,* ten years later), but he also had important business interests to look after, for he was at this time involved in projects to sell slaves to the Spanish colony of Louisiana, to supply the Spanish army with munitions, and the heir to the Spanish throne with a French mistress. Returning to France, Beaumarchais wrote a play, *Eugénie*, which made use of the episode of his sister and Clavijo. *Eugénie* was successfully staged by the Comédie Française in 1767, and two years later was produced in London by David Garrick as *The School for Rakes*.

Beaumarchais had meanwhile married another rich widow, but the marriage did not last, and a number of business reverses led him into law-suits which dragged on for several years, and which inspired him to write a series of *Mémoires* accusing the entire judicial system of corruption. He finally emerged from the legal process beaten, bankrupt, branded as a criminal and deprived of his civil rights. Undeterred, Beaumarchais continued to attack his accusers and enemies, found time and energy to write his play, *The Barber of Seville*, and in due course managed to rehabilitate himself, though not until 1778. But before then he visited London on two occasions on secret missions: once to obtain and suppress certain scandalous documents relating to Madame Dubarry, and later on business involving the transvestite spy, the Chevalier d'Éon. A life crowded with incident.

Le Barbier de Séville was first conceived by Beaumarchais as an *opéra comique*, in which form it was rejected. (The playwright, it will be remembered, was also something of a musician, and had composed the music for several songs in the libretto.) After his return from London, he re-wrote his *opéra comique* as a five-act play. It was performed, failed, was re-shaped into four acts and produced again two days later at the Comédie Française, and has been in the repertory of that theatre ever since. Five years later, it was used as the libretto of an opera by Paisiello, and of course much later, in 1816, it was to become the basis of Rossini's *Barbiere di Siviglia*.

In 1776, the year following the première of *Le Barbier de Séville*, Beaumarchais raised a large capital sum and formed a company to supply arms and munitions to the American colonials fighting the British, and managed to persuade the French Government secretly to support his enterprise. At the same time, his quarrel with the actors of the Comédie Française, which he brought to a successful outcome, led to the placing of authors' rights on an equitable legal basis. When Voltaire died in 1778, Beaumarchais purchased all his manuscripts, and set up his own publishing house in Germany to produce a definitive edition of the great man's works. He had also been at work on a sequel to *Le Barbier de Séville*, a play in which the barber Figaro is now a valet in the service of that Count Almaviva whom he had helped to win Rosina from her guardian. *La Folle Journée, ou Le Mariage de Figaro* was produced by the Comédie Française in 1784, but only after a number of alterations and modifications to its plot had been made, and permission for its performance had been obtained from Louis XVI himself. The French public acclaimed the play which was an unprecedented success and ran for sixty-eight performances. But, even at the height of his triumph, Beaumarchais found himself in trouble again. For having made a remark referring to the difficulties he had experienced in getting his play staged, a remark thought to be critical of the King and Queen, he was imprisoned for five days in a house of correction for juvenile delinquents!

Le Mariage de Figaro was immediately translated into English and German, and performed abroad. In 1786, its author married for the third time. This marriage endured. His wife, by whom he had had a daughter nine years before they married, was to survive him. Three years after *Figaro*, in 1787, Beaumarchais collaborated with Mozart's rival Salieri in an opera, *Tarare*, which was produced with great success at the Paris Opéra, and even more successfully in Vienna the following year in an Italian adaptation by Da Ponte. It was to prove Beaumarchais' last triumph, for the wealth he had accrued in these latter years was to lead to his downfall as France headed inexorably towards revolution, a revolution Beaumarchais had played his small but vital part in helping to bring about. After seeing many of his old acquaintances denounced and guillotined, he was finally forced into exile, and his wife, sister and daughter thrown into prison. In 1796 he returned to France, where the final play of his trilogy about the Almavivas, *La mère coupable*, was produced the following year. Beaumarchais died of apoplexy in 1799, at the age of seventy-seven.

Le Barbier de Séville, Le Mariage de Figaro and *La mère coupable*, though not planned as such, constitute a kind of *Almaviva Saga*, following the relationship of Rosina and Count Almaviva through courtship, marriage and disillusion. In the first play (like *Figaro*, known to audiences outside France mainly in its operatic metamorphosis), the barber Figaro helps young Almaviva in his plan to marry Rosina against the wishes of her guardian, Dr Bartolo. The action is carried forward wittily and swiftly within the framework of light-hearted, inconsequential comedy. The sequel, *Le Mariage de Figaro*, written some years later, has changed its tone. Basically still a comedy, it is a less farcical, more serious comedy than *Le Barbier de Séville*. Life is more earnest after marriage than it was before, and Beaumarchais had also had plenty of opportunity to become a sadder and wiser man. Also, France was moving nearer to cataclysmic social change. Figaro's comments on class differences have more edge in the second play than in the first, and his jokes are more pointed. *The Guilty Mother* (1796), one of Napoleon's favourite plays, is the least successful of the three. The revolution is past, the Almavivas have survived and, twenty years later, are now plain 'Monsieur et Madame Almaviva'. They have sold their estate at Aguas-Frescas, three leagues from Seville, where the events of *Le Mariage de Figaro* took place. The Count's eldest son has been killed in a duel, and it is discovered that his second son, Léon, is in fact the offspring of the Countess and Chérubin. (The Countess is the guilty mother of the title.) Chérubin, meanwhile, has died on the field of battle, 'al concerto di tromboni, di bombardi, di cannoni' as Figaro had jokingly almost prophesied.[1] The count has brought his own illegitimate daughter, Florestine, into the household, as his ward, and she and Léon are lovers. Figaro's cunning is still useful to the family, for he is able to prevent an Irish villain from marrying Almaviva's ward and getting hold of his three million francs' worth of Mexican gold shares! The tone of the play is *larmoyante*, and its situations are as contrived as its dialogue is stilted. *Le Mariage de Figaro*, the central play of the trilogy, is by far the most successful of the three, and certainly the most influential.

Da Ponte's libretto for Mozart's opera is generally acknowledged to be a masterpiece of the librettist's art. The one criticism that is levelled against it is that it blunts the revolutionary edge of Beaumarchais' original. Of course it does: Da Ponte himself was the first to admit this.[2]

In a Preface to the first edition of his libretto (which was printed in both Italian and German), Da Ponte describes his intentions quite clearly:

The duration prescribed by general usage for dramatic performances, the given number of characters to which one is confined, as well as certain other considerations of prudence, morality, place and public constituted the reasons why I have not made a translation of this excellent comedy, but rather an adaptation or, let us say, an extract.

For this purpose I was obliged to reduce the original sixteen characters to eleven, two of which may be performed by a single person, and to omit not only an entire act but also many extremely effective scenes and a number of those good jokes with which the original play teems. In place of these I have had to insert canzonettes, arias, choruses and other forms of words susceptible of being set to music: things which can be managed only in verse, and never in prose. In spite, however, of every effort and of all the zealous care the composer and I exercised in order to be brief, the opera will not be one of the shortest to have been performed on our stages. We hope that sufficient excuse for this will be found in the variety of the dramatic strands by which the drama is woven together, the vastness and scope of the same, the multiplicity of musical numbers necessary in order not to leave the performers idle, and also in order to avoid the boredom and monotony of long recitatives, and to paint faithfully and in varied colours the different emotions that are aroused. Above all, we hope to have realized our special

---

[1] 'To the music of trumpets, shells and cannon' (in Figaro's 'Non più andrai' which ends Act I of Mozart's opera).

[2] See also p. 224.

desire to offer a new kind of entertainment to a public of such refined taste and such good judgment.[1]

To read Da Ponte's libretto alongside Beaumarchais' play is to realize that he was forced to emasculate the play in order to bring it down to manageable length for setting to music. This was to be expected. Nor is it surprising that passages of revolutionary sentiment which would have offended the Austrian Emperor were expunged. Clearly, Da Ponte's *Figaro*, lacking much of Beaumarchais' detail of plot, his social and legal satire, and even some of his characters, is a work with lesser resonances than its French original. It is also more tightly-knit, less rambling, as befits an opera libretto. Those critics who bemoan the loss of the revolutionary wind which sweeps through Beaumarchais are as misguided as those who proclaim, on the other hand, that the opera itself is revolutionary in a political sense (it is not even revolutionary in musical-dramatic terms, but a logical development from earlier eighteenth-century opera). I can even recall reading a programme note which described *Le nozze di Figaro* as 'a left-wing opera' thus belittling a great work of the creative imagination by forcing it into the narrow arena of twentieth-century politics.

The truth is that, despite the political uproar it caused on its opening night in Paris, Beaumarchais' play is not overtly political. It would even be going too far to describe it as a domestic comedy with political overtones. That Figaro held his master, Count Almaviva, in amiable contempt was a state of affairs which the playwright took for granted. After all, Figaro knew the Count well. Had he not helped him (in *Le Barbier de Séville*) to outwit Bartolo and marry Rosina? There is nothing in the play to fan the winds of revolution, nothing to incite the poor to rebellion. What there is in the play is a ready acceptance of the idea of equality which the upper class found shocking to contemplate when it was revealed to them in that performance of 27 April, 1784. It needs to be stressed today, in the face of facile political interpretations of Mozart's opera, that Beaumarchais' Figaro is no more revolutionary a character than the cheeky servants of *commedia dell' arte*. *Figaro* both as play and as opera is no political tract, nor is it an early example of 'women's lib.' propaganda: it deals with larger concerns, with life, love, dignity and self-respect. Some of Figaro's sharper retorts have been tempered by Da Ponte, and of course the librettist has had to shorten considerably Figaro's long soliloquy in Act V, which is the closest that character comes to articulating a political attitude. In the soliloquy, which begins 'O femme! femme! femme!, créature faible et décevante! Nul animal créé ne peut manquer à son instinct: le tien est-il donc de

---

[1] Copies of the Italian libretto are in the Library of Congress, Washington, and the Istituto Musicale, Florence. Two copies of the German libretto (a prose translation of Da Ponte's Italian) are in the City Library, Vienna.

tromper?',[1] Figaro describes his past life, revealing that he has followed several professions, among them veterinary surgeon, playwright, banker and barber before entering Almaviva's service. His experiences have left him cynical but essentially undefeated, and his summing-up is philosophical rather than political in tone:

O bizarre suite d'événements! Comment cela m'est-il arrivé? Pourquoi ces choses et non pas d'autres? Qui les a fixées sur ma tête? Forcé de parcourir la route où je suis entré sans le savoir, comme j'en sortirai sans le vouloir, je l'ai jonchée d'autant de fleurs que ma gaieté me l'a permis: encore je dis ma gaieté sans savoir si elle est à moi plus que le reste, ni même quel est ce *moi* dont je m'occupe: un assemblage informe de parties inconnues; puis un chétif être imbécile; un petit animal folâtre; un jeune homme ardent au plaisir, ayant tous les goûts pour jouir, faisant tous les métiers pour vivre; maître ici, valet là, selon qu'il plaît à la fortune; ambitieux par vanité, laborieux par nécessité, mais paresseux avec délices! Orateur selon le danger; poète par délassement; musicien par occasion; amoureux par folles bouffées; j'ai tout vu, tout fait, tout usé. Puis l'illusion s'est détruite, et, trop désabusé – désabusé! Suzon, Suzon, Suzon! que tu me donnes de tourments![2]

In the process of turning a five-act play into an opera libretto, Da Ponte had necessarily to make a large number of cuts. In order to avoid giving offence to the Emperor, he availed himself of the opportunity to delete several of Figaro's more impudent utterances, and also to dispense with several of Beaumarchais' minor characters. However, a comparison of the text of *Le nozze di Figaro* with that of *Le Mariage de Figaro* reveals that the librettist has dealt fairly with the playwright, has retained the feeling and flavour of the original play, and has indeed carried over into his libretto a good many lines which are not paraphrases or précis, but direct translations of the French.[3]

---

[1] O woman, woman, woman, weak and deceptive creature. No living being can fail to be true to its nature: is yours, then, deception?

[2] What a bizarre series of events! How did all this come to happen to me? Why these things and not others? Who is responsible for them? Forced to follow a road I set out upon in ignorance and which I shall leave involuntarily, I have strewn it with such flowers as my good humour has allowed. Again, I say my good humour without knowing whether it is mine any more than the rest, or even who this 'me' is that I'm concerned about: a formless assemblage of unknown parts, then a stupid, weak individual, a frisky little animal, a young man bent on pleasure and trying out everything. Master here, valet there, as it pleases fortune. Ambitious through vanity, industrious through necessity, but lazy by choice! Orator when I had to be, poet for relaxation, occasional musician, often crazy with love, I've seen everything, done everything, been everything. Then, my illusions destroyed, and too much disabused – disabused! Suzanne, Suzanne, Suzanne, what torments you make me suffer.

[3] Though irrelevant, it is interesting to note that the composer Carl Davis, who provided the music for a production of Beaumarchais' play by the National Theatre of Great Britain in 1974, discovered from the Beaumarchis family archives in Paris that

IV

As the play's sub-title, *La Folle Journée*, indicates, the action takes place during one day. The opera is in four acts, set in Count Almaviva's castle and its grounds, near Seville. Having been helped by the barber Figaro to win Rosina from her guardian Dr Bartolo in Seville, Almaviva has taken up residence with his bride on his estates, and has taken Figaro into his service as valet. Figaro has fallen in love with the Countess's maid, Susanna, and the 'crazy day' is, in fact, the day of their wedding.

When the curtain rises on Act I, Figaro is discovered in a partly furnished room, measuring the floor. Susanna is trying on her bridal headdress in front of a mirror. When she asks him why and what he is measuring, Figaro informs her that the Count intends to give them this room, and a splendid bed to furnish it. He is surprised to hear Susanna voice her suspicions of the Count's intentions, and points out that the room is very conveniently placed between the suites of the Count and the Countess. If the Countess should require Susanna in the night, a hop and a skip will take her to her mistress. Susanna's reply is that, should the Count send Figaro off on some errand or other, a similar hop and skip will bring his Lordship to her door. The Count, tiring of marital fidelity, has designs upon her, and has even enlisted the help of Don Basilio, the Countess's singing teacher, who is continually pressing his master's claim.

Susanna leaves to answer a summons from her mistress, while Figaro, stunned to learn of his master's duplicity, determines to outwit the Count and Basilio. As Figaro goes out, Dr Bartolo, the Countess's old ex-guardian, enters with the Almavivas' housekeeper, Marcellina, who years ago used to be Bartolo's housekeeper in Seville. They are plotting to prevent Figaro from marrying Susanna. Bartolo has a score to settle, for it was Figaro who (in *The Barber of Seville*) had helped Almaviva to steal his ward Rosina away from him. Marcellina needs no reason other than that she is an old maid in search of a husband. Figaro, who is young enough to be her son, is already in her clutches, for he had foolishly, and no doubt frivolously, signed a document agreeing to marry her if he was unable to repay a loan she had advanced. Marcellina reveals herself as a veritable Shylock, for she intends to hold the young man to his bond. Bartolo promises himself revenge on Figaro, even if he has to pore over all the law books in Seville (and he is a doctor of medicine, not of law!)

---

much of the music for the dances and marches in the first production of the play in 1784 was by the young Mozart. The pieces were no doubt used without the composer's knowledge, and may even have been chosen from music he composed in Paris during his stay there in 1778. Mozart's *conscious* connection with the Figaro plays also dates from his Paris stay of 1778, when he composed a set of variations, for piano (K. 354) on the arietta 'Je suis Lindor' from Beaumarchais' *Le Barbier de Séville*.

Title-pages from two early piano scores of *Die Zauberflöte*.

Stage designs by Karl Friedrich Schinkel for a production of
Die Zauberflöte in Berlin, 1829.

M.73a

M.73b

Further designs by Karl Friedrich Schinkel for *Die Zauberflöte*.

'Monostatos and Pamina' by Moritz von Schwind (1869). Part of
Schwind's fresco of scenes from *Die Zauberflöte* in a loggia of
the Vienna State Opera House.

and delights in the prospect of marrying off his old housekeeper to the man who had robbed him of the girl who is now the Countess Almaviva. As he leaves, Susanna enters. She and Marcellina lose no time in exchanging incivilities. Marcellina goes off in a bad temper, and the young page Cherubino arrives. He is in a state of adolescent despair, having been dismissed by the Count who had caught him making advances to the gardener's daugher, Barbarina. Cherubino is at the age when he fancies himself in love with virtually every woman he encounters, but his most serious, and most hopeless infatuation is with the Countess. Snatching from Susanna a ribbon because it belongs to his beloved Countess, he offers in return a song he has written, and tells Susanna to read it to every woman in the castle! All his waking thoughts, he confesses, are of love.

The Count is heard approaching, so Cherubino quickly hides behind an armchair. Upon entering, Almaviva, thinking himself alone with Susanna, beings to flirt with her. Reminding her that the King of Spain has appointed him Ambassador to England, and that she and Figaro will accompany him, he claims to be in love with her, and asks her to meet him that evening in the garden. At this moment, Basilio is heard outside the door, asking for the Count. Almaviva, not wishing to be caught alone with Susanna, hides behind the armchair, while Cherubino, unobserved by him, skips round the chair and sits in it. Susanna hastily covers him with a length of material. Basilio now enters and, acting upon orders, tells Susanna how greatly the Count loves her. Unfortunately, he goes on to gossip about Cherubino who, he says, is in love with both Susanna and the Countess. This indiscretion brings the Count from his hiding place. Now more determined than ever that the page shall leave the castle immediately, he begins to describe to Susanna and Basilio how he had discovered Cherubino with Barbarina. By way of demonstration, he whisks the cover off the chair, revealing a frightened Cherubino. Thinking that he has caught Susanna and Cherubino in a compromising situation, the Count is about to send Basilio to fetch Figaro, when Cherubino makes it clear to him that he has overheard all that has passed between him and Susanna.

Figaro now enters with a group of the Count's villagers who sing their master's praises for having abolished the long-established *droit de seigneur* by which a nobleman was entitled to the services, on her wedding night, of any girl on his estate. Figaro now asks Almaviva to perform the wedding ceremony. Playing for time, Almaviva repeats that the old *droit de seigneur* has gone forever, but that he needs time to organize a proper celebration for Figaro and Susanna. In an aside, he wonders where Marcellina can be, for she had mentioned to him something of her scheme to thwart the young lovers. Meanwhile, he finds it expedient to forgive Cherubino. Instead of dismissing him, the Count makes him an officer in his regiment, which he orders him to join immediately. Whispering to Cherubino that he must speak to him before he departs, Figaro then loudly pretends to mock the lad who will now have to exchange his amorous pursuits for the rigorous, indeed highly dangerous, life of the soldier.

Act II takes place later in the day, in the Countess's boudoir. After lamenting that she has lost the love of her husband, the Countess questions Susanna who has already informed her mistress of the Count's attempts to seduce her. Figaro enters, and confirms that, thwarted in his designs on Susanna, the Count is now threatening to retaliate by marrying Figaro off to Marcellina. The Countess, Susanna and Figaro together concoct a plan to trap the Count. He will receive a letter from Susanna, agreeing to an assignation in the garden that evening, but the appointment will be kept not by Susanna but by Cherubino dressed as a woman. At the appropriate moment the Countess will interrupt them.

Figaro leaves in high spirits, delighted at the prospect of settling his score with the Count, and agrees to send Cherubino to the two women, to be fitted for his costume. When the page enters, he is first made to sing the song he had given earlier in the day to Susanna. The Countess and Susanna then proceed to dress him up in one of Susanna's frocks. During this process, Cherubino drops a paper which is revealed to be his commission to the Count's regiment. In handing it back to him, the Countess comments that, in his hurry, the Count has neglected to seal it. Noticing also that Cherubino had scratched his arm, and bandaged it with her ribbon, the Countess sends Susanna to fetch sticking plaster and another ribbon from her own room which adjoins the Countess's. While she is gone, Cherubino attempts to stammer out a confession of love to the Countess, but is interrupted by the Count knocking to demand admittance. Rather than allow herself to be discovered with Cherubino who is still *en travestie*, the Countess pushes him into her dressing-room, throws his own clothes after him, then opens her door to admit the Count. He has heard voices, and asks who was with her. The Countess says it must have been Susanna, who has now gone to her own room. Suddenly a noise is heard from the dressing-room, and the Countess hurriedly changes her story and claims that Susanna is in there. Highly suspicious, the Count orders Susanna to come out from the dressing room, while the Countess, feigning indignation, orders her to stay where she is, Meanwhile, unseen by either of them, Susanna has returned from her own room, and is hidden in an alcove in the Countess's room. The Countess fails to convince the Count that the occupant of the dressing-room is Susanna trying on her wedding gown, and the Count announces that he will force the door open. He leaves to procure the necessary implements, insisting that the Countess accompany him. As soon as they have gone, Susanna summons Cherubino, now properly dressed again, and urges him to flee. The Count has locked the only exit from the Countess's boudoir, so the only means of escape for Cherubino is by the balcony. In a panic, he leaps down into the garden, and runs for his life. Susanna now enters the dressing-room to await the Count's return.

When the Count and Countess return, he is carrying a crowbar to force the door open. The Countess decides to confess that it is Cherubino who is in the dressing-room, but her confession only increases the Count's anger. He demands the key from her, but before he can use it the door opens and Susanna steps demurely out. She wonders aloud what all the commotion is about, and the Count finds himself obliged to apologize for having suspected the Countess of duplicity. He is perplexed, however, by the letter he has received, and the women are obliged to confess that they had intended to trick him and that the letter was in fact written by Figaro. The Countess and Susanna make much of his discomfiture, but when Figaro enters to announce that everyone has assembled for his wedding to Susanna, and urges the Count to perform the ceremony, the Count instead begins to question him about the letter. Figaro, of course, denies all knowledge of it, despite the women's attempts to prompt him. At this point, Antonio the gardener enters, rather the worse for drink, and brandishing a pot of carnations. He has seen several things thrown down from the balcony in his time, he says, but now someone has thrown down into the garden a man, who landed on his carnations and damaged them. Figaro claims that it was he, and Antonio then offers him a document which had fallen from the pocket of whoever dropped from the balcony. The Count deftly seizes the document, which he notes is Cherubino's army commission, and asks Figaro to prove the paper is his by identifying it. Figaro is at a loss but the Countess manages to snatch a glance at the piece of paper, and prompts him to give the correct answers.

Marcellina, Bartolo and Basilio now enter and raise the matter of Figaro's indebtedness to Marcellina. She flourishes the contract by which Figaro has promised to marry her if he cannot repay the money he owes. Bartolo will act as her lawyer, and Basilio is a witness to the transaction. The Count promises to investigate the matter that very day, and the act ends with Marcellina and her colleagues confident, and Figaro, Susanna and the Countess in a state of confusion.

The third act takes place in a large salon, decorated for the wedding festivities. Alone, the Count soliloquizes on the perplexing events of the day so far. Unobserved by him, the Countess and Susanna appear at the back of the salon, the Countess encouraging Susanna to proceed with their plan of laying a trap for the Count. Susanna comes forward, and at first the Count speaks sharply to her. However, she manages to persuade him that she returns his affection, and that she will meet him that evening in the garden. Almost immediately afterwards, he overhears a remark of Susanna to Figaro and realizes he is being fooled again.

Marcellina and the others now assemble for the hearing the Count has promised them. The notary, Don Curzio, has been summoned and gives it as his opinion that Figaro is bound by the terms of his agreement to marry Marcellina. Figaro now asserts that he cannot possibly marry without the consent of his parents, whom he does not know, for he is of noble birth and was stolen by gipsies as a child. When Bartolo demands proof, Figaro shows him a birthmark on his arm. Marcellina straightway identifies Figaro as her long-lost son, and informs him that Bartolo is his father. A joyous reunion ensues. When Susanna enters with money to rescue Figaro from Marcellina, only to find them locked in an embrace, she slaps Figaro's face. But the situation is soon made clear to her, and she and Figaro look forward happily to their imminent wedding.

When all have left the salon, Barbarina enters with Cherubino who is seeking somewhere to hide from the Count. She promises to dress him as a girl and allow him to join the maidens of the estate when they present their bouquets to the Countess during the wedding festivities. They leave, and the Countess enters, lamenting that she has lost her husband's love, and recalling her earlier happiness. When she leaves, the Count enters with Antonio who informs him that Cherubino is still somewhere in the castle grounds. They go to search for him, and the Countess returns with Susanna. Together the two women concoct a letter confirming the assignation which Susanna has made with the Count that evening. They seal the letter with a pin, which is to be returned as a token that the message has been received.

The village girls now enter, and sing a chorus in praise of the Countess to whom they present flowers. The Countess comments on one particularly charming girl, who is immediately revealed by Antonio and the Count to be Cherubino. The Count's anger is deflected by Barbarina who coyly blackmails him (for he has flirted with her in his time) into agreeing to her marriage to Cherubino. At last, the other marriage, that of Figaro and Susanna, can take place. During the ceremony, Susanna surreptitiously hands the Count the note she and the Countess have written.

Act IV takes place that night in the garden of the castle. Barbarina enters with a lantern, searching for the pin which she has been entrusted by the Count to return to Susanna, but which she has dropped. Figaro and Marcellina enter, and Barbarina unwittingly betrays that she is bearing an answer from the Count to Susanna. Under the impression that his newly-won bride is already deceiving him, Figaro angrily and bitterly rails against all womankind.

Basilio and Bartolo now arrive to witness the various intrigues, and later the Countess and Susanna also appear, each dressed in the other's clothes. In the darkness of the garden, all the would-be lovers mistake one another's identity. Cherubino flirts with the Countess, thinking she is Susanna, and is chased away by the Count who proceeds to woo his own wife in error. Figaro mistakes Susanna for the Countess, but soon recognizes her, and makes his peace. The Count thinks he has discovered Figaro and the Countess in a compromising situation, and calls for vengeance. Feigning the Countess's voice, Susanna asks for pardon, which the Count angrily refuses. Then the Countess appears, with the words 'Perhaps I may obtain their pardon'. Dumbfounded, the Count in turn humbly begs forgiveness of the Countess, who generously gives it. The opera ends with a chorus in which all the characters sing that only love can resolve this day of torments, caprice and folly.

v

The Overture to *Le nozze di Figaro*, a gaily bustling *presto* in D major, admirably sets the opera's mood, while remaining a self-contained piece, none of whose themes recur in the course of the work. There is no middle section in a slower tempo: Mozart's concern appears to have been to give his audience an immediate indication of the opera's inner pace, and of the hectic events of the 'folle journée' which they were about to witness. Without pausing for applause after the Overture, the conductor should attack swiftly the opening *duettino*, as Mozart calls it, for Susanna and Figaro, a lively G major piece ('Cinque . . . dieci . . .': No. 1). Gone is the unnecessary and inhibiting formality of the older comedies: in its place is a charming and simple duet whose very naturalness marks the skill with which it is composed. The loving and companionable relationship between Susanna and Figaro is effortlessly conveyed in the music, as is the fact that the lady usually gets her own way. The duet begins with Figaro's 'counting' theme, as he measures the room, but Susanna's insistent phrase in which she begs him to admire her new hat soons wins the day, and Figaro's capitulation is sung to her theme. The mood is one of unblemished affection and concord. But dramatic tension is introduced in the ensuing *secco* recitative in which Susanna opens Figaro's eyes to the Count's intentions. In their second *duettino* ('Se a caso madama la notte ti chiama': No. 2), the lovers may not be actually quarrelling, but they are ready for conflict. Susanna alerts Figaro to the dangers of the day that lies before them, and the duet's *allegro* hesitates, resorts to recitative for a bar or so, then continues on its way in a more serious humour. Some of the solo arias in *Figaro*, we shall see, are there to express character rather than to advance action; but the duets and ensembles move the plot along confidently, while contriving to present themselves also as self-contained, and highly mellifluous musical entities.

Left alone, Figaro expresses his opinion of the Count in a forceful F major cavatina ('Se vuol ballare': No. 3). The recitative which precedes the cavatina is a reasonable précis of Beaumarchais, and set most meaningfully by Mozart; the song itself, though its menacing words are not to be found in the play (If you wish to dance, my dear Count, my

guitar will accompany you. Come to my school, and I'll teach you how
to dance), is perfectly in accord with Figaro's mood at this point.
Mozart's music exudes force and determination, and all within the
formal framework of an aristocratic minuet [Ex. 35].

Ex. 35

After Figaro's declaration of war upon Almaviva comes Dr Bartolo's
declaration of war upon Figaro, 'La vendetta' (No. 4). This spirited
allegro aria is thought by many to be one of the comparatively weaker
pieces in *Le nozze di Figaro*: 'the dullest thing in the opera – until we reach
Marcellina's aria in Act IV', in the words of a recent commentator.[1] But,
despite the fact that it is a more old-fashioned aria than Figaro's
menacing song, 'La vendetta' serves its purpose well, and is a tuneful,
enjoyable piece into the bargain. Bartolo begins with vigorous
determination in a bluff D major: the man of good judgment, roused to
righteous anger. But, as he proceeds, his anger gets the better of him,
and he begins to splutter, losing his dignity and his self-control in a riot
of inane and small-minded patter. He recovers himself, to end the aria
in more measured notes. 'Tutto Siviglia conosce Bartolo',[2] he exclaims
complacently. It is all too likely that all Seville does know him, and
probably much better than he knows himself. It is too late for this, and
for the judicial tone of 'Il birbo Figaro vinto sarà';[3] the quicker, shorter
notes of 'Se tutto il codisce' have revealed the essential Bartolo to be a
mean and pompous buffoon. All this in a jolly bass aria, rousingly
accompanied!

Marcellina and Susanna attempt acidulous politeness to each other in
their *duettino*, 'Via resti servita' (No. 5), its opening violin figure
suggestive of a hasty and insincere exchange of curtsies, but their formal
politeness disintegrates as the duet proceeds. Marcellina and Susanna
keep up appearances longer than the orchestra does, until Susanna
breaks down the older woman's defences by referring unkindly to her
age. From then on, Marcellina flounders, while Susanna mocks her in
light-hearted staccato triplets. 'Via resti servita' has none of the
formality of structure of Bartolo's 'La vendetta', nor would it make
sense away from the opera. But, in its proper context, what a delightful
scene it makes, and what a remarkable example of Mozart's genius for

[1] R. B. Moberly: *Three Mozart Operas* (London, 1967).
[2] 'All Seville knows Bartolo'.   [3] 'That rascal Figaro will be beaten'.

characterization. Euphonious, witty and dramatically to the point, this duet, brief though it is, is one of the highlights of the opera.

Cherubino's 'Non so più cosa son, cosa faccio' (No. 6) is another. Both an entrancing and joyous song and a perceptive evocation of a young man's pubescence, Cherubino's arietta sums up the young page's personality with vivid immediacy. In his notes on the characters in the play, Beaumarchais says of Cherubino that 'the basis of his character is an undefined and restless desire. He is entering on adolescence all unheeding, and with no understanding of what is happening to him, and throws himself eagerly into everything that comes along.'[1] Mozart, in the restless and excited movement of the violins in 'Non so più cosa son', has caught this characteristic to perfection, and the effervescent sexuality of the page's song underlines its text with wit and tact. Cherubino, though he professes to be in love with the Countess, is in love with love, or more likely, with sex, and his heart throbs, he says, at the very mention of his beloved ones. These include virtually every female on the estate. At the end of the song, the tempo slows from its *allegro vivace* to *adagio* as Cherubino murmurs sensually, 'E se non ho chi m'oda' (and if there is no one to listen to me) and then quickens excitedly for the abrupt conclusion of 'parlo d'amor con me' (then I talk of love to myself). (He may even be referring to solitary masturbation.)

The trio, 'Cosa sento' (No. 7), in which the Count expresses his anger, Susanna her confusion and Basilio his delight in the situation, is a masterly piece of writing for the stage, advancing the action while at the same time expertly delineating the characters and their idiosyncrasies, and in music whose tunes and themes follow one another in generous profusion. Even the interpolated recitative within the trio, when the Count breaks off to narrate an incident of the previous day, contrives to be as memorable as the rest. As the Count describes how he had caught Cherubino in a compromising situation, he unwittingly pulls aside a chair-cover to reveal the page again, and the long-held F on oboe, horns and violas is like the holding of one's breath in suspense. The interplay of themes, the Count's blustering, Basilio's oily and malicious, Susanna's nervously trembling, is masterly, as is the apparent ease with which Mozart dovetails all within a perfect formal framework. Incidentally, Hans Gal[2] has pointed out that, in this trio, Basilio sings the phrase 'Così fan tutte le belle', not only anticipating a future Mozart opera title, but doing so to a melodic phrase which is in fact quoted in the Overture to *Così fan tutte*.

The chorus of retainers ('Giovani liete'; No. 8) is, like the other choral comments of the servants later in the opera, simple and homely. Shorn of its few bars of orchestral introduction, it is repeated as the servants and retainers, denied an immediate wedding ceremony, take their leave of the Count. The act ends with the popular 'Non più andrai' (No. 9) in

[1] Beaumarchais: *Le Mariage de Figaro* (1785).   [2] In *The Golden Age of Vienna* (1949).

which, to a lively C major marching tune, Figaro teases Cherubino, contrasting his present sybaritic circumstances with future military horrors.

Act II introduces us to the Countess. Her cavatina, 'Porgi, amor, qualche ristoro' (No. 10), with which the act begins, is solemn and dignified rather than sad, though the Countess certainly has cause for sadness in her husband's infidelities. Of course, she herself is not above flirting with young Cherubino, but one's emotions are, by definition, not rational. 'Porgi amor' becomes somewhat agitated in its middle section [Ex. 36], before progressing to the calm, now distinctly tinged with

Ex. 36

Por-gi, a mor, qual-che   ri - sto - ro   al mio duo-lo, a' miei so - spir!

melancholy, of its final bars [Ex. 37]. During the scene which follows,

Ex. 37

o mi   ren - di il mio   te - so - ro,   o mi   la scia al-men   mo - rir!

Figaro enters singing the last bars of his 'Se vuol ballare', and, after outlining his plan to confuse the Count, exits with a few more bars of his song, which the orchestra obligingly accompanies. The song which Cherubino has composed ('Voi che sapete': No. 11), and which he sings to the Countess and Susanna, is ostensibly accompanied by Susanna on the Countess's guitar, though again Mozart's orchestra joins in, the theme itself being announced by the clarinet, an unlikely sound to be produced by Susanna's strumming. Cherubino's song is a simple but appealing tune, and its romantic harmonies suggest the youth's awakening pubescent desires. The device of having a character in opera sing, and be understood by the other characters to be singing, presents the composer with an interesting aesthetic problem. If Susanna and the Countess know Cherubino is singing, performing for them, in 'Voi che sapete', how do they think he and they are expressing themselves throughout the rest of the opera? Mozart solves the problem by ignoring it, or perhaps it would be fairer to say he minimizes it by the deliberate simplicity of Cherubino's song.

The aria which Susanna sings (No. 12: 'Venite, inginocchiatevi') as she dresses Cherubino in her own clothes is really an orchestral piece with voice obbligato. Unlike those arias which occur at moments of reflection, it actually advances the action, and obviously was constructed by Mozart for precisely this purpose. It is not an aria which any singer would be tempted to perform out of context as a concert item, precisely because it fulfils its purpose so admirably in the opera. In the C major *Terzetto* (No. 13: 'Susanna, or via sortite!'), to which Susanna contributes though she is hiding from the Count, she twice sings a rising chromatic scale which takes her up to a high C [Ex. 38]. Originally, these passages

Ex. 38

qui   cer - to   na - sce - rà,

were sung by the Countess, which dramatically makes better sense. Mozart changed the two sopranos' parts for a performance in which it was desirable that the Susanna should sing the higher line in the trio, but some modern productions sensibly change back to the original. The piece is a model of concerted writing for the lyric stage, the feelings of the characters and the requirements of the form appearing not to conflict at any point. A similar mastery of dramatic form is apparent in the *duettino* 'Aprite, presto aprite' (No. 14) for Susanna and Cherubino, where the short, agitated motifs perfectly express the characters' frenzy.

The twenty-minute-long finale to Act II (No. 15: 'Esci omai, garzon malnato'), the most extended number in the opera, is a complete musical entity in itself. Beginning as a duet for the Count and Countess, it ends as a septet with all the principal characters taking part. This finale is often, and rightly, pointed to as a perfect example of the marriage of music and drama in opera. Basically in E flat, the key with which it begins and ends, the finale can be divided into three distinct movements which sub-divide into eight sections. The opening angry *allegro* for the Count and Countess is followed by a modulation to B flat and a change of tempo to *andante con moto* (section two) when Susanna emerges from the locked room to confound the suspicious Count, her entrance preceded by a few simple chords which are strangely eloquent and moving [Ex. 39]. The trio proceeds to quicken to an *allegro* (section

Ex. 39

Andante con moto   SUSANNA

Si - gno - re!

three). The fourth section, or second movement, a G major *allegro*, begins with Figaro's entrance, and moves through C major (*andante*) to F major (*allegro molto*) with the entrance of Antonio, the gardener. The B flat *andante* which follows is a kind of bridge to the final movement, a return to the opening key of E flat and a fast tempo, as Marcellina, Basilio and Bartolo enter to add to the confusion. Superbly constructed though it is, the finale does not in performance draw one's attention to its formal perfection; it simply advances the action with a fine pace and variety.

The duet for the Count and Susanna, 'Crudel! perchè finora' (No. 16), which, after the opening *recitativo secco*, begins Act III, reveals the Count to be seriously smitten with Susanna, while she treats him quite casually, delivering answers of almost Freudian erroneousness to his ardent questions. Again, Mozart's musical characterization is remarkable for its psychological insight, yet contrives to be expressed through the most beguiling of melodic material. When Susanna finally agrees to meet him in the garden, the Count's music relaxes into a blissful A major melody.

It has been convincingly argued[1] that the order of two of the numbers in Act III was altered by Mozart before the first performance, to allow the singer who was doubling the rôles of Bartolo and Antonio time to change costumes, and that the altered order, as found in scores and libretti, weakens the dramatic structure, and indeed the sense, of Act III. Though I think the act is in any case structurally weaker than Acts I and II (and Act IV is weaker still), I am sure that a change must have been made by Mozart and Da Ponte and that, in modern performances in which the rôles of Bartolo and Antonio are not doubled, numbers 17 to 20 should be performed in the following order: 17, 19, 18, 20. In other words, the Countess's great aria 'Dove sono?' should come before the sextet instead of after it.[2]

Only four of the fourteen solo arias in *Le nozze di Figaro* are preceded by accompanied recitative, and the Count's 'Vedrò mentr'io sospiro' (No. 17) is the first of them. The forthright C major anger of the recitative ('Hai già vinta la causa!') is followed by the passionate D major of the aria in which the Count's injured feelings burst forth. It is here that the Count reveals himself as a really dangerous opponent to Figaro, certainly more positively than at the corresponding point in Beaumarchais. 'Vedrò mentr'io sospiro' is his answer to the challenge of Figaro's 'Se vuol ballare' in Act I. The Countess's aria, 'Dove sono' (No. 19), also preceded by wonderfully expressive *recitativo accompagnato*, is, in a way, her answer to the challenge of her husband's infidelities. The aria begins in calm despair [Ex. 40] but ends optimistically, as the Countess

Ex. 40

Do - ve so - no   i bei mo - men - ti,

---

[1] By Robert Moberly and Christopher Raeburn (in *Music and Letters*, April, 1965).

[2] Changes in the *recitativo secco* are, of course, also involved. The interested reader is referred to the article in *Music and Letters* (April, 1965), where the changes are fully discussed.

considers the possibility of regaining his love [Ex. 41]. The aria's C major easily encompasses both moods.

Ex. 41

Ah! se al - men la mia co - stan - za nel lan - gui re a - man - do o - gnor,

In the F major sextet, 'Riconosci in quest' amplesso' (No. 18), Mozart has created one of the finest of all operatic ensembles, in which the different thoughts and emotions of the six characters are simultaneously portrayed, their differences being used to motivate the contrasts of rhythm and tempo in the music. At the same time the action is greatly advanced, but always on the wings of Mozart's seemingly effortless melody, which embraces not only Susanna's momentary misunderstanding when she enters to find Figaro and Marcellina embracing, and expresses her despair in four bars which are almost heartbreaking [Ex. 42], but also the rich comedy of the explanation that Marcellina

Ex. 42

Già d'ac-cor-do col-la spo-sa? Giu - sti Dei, che in-fe - del - tà, che in-fe - del tà!

and Bartolo are Figaro's parents [Ex. 43]. This sextet is the piece which, according to Michael Kelly,[1] was Mozart's favourite in the entire opera.

One of the most serenely beautiful numbers in the score is the little B flat duet for the Countess and Susanna ('Che soave zeffiretto': No. 20) in which the Countess dictates and Susanna writes the note which is to lure the Count to an assignation that evening in the garden. It emerges simply and naturally from the preceding recitative, the strings alone accompanying the dictation, the oboe and bassoon coming in only when Susanna repeats the words, phrase by phrase, as she writes them. The text of the letter is repeated as the two women read it over together. The music exudes a tender confidence, suggesting the closeness of the relationship between mistress and maid and also an unclouded certainty that their ruse will succeed.

The chorus 'Ricevete, o padroncina' (No. 21) is as simple and homely a piece as the earlier chorus of servants in Act I, and the Finale to the act ('Ecco la marcia': No. 22), though not constructed on the vast scale of the finale to the preceding act, is free in form. It begins with a march to which the wedding procession enters, and follows it with a short duet for two of the young female servants, a full chorus, and then a fandango whose melody is clearly Spanish in origin and would already have been known to the Viennese through its use in Gluck's *Don Juan* ballet music (produced in Vienna in 1761). After a passage of recitative, the act ends

---

[1] See p. 228.

Ex. 43

with a repeat of the chorus. The fandango is not used merely as a formal dance: during it the Count receives Susanna's note, pricks his fingers on the pin with which it is sealed, and is observed by Figaro. The asides of the Count and Figaro are sung over the courtly dance rhythm.

It has to be admitted that *Le nozze di Figaro* does show a certain falling off in Act IV, not so much in the quality of Mozart's musical invention as in the confident shape of Da Ponte's libretto. The act contains two of the finest numbers in the score, but it is slow to get under way because of the arias which had to be provided for those principals who had not yet been given one. When it does get going, the action, with all those mistaken identities in the garden, tends to veer towards farce rather than the elegant and humane comedy of the earlier acts. The curtain rises on Barbarina's cavatina, 'L'ho perduta' (No. 23) as she searches for the pin which has dropped from the Count's reply to Susanna's note. This does have dramatic justification, and was not something inserted for the singer. The F minor key gives the cavatina a mood of sorrow somewhat out of proportion, but it is likely that Mozart intended gently to caricature the serving maid's distress at losing a pin. The piece ends with a vocal phrase in mid-air, on the dominant, and the *recitativo secco* begins immediately in the next bar. The following two arias are frequently omitted in performance, and it is difficult to argue for their inclusion. Marcellina's 'Il capro e la capretta' (No. 24) is a conventional piece of writing. It gives the singer a chance to show her coloratura technique, but its *tempo di minuetto* and old-fashioned baroque style seem out of place in *Figaro*. Basilio's 'In quegli anni' (No. 25) is an agreeable enough formal aria, and it does quite neatly characterize the smooth but small-minded Basilio; but, like Marcellina's aria, it makes no attempt to integrate itself into the fabric of the comedy.

With a return to the plot and the immediate concerns of the leading characters, Mozart also returns to form in Figaro's great recitative ('Tutto è disposto') and aria, 'Aprite un po' quegli' occhi' (No. 26). At this point in Beaumarchais' play, Figaro rants against the existing social order in an extremely long soliloquy. Mozart and Da Ponte confine his ranting to the subject of the faithless female sex. The accompanied recitative is superb in its close reflection of Figaro's rapidly changing moods, and the aria, in which his bitter jealousy finds passionate utterance, is a magnificent character study, exact in its psychological comment and in its witty but not unsympathetic exposition of Figaro's plight. The horn fanfares at the end are, of course, a reference to the cuckold's horns.

Susanna's real nature, warm, simple, loving, is revealed in the music of her aria, 'Deh vieni, non tardar' (No. 27), and her delight in mischief is pointed to by the dramatic situation, for this song of tender love is in reality addressed by Susanna to Figaro, though he, overhearing it, is meant to believe she is anticipating her assignation with the Count. The accompanied recitative preceding the aria sounds a note of passion; the aria itself is one of Mozart's ambivalent *andantes*, a tune which breathes a contentment which is yet close to tears. The pizzicato string accompaniment, with flute, oboe and bassoon, contributes to a mood of sheer poetry and stillness.

The finale to the opera (No. 28: 'Pian, pianin le andrò più presso') involves all eleven principal singers, but not the chorus of retainers, and is musically, though not dramatically, almost the equal of the great Act II finale. The tangled skeins of plot are unravelled, and finally the moment of reconciliation between Count and Countess is reached. With the simplest of means, Mozart effects a moving moment of reunion [Ex. 44],

Ex. 44

bringing a seriousness and sincerity to Da Ponte's perfunctory and unconvincing verbal exchange. In a quick closing *stretta*, all eleven principal characters endorse the message of happiness and love.

For a revival of *Le nozze di Figaro* at the Burgtheater in 1789, three years after its première, Mozart added two arias for Adriana Ferrarese del Bene, who now sang Susanna, and who the following year was to create the role of Fiordiligi in *Così fan tutte*. 'Al desio di chi t'adora' (K. 577) followed the recitative 'Giunse alfin il momento', replacing 'Deh vieni, non tardar'. Unlike the serenely beautiful 'Deh vieni', it is a conventional bravura piece, a slow first section followed by a fast cabaletta-like conclusion. Though it sounds quite pleasing out of context, it is both vastly inferior to (and much less suitable for Susanna than) 'Deh vieni'. 'Un moto di gioia mi sento nel petto' (K. 579) was probably used in place of 'Venite, inginocchiatevi' in Act II. It too is less effective than the aria it replaced, but is quite in character for Susanna in its sweetness and simplicity. The words for both arias are presumably by Da Ponte. While he was rehearsing the 1789 revival of *Figaro*, Mozart wrote to his wife who had gone to nearby Baden for her health, 'The little aria which I composed for Madame Ferrarese should, I think, be a success, so long as she is able to sing it in an artless manner, which, however, I doubt very much.'[1] This must refer to 'Un moto di gioia', for the other aria could hardly be sung artlessly. It is somewhat disconcerting that Mozart appears not to have minded the substitution of 'Al desio' for 'Deh vieni'.

Mozart made several other minor changes to his score for the 1789 performances, and also took the opportunity to change the tessitura of the Count's aria, 'Vedrò mentr' io sospiro' in order to accommodate the new performer who must have had a higher and more flexible baritone than Stefano Mandini, the original singer, for the revised version is studded with high Gs and is considerably more florid in style.[2]

[1] Letter written in August, 1789.

[2] The revised version of the Count's aria was found by Christopher Raeburn in 1959, and has since been recorded by Dietrich Fischer-Dieskau.

XVIII

Don Giovanni
opera buffa in two acts
K. 527

Dramatis personae:

Don Giovanni, an extremely licentious young nobleman	(baritone)
Il Commendatore (The Commander)	(bass)
Donna Anna, his daughter	(soprano)
Don Ottavio (her betrothed)	(tenor)
Donna Elvira, a noblewoman from Burgos, abandoned by Don Giovanni	(soprano)
Leporello, servant of Don Giovanni	(bass)
Masetto, a peasant, betrothed to	(bass).
Zerlina	(soprano)

LIBRETTO by Lorenzo da Ponte, based on several earlier sources

TIME: Mid-seventeenth century
PLACE: Seville

FIRST PERFORMED in Prague, 29 October, 1787, at the Nationaltheater (now Tyl Theatre), with Luigi Bassi (Don Giovanni), Giuseppe Lolli (Commendatore and Masetto), Teresa Saporiti (Donna Anna), Caterina Micelli (Donna Elvira), Antonio Baglioni (Don Ottavio), Felice Ponziani (Leporello), Caterina Bondini (Zerlina)

Don Giovanni

A THIRD CHILD, Johann Thomas Leopold, had been born to the Mozarts on 18 October, 1786, but had died less than a month later. Mozart's journey to Prague in the following January, to see the Prague production of *Le nozze di Figaro* has already been mentioned. Most of his time in Prague was spent with the family of his Viennese Masonic patron and friend Count Thun, but he found time also to conduct business. He gave a pianoforte recital in the Nationaltheater, at which both his music and his performance roused the audience to the most frenzied enthusiasm. At the end of the recital he was forced to improvise upon the piano for more than half an hour, after which, in response to a shouted request to play something from *Figaro*, he improvised a set of variations from Figaro's 'Non più andrai farfallone amoroso'. A recently completed symphony was played to great applause at another concert, and has since been known as the 'Prague' Symphony. Mozart happily agreed to compose a new opera for the Prague Nationaltheater, and he and Constanze returned to Vienna in mid-February.

Mozart consulted Da Ponte regarding the new opera for Prague, and agreed upon Don Juan as a subject. Da Ponte set to work on the libretto, but was simultaneously working on libretti for two other composers, Salieri and Martin y Soler. He has left a highly coloured account of his labours:

> I returned home and went to work. I sat down at my table and did not leave it for twelve hours continuous – a bottle of Tokay to my right, a box of Seville to my left, in the middle an inkwell. A beautiful girl of sixteen – I should have preferred to love her only as a daughter, but alas . . . ! – was living in the house with her mother, who took care of the family, and came to my room at the sound of the bell. To tell the truth the bell rang rather frequently, especially at moments when I felt my inspiration waning. She would bring me now a little cake, now a cup of coffee, now nothing but her pretty face, a face always gay, always smiling, just the thing to inspire poetical emotion and witty thoughts. I worked twelve hours a day every day, with a few interruptions, for two months on end; and through all that time she sat in an adjoining room, now with a book in hand, now with needle or embroidery, but ever ready to come to my aid at the first touch of the bell. Sometimes she would sit at my side without stirring, without opening her lips, or batting an

eyelash, gazing at me fixedly, or blandly smiling, or now it would be a sigh, or a menace of tears. In a word, this girl was my Calliope for those three operas, as she was afterwards for all the verse I wrote during the next six years. At first I permitted such visits very often; later I had to make them less frequent, in order not to lose too much time in amorous nonsense, of which she was perfect mistress. The first day, between the Tokay, the snuff, the coffee, the bell, and my young muse, I wrote the first two scenes of *Don Giovanni*, two more for the *Arbore di Diana*, and more than half of the first act of *Tarar*, a title I changed to *Assur*. I presented those scenes to the three composers the next morning. They could scarcely be brought to believe that what they were reading with their own eyes was possible. In sixty-three days the first two operas were entirely finished and about two thirds of the last.[1]

Meanwhile, Mozart was attempting to brush up his English, with a view to visiting London, whither his English friends the Storaces, Michael Kelly and Thomas Attwood had already returned. Losing no opportunity to practise, he wrote in another friend's album, with more fervour than grammar, 'Don't never forget your true and faithfull friend'.[2] In the spring he took on a new pupil in composition, a short, stocky sixteen-year-old German who had come to Vienna especially to study with Mozart. But the lad stayed no longer than two weeks, and was then recalled to Germany by the serious illness of his mother. Although he later returned to Vienna to live, he and Mozart never met again. His name was Beethoven.

In May, Leopold Mozart died in Salzburg. An illness of his own prevented Wolfgang from being with his father at the end, and poverty forced him to move his lodgings from the centre of Vienna to the suburb of Landstrasse. A few days after his father's death, Mozart had to bury his pet starling. Throughout these emotional upsets he worked steadily on *Don Giovanni*. At the beginning of October, Mozart and Constanze journeyed to Prague to prepare for the rehearsals of the new opera. The première had originally been planned for 14 October to celebrate the marriage of the Archduchess Maria Theresia, the Emperor's niece, and Prince Anton Clemens of Saxony. However, *Don Giovanni* not being ready on the 14th, the royal couple saw a performance of *Le nozze di Figaro* instead. The first performance of *Il dissoluto punito o sia Il Don Giovanni*, to give the new opera its correct title, took place in Count Nostitz's National Theatre (Still in use in Prague, now called the Tyl Theatre) on 29 October, conducted by the composer. There are several stories concerning Mozart's last-minute composition of the Overture, the least improbable of which is Constanze's. According to her, Mozart wrote the Overture the night before the first performance, while she

---

[1] Da Ponte: op. cit.

[2] In Joseph Franz von Jacquin's Album. The Album is now in the Salzburg Mozarteum.

plied him with punch which made him drowsy, and stories which woke him up again. By seven the next morning the Overture was finished just as the copyist arrived to collect it.

Don Giovanni was received by its Prague audiences with wild enthusiasm, and the Prague *Oberpostamtszeitung* of 3 November carried the following notice:

> On Monday the 29th, the Italian opera company gave the ardently awaited opera by Maestro Mozard [*sic*], *Don Giovanni*, or *das steinerne Gastmahl*. Connoisseurs and musicians say that Prague has never yet heard the like. Herr Mozard conducted in person: when he entered the orchestra, he was received with threefold cheers, which again happened when he left it. The opera is, moreover, extremely difficult to perform, and everyone admired the good performance given in spite of this, after such a short period of study. Everybody, on the stage and in the orchestra, strained every nerve to thank Mozard by rewarding him with a good performance. There were also heavy additional costs, caused by several choruses and changes of scenery, all of which Herr Guardasoni had brilliantly attended to. The unusually large attendance testifies to a unanimous approbation.[1]

Mozart and Constanze remained in Prague for two weeks after the *Don Giovanni* première, returning to Vienna in mid-November. It was several months before the opera was staged in Vienna, with certain changes (discussed on pp. 268 and 271–72). It did not at first repeat its Prague success, and the Emperor told Da Ponte, 'It is not meant for the teeth of my Viennese.' Da Ponte repeated the remark to Mozart who replied quietly, 'Give them time to chew on it.' He was right, for in due course the Viennese came to appreciate *Don Giovanni* as greatly as the citizens of Prague.

II

The Don Giovanni or Don Juan story was not invented by Da Ponte: it had been made use of by dramatists for more than a century and a half before Mozart's librettist came to it. The old legend of the compulsive seducer who is finally dragged down to hell seems to have first made its way into dramatic literature with *El Burlador de Seville*, a comedy by the Spanish monk Gabriel Tellez (1571–1648) who wrote plays under the name Tirso de Molina.[2] *El Burlador de Seville*, which had already become popular on the stage by the time of its first publication in Barcelona in 1630, served as the basis for other Don Juan plays, by Molière (*Don Juan, ou Le Festin de Pierre*, 1665), Shadwell (*The Libertine*, 1676) and Goldoni (*Don Giovanni Tenorio, o sia Il Dissoluto*, 1736) as well as by several lesser-known Italian, French and German playwrights. From the spoken

---

[1] Quoted in Deutsch, op. cit.
[2] Ernest Newman recounts the plot of Tirso de Molina's play in detail, in his chapter on *Don Giovanni* in *More Opera Nights* (London, 1954).

theatre, the story had found its way into ballet and opera. Mozart knew Gluck's ballet, *Don Juan*, based on Molière and first staged at the Kärntnertor Theater in Vienna, in 1761, and Da Ponte knew the one-act opera, *Don Giovanni o sia Il convitato di pietra* by Giuseppe Gazzaniga, performed in Venice on 5 February, 1787, for he drew upon its libretto by Giovanni Bertati in writing his own libretto for Mozart. The legend continued to be used in art and literature: Byron's unfinished *Don Juan* (1819–1824), written in order to 'strip the tinsel off sentiment', is one of the greatest poems in the English language.

Even more so than with his other two operas composed to libretti by Da Ponte, Mozart is primarily responsible for the stature of the completed work. Da Ponte's *Le nozze di Figaro* and *Così fan tutte* are amusing and well-planned, but it has to be admitted that his *Don Giovanni* is more primitively structured, and less successful in bringing the characters to life on the page. This latter failing is obscured, fortunately, by Mozart's music which most emphatically does give life to Da Ponte's cardboard creations, even to the impossibly colourless Don Ottavio. It may be that Da Ponte would have done better to cast himself adrift from the Gazzaniga libretto more boldly, for in the process of expanding a one-act libretto into one with two acts, he seems merely to have duplicated in his Act II the sequence of events, or at least of feelings, in Act I. Read in the study, Da Ponte's *Don Giovanni* is revealed to be full of padding. However, since some of the padding inspired Mozart to his greatest heights, one can hardly complain!

Don Giovanni has been the subject of more abstruse and irrelevant speculation or inquiry on the part of German musicologists and musical philosophers than any other opera, with the exception of Wagner's *Ring*. Though I think it important not to be diverted along the paths of the higher nonsense, I shall comment briefly, in Part III of this chapter, on the difficulty some critics have found in reconciling the tragic and the comic aspects of the opera which Mozart and his librettist called a 'dramma giocoso' or light-hearted drama.

Although it is possible to stage *Don Giovanni* as though the entire action took place during the course of twenty-four hours, Giovanni's last day on earth, this can only be achieved at some cost to dramatic credibility. It is more sensible to assume that the action is spread over a period of at least several days.

The opera, set in Seville in the seventeenth century, is in two acts. The first act begins, at night, in the garden of Donna Anna's house. Don Giovanni's servant, Leporello, is standing with a lantern, and grumbling that, while his master is engaged indoors in amorous pursuits, he, Leporello, is forced to wait about in the cold, overworked and underpaid. Suddenly, Giovanni, his face masked, emerges from the house pursued by Donna Anna who has grabbed hold of him to prevent him from escaping and to discover his identity. She calls out for help as she struggles with him, and soon her father, the Commendatore (or Commander), appears, sword in hand. He and Giovanni fight while Donna Anna goes into the house to rouse the servants. The Commendatore is killed, and Giovanni and Leporello make their escape. When Donna Anna returns, she is accompanied by her betrothed, Don Ottavio, as well as by a few servants. They find the Commendatore's dead body, and Donna Anna faints from shock. After the body has been removed and Anna has revived, she extracts from Ottavio an oath that he will avenge her father's death.

Act I Scene II is set in a street. Leporello is making a half-hearted attempt to persuade Giovanni to give up his obsessive pursuit of women, when suddenly Giovanni declares he can scent a woman approaching. They hide, and Donna Elvira enters. She has travelled from Burgos in search of her lover who has abandoned her. Giovanni moves forward to console her, only to discover that she is one of his discarded mistresses and that he is the scoundrel she is pursuing. As soon as he can, he retreats, leaving Leporello to console Elvira by revealing to her that she is neither the first nor the last of his master's conquests, but merely one of a long list. Leporello shows her the list: six hundred and forty women in Italy, two hundred and thirty-one in Germany, a hundred in France, ninety-one in Turkey and, at home in Spain, already one thousand and three. The scene ends with Elvira swearing to take her revenge on Giovanni.

The third scene takes place in the open country, near Don Giovanni's villa. A rustic wedding party is in progress. Two young villagers, Zerlina and Masetto, about to marry, are singing and dancing, surrounded by their friends. Giovanni and Leporello enter, and Giovanni immediately begins to flirt with Zerlina. Leporello is ordered to take everyone else, including Masetto, to Giovanni's villa for an impromptu feast. When Masetto appears reluctant to leave his Zerlina alone with a strange gentleman, Giovanni makes it clear to him that he has no choice in the matter. Left alone with Zerlina, Giovanni soon breaks through her not very formidable defences. She is far too good to be wasted on a country bumpkin, he tells her. He, Giovanni, loves her and will marry her immediately. Though she only half believes him, Zerlina is ready to be led off to his villa. Before they can depart, however, Elvira makes a sudden appearance, and declares she will not allow an obviously innocent maiden to be deceived by Giovanni. He attempts to convince Zerlina that Elvira is a poor, unhappy creature who is infatuated with him and whom he must pretend to love, but Elvira leaves, taking Zerlina with her. Don Ottavio now arrives with Donna Anna in mourning. Anna begins to ask Giovanni, as a nobleman, to help her find the murderer of her father, when Elvira returns and warns her against him. Giovanni whispers that Elvira is demented, but Donna Anna and Don Ottavio find her sane and convincing. Elvira leaves, and Giovanni hastens after her with the excuse that she may commit some folly if left to herself. He takes a hurried leave of Donna Anna and Don Ottavio.

As soon as he has gone, Anna exclaims that Don Giovanni's last words, or the tone in which they were uttered, have made her suddenly convinced that he was the masked intruder who had broken into her bedchamber and assaulted her. She tells Ottavio how she struggled free, raised an alarm, and then pursued him into the street to stop him from escaping. She is certain now that Giovanni was her attacker and the killer of her father. Again she calls on Ottavio to avenge her. When she has departed, Ottavio soliloquizes that he can scarcely believe a nobleman capable of committing so villainous a crime, but that he will do all he can to discover the truth, for his peace of mind depends on that of his beloved Donna Anna.

He departs, and Giovanni and Leporello now reappear to plan the magnificent party which is about to take place at Giovanni's villa. Zerlina is there already, and Leporello has managed to lock Elvira out. Giovanni encourages Leporello to invite any other young women he may encounter, and looks forward during the course of the evening to adding a good ten names to his list of conquests.

The scene changes to the garden of Giovanni's villa. Masetto is furious with Zerlina, but she assures him that she remains unsullied by Don Giovanni. They make up their lovers' quarrel, but when Giovanni is heard to approach, Zerlina becomes nervous of meeting him again, and Masetto's suspicions are reawakened. He hides quickly, and overhears Giovanni's renewed attempt at the seduction of Zerlina. When Masetto suddenly reveals himself, Giovanni suavely conducts them both into his villa. Three masked figures now enter. They are Donna Elvira, Donna Anna and Don Ottavio, and, when Leporello conveys to them an invitation from Don Giovanni to join the party in his villa, they accept with alacrity.

The scene moves to the interior of the villa, where the party is in progress. A dance has just ended, and Giovanni escorts several girls to their places while Leporello presses refreshments upon the men. Giovanni continues to flirt with Zerlina, but finds time to greet the three masked strangers as they enter. The music strikes up again, and Giovanni takes Zerlina as his partner while Leporello forces Masetto to dance. Giovanni succeeds in leading Zerlina into another room, and Leporello, fearing disaster, hastily follows. Suddenly Zerlina's voice is heard, calling for help. Anna, Elvira and Ottavio are about to force an entry into the off-stage room when suddenly Giovanni emerges, dragging with him Leporello whom he claims is the offender. But no one is deceived by this, and one by one, Anna, Elvira and Ottavio remove their masks and threaten their host. They are now aware of his true character and will reveal it to the world.

In most productions of the opera, Giovanni is seen to make his escape before the curtain falls. But there is nothing in the text to support such a reading. Da Ponte and Mozart presumably expected their audiences to understand that Giovanni was now unmasked and disgraced and that his accusers would proceed to the due processes of law. It is unlikely that Don Ottavio would have attempted a 'citizen's arrest' on the spot, though he might have challenged Giovanni to fight. It is clear from the events of Act II that Giovanni has not fled from his villa or gone into hiding, except momentarily to avoid Masetto and his friends.

Act II begins in the street, outside an inn where Donna Elvira and her maid are lodging. Leporello wants to leave Don Giovanni's service, but is persuaded by a bribe to remain. Giovanni now has his eye on Elvira's maid. In order to serenade her he exchanges cloaks and hats with Leporello, for, as Giovanni puts it, 'a nobleman's costume is not very popular among people of that class'. When Donna Elvira appears on the balcony of the inn, Giovanni, hidden behind Leporello, calls on her to come down to him, for he is penitent. When she comes out into the street she is greeted by the disguised Leporello who leads her smartly away so that Giovanni can proceed to serenade the maid. Masetto and a number of his friends now arrive in search of Giovanni, who, passing himself off as a disgruntled Leporello, sends the others on a false trail, and then assaults Masetto and runs away. Zerlina enters, helps the badly shaken Masetto to his feet, and archly promises him a better cure for his wounds than any chemist can prescribe.

The next scene takes place in a dark courtyard in front of Donna Anna's house. Leporello enters with Elvira whom he has been unable to shake off, and shortly afterwards Anna and Ottavio appear. As Leporello is about to slip out through the door, he is confronted by Zerlina and Masetto who, imagining him to be Giovanni, threaten him with death. Elvira begs them to be merciful to him, but Leporello is taking no chances and, flinging off his disguise, manages to make a quick escape. Don Ottavio asks the others to comfort Donna Anna while he goes to avenge her father's murder. (It is at this point that the Viennese additions to Act II were inserted: the aria in which Elvira sings of her unhappiness, and of the ambivalence of her feelings towards Giovanni; and the duet in which Zerlina captures Leporello, ties him up and threatens him with a razor.)

The scene changes to a cemetery, later that evening. Among several statues, there is one of the Commendatore, seated on a horse. Don Giovanni enters, and is joined by Leporello. They re-exchange garments, and Giovanni begins to boast of his amorous exploits since they parted, one of which was with a current sweetheart of Leporello. Indignantly, Leporello asks, 'What if she had been my wife!' At this, Giovanni laughs loudly, only to be rebuked by a voice which seems to come from the statue of the Commendatore. 'By dawn you will have laughed for the last time,' it promises. At first amused, Giovanni orders Leporello to invite the statue to supper. The terrified Leporello does so, and even Giovanni is somewhat shaken when the statue nods its head in acceptance.

A short scene follows, in a room in Donna Anna's house, in which Ottavio suggests they should now marry. Donna Anna insists on a longer period of mourning, and, accused by Ottavio of treating him cruelly, refutes the charge.

The final scene takes place in the banquet hall of Don Giovanni's villa. Giovanni is seated at supper, Leporello waits upon him, and musicians play for him. Leporello surreptitiously tries to procure a few scraps of food for himself. Suddenly Donna Elvira rushes in and implores Giovanni to change his ways before it is too late. He pays no heed to her, and she is about to leave when suddenly, frightened by something outside, she screams, recoils and runs out by another door. Giovanni sends Leporello outside to discover what has frightened her, and Leporello himself screams and comes running back in terror to say that 'the man of stone' is approaching the banqueting hall. He hides under the table as a loud knocking is heard, and Giovanni himself admits the statue of the Commendatore. Giovanni flippantly requests Leporello to lay another place at table, but the statue says he has come to invite Giovanni to dine with him: 'Give me your hand upon it,' says the statue, and his grip upon Giovanni brings the chill of the grave into the room. The statue orders Giovanni to repent his crimes, but Giovanni faces eternity with courage, and replies, 'No, you old fool'. The flames of hell torment him, and demons' voices are heard promising him the horrors of hell, as the flames increase and engulf him.

After Giovanni's disappearance, the flames subside and the room assumes its normal aspect again. Accompanied by a Minister of Justice, Elvira, Anna and the other characters arrive to confront Giovanni, only to be informed by Leporello that he has been dragged down to eternal damnation by the Commendatore's statue. Ottavio and Anna agree to marry in one year's time, Elvira announces her intention of retiring to a convent, Zerlina and Masetto plan a cosy supper at home, Leporello thinks of looking for a better master, and they all then turn to address the audience with the moral of the story, which is that all evildoers end thus, and that sinners inevitably get their just deserts in the long run.

III

The Overture to *Don Giovanni*, whether or not Mozart composed it after midnight on the eve of the première, is an integral part of the opera, in a way that earlier Mozart overtures are not. In the so-called French form, a solemn introduction followed by an *allegro*, it begins with the full orchestra sounding the chords which we are to hear again, reinforced by trombones, when the statue of the Commendatore arrives to sup with Don Giovanni in the finale of Act II. The D minor *andante* of the Overture is drawn from this scene, but the *allegro* in D major which follows is not based on themes from the opera, though its agitation and turbulent energy are clearly intended as a portrait of Giovanni. The Overture ends quietly and inconclusively, modulating into the F major of Leporello's opening scene, and continuing into it without a pause, as the curtain rises. The Introduction (No. 1) encompasses Leporello's grumbling soliloquy, 'Notte e giorno faticar', an animated trio when Don Giovanni enters with Donna Anna, and a grave *andante* in F minor for the three men after the Commendatore has been mortally wounded by Giovanni. Just as the Overture had merged into the opening scene, so too the Introduction dispenses with any punctuating final chords, moving straight from its last chromatic bars with their prominent oboe and flute parts into the *secco* recitative exchange between Giovanni and Leporello. As they depart, Donna Anna reappears with Don Ottavio, and, after a further four bars of *secco* recitative, the orchestra launches into a furious *allegro assai* to introduce the recitative and duet 'Fuggi, crudele, fuggi' (No. 2) whose sense of onward movement is in no way vitiated by its frequent interjection of accompanied recitative. Donna Elvira is introduced in 'Ah, chi mi dice mai quel barbaro dov'è?' (No. 3), an aria during whose orchestral *ritornelli* Don Giovanni and Leporello exchange *sotto voce* comments. Mozart's musical characterization is at its height in *Don Giovanni*. To distinguish between the musical styles of soubrette and leading lady is not difficult, but to create two totally different characters who use the same style of utterance is another matter. The music of Donna Elvira has more in common with that of Donna Anna than with that of Zerlina, whom we have yet to meet in the opera; it could not, however, be mistaken for Donna Anna's music, for it has none of her well-bred reserve in grief. Donna Elvira is sometimes played as a virago: this is wrong, surely, but she should certainly be played with the passionate determination which pervades this, her first aria. She may not, at any given moment, know whether she is more steadfast in her love for Giovanni or her desire for vengeance, but she is driven on by furies. The orchestra in 'Ah, chi mi dice mai' uses clarinets for the first time in the opera, and they combine with horns and bassoons to emphasize the passionate warmth of the music. The aria does not come to a full close, for Don Giovanni approaches Donna Elvira immediately after her final cadence, and the action proceeds in *secco* recitative. Leporello's Catalogue aria ('Madamina': No. 4), sung to Elvira to reveal to her the extent of Giovanni's sexual athleticism, lists the women he has had in various countries: 'In Italia sei cento e quaranta, in Almagna due cento e trent' una, cento in Francia, in Turchia novant' una, ma in Ispagna son già mille e tre.' This adds up to a grand total of two thousand and sixty-five, and Leporello describes the different types, baronesses, countesses, ladies' maids, dark, fair, plump, thin, in a witty, light-hearted song, whose opening *allegro* is followed by an *andante* which matches the mock tenderness of the words with music of an insinuating eroticism. 'You know what he does to young virgins,' Leporello sniggers at the end of the song: 'Voi sapete quel che fa.' The last three words are repeated twice, and it appears to have been Luigi Lablache in the nineteenth century who began the custom of nasally and knowingly humming the second repetition, which most Leporellos adopt today.

Zerlina and Masetto are introduced in 'Giovinette, che fate all'amore' (No. 5), a good-humoured duet with a chorus refrain, in a rustic 6/8 rhythm and a bright G major. The aria in which Masetto responds to Giovanni's not very heavily veiled threat ('Ho capito': No. 6) is a bluff *allegro di molto* in which the lad's angry jealousy barely contains itself in irony and sarcasm. The 'duettino', 'Là ci darem la mano' (No. 7), preceded by recitative which is almost as seductively caressing as the duet itself, is a miracle of invention and musical characterization. Within its light bantering A major melody [Ex. 45] are embedded a number

Ex. 45

of verbal and musical subtleties, of phrasing, of inflection, of orchestration. Though Giovanni begins the duet without instrumental preamble, there is no sense of urgency. The tone contrives to be both elegant and sensuous, and the tempo indication is *andante*. Mozart did not indicate any change of tempo for the conclusion of the duet, after Zerlina has yielded, and those conductors who take it faster merely destroy its mood, introducing a suggestion of unseemly haste to get into bed. The eroticism of the recitative and the duet is best conveyed by keeping to Mozart's tempo. He has, after all, indicated the state of affairs with a time change from 2/4 to 6/8.

Elvira's 'Ah! fuggi il traditor' (No. 8), a vigorous warning to Zerlina, is a very practical aria. It is short, vigorous and passionate, but it does not draw attention to itself. Instead, it advances the drama. Its angular severity has led to the suggestion that Mozart deliberately wrote it in the style of Handel, but there is no evidence to support this. Its sternness is surely a dramatic attribute: Elvira is uttering a kind of warning to wantons. She begins the great quartet, 'Non ti fidar, o misera' (No. 9), with a phrase of melting tenderness [Ex. 46], quite different in mood from her aria. The quartet is yet another remarkable instance of

Ex. 46

Mozart's genius for characterization allied to musical beauty. The situation has its comic aspect, as Giovanni attempts to convince Donna Anna and Don Ottavio that Elvira is mad, while simultaneously doing his best to prevent her from making any more damaging utterances. Yet the total effect is ambivalent, and at the end the orchestra's comment is made in sympathy with Elvira, to the phrase [Ex. 47] which she had first

Ex. 47

sung to the words 'Te vuol tradir ancor', ['He has already betrayed me,] and now he wishes to betray you.'

In a few bars of *secco* recitative after the quartet, Don Giovanni takes his leave of Donna Anna, and something in the caressing tone of his voice makes her suddenly quite certain that he is the murderer of her father. As he walks off, the realization comes to her, expressed musically by a two-bar phrase low in the double basses, slow and as though awakening, then the fortissimo crash of the full orchestra tells us that the dreadful certainty has burst up into her consciousness [Ex. 48], and we

Ex. 48

are launched on the accompanied recitative which precedes her aria, 'Or sai chi l'onore rapire a me volse' (No. 10).[1] Commentators have been known to ponder on whether or not Anna is really telling the entire truth to her betrothed, when, in her recitative, she says she managed to struggle free from her attacker. Let us beware of bringing a twentieth-century sophistication to bear on an eighteenth-century convention. Mozart and Da Ponte, who created the character, quite clearly mean us to believe the lady's story. They would have left us, and their own contemporary audiences, in no doubt if they had intended otherwise.

The orchestral punctuation of Donna Anna's words in the recitative is charged with drama, and the sweeping vehemence of her aria would have aroused a less placid lover than Ottavio to instant revenge. Instead, however, he voices his unwillingness to believe that a nobleman could be capable of such villainy, and perhaps the final two chords in the orchestra at the end of the aria, as Anna departs, are meant to prepare us for Ottavio's vacillation, for they have the effect of softening the sound and slowing the pace. The hushed stillness of the aria ('Dalla sua pace': No. 11) in which Ottavio sings of his love for Anna is so beautiful in itself that it seems almost churlish to point out that something more resolute might have been welcome here. In any case, Ottavio is not presented to us as the most resolute of characters. The aria is one of Mozart's finest expressions of tenderness rather than of passionate love, and one cherishes it as such. It is not in the original Prague score, but was composed for the Vienna production to replace the tenor's Act II aria, 'Il mio tesoro' which was too difficult for him. Nowadays, though many tenors are defeated by 'Il mio tesoro', none are willing to admit it, and, since none would want to be deprived of the opportunity to sing 'Dalla sua pace', we therefore invariably hear both arias. In fact, most performances of *Don Giovanni* now conflate the Prague and Vienna scores, omitting one number only, which makes for a long opera, and in particular a long second act. It is not known why, in substituting a simpler aria for 'Il mio tesoro', Mozart inserted it in a different place and a different act, but it may be that he felt the drama already tended to sag in Act II.

The contrast between the characters of Ottavio and Giovanni could hardly be more strongly emphasized than by the next number in the score, for, as Ottavio leaves, Giovanni and Leporello enter, and, after a short passage of recitative, Giovanni bursts into song with the magically energetic 'Finch' han dal vino' calda la testa' (No. 12), a feverish explosion of sheer sexual drive, which seems suddenly to lay bare before us Giovanni's innermost being, his *raison d'être*. The song is sometimes referred to as the 'Champagne aria', and producers of the opera have

---

[1] Literally: 'Now you know who tried to steal my honour.' One often finds the title quoted illiterately as 'Or sai chi l'onore' ('Now you know who the honour'!) Better, if one must abbreviate, to refer simply to 'Or sai' ('Now you know').

thus been led to give Giovanni a goblet to wave around while he is singing it. But, in the song, he is merely instructing Leporello to lay on food and drink for the guests at his villa. There is no suggestion that he himself is drinking in a public street in Seville, nor does the Italian text stipulate what kind of wine is to be offered; champagne has crept in only with a bad German translation ('Treibt der Champagner das Blut erst im Kreise') which does not even fit the notes very comfortably.

Zerlina's delightful song, 'Batti, batti, o bel Masetto' (No. 13), in which she insinuates herself into Masetto's affections again, is an apt musical depiction of her character, lightly flirtatious yet capable of tenderness. In the first part of the song – it is too simple to be called an aria – Zerlina invites Masetto to beat her for being so naughty; when he fails to respond to this masochistic invitation, she makes her peace with him, with a change from 2/4 to 6/8. Throughout, a graceful cello obbligato has woven its way through the scoring of the accompaniment. Then, after a short passage of recitative, in which his suspicions are aroused again by Zerlina's nervousness at the imminent return of Don Giovanni, Masetto begins the superb Act I finale (No. 14).

Mozart has already proved, with the second act finale of *Le nozze di Figaro*, his genius in the construction of extended dramatic finales, and that of the first act of *Don Giovanni* is in no way inferior, despite the necessity of a scene-change in the middle of it. The beginning of the finale, with Masetto watchful, Zerlina nervous and Don Giovanni cautious, is dramatic; after the chorus of servants has gone inside the villa with Giovanni's peasant-guests, the tempo slows to *andante*, but quickens again for the exit of Giovanni, Zerlina and Masetto. The famous minuet played by Giovanni's musicians is first heard (off stage) played by strings, oboes and horns, as an accompaniment to Leporello's invitation to three masked strangers to join the festivities. The maskers' trio, 'Protegga il giusto cielo', an island of introspective calm in the midst of this ocean of extrovert merriment, is sublimely beautiful in the manner of Mozart's piano concerto slow movements, its meltingly lovely accompaniment provided by the orchestra's wind instruments alone. The scene now changes to Don Giovanni's ballroom, with its three orchestras playing simultaneously for three different dances: for the aristocracy a minuet (now in G major, whereas it had earlier been heard in F), a contre-danse in 2/4 time for the burgers, should there be any present, and what the stage directions call a 'Teitsch' (Deutsche Tanze, or waltz) for the peasants. Mozart enjoys weaving all three dances into a contrapuntal unity, until the gaiety is disrupted by Giovanni's latest attempt to seduce Zerlina, and the act ends in his exposure, to music which, while never inappropriate, is disappointingly conventional after the finale's earlier felicities.

Act II opens briskly, but conventionally, with a *buffo* duet for Giovanni and Leporello ('Eh via, buffone': No. 15). The trio which follows ('Ah taci, ingiusto core': No. 16) in which Giovanni and Leporello cruelly mock Elvira while she sings reproachfully of her love for Giovanni, is a more complex piece. Musically, it is very beautiful; if one listened to it without understanding the words, one would think it uttered none but the tenderest sentiments. The words tell us, however, that the three singers are voicing widely different thoughts. In his ironic serenade to Elvira, Giovanni anticipates [Ex. 49] the beginning of the

Ex. 49

serenade he will sing a few minutes later in his 'sincere' attempt to seduce Elvira's maid. Perhaps it is his all-purpose serenade tune. In a production of the opera, if the comedy is not over-played, the trio is seen and heard to work. But it is Da Ponte who is responsible for this: we may have to admit that Mozart, or that music, is incapable of irony. Giovanni's serenade ('Deh, vieni alla finestra': No. 17) is a gentle canzonetta in two stanzas, accompanied (ostensibly by Giovanni himself) on the mandoline, with a background of pizzicato strings. Suitable to the dramatic situation, it is also an enchanting little love song for any occasion.

The next musical number is a solo for Giovanni ('Metà di voi quà vadano': No. 18), but it is also a means of advancing the action which, at this point in the plot, is badly in need of advancement. Giovanni, disguised as Leporello, is busily sending Masetto and his friends off on a false trail. He begins in the musical accents of Leporello, but the more aristocratic phrasing of Giovanni creeps into the melody as he warms to the task. The purely musical interest of the aria is not quite sufficient to sustain its length. The earthy sentiments expressed by Zerlina in her 'Vedrai, carino' (No. 19) are dressed up by Mozart in a gracious tune [Ex. 50] in whose mouth butter would hardly melt, though the strings of the orchestra give it a certain warmth in the postlude.

Ex. 50

There is little dramatic justification for the following scene which musically consists only of the sextet (No. 20), but one would be unwilling to lose this great ensemble, begun by Elvira and the disguised Leporello, who are soon joined by Anna and Ottavio who enter to a masterly modulation from B flat to D and a heavenly consolatory phrase addressed to Anna by Ottavio [Ex. 51]. After the entrance of Zerlina and Masetto, the unmasking of Leporello begins, and the tempo quickens

Ex. 51

OTTAVIO

Tergi il ci - glio, o vi - ta mi - a, e dà cal — ma al tuo do - lo - re;

from *andante* to *allegro molto*. Leporello makes his escape at the end of his simple but highly effective aria ('Ah pietà, signori miei': No. 21), as the orchestra illustrates his stealth in four bars of quiet postlude. It is now that Ottavio sings 'Il mio tesoro' (No. 22), which, as everyone points out, is dramatically insupportable. As long as the tenor's voice is flexible enough, it ought not to be a fiendishly difficult aria to sing. It should be omitted rather than allowed to sound difficult; but, if the tenor can sing it, 'Il mio tesoro' is surely the most purely beautiful aria in the score, and expressive of Ottavio's gentleness, even when he swears vengeance in the second part of the aria. The six bars of fioriture on the second syllable of 'tornar' [Ex. 52] are but rarely managed in one breath by the tenor.

Ex. 52

nun - zio vo - gl'io tor - nar!

In the Vienna production, Leporello did not sing his 'escape' aria (No. 21). Instead, he made his getaway after the sextet, in recitative, ending, however, with the same melodic phrase with which No. 21 ends, to the words 'fuggia per là'. 'Il mio tesoro' being omitted, the Vienna production added a duet, preceded by *recitativo secco* in which Zerlina, having pursued Leporello, re-enters immediately, dragging him by the hair. She ties him to a chair and threatens him with a razor, in the duet 'Per queste tue manine' (No. 22b). The recitative begins with the 'Fuggia per là' phrase, which Zerlina sings to the words 'Restati quà'. The duet [Ex. 53] is a charming and amusing piece, and it is a pity that one never

Ex. 53

Allegro moderato

LEPORELLO

Per que - ste tue ma - ni - ne, can - di - de e te - ne - rel - le, per que - sta fre - sca pel - le, ab - bi pie - tà di me,_____ ab - bi pie - tà di___ me!

hears it. But if the price to be paid is the loss of 'Il mio tesoro', that is too high.

The recitative and aria which follow ('In quali eccessi . . . Mi tradì quell' alma ingrata': No. 23), sung by Donna Elvira, are also additions to the Prague score, inserted at the insistence of the Viennese Elvira, Caterina Cavalieri (who had been the first Constanze in *Die Entführung aus dem Serail*). Though it is dramatically irrelevant, indeed damaging to the dramatic tension at this stage of the proceedings, Cavalieri's scena is, in itself, both effective and extremely beautiful. The complex feeling it expresses of unrequited love mingled with pity for her betrayer is by no means out of keeping with the character of Elvira. The recitative, accompanied by the strings of the orchestra, begins with an imposing figure [Ex. 54] which persists until the aria, which is a magnificent

Ex. 54

allegretto, its vocal melody enhanced and supplemented by passages for solo clarinet and flute.

It is in the following scene, in which Don Giovanni and Leporello meet in a cemetery after night has fallen, that we hear for the first time the post mortem voice of the Commendatore. Giovanni and Leporello have been discussing, in *recitativo secco*, Giovanni's latest seduction attempt, when suddenly Giovanni's ribald laughter is interrupted by the Commendatore's voice in a declamatory passage accompanied by three trombones, an instrument we have not heard earlier in the opera [Ex. 55]. The deeply solemn timbre of the trombones (supported by other

Ex. 55

wind instruments) give to the Commendatore's words an awesome authority, for in Mozart's day this instrument was not normally heard in a theatre, but only in a church orchestra. Twice later in this recitative scene, the voice of the Commendatore is heard, accompanied by his chilling trombones, the second time when, with one word, he accepts Giovanni's invitation to supper. In an *allegro* duet, 'O statua gentilissima' (No. 24), Giovanni sings with bravado and Leporello with fearful apprehension as he is made to address the Commendatore's statue. Other commentators have pointed out how, at Giovanni's observation about the strangeness of the scene ('bizarra è inver la scena') the accompaniment sounds like a strange anticipation of nineteenth-century romanticism.

Donna Anna's 'Non mi dir' (No. 25) is a formal two-part aria, preceded by recitative at the beginning of which the orchestra anticipates and quotes the beautiful opening vocal phrase of the aria. It is moving and also highly effective dramatically, and, given a soprano who can manage the coloratura of the fast second part, audiences always respond enthusiastically to it. Some very eminent critics have misguidedly bewailed what they regard as the bad taste of the coloratura in this aria. Berlioz called it 'shocking impropriety', and wrote that he would willingly give some of his own blood to erase that shameful page, in which Mozart had commited 'one of the most odious and idiotic crimes against passion, taste and common sense of which the history of art provides an example'.[1] One is tempted to exclaim, 'Look who's talking!' Ernest Newman sadly and ill-advisedly follows Berlioz by referring to the 'bravura second section that has always been a source of pain to most of [Mozart's] admirers, who find it difficult to understand why the singer should suddenly cease to be the sympathetic and noble Donna Anna and become transformed into a mere Madame This or Madame That, angling for applause'.[2] This admirer of Mozart can only comment that, untainted as he is by the puritan tradition, he has never found the second part of 'Non mi dir' a source of pain to himself, and begs leave to doubt that Mr Newman could have been speaking for very many admirers of the composer. Coloratura can be as effective in conveying emotion as passages not requiring vocal agility from the singer, and there is, to my knowledge, no musical rule which equates plainness with quality.

In the second act Finale (No. 26) can be found those conflicting elements of the opera which have led to so much controversy and confusion among critics. Many German (and some Anglo-Saxon) commentators have found difficulty in reconciling the tragic and the 'giocoso' parts of *Don Giovanni*; they feel that an opera must fit neatly into either the tragic or the comic pigeon-hole. Volumes have been written to prove that Mozart's intention was to write a tragic opera and to explain away the comic episodes; or conversely to explain away the more sombre aspects of the drama, such as Giovanni being dragged screaming to hell, and to prove that Mozart's opera is a delightful comedy. Many excellent operas do fit neatly into such categories, and among them are several by Mozart; but genius tends to make its own rules, and even to break its own rules, and the Mozart of *Le nozze di Figaro*, *Don Giovanni* and *Die Zauberflöte*, whatever the title-pages of his

[1] *The Memoirs of Hector Berlioz* (trans. and ed. David Cairns; Victor Gollancz Ltd, 1969).
[2] Ernest Newman: *More Opera Nights* (Putnam, 1954).

scores may say, has chosen to ignore this particular distinction. Also, the aesthetic conventions of the eighteenth century are different from those of the nineteenth and even more different from those, if they still exist, of today. Accused of inconsistency of aim, would Mozart have known how to reply? The Act II finale of *Don Giovanni* begins as *opera buffa*, develops into drama of the highest seriousness, and, with the concluding sextet, re-enters the realm of comic opera. There is a larger consistency than that of the narrow paths of drama and comedy, and *Don Giovanni* does not betray it. There is the wholeness of life itself, of which *Don Giovanni* might be considered a microcosm. Whether one considers life or Mozart's opera comic or tragic, or diverse, depends, surely, upon one's own temperament.

The finale begins joyously, as Giovanni prepares to eat his supper while the ravenous Leporello tries surreptitiously to snatch some for himself. Giovanni's table musicians begin to play a tune[1] from Martín y Soler's opera *Una cosa rara*, which had been produced in Vienna with great success in 1786, and in Prague in the autumn of 1787 only a few weeks before the première of *Don Giovanni*. The audience would have recognized the tune: Leporello certainly does, and comments 'Bravi! Cosa Rara.' Above the melody, played by the wind band on stage, Giovanni and Leporello continue their exchange of pleasantries. The band now moves on to another song, 'Come un agnello' from Sarti's opera, *Fra due Litiganti il terzo gode*, which had been heard in both Prague and Vienna in 1783 and frequently revived. 'Evvivano i litiganti' exclaims Leporello, who is remarkably well versed in contemporary opera. The third tune causes him to mutter 'Questa poi la conosco pur troppo!' ('I know that one only too well'), for it is Figaro's 'Non più andrai' from *Le nozze di Figaro* which Prague and Vienna had heard the previous year. Felice Ponziani, the Leporello of the Prague première, had been Prague's Figaro as well, so the audience, most of whom knew 'Non più andrai' as well as he did, would have appreciated the joke. As the stage band ends the *Figaro* aria, the mood changes abruptly from comic to dramatic with the entrance of Elvira. In the trio in which she implores him to repent, Giovanni sums up his philosophy with taut defiance in a superb phrase [Ex. 56] extolling woman as the sustenance

Ex. 56

So - steg - no e glo - ri - a   d'u - ma - ni - tà,___   so - steg - no e glo - ri - a   d'u - ma - ni - tà,

and glory of mankind. The appearance of the Commendatore's statue is heralded by off-stage knocks and accompanied by a wild outburst from the entire orchestra, including the trombones (which are only ever heard in the opera in conjunction with the Statue's appearances). The D minor

---

[1] 'O quanto un si bel giubilo', the conclusion of the Act I finale of *Una cosa rara*.

andante of Giovanni's final earthly encounter quickens as the flames of hell appear, and a chorus of voices from below sings of the horrors awaiting him there. Mozart's depiction of Giovanni's brave defiance catches miraculously the heroic fatalism of his character as he faces eternity. (His final 'No' is occasionally sung on the A natural an octave higher than written, by baritones who have the range for it – Dietrich Fischer-Dieskau, for instance – and who can blame them?)

The serious opera ends, but there is a return to the world of *opera buffa* with the entrance of Anna, Ottavio, Elvira, Zerlina and Masetto, who join Leporello in a sextet in which he tells them what has happened to Giovanni, and they express their astonishment, muse severally on their future plans, and combine again to inform the audience that all evildoers will end as Giovanni did. Productions of the opera used sometimes to omit the sextet, a barbarous practice which was at one time thought to have originated with the first Viennese production of the opera, six months after Prague. It is now known, however, that the sextet was performed in Vienna, and no producer of *Don Giovanni* today would dream of truncating this great opera merely in pursuit of so dubious a concept as artistic unity.

XIX

Così fan tutte
comic opera in two acts
K. 588

Dramatis personae:

Fiordiligi	(sisters) from Ferrara,	(soprano)
Dorabella	living in Naples	(soprano)
Ferrando	(their suitors)	(tenor)
Guglielmo		(baritone)
Don Alfonso, an elderly philosopher		(bass)
Despina, servant to the sisters		(soprano)

LIBRETTO by Lorenzo da Ponte

TIME: the late eighteenth century
PLACE: Naples

FIRST PERFORMED in Vienna, 26 January, 1790, at the Burgtheater, with Adriana Ferrarese del Bene (Fiordiligi), Louise Villeneuve (Dorabella), Dorotea Bussani (Despina), Vincenzio Calvesi (Ferrando), Francesco Benucci (Guglielmo), Francesco Bussani (Alfonso)

Così fan tutte

I

WHEN MOZART AND Constanze arrived back in Vienna in mid-November, 1787, after the Prague première of *Don Giovanni*, it was to learn that the doyen of living composers, Gluck, had died a day or so previously. Presumably Mozart attended his funeral. Three weeks later he was appointed by the Emperor to succeed Gluck as Imperial and Royal Court Composer, at a salary of eight hundred gulden per annum, which was approximately twice the sum he would normally be paid for composing an opera for the Imperial theatres. There were no formal duties, but he was expected to write dance music each year for the Court Balls. In fact, during the four years of life remaining to him he composed thirty-six minuets and more than thirty German dances for these entertainments.

In December the Mozarts moved again, this time to an apartment in Tuchlauben, a street in the Inner Town, and there on 27 December Constanze gave birth to a daughter, Therese, who died six months later of intestinal cramp. In May, 1788, *Don Giovanni* was produced in Vienna, Mozart having, in April, composed three new pieces of music for it. Despite his court appointment, he was still finding it extremely difficult to live on his earnings. Unable to keep up the payments of rent for their apartment, in June he and Constanze moved yet again, this time outside the city walls to the Währingerstrasse. It was here that, within a few weeks between mid-June and early August, Mozart miraculously composed his last three symphonies, and arguably his greatest: those in E flat major (K. 543), G minor (K. 550) and C major (the 'Jupiter', K. 551). At the same time, he was forced to write begging letters to a fellow-Mason, Michael Puchberg. The rest of the year was spent composing and giving concerts, but Mozart's concert appearances had ceased to be fashionable, and his financial situation steadily worsened. Early in 1789 the family moved back to the inner city, and took rooms in the Judenplatz. When Prince Karl Lichnowsky, a Mason and member of the same lodge as Mozart, invited the composer to accompany him on a visit to the court of Frederick William II of Prussia, Mozart accepted with enthusiasm. On 7 April they set out for Berlin and Potsdam, via Prague, Dresden and Leipzig. In Prague and Dresden Mozart renewed acquaintance with old friends, and in Dresden gave a concert at his hotel, at which a number of fellow-Austrian musicians took part. For the Saxon Elector, he played his recent D major piano concerto, K. 537, and was rewarded with a snuff-box and 100 ducats. In Leipzig he played on the organ in Bach's old church of St Thomas, in the presence of a pupil of Bach. An eyewitness relates that Mozart played quite beautifully for about an hour, and that Bach's pupil was delighted and thought that his old master had been resurrected. In Berlin, after having played before Queen Frederike, Mozart received a commission from the King to compose six string quartets and six piano sonatas for the young Princess Frederike Charlotte to play. Throughout his journey, he wrote loving, and teasingly erotic letters to Constanze. He arrived back in Vienna on 4 June. Within weeks he was having to appeal again to Puchberg for a further loan, although he had not been able to repay the money he had borrowed earlier. Constanze was unwell and had gone to take a cure at Baden, about seventeen miles south of Vienna, where Mozart visited her frequently. After several minor commissions and engagements which brought him very little money, Mozart at last received, in October, another commission for an opera.

This new request from the Emperor Joseph II probably resulted from the revival of *Le nozze di Figaro* at the Burgtheater in the summer, in which Susanna was sung by Adriana Ferrarese del Bene, for whom Mozart composed two new arias. For the new opera, Lorenzo da Ponte was again called on to provide a libretto, and this time he produced an original work, though it may possibly have been based on a real incident which is said to have amused Viennese society not long before. Perhaps there is a clue offered in the fact that Da Ponte's libretto concerns two sisters from Ferrara who are seduced into apparent infidelity by their disguised lovers, and that these roles were sung at the première by singers who were thought to be two sisters from Ferrara, one of whom, Adriana Ferrarese del Bene, was known to be Da Ponte's mistress. Mozart must have given his agreement for 'La Ferrarese' to sing the leading role of Fiordiligi, although he did not think highly of her as a singer. ('The leading woman singer, Madame Allegranti is far better than Madame Ferrarese, which, I admit, is not saying very much,' he had written to Constanze of a singer he heard in Dresden.[1]) The singer of Dorabella at the première, Louise Villeneuve, was apparently not the real-life sister of La Ferrarese.

Mozart worked on the opera, *Così fan tutte*, throughout the autumn and early winter, during which time a fifth child, Anna Maria, was born to the Mozarts on 17 November, 1789, only to die of cramp an hour later. On New Year's Eve, the opera was sufficiently advanced for Mozart to hold a brief rehearsal to which he invited Michael Puchberg and Haydn. The first rehearsal with orchestra took place on 21 January, 1790, and again Haydn and Puchberg, from whom Mozart took the

[1] Letter from Dresden, 16 April, 1789.

opportunity to borrow more money, were invited. The first performance of *Così fan tutte* was given in the Burgtheater on 26 January. The Burgtheater poster described the new opera as a comic *Singspiel* in two acts, and gave its sub-title as *La scuola degli amanti* (The school for lovers). It was enthusiastically received, even by Count Zinzendorf ('The music by Mozart is charming, and the subject rather amusing'[1]), ten performances were given between January and August, and no doubt there would have been more had not the court gone into mourning for the Emperor Joseph, who died about a month after the première, to be succeeded by his brother Leopold.

II

Disappointingly, Da Ponte makes virtually no mention of *Così fan tutte* in his *Memoirs*. In one half-sentence he refers to the opera (by its sub-title, *La Scuola degli amanti*) as 'an opera that holds third place among the three sisters born of that most celebrated father of harmony' (i.e. Mozart). He mentions it only because he had written the leading role to be sung by his-mistress, Adriana Ferrarese del Bene, though he curiously omits to mention her name.

Da Ponte's libretto is an original work, but it has only fairly recently come to light[2] that the librettist, having plundered the Spanish playwright Tirso de Molina for *Don Giovanni*, appears to have done so again, for at least one or two details of the plot of *Così fan tutte* owe something to incidents in two plays by Tirso: *El amor medico* (a title borrowed by Molière for *L'Amour médecin*) and *La celosa de si misma*. The similarity of Da Ponte's plot to a story in Ariosto's *Orlando Furioso* has also been commented upon, and it has further been suggested that an earlier derivation is the tale of Cephalus and Procris in Ovid's *Metamorphoses*. Truly, there is nothing new under the sun. In any case, until the nineteenth century no one expected plots to be entirely new. Whether original or not, Da Ponte's libretto is neat and amusing. Only those who approach it expecting a profound dissertation on the nature of love and fidelity are likely to find it seriously disappointing.

The action of the opera takes place in Naples in the late eighteenth century, and the opening scene of Act I is set in a café where two young officers, Ferrando and Guglielmo, are boasting about the fidelity of the young women to whom they are betrothed. Their friend, Don Alfonso, an old philosopher, is sceptical. In his view, all women are fickle. The young officers indignantly but confidently enter into a wager with him. He will prove the two ladies capable of infidelity when put to the test, or lose one hundred zecchini. The only condition is that Ferrando and

---

[1] Zinzendorf: op. cit.
[2] In an article by Anna Livermore in *Music and Letters*, Vol. XLVI, No. 4.

Guglielmo are to do whatever Alfonso asks, and of course to breathe no word of the wager to the two young ladies.

The scene changes to the garden of the villa on the Bay of Naples, where the two girls, who are sisters, live. The sisters, Fiordiligi and Dorabella, sit gazing at their lockets which contain portraits of their lovers, whose apparently daily visit they await. Suddenly Don Alfonso enters with, he says, bad news. The two officers have been ordered to report to their regiment immediately for active service on the battlefield, and even now are waiting outside to say farewell. The two young men, now in military uniform, enter, and an exaggeratedly tearful farewell is taken. Fiordiligi threatens to die at Guglielmo's feet rather than allow him to go, while Dorabella swears she will tear her heart out before parting from Ferrando. However, the sound of a drum, calling the officers, brings them somewhat to their senses, and the two men attempt to leave, as a chorus, off stage, is heard singing of the glories of war and the military life. Even now, the girls persuade them to stay a little longer, but Alfonso points out that, as their regiment's ship has just left, they had better catch it up with a few friends who fortunately are waiting with a smaller vessel. A final embrace, and the promise to write twice a day, and finally Ferrando and Guglielmo are allowed to depart. Fiordiligi, Dorabella and Alfonso watch their ship disappear in the distance, and wish it a calm sea and a safe voyage. The girls withdraw to mourn the loss of their lovers, and Alfonso observes that he must now hurry off to the prearranged spot to meet the 'two champions of Venus and Mars' and bring them back disguised.

Inside the villa, their maid-of-all-work, Despina, is trying to serve her mistresses with their breakfast chocolate. Brushing aside their tragic posturings, she briskly assures them that their men are not likely to remain faithful once they are away, and that the young ladies had better make up their minds to enjoy themselves with new lovers. The sisters indignantly stalk out of the room, followed by Despina. Alfonso enters, and in a soliloquy decides to enlist the aid of the maid, whom he fears may be smart enough to recognize the disguised lovers. When Despina reappears, Alfonso bribes her to help him console the reluctant young ladies by introducing into the house two friends of his, who have everything that could possibly appeal to ladies of good judgment. He calls to the two men, who enter disguised in exotic Muslim costumes. Despina does not recognize them, and thinks they look very peculiar and likely to prove 'vero antidoto d'amor', the absolute antidote to love. But she agrees to help, and Alfonso momentarily departs.

Hearing strange voices, Fiordiligi and Dorabella return, and are outraged to find two male foreigners in their drawing-room. They order Despina to turn them out of the house, but the two men immediately begin to pay elaborate court to them, changing partners. Ferrando addresses himself to Guglielmo's Fiordiligi, and Guglielmo to

Dorabella. Alfonso re-enters, greeting the strangers as old friends of his, and commending them to Fiordiligi and Dorabella. In indignant confusion, the sisters sweep out, and the young officers cheerfully assume that they have won their bet. But Alfonso assures them the game has just begun, and reminds them that the time-limit is twenty-four hours. They must keep up their attack on the girls' virtue until the following morning. The two officers retire, confident of the women's fidelity, and Alfonso consults Despina who has by now entered into the spirit of the game, and is as determined as Don Alfonso that her mistresses shall succumb to the advances of the colourful foreigners.

The scene changes to the garden. The two foreigners rush in, each with a little bottle in his hand, pursued by Don Alfonso who implores them not to kill themselves. But the unrequited lovers toss down what they claim is arsenic, and then collapse at the feet of Fiordiligi and Dorabella. Despina is sent for a doctor, and the sisters are left to bring some comfort to what may be the last living moments of the men whose love for them has taken so desperate a turn. Despina now reappears, disguised as a doctor, and revives the dying men with the aid of an enormous magnet, or 'pietra mesmerica' (mesmeric stone). As the men slowly recover and beg for signs of affection, the sisters begin to weaken, out of sheer compassion. But when they are asked for a kiss, their indignation returns, and the first act ends with no further advantage to Alfonso's scheme.

Act II begins indoors, with Despina urging her mistresses to enjoy themselves. Once she has left them alone, the sisters consider the possibility of indulging in a little harmless flirtation. Fiordiligi's scruples delay her momentarily, but soon they decide: Dorabella will amuse herself with 'the little dark one', who is the disguised Gùglielmo, Fiordiligi's betrothed, while Fiordiligi chooses 'the little fair one', Ferrando.

The scene now changes back to the garden, where the suitors have gone to some trouble to produce an appropriate atmosphere. A barge is moored at the landing-stage, from which the disguised Ferrando and Guglielmo, accompanied by other singers and musicians, serenade the ladies. Alfonso gives directions to the servants to decorate the scene with flowers. Fiordiligi and Dorabella arrive, but find themselves tongue-tied, and faced with an apparent change of heart the men are disconcerted and unsure of how to proceed. Eventually, with the help of Alfonso and Despina, the couples are sorted out, and Fiordiligi and Ferrando wander off among the trees while Guglielmo makes love to Dorabella and is somewhat surprised to find that she responds. They exchange tokens: he gives her a heart-shaped locket, and she allows him in return to keep the locket which Ferrando had given her. They walk off together, arm in arm, after which Fiordiligi enters in some agitation, pursued by Ferrando. Fiordiligi feels her fidelity to Guglielmo threatened by her new admirer. Although she repulses him, when she is alone she admits to a guilty passion for him.

Ferrando and Guglielmo meet to compare notes. Ferrando assures Guglielmo that his Fiordiligi is purity incarnate, and waits to hear the same said of Dorabella. Instead, Guglielmo dangles in front of his friend the locket he has been given, and expresses himself cynically on the subject of that feminine virtue he had earlier been so quick to defend. Goaded by jealousy, by Alfonso, and by Guglielmo's complacent assurance that Fiordiligi will remain faithful to him, Ferrando resolves to make a fresh assault upon Fiordiligi's virtue.

Inside the villa, Dorabella confesses that she is enjoying herself, but Fiordiligi is determined to escape from temptation, and decides to dress in a uniform belonging to Ferrando (not, curiously, a uniform of her own lover, Guglielmo) and go to the battlefield to be with Guglielmo. She is about to assume her disguise when Ferrando enters, and she finds she can no longer defend herself against his charms. She admits her love for him.

Guglielmo, who has overheard, is in despair, and asks how they should punish the women. Alfonso's advice is to marry them. He will arrange a double ceremony, in which all will end happily, for, deep down, despite their infidelities, he is sure the original couples love each other.

The wedding is celebrated in the final scene of the opera, the notary being Despina in another of her disguises, who marries Fiordiligi to Ferrando and Dorabella to Guglielmo in a mock ceremony. At the height of the festivities, the familiar military march is heard off-stage, and the women immediately realize that it heralds the return of the two officers. Their newly acquired husbands flee in terror, and soon the familiar faces of Ferrando and Guglielmo appear to confront two very frightened young women. The men find the marriage contract, which Alfonso has conveniently dropped, and angrily accuse the women. Alfonso blandly assures them that it is true that a double wedding has just taken place, and that they will find proof in the next room. The two young men leave, and return wearing half of their Muslim costumes. 'The Albanian cavalier bows before you,' is Ferrando's ironic greeting to Fiordiligi, while Guglielmo sings a phrase of the serenade with which he had wooed Dorabella. The sisters, and indeed Despina, are dumbfounded, but Alfonso restores everyone's good humour by asserting that all of them will be the wiser for the experience they have undergone. The girls swear that they will now be true to their original lovers, who reply that they believe it but have no wish to put it to the test. In a final chorus, all six characters sing in praise of the optimistic rationalist whose temperament is the one best suited to weather the storms of life.

III

The Overture is in C major, the basic tonality of *Così fan tutte*, to which the opera keeps returning. After two quick chords from the full orchestra to gain the audience's attention, it begins with a short *andante* in which the oboe, associated in the opera with the cynical comments of Don Alfonso, plays a phrase of such tenderness that it can have no connection with Alfonso. The only actual theme from the opera to be heard in the Overture is that sung in Act II by the three men to the words of the title, 'Così fan tutte' (All women are like that). (In No. 30; see Ex. 64.) In the Overture this phrase is blared forth loudly by the wind instruments at the end of the *andante*, and followed immediately by a bustling *presto* which sets the superficially light-hearted mood of the opera, and persists until the end of the Overture, pausing only momentarily to repeat the 'Così fan tutte' phrase.

The first scene consists of three trios for the male characters, separated by *secco* recitative. We shall be some way into the opera before we hear any accompanied recitative, and then, at least in Act I, it will be used satirically. As the curtain rises on the first scene the orchestra announces the tune to which first Ferrando (tenor) and then Guglielmo (baritone) will sing the praises of his beloved, thus provoking their friend Alfonso to cast doubt on such paragons of female virtue. This first trio (No. 1: 'La mia Dorabella capace non è') is dominated by the high-spirited confidence of the two young officers, just as the tone of the second (No. 2: 'È la fede delle feminine come l'araba Fenice') is set by Alfonso's disbelieving laughter which he shares with the flute and bassoon. The third trio (No. 3: 'Una bella serenata') is launched confidently by Ferrando who is announced by trumpets and drums, and ends with an extended coda, in contrast to the two earlier trios which glide easily into the recitative. The three trios are a unified whole, and the recitative between them should be performed briskly enough to make this clear to the audience.

The sisters are introduced in a duet (No. 4: 'Ah guarda, sorella') in which they sigh ecstatically over the miniature portraits of their lovers. The words make it clear that we are to laugh at their exaggerated protestations of love, but here, as elsewhere throughout the opera, Mozart's music is either ambiguous or, more likely, deliberately ambivalent in tone, for the gentle warmth of the orchestral introduction, clarinets and bassoons predominant, persists through the *andante* of the duet, while the *allegro* continues the mood of serene confidence in which the young ladies bask in their condition of happy, unclouded love. It is not unclouded for long: Don Alfonso bursts in with his only separate solo number in the entire score (No. 5: 'Vorrei dir'), an F minor aria which is over so quickly it hardly deserves to be called an aria. To an accompaniment of syncopated strings depicting his breathless agitation, he simulates and communicates distress in a series of broken phrases [Ex. 57]. The quintet (No. 6, 'Sento, o Dio') is the first

Ex. 57

of the masterly ensembles to be found in *Così fan tutte*. The two sisters voice their real grief, while the men pretend, though the sentimental Ferrando adopts the sisters' lyrical accents more frequently than he does the *buffo* style of his colleagues. The opening of the quintet lends itself to comic exaggeration, but the development is of such beauty that only the grumbling of the two lower male voices prevents the situation from becoming unsuitably serious.

An attractive short duet or 'duettino' (No. 7, 'Al fato dan legge quegli occhi vezzosi') for Ferrando and Guglielmo, preceded by a passage of *secco* recitative which the two men also sing in duet, is almost invariably omitted from performances of the opera. While I can hardly claim that the work is damaged greatly by its omission, this is only the first of three numbers which are usually cut, on the grounds that they are not up to the general standard of excellence and that *Così fan tutte* is a long opera. It *is* a long opera, but not all that long. A performance without cuts takes almost exactly three hours without interval (each of the two acts lasts about ninety minutes), and the total time saved by making the usual cuts of Nos. 7, 24 and 27 is less than ten minutes. The men's duettino, *pace* those Mozart commentators who have found it 'poor both in musical substance and in characterization'[1] or 'hardly worthy of Da Ponte and not at all worthy of Mozart',[2] fits appropriately into the dramatic situation, is not uncharming, and takes less than a minute and a half to perform.

Equally suited to the dramatic situation, but no stronger in musical substance or characterization, is the delightful march chorus which follows (No. 8: 'Bella vita militar'), which no conductor or director would dream of omitting (unless he were attempting to perform the opera without the expense of engaging a chorus).[3] The march, to which the villagers sing of the glory of the military life, is no more belligerent than a toy soldier, despite its trumpets and drums. In the quintet which follows (No. 9: 'Di scrivermi ogni giorno') the quartet of lovers take

[1] Jahn: *Life of Mozart*.   [2] Newman: *Opera Nights*.
[3] The present writer, in his misguided youth, stage-managed such a production of the opera.

their farewells, to music of almost heart-breaking loveliness, while the bass voice of Alfonso, silent for most of their leave-taking, comments at the beginning and end of the ensemble that he is about to burst with suppressed laughter. His muttering does little to disturb the serene beauty of the moment, for the music speaks eloquently of the anguish of parting, even though that anguish is felt only by the two sisters. That the quintet is so moving, the long phrases of the lovers and the gently pulsating, almost sobbing accompaniment so perfectly in accord with the sisters' view of the situation, would suggest either that we are meant to believe Ferrando and Guglielmo to be consummate actors, greatly experienced in deception, or that Mozart, finding it too complex a task, made no attempt to portray their duplicity.

The march (No. 8) is heard again immediately the quintet has ended, and the two young officers depart. There follows a most beautiful trio (No. 10: 'Soave sia il vento') in which the sisters and Alfonso pray that the travellers be transported safely by a gentle breeze and a calm sea. This time even Alfonso's cynicism is stilled, and he contributes to the trio not as a character but simply as a voice. The muted violins and soft wind chords of the accompaniment suggest the murmur of wind and wave, while the voices breathe a heavenly, transfiguring calm of the kind often found in the *andantes* of Mozart's piano concerti. At this moment we are far removed from *opera buffa*, and it is necessary for Alfonso to bring us back to it briskly, after the trio, with a passage of recitative which begins as *secco*, but into which the orchestra suddenly enters to support him for the last thirteen bars as he rages against woman's infidelity.

In Dorabella's recitative and aria (No. 11: 'Smanie implacabile'), both Da Ponte in his text and Mozart in his music satirize the high passions of *opera seria*, though to a modern audience the element of parody requires to be exaggerated by the mezzo-soprano in performance if it is not to be lost, for it is quite possible to listen to 'Smanie implacabile' as a perfectly serious aria inserted into a comic opera. (Fiordiligi's 'Come scoglio', yet to come, is too broad to be misunderstood or to require additional emphasis in performance.) Indeed, there is no reason why the aria should not be performed 'straight', for Dorabella's grief is no less real for being over-indulged. It is immediately put in its place by Despina's 'In uomini, in soldati' (No. 12), a cheerful little *allegretto* in which the typical soubrette's amoral philosophy is expounded in an introductory passage in 2/4 and in the aria proper in a jovial 6/8.

The sextet (No. 13: 'Alla bella Despinetta') sounds as though it was intended as an act finale, and it is possible that, while he was writing it, Mozart may have thought of dividing the opera into four acts, similar to *Le nozze di Figaro*. Like the *Figaro* finales this sextet advances the action, and is more unashamedly comical in tone than the earlier numbers in the opera. It retains, throughout, its key of C major and its *allegro* tempo, indicating developments in the action by changes of time.

Alfonso's recitative, as he pretends to recognize his old friends from Albania, is supported by the orchestra. The harpsichord takes over for a few bars, but the orchestra is called in again to lend artistic verisimilitude to the otherwise bald and unconvincing narrative of Ferrando's and Guglielmo's declarations of love to, respectively, Fiordiligi and Dorabella, and this leads into Fiordiligi's recitative preceding her aria, 'Come scoglio' (No. 14). That Madame Ferrarese del Bene was a singer of prodigious gifts is evident from the demands made in 'Come scoglio' upon her range (from the A below middle C to high C) and flexibility. The formal display aria of *opera seria* is parodied wittily, but simultaneously taken seriously as a model, and the soprano who can negotiate the rapids of this formidable aria is assured of enthusiastic applause. As in *Don Giovanni* and *Le nozze di Figaro*, Mozart has sharply differentiated between types of soprano in *Così fan tutte*, making a distinction between temperaments as well as between social classes.

Guglielmo's response to Fiordiligi's grandiloquent outburst was originally in an aria, 'Rivolgete a lui lo sguardo',[1] but Mozart had second thoughts and replaced it with a shorter, less formal aria, 'Non siate ritrosi' (No. 15), whose informality is more in accord with Guglielmo's temperament, and which makes a more effective contrast with 'Come scoglio'. At its conclusion, Guglielmo collapses with laughter, and this leads directly into the delightful little laughing trio, 'E voi ridete?' (No. 16) in which the two young officers' amusement is set off against Alfonso's irritated discomfiture. Ferrando's aria, 'Un' aura amorosa' (No. 17), follows. Whether one agrees with Ernest Newman that it is sickly-sentimental, excessively long, and commonplace, or delights, like Alfred Einstein, in its lyric tenderness, presumably depends upon one's temperament. Certainly the aria is superfluous, but that could be said of the majority of arias in opera. Ferrando *is* more sentimental than his friend Guglielmo, and 'Un' aura amorosa' is a love song, conventional in the feelings it expresses, though surely anything but commonplace in the musical language in which those feelings are conveyed.

The Act I finale ('Ah! che tutta in un momento si cangiò la sorte mia': No. 18) moves from the sensuous mood of the sisters' duet with its delicate accompaniment in which flutes and bassoons are prominent, through the drama of the pretended suicide attempt on the part of the disguised lovers, the appearance of Despina as a comical doctor, and the gradual weakening of the sisters, to their outraged reaction when a kiss is required of them. In case we do not immediately realize that the medical gentleman is Despina, 'his' entrance is accompanied by the orchestral introduction to the maid's aria (No. 12) now in 3/4 time. (The

---

[1] Listed in the Mozart catalogue separately as K.584.

doctor cures Ferrando and Guglielmo by means of a huge magnet and a reference to mesmerism; a private Mozart-Da Ponte joke, for Doctor Mesmer had been a friend of the Mozart family, and it was in his house that the twelve-year-old Mozart's *Bastien und Bastienne* was first performed.) As the finale develops, Mozart's ideas proliferate, following one another in swift profusion. Dr Mesmer's magnet revives the lovers to the trilling of flutes, oboes and bassoons as its mysterious current flows through them, and the turbulent *presto* which follows the convalescents' request for 'un bacio' (a kiss) works itself up to a magnificent climax.

To begin any act of an opera with *recitativo secco* is generally thought today to be a miscalculation, though less so when the performance is in one's vernacular. Act II of *Così fan tutte* begins with a rather too long dialogue scene between the two sisters and Despina, but when Despina sings her lighthearted advice on how to deal with the opposite sex (No. 19: 'Una donna a quindici anni') she does so in an *andante-allegretto* aria of pert charm. The sisters' defences begin audibly to weaken in 'Prenderò quel brunettino' (No. 20), a delightfully irresponsible duet in which, accompanied by the cynical oboes of Alfonso instead of the romantic-sentimental clarinets, the girls anticipate a little mild flirtation. Their voices blend in thirds and sixths, and follow each other in canon and imitation. It is Dorabella who leads, in choosing to take the dark one ('quel brunettino'), but her sister is a willing partner in the adventure, singing with equally delighted anticipation of the 'biondino'. After the duet, Alfonso enters to invite the ladies into the garden where the 'Albanians' are waiting to serenade them. In the German translation made by Eduard Devrient in 1860, an attempt was made at this point to 'clean up' the plot by the insertion of a scene in which Despina reveals to the sisters the real identity of their new suitors [Ex. 58], thus making

Ex. 58

nonsense of the remainder of the action, Fiordiligi and Dorabella now being saved from immorality by the knowledge that they are outwitting the men. (In Da Ponte's libretto, Despina thinks she is aiding and abetting infidelity, and does not know that the 'Albanians' are Ferrando and Guglielmo.)

The serenade arranged by Guglielmo and Ferrando (No. 21: 'Secondate, aurette amiche') is a serene *andante*, first played by clarinets, horns and bassoons, and then sung by the two men themselves. A chorus of guests joins in the postlude, in which flutes are added to the accompaniment. The mood conjured up is of Arcadian contentment. But the young lovers do not know how to carry their flirtation forward, so Alfonso and Despina tutor them in the quartet, 'La mano a me date' (No. 22), which is virtually a duet for the tutors, the tutored contributing very little to the graceful banter and cheerful patter of the lesson. Dorabella, the first of the sisters to succumb, does so in a charming, sentimental duet with Guglielmo, 'Il core vi dono' (No. 23), in which the orchestra at one point imitates the heartbeats of the lovers as they coyly sing of their palpitating hearts.

Ferrando's aria, 'Ah! io veggio' (No. 24), is more often than not omitted from performances of the opera, though the preceding recitative, in which Fiordiligi begins to realize she is in grave danger of weakening, is usually performed. A formal and elaborate display aria, 'Ah! io veggio' nevertheless conveys Ferrando's excitement as he finds himself carried away by the dangerous game of pretence he has been playing [Ex. 59]. It is also a highly attractive piece of music, and

Ex. 59

Ferrando ought not to be deprived of the chance to sing it. Left alone, Fiordiligi now accuses herself of mental infidelity to Guglielmo, in her great recitative and aria, 'Per pietà, ben mio' (No. 25), the aria a magnificent E major rondo, with two horns playing a prominent part. Ernest Newman referred to the opening *adagio* [Ex. 60] as 'pseudo-

Ex. 60

pathetic': I hear nothing 'pseudo' in it, despite the prevalence of notes below middle C which the originator of the rôle must have delighted in. The concluding *allegro*, with its coloratura passages and wide leaps, is less touching, though wonderfully effective and exciting in performance. Some commentators take it for granted that Beethoven consciously imitated 'Per pietà, ben mio' in Leonora's 'Komm', Hoffnung' in *Fidelio*, with its obbligato horns. He may have done, though it seems hardly likely.

'Donne mie la fate a tanti' (No. 26), Guglielmo's delightful *buffo* aria, is preceded by accompanied recitative in which Ferrando proves himself less capable of receiving unpleasant news than of giving it, and is followed by Ferrando's recitative and aria, 'Tradito, schernito' (No. 27). The tenor is unfairly treated in truncated performances of *Così fan tutte*, for this is another number which is frequently omitted, though it is a splendidly virile expression of Ferrando's bitterness [Ex. 61].

Ex. 61

In a delightful *allegretto* aria, 'È amore un ladroncello' (No. 28), Dorabella expresses her frivolous philosophy of love. Curiously, Newman dismisses this aria as 'uninteresting', while Dent snobbishly affects to find in it a 'warmth of feeling and distinction that is quite foreign to the backstairs mind of the lady's-maid'. But 'È amore un ladroncello' is, in fact, extremely Despina-like in its style and content, and none the worse for it. In fact, both Dorabella and Guglielmo are closer in character and personality to the amoral Despina than they are to Fiordiligi and Ferrando. The latter pair, a pair only while the Albanian masquerade lasts, are slower to change their affections, but more deeply moved when they make the change. The duet, 'Fra gli amplessi' (No. 29), in which the disguised Ferrando finally wins the love of Fiordiligi, is so beautiful and deeply felt that one cannot in any sense think of it as pretence. It is begun by Fiordiligi alone, expressing, as she thinks, her determination not to yield. However, when she hears Ferrando's voice she begins to weaken. As she does so, his pleading becomes more urgent, and he presses his advantage in an especially sensuous passage [Ex. 62] after which, to the tenderest of comments on

Ex. 62

the oboe, Fiordiligi yields in a simple phrase into which Mozart miraculously injects an immensity of feeling [Ex. 63]. In the brief *arioso*,

Ex. 63

'Tutti accusan le donne' (No. 30), Alfonso advises his two friends to appreciate women for what they are, and invites them to repeat after him the words, 'Così fan tutte'. The words and their repetition are sung to the musical phrase which was quoted in the Overture [Ex. 64].

Ex. 64

The Finale (No. 31), an extended number which occupies the last twenty minutes or more of the opera, is constructed in several sections which, however, interlock in a less complex manner than the finales of *Don Giovanni* or the second act of *Le nozze di Figaro*. In fact, the sections hardly interlock at all, but simply follow one another. The opening *allegro assai* in which bustling preparation is made for the double wedding is succeeded by an *andante* in which a chorus sung by the guests frames a quartet for the two couples. This leads into a beautiful *larghetto* quartet in which, while the three higher voices sing of their hopes for future happiness, Guglielmo's baritone grumbles about the ladies' infidelity. This is perfectly in character, provides a slight touch of acerbity to flavour the sweetness, and also relieves Mozart of the need to give to Guglielmo the tune which the other three have sung in canon [Ex. 65],

Ex. 65

for its tessitura is rather high for him: one note in it, the A flat, would take him higher than he is required to sing elsewhere in the opera, and is not in every baritone's range. Despina imitates the Notary in a nasal voice in the following *allegro*, and the tempo later undergoes several fluctuations between *andante* and *allegro* before the final reconciliation of the lovers in a brisk *allegro molto* sextet which ends the opera.

Così fan tutte, though no one nowadays denies its greatness, has never achieved the popularity of *Don Giovanni* or *Le nozze di Figaro*. The nineteenth century thought it too frivolous, or even improper, and this opinion is still occasionally encountered. The late Cyril Connolly once confessed to me that it was the one Mozart opera he could not stand, because it condoned the corruption of innocence. I do not think it condones anything of the kind, nor do I think Fiordiligi and Dorabella essentially innocent. *Così fan tutte*, as I experience it, has a formal perfection denied to *Giovanni* or *Figaro*, though the range of musical and dramatic characterization is much wider in the two earlier operas. *Così fan tutte* deals with human relationships sympathetically, even profoundly, though totally without sentimentality. It is as serious a comedy as *Figaro*, and Mozart wrote for it some of his most deeply moving music as well as some of his most delightful. Perhaps it is an opera for the connoisseur of music rather than of opera, for the characters in the other two Da Ponte operas are more interesting, and the action in them is more complex. But the music of *Così fan tutte* is certainly the equal of the other two operas, and in some moods it is easy to think it superior. The opera's musical statement is unique. There is no way of paraphrasing it: all one can do is go back to the notes.

XX

La clemenza di Tito

opera seria in two acts

K. 621

Dramatis personae:

Tito Vespasiano, Emperor of Rome	(tenor)
Vitellia, daughter of the Emperor Vitellio	(soprano)
Servilia, sister of Sesto	(soprano)
Sesto, friend of Tito	(soprano)
Annio, friend of Sesto	(soprano)
Publio, Commander of the Praetorian Guard	(bass)

LIBRETTO by Pietro Metastasio, revised by Caterino Mazzolà

TIME: A.D. 80

PLACE: Rome

FIRST PERFORMED in Prague, 6 September, 1791, at the Nationaltheater (now Tyl Theatre), with Antonio Baglioni (Tito), Maria Marchetti-Fantozzi (Vitellia), Signora Antonini (Servilia), Domenico Bedini (Sesto), Carolina Perini (Annio), Gaetano Campi (Publio)

La clemenza di Tito

I

WITHIN A FEW months of the first performance of *Così fan tutte*, Mozart was again forced to appeal to Puchberg:

> I am now standing at the threshold of my fortune, but if I fail of my goal this time I shall be defeated forever. My present circumstances are such that, despite my auspicious prospects, I should have to abandon all hope of success unless I could depend on the help of a staunch friend. For some time now you must have noticed a certain melancholy about me, and only the very many kindnesses you have already shown me have prevented me from speaking frankly to you. But once again, for the last time, in this moment of my greatest need, when my future happiness hangs in the balance, I appeal to you to help me to the fullest extent of your ability. You know that, if my present circumstances were to become known, it would damage the chances of my application to the Court. . . .[1]

He goes on to speak optimistically of his hopes of further advancement under the new Emperor. In return, Puchberg sent 150 gulden, but within days Mozart was begging for more, and was sent a further 25 gulden. So it went on. Mozart at this time was suffering from severe rheumatic pains in the head ('I would have come to see you myself, but my head is covered in bandages due to rheumatic pains, which makes me feel my situation even more acutely'[2]), and was finding it difficult and painful to work. The tone of his letters to Puchberg grew even more desperate. The advancement he was hoping for was the post of second Kapellmeister, for which he had petitioned the new Emperor. At Puchberg's suggestion he began to take pupils again: in the postscript of a begging letter to him in the middle of May, Mozart mentioned that he already had two pupils, but would very much like to raise the number to eight. 'Try to spread the word that I am willing to give lessons.'[3] It was at this time that Franz Xaver Süssmayr became Mozart's pupil. Süssmayr, born at Schwanenstadt in Upper Austria in 1766, was therefore twenty-five when he began to take lessons in composition

---

[1] Letter written at the beginning of April, 1790.
[2] Letter to Puchberg, early April, 1790.
[3] Letter to Puchberg, middle of May, 1790.

from Mozart, who became very fond of him and admitted him to the family circle.

In June, Mozart accompanied Constanze to the spa at Baden, and for the sake of economy stayed there with her, returning to Vienna only when engagements required him to. He composed a Mass for a church in Baden, but by September he was back in Vienna organizing another move, from the Judengasse to No. 8, Rauhensteingasse, just behind the Cathedral. In October, Leopold II was crowned Holy Roman Emperor in Frankfurt-am-Main, and a number of Viennese musicians, led by Salieri, Kapellmeister to the Court, travelled to Frankfurt. Mozart went, too; but at his own expense. He took with him his brother-in-law, the violinist Franz Hofer, who had married Constanze's sister Josepha. Mozart's hope was that, by being present where so many of the European nobility would be assembled, he might attract a few commissions. Pawning his silver in order to buy a carriage, he set out with Hofer on 22 September. The journey took six days, and Mozart wrote to Constanze the moment they arrived in Frankfurt: 'The journey was very pleasant. . . . In Regensburg we lunched magnificently to the accompaniment of divine music. The cooking was superb, and the Moselle glorious. We had breakfast in Nuremberg, an ugly town, and in Würzburg, a beautiful, magnificent town, we fortified our precious stomachs with coffee. Everywhere, the food was tolerable, but at Aschaffenburg, two and a half stages from here, the innkeeper was kind enough to fleece us disgracefully.'[1]

Leopold II's coronation took place in Frankfurt on 9 October, and a week later Mozart gave a concert in the Stadttheater at which he played two of his piano concerti, and accompanied Hofer in a violin sonata, 'a splendid success from the point of view of honour and glory, but a failure as far as money was concerned'.[2] He returned to Vienna via Mainz where he gave a concert at the Elector's Palace; Mannheim where he heard his *Figaro* performed; Augsburg, and Munich where he performed at a concert given by the Bavarian Elector for the King of Naples. He arrived back in Vienna to find awaiting him a letter (in French) from Robert May O'Reilly, the manager of an Italian opera season in London:

Through a person attached to His Royal Highness, the Prince of Wales, I have learned of your intention to undertake a journey to England. As I desire to know people of talent personally, and am at present in a position to be of advantage to them, I am able to offer you, sir, a position as composer in England. If, therefore, you are able to be in London towards the end of this coming December, 1790, and can stay until the end of June, 1791, and compose during that time at least two operas, serious or comic, as the management may decide, I offer you three hundred pounds sterling. You

[1] Letter of 28 September, 1790.   [2] Letter to Constanze, 15 October, 1790.

would also be free to write for the professional concerts or any other concert-hall though not for other theatres. If this proposal seems agreeable to you and you are in a position to accept it, please do me the favour of replying by return, and this letter will then serve as a contract.

How Mozart replied, if he did reply, is not known. He certainly had no firm intention to visit England at this time. A few weeks later, at a farewell dinner for Haydn who was about to leave for London at the instigation of Johann Peter Salomon, that impresario also invited Mozart to London. But the story has come down to us that, at the door of Haydn's carriage, Mozart said to him: 'I fear this is the last time we shall see each other.' Mozart stayed in Vienna for the winter, composing, teaching, and occasionally performing in public. He also renewed his friendship with Emanuel Schikaneder, the actor-manager whom he had known in his Salzburg days, for Schikaneder was now in Vienna where he was running a suburban theatre, the Theater im Starhembergschen Freihaus auf der Wieden. (The 'theatre in the Starhemberg family's tax-exempt building in the district of Wieden' is more familiarly referred to as the Theater auf der Wieden.)

The details of how Mozart came to write *Die Zauberflöte* for Schikaneder's Theater auf der Wieden properly belong in the next chapter. The two old friends, librettist and composer, collaborating as such for the first time, worked on the opera throughout the summer of 1791, and Mozart composed much of it in June and July, partly at Baden, where he spent some time with the still semi-invalid but now also pregnant Constanze. Towards the end of July, Mozart took her back to Vienna where their sixth child, Franz Xaver Wolfgang, was born on 26 July. He and their second-born, Karl, were the only two Mozart children to survive childhood. Karl died in Milan in 1858 where he had been an official in the Austrian finance department, while Franz Xaver Wolfgang followed his father's profession of composer, pianist and teacher. He enjoyed a successful career, and died in 1844 while taking a cure in Karlsbad.

Two events during that summer of 1791 occurred to interrupt Mozart's work on *Die Zauberflöte*. The first was a visit from a stranger whom Mozart described to Constanze as an odd-looking man, very tall, slender and immensely grave, and dressed from head to foot in grey. The mysterious stranger presented him with an anonymous letter commissioning a Requiem Mass and offering a generous financial inducement. After consulting Constanze, Mozart accepted the commission, though the work was required to be completed in the shortest possible time; the stranger returned to pay the fee and to promise an additional payment upon completion of the Mass. One condition was that Mozart would make no attempt to discover the identity of his patron.

Apart from the financial reason, Mozart may especially have wanted to compose a liturgical work at this time, for he had some weeks earlier applied to the Municipal Council of Vienna to be appointed as unpaid assistant to the Kapellmeister at St Stephen's Cathedral, in the hope of eventually replacing the existing elderly incumbent. Mozart's request was granted, but Kapellmeister Hofmann outlived him.

It subsequently transpired, after Mozart's death, that the odd-looking man who had ordered the Requiem was one Anton Leitgeb, acting on behalf of Count Franz von Walsegg-Stuppach. The Count was a moderately gifted amateur musician who gave musical parties two or three times a week, in which his family and staff played an active part. He was also anxious to be accepted as a composer of merit, and was in the habit of commissioning quartets from different composers, always anonymously. The Count would then copy the works in his own hand, and parts would be made from his score. After the performance, he would ask the assembled company to guess the composer. They invariably suggested himself, and with a modest smile he would tacitly admit the imputation. Count Walsegg-Stuppach ordered the Requiem from Mozart for his wife who had died in February. When, sometime after Mozart's death, he received the score which had been completed by Süssmayr, the Count followed his usual practice, and himself conducted the first performance of the 'Requiem composto del Conte Walsegg' in December, 1793. Mozart, however, in his condition of overwork and serious ill-health, half-seriously imagined that the mysterious stranger may have been from another world, and that the Requiem he was now composing was destined to be sung for the repose of his own soul.

Mozart worked on the Requiem and *Die Zauberflöte* simultaneously. But a second interruption, another commission but a less mysterious one, led him to put aside both works for several weeks. Leopold II was about to undergo another coronation, this time as King of Bohemia, and the ceremony was to take place in Prague in September. For the coronation opera, the Bohemian nobility had chosen an *opera seria* libretto, *La clemenza di Tito*, by Metastasio, adapted and abridged for the occasion by the Dresden court poet Caterino Mazzolà. Mozart was commissioned by Domenico Guardasoni, the impresario acting for an association of Bohemian noblemen, to provide the music for the opera. Though he was not excited by the prospect of returning to the outmoded form of *opera seria*, Mozart enthusiastically grasped the opportunity to produce a work which would be given its first performance on so important an occasion. The libretto was given to him in Vienna in mid-July, and he immediately put aside *Die Zauberflöte* and the Requiem, and set to work on *La clemenza di Tito*. By the middle of August he had composed part of the opera, and set out for Prague accompanied by Constanze and young Süssmayr. As Mozart was stepping into the carriage, the tall man in grey suddenly appeared, and asked what would now happen to the Requiem. Mozart assured him that he would give it priority on his return, and the stranger appeared to be satisfied with this information. Perhaps in order to put disturbing thoughts about the Requiem out of his mind, Mozart continued to work on *La clemenza di Tito* during the three-day journey, by day in the carriage and at night in the inns in which they stayed. He began to write the role of Sextus for tenor voice, but on arrival in Prague discovered that the role had been assigned to a castrato. Working against time, he completed the opera in Prague with the aid of Süssmayr who composed the *secco* recitatives and who may have had a hand in one or two numbers in the score.

On 29 August, the Emperor Leopold II arrived in Prague, followed next day by his Empress. There was a Grand Procession and a High Mass in the cathedral on 31 August, with music provided by Salieri and the musicians of the Vienna court orchestra. A festival performance of *Don Giovanni*, Prague's other Mozart opera, was given on 2 September, conducted by Mozart and attended by the Emperor. The coronation itself took place on 6 September, and in the evening *La clemenza di Tito* was performed, conducted by Mozart. The occasion is described in the *Krönungsjournal für Prag*, published in Prague immediately after the festivities:

> On the 6th, that is the day of the Coronation, the Estates[1] gave a quite newly composed opera (the text of which, however, had been arranged from the Italian of Metastasio, by Herr Mazzolà, theatre poet in Dresden) to glorify His Majesty's day. The composition is by the famous Mozart, and does him honour, though he did not have much time for it and was also the victim of an illness, during which he had to complete the last part of the same.
>
> The Estates had spared no pains over the performance of the same; they had sent the manager to Italy, who brought back with him a *prima donna* and a *primo uomo*. The title of the opera itself was *La clemenza di Tito*. The entry was free, and many tickets were distributed. The house holds a great number of persons, and yet, as one may well imagine, the demand for tickets was on such an occasion so great, that the supply came to an end, because of which many natives and visitors, among them persons of quality, had to go away again as they had not provided themselves with tickets.
>
> His Majesty appeared at half past seven o'clock and was received with the loud applause of those present. The Members of the Estates themselves took in the tickets and were responsible for the necessary arrangements, so that no one having a ticket was refused admission, and no one having no ticket was able to force his way in.[2]

The opera was given a few performances, the last being on 30 September, the day of the first performance of *Die Zauberflöte* in Vienna. Mozart, Constanze and Süssmayr returned to Vienna earlier, in mid-

[1] i.e. The Nobility of Bohemia.
[2] Copy in University Library, Prague. Quoted in Deutsch: op. cit.

September, for Mozart still had much work to do on *Die Zauberflöte*. Before leaving Prague, however, he paid a visit to the Masonic *Wahrheit und Einigkeit* (Truth and Unity) lodge, where his cantata *Die Maurerfreude* (K. 471) was performed, and promised his brethren he would shortly be offering a better tribute to the Masonic spirit. Presumably, he was referring to *Die Zauberflöte*. When the time came for him to say farewell to his circle of friends in Prague, Mozart became so melancholy that he shed tears. 'A sense of premonition of his approaching end seemed to have produced this sad mood, for he already bore within him the germ of the disease which was soon to lead to his death.'[1]

The first performances of *La clemenza di Tito* were coolly received, and the Empress, born an Infanta of Spain, is said to have described the work, oddly, as 'una porcheria tedesca' or 'German swinishness'. The egregious Count Zinzendorf, who had travelled from Vienna for the coronation, noted in his diary[2] that 'we were regaled with the most tedious spectacle, *La clemenza di Tito*'. The opera was not heard in Vienna until three years later, after which, usually in German translation, it became popular in German and Austrian theatres until well into the nineteenth century. It was revived in Prague in 1848 to celebrate the accession of the Emperor Franz Josef to the throne.

II

Metastasio's libretto, originally in three acts, had first been used by Antonio Caldara, whose *Clemenza di Tito* was produced in Vienna in 1734. A setting by Gluck was staged in Naples in 1752, and other composers who produced settings of the same libretto in various European cities include Leonardo Leo (1735), Francesco Veracini (1737), Georg Wagenseil (1746), Davide Perez (1749), Andrea Adolfati (1753), Niccolò Jommelli (1753), Vincenzo Ciampi (1757), Baldassare Galuppi (1760), Giuseppe Scarlatti, grandson of Alessandro and nephew of Domenico (1760), Gioacchino Cocchi (1765), Johann Naumann (1769) and Giuseppe Sarti (1771). After Mozart, Metastasio's libretto appears to have been used only once more, by Bernardino Ottani in Turin in 1798. Mozart, in the catalogue he kept of his own works, noted that the libretto had been 'ridotta a vera opera', made into a real opera, by Caterino Mazzolà. Mazzolà's revisions consisted not only of reshaping three acts into two but also of shortening the lengthy recitatives, and writing verses for new arias and ensembles.

The action of the opera takes place in Rome, in A.D. 80. At the beginning of Act I, in her apartments, Vitellia, daughter of the late Emperor Vitellio, incites Sesto, who is in love with her, to assassinate the emperor Tito, for she is enraged at not having been chosen by Tito as his empress. Though Sesto is a friend of Tito, he is willing to carry out

---

[1] Niemetschek: *Memoirs*. [2] Zinzendorf: op. cit.

Vittelia's commands, love being stronger than friendship. Sesto's friend Annio enters, to announce that Tito will not, after all, marry Queen Berenice. Vitellia hastily instructs Sesto to defer carrying out her orders, since this means that she may yet be chosen by Tito. When Sesto voices his suspicion that she does not return his love, Vitellia angrily retorts that she is weary of his doubts. She leaves, and Annio asks Sesto for the hand of his sister, Servilia, in marriage. Sesto assures his friend that he will seek the Emperor's consent to this.

The scene changes to part of the Roman Forum. Tito enters from the Capitol and takes his place on the throne, and the assembled populace sings his praises. Dismissing everyone else, Tito addresses himself to Sesto and Annio alone, and announces that he has decided to marry Servilia immediately. Noting his friend's obvious embarrassment, Annio hastily speaks up in favour of the marriage. Tito sings of the happiness it gives him to benefit the oppressed and elevate his friends, and he and Sesto leave together. Servilia enters, and Annio informs her she is to be Empress. They sing of their unhappy love.

The next scene takes place in the Imperial Gardens on the Palatine Hill, where Publio, Commander of the Praetorian Guard, warns Tito that there is a conspiracy against him. Servilia enters and tells Tito that she is in love with Annio, to which he replies that he welcomes her frankness and will not come between her and the man she loves. Vitellia enters and, now under the impression that she has been passed over in favour of Servilia, renews her command to Sesto to kill Tito and set the Capitol alight. He hastens off to carry out her commands, but not before he has sung an aria begging her to love him. Immediately he has left, Publio and Annio enter to inform Vitellia that Tito has now decided she shall be his consort. Horrified, Vitellia attempts to call Sesto back, but she is too late.

The final scene of Act I is set in the square before the Capitol. Sesto has passed on instructions to his fellow conspirators, and already the Capitol is ablaze. But he is in anguish at having agreed to carry out a plot against his friend the Emperor, and goes off most reluctantly to play his part in it. As the cries of the populace can be heard in the distance, Servilia, Annio, Publio and Vitellia arrive on the scene to ask each other what has occurred. Sesto returns to announce that Tito has been stabbed to death, and Vitellia is just in time to stop him from confessing that it was he who committed the murder.

Act II opens in the Imperial Gardens. Sesto, having discovered that Tito is not dead, confesses his treachery to Annio, who advises him to make a clean breast of it to Tito. But Vitellia enters and asks him to flee from Rome to protect his life and her honour. Publio and members of the guard enter, and Publio announces that the man stabbed was not Tito but, in error, Lentulus, who has survived to accuse Sesto. He arrests Sesto and takes him before the Senate.

In the great hall of the Senate, the populace renders thanks to the gods for the preservation of Tito's life. Tito sends Publio to discover the Senate's verdict: he himself is still convinced of his friend Sesto's innocence. When Publio returns, it is to confirm Sesto's guilt, and Annio pleads on his friend's behalf. Tito cannot bring himself to sign the death sentence before first speaking to Sesto, whom he orders to be brought before him. Tito tries to find a way to save Sesto, but Sesto cannot offer any explanation without incriminating Vitellia, As he is led off to die in the arena, Sesto asks Tito to remember for a moment their former friendship. Tito departs for the arena with Publio. Servilia and Annio now enter and encounter Vitellia, whom they ask to intercede on behalf of Sesto. Left alone, Vitellia realizes she cannot allow herself to become Empress and see Sesto, who loves her, put to death for a crime to which she had incited him.

The final scene takes place in a great amphitheatre. Sesto is brought before Tito who has already decided to spare him. Vitellia now enters and, throwing herself at Tito's feet, confesses her part in the crime. Astonished at the number of people who appear to have wanted to betray him, the magnanimous Emperor nevertheless refuses to take refuge in cruelty. He pardons everyone, and the opera ends with the entire populace praising the clemency of their Emperor.

III

When one considers that La clemenza di Tito is Mozart's penultimate opera, composed after the three great Da Ponte operas at a time when he had also written the greater part of Die Zauberflöte, one is inclined not to appreciate it at its true worth. As an opera seria, it cannot fail to appear stiffly formal in the light of Le nozze di Figaro and Don Giovanni, and it is hardly surprising that most commentators on Mozart refer to it unenthusiastically. 'Mozart did what he could,' says Einstein.[1] In the opinion of Dent, 'it can only be considered as a museum piece'.[2] If, however, La clemenza di Tito had been written before Idomeneo, it is likely that critical opinion would rate it more highly than at present it does, for it would then be seen as a fine example of opera seria without being required to compete for our affection against the more modern operas which followed it.

By this, I do not mean to say that I think La clemenza di Tito the equal of Idomeneo. After Idomeneo, Mozart must surely have felt that he had exhausted the old forms: certainly the earlier opera breathes more life into those forms than the later one. Also, La clemenza di Tito was composed under a greater than usual pressure. It was a rushed job, dashed off in three weeks to a libretto thrust upon the composer while he was still trying to complete Die Zauberflöte. And, by this time, he was in

---

[1] Alfred Einstein: Mozart, His Character, His Work.   [2] Dent: Mozart's Operas.

very poor health. The wonder is that the opera contains as much beautiful music as it does. To expect it to be a dramatic work of the first magnitude, as well, is unrealistic.

Composed at the last moment, the Overture nevertheless does not make use of any themes from the opera: instead it establishes a mood which, though formal, is also festive. Its contrapuntal development section links it in mood with the *Zauberflöte* Overture which must have been composed only a week or two later. The individual numbers of *La clemenza di Tito* are, of course, separated by *recitativo secco*, and immediately after the Overture the curtain goes up on a conversation in recitative between Vitellia and Sesto. (Mozart's young pupil Franz Süssmayr is thought to have written all the recitative in the opera.) Their duet (No. 1: 'Come ti piace, imponi') consists of an *andante* section in which the two characters sing separately, the music appropriately portraying first Sesto's love and then Vitellia's fury, and an *allegro* in which they sing together, the music now having to render the dramatic situation somewhat more ambiguously. Two of the male characters in the opera, Sesto and Annio, are written for soprano voices. In the Prague production, Sesto was sung by a castrato and Annio by a female soprano, though it is clear from his early sketches that Mozart initially planned the role for a tenor voice. To have two male roles sung by female voices is not exactly a help to the opera in modern productions, even when, as often happens, mezzos are used instead of sopranos. To use tenors, however, would do violence to the texture of the music.

The soprano Vitellia's music has a very low tessitura which is equally well suited to a mezzo-soprano, except that in the trio, 'Vengo aspettate', she has to produce a top D, at which even some sopranos might baulk.[1] The first of Vitellia's two arias (No. 2: 'Deh se piacer mi vuoi') is a two-part *larghetto-allegro*, and musically rather too charming for the sentiments it expresses. There is characterization of a kind here, but it seems as though Mozart has been content to take Vitellia's words at their face value. In the duettino (No. 3), 'Deh prendi un dolce amplesso', the two friends Sesto and Annio (both adult males, one has to remember, despite their soprano voices) express their feelings of warm friendship. Only twenty-four bars long, this simple little piece became immensely popular out of its operatic context; though only, one imagines, because of its simplicity. It might almost have been intended for *Die Zauberflöte* and have strayed into *La clemenza di Tito* by mistake!

A brilliantly scored festive march (No. 4) is followed by a chorus (No. 5: 'Serbate, o Dei custodi'), a vigorous and joyous *allegro* in praise of Tito. After recitative, the chorus is repeated, and then the march. Tito replies in his first aria (No. 6: 'Del più sublime soglio'), a simple *andante* which begins without any orchestral introduction [Ex. 66], and proceeds

---

[1] When Dame Janet Baker (mezzo-soprano) sang Vitellia in the Royal Opera production in London in 1974, she did not always attempt the note.

Ex. 66

upon its stately way with something of the serenity of Gluck rather than of anything in Mozart's own earlier *opere serie*. Most of the arias in this opera are concise to the point almost of terseness. This, together with a general absence of accompanied recitative, tends to give *La clemenza di Tito* the appearance more of a court masque than of a piece of drama through music.

Even more popular with its first audiences than the duettino for Sesto and Annio was the Duet (No. 7: 'Ah, perdona al primo affetto') for Annio and Servilia, a touchingly innocent love duet without a trace of passion or sensuousness. Dent thought it 'one of Mozart's loveliest inspirations',[1] and perhaps it is, though I would not place it on my personal short list. Its 2/4 time and key of A major call to mind the duet 'Là ci darem la mano', and so does its orchestration, but it seems to me dull when set beside that inspired piece. Still, Beethoven admired 'Ah, perdona al primo affetto', and improvised a fantasia on it at a concert he gave in Prague seven years after the première of *La clemenza di Tito*; its opening melody is said to be the tune to which Shelley wrote 'I arise from dreams of thee', but I can only echo the observation of Edward Dent[2] that 'it cannot be said that the words go well with the tune.'

Tito's second aria (No. 8: 'Ah, se fosse intorno al trono'), a short, quite lively, but conventional *allegro*, is followed by the first of the three really impressive arias in the opera (the others are Nos. 19 and 23), Sesto's 'Parto, parto' (No. 9). This is the aria today best known outside the opera [Ex. 67]. Though dramatically no more convincing than any

Ex. 67

other number in the score, 'Parto, parto' is a magnificent virtuoso aria in three parts, *adagio-allegro-allegro assai*, and its virtuosity is instrumental as well as vocal, for it contains an obbligato part for clarinet which Mozart wrote for his friend and fellow-Mason Anton Stadler who played in the orchestra at the first performance. (It was for Stadler that Mozart

[1] Dent: op. cit.   [2] Dent: op. cit.

composed his beautiful Clarinet Concerto, only a few weeks later.) The elaborate clarinet part goes down into the bass clef, for Stadler's instrument played several notes below the clarinet's normal range. These passages are today played an octave higher. Sesto's aria makes as fine an effect in the concert hall as in the theatre, which I suppose is a criticism of it, or rather of Mozart's essentially undramatic opera.

Dramatically, the finest piece in the score is undoubtedly the trio (No. 10: 'Vengo, aspettate!') in which Annio and Publio, who sing together throughout the trio, mistake for joy the anguish expressed by Vitellia in her fierce *allegro*, which is virtually a solo aria. Here the orchestra is used to masterly dramatic effect, the urgent violin figures emphasizing Vitellia's terror and remorse. Sesto's accompanied recitative (No. 11) leads not into an aria but directly into the Act I Finale (No. 12: 'Deh conservate, o Dei'). It is here, both in the recitative with its passionate intensity and in the finale itself, that the opera leaps from conventionality into life. The chorus of Roman citizens remain off-stage, but their cries of lament alternate with and interrupt the on-stage solos and ensembles. An opening *allegro* quintet, launched by Sesto, leads by way of a short passage of recitative to an *andante* section. There is no concluding *stretta*: the act finishes slowly, quietly and uneasily, the final bars for the principal characters still punctuated by off-stage cries of lament from the chorus. The end is unexpected, and unexpectedly poignant.

Act II begins, like Act I, with *secco* recitative. Annio's aria (No. 13: 'Torna di Tito a lato') is a simple little piece, gentle in manner and quite lively in tempo. It is followed by a trio (No. 14: 'Se a volto mai ti senti') for Vitellia, Sesto and Publio, which is musically striking and dramatically less static than most of the solo numbers in the score. When the chorus expresses its delight that Tito has been preserved (No. 15: 'Ah, grazie si rendano') it does so not in a jubilant *allegro* but in a pleasantly gracious little *andante* which breathes relief and contentment. Between its two stanzas, Tito adds his voice in a solo passage in similar vein. Publio's aria (No. 16: 'Tardi s'avvede') is an innocuous little song, too brief to outstay its welcome, but Annio's 'Tu fosti tradito' (No. 17), though its opening phrase is virtually identical with that of No. 16, is a piece of stronger musical character, a flowing *andante* of great charm. It is followed immediately by solo accompanied recitative for Tito which begins promisingly but which later dwindles into *recitativo secco*. The trio, 'Quello di Tito è il volto' (No. 18), *andante* followed by *allegro*, is both beautiful and expressive, and in performance comes across as one of the most effective numbers in the opera. Like his earlier aria, Sesto's 'Deh, per questo istante' (No. 19) consists of a slow first section followed by an *allegro*, with an even faster coda. The opening *adagio* is deeply felt, but the *allegro* sounds incongruously joyful, given that the dramatic situation is of a man suffering remorse for the crime for which he is about to be put to death. As a piece of euphonious music, however, Sesto's aria is quite beautiful.

Tito's great aria, 'Se all' impero' (No. 20), is distinctly superior to his two earlier arias, a strongly constructed *da capo* with an imperious *allegro* opening, and a contrasting *andantino* middle section which comes from the world of *Così fan tutte* and in fact begins with a near-quote from the *Larghetto* of that opera's second-act finale. The florid passages in the *allegro* are not easy to sing in tempo, but Mozart's tenor Antonio Baglioni had created the role of Ottavio in *Don Giovanni* four years earlier and had not been defeated by 'Il mio tesoro', so presumably 'Se all' impero' held no difficulties for him.

Since each principal characer had to be given his or her aria, Servilia now sings a sweetly innocuous minuet, 'S'altro che lagrime' (No. 21), with the woodwind prominent in its delicately scored accompaniment. This short song, for it is hardly an aria, is followed by Vitellia's accompanied recitative (No. 22: 'Ecco il punto, o Vitellia') and aria (No. 23: 'Non più di fiori'). The recitative is not particularly remarkable, but the aria [Ex. 68] is a superb rondo which became popular in the

Ex. 68

Non più di fio - ri va - ghe ca - te - ne   di - scenda I   me - ne   ad in - trec - ciar.

nineteenth century outside the opera. The obbligato part for basset-horn was played by the clarinettist Stadler at the first performance. The basset-horn's watery, plangent tone gives an individual colour to the accompaniment when it is used with the strings: on its own, the instrument tends to draw attention to itself and away from the voice, though Mozart is careful not to give it too great a prominence. Somewhat too extended a piece to be completely effective dramatically, Vitellia's aria is musically one of the highlights of the opera. It does not come to a full close, but leads straight into the brief but majestic chorus, 'Che del ciel, che degli Dei' (No. 24), in which the citizens pay homage to Tito. The somewhat dull accompanied recitative (No. 25) in which Tito reveals his clemency is followed by the finale (No. 26: 'Tu, è ver, m'assolvi Augusto?'), a lightly scored *allegretto* for the principal soloists and chorus which brings the work to a perfunctory conclusion.

For many years after Mozart's death, *La clemenza di Tito* remained one of his most popular operas. Now, critical and popular opinion places it decidedly below the three great operas which immediately precede it (*Le nozze di Figaro, Don Giovanni* and *Così fan tutte*), the hybrid work written contemporaneously with it (*Die Zauberflöte*) and even the *opera seria*, *Idomeneo*, of eleven years earlier. It would be pleasing if one could redress the balance slightly by suggesting that, in recent years, *La clemenza di Tito* has been unjustly neglected; but, except in the sense that it is unjust, also unwise, to neglect any work by Mozart, there is surely not much of a case to be made. *La clemenza di Tito* is performed nowadays, and I have seen three very fine productions: by Jean-Pierre Ponnelle at Cologne in the 1960s, and more recently at Salzburg, and by Anthony Besch at the Royal Opera, Covent Garden. Anthony Besch's production, especially, brought the opera to vivid life for the period that one was in the theatre, but it does not resonate in my memory, nor, when I return to the opera in the excellent recording conducted by Istvan Kertesz, do I find my respect for Mozart's score ripening into love.

XXI

Die Zauberflöte

opera in two acts

K. 620

Dramatis personae:

The Queen of Night	(soprano)
Pamina, her daughter	(soprano)
Papagena	(soprano)
Three Ladies of the Queen of Night	(soprano; soprano; mezzo-soprano)
Three Boys	(soprano; mezzo-soprano; alto)
Tamino	(tenor)
Monostatos, a Moor	(tenor)
Sarastro	(bass)
Papageno	(baritone)
The Speaker of the Temple	(bass)
Two Priests	(tenor; bass)
Two Men in Armour	(tenor; bass)

LIBRETTO by Emanuel Schikaneder, derived from a number of sources

TIME and PLACE: Ancient Egypt

FIRST PERFORMED in Vienna, 30 September, 1791, at the Theater auf der Wieden, with Josepha Hofer (Queen of Night), Anna Gottlieb (Pamina), Barbara Gerl (Papagena), Benedikt Schack (Tamino), Johann Joseph Nouseul (Monostatos), Franz Xaver Gerl (Sarastro), Emanuel Schikaneder (Papageno), Herr Winter (Speaker)

Die Zauberflöte

I

MOZART HAD RENEWED his friendship with Emanuel Schikaneder when the latter settled in Vienna in 1789 to run the Theater auf der Wieden, and it is hardly surprising that Schikaneder should have wanted Mozart to collaborate with him on a play with music. How the subject of *Die Zauberflöte* was chosen is described in the third section of this chapter. When it was chosen is not absolutely certain. It is usually assumed that Schikaneder, a fellow-Mason, approached Mozart in May, 1791, and persuaded him to write an opera for his theatre to help him avert a serious financial crisis. Mozart, by this time in a state of permanent financial crisis, was in no position to refuse, though he warned Schikaneder that they might find themselves with a flop on their hands, for he had never before attempted a *Zauberoper*, or magic opera. But a letter from Schikaneder –

> Dear Wolfgang,
>   Herewith I return your 'Pa-pa-pa', which I like fairly well. It will do at any rate. We shall meet this evening at the usual place.
>   Yours, E. Schikaneder[1]

– which clearly refers to the Papageno–Papagena duet in Act II of *Die Zauberflöte* is said[2] to have been dated 5 October, 1790. The opera may, therefore, have been begun in that autumn, though Schikaneder's letter, referring to a meeting that evening, cannot possibly have been dated 5 October, for Mozart was in Frankfurt on that date and was away from Vienna from 23 September to 10 November.

Whenever he may have begun work on *Die Zauberflöte*, Mozart had finished the first of the opera's two acts before 2 July, 1791, when he asked Constanze to 'tell that idiotic fellow Süssmayr to send me my score of the first act, from the introduction to the finale, so that I may orchestrate it'.[3] Süssmayr, also in Baden, was copying parts of the score for him. Mozart wrote much of the opera in a small wooden summer-

---

[1] Quoted in Jahn: op. cit.
[2] According to Erich Schenk: op. cit. Deutsch (op. cit) says the letter, which according to him is dated 5 September, is a forgery. The original is in the Vienna City Library.
[3] Letter of 2 July, 1791.

house in the garden of the Theater auf der Wieden. Prince Starhemberg later gave the summer-house, a one-roomed hut, to the city of Salzburg where today it stands in the garden of the Mozarteum.

Mozart was able to send money to Constanze for her expenses in Baden only by continuing to apply to Puchberg. The increasing lack of self-respect indicated by his letters to Puchberg is painful to contemplate. His situation was indeed a desperate one, but the fecklessness in his character which his father had referred to on more than one occasion clearly contributed to his difficulties, though there is no certain evidence that he was, at this stage of his life, the compulsive gambler and libertine suggested by gossip immediately after his death.

The interruptions to Mozart's work on *Die Zauberflöte*, first the commissioning of the Requiem, and then *La clemenza di Tito*, have been described in the previous chapter. When he returned to Vienna in mid-September, Mozart still had several numbers to write for *Die Zauberflöte*. On 28 September he was at work on the march of the priests and the Overture. On the 29th he noted in his private catalogue that the opera had been completed. On the 30th, he conducted its first performance at Schikaneder's theatre. No doubt, rehearsals had begun much earlier of most of the musical numbers in the opera, many of them directed by the theatre's young Kapellmeister, Johann Henneberg, who conducted the opera from the third performance onwards. Schikaneder himself sang the role of Papageno, which Mozart had fashioned for him by keeping the music simple in style and narrow of range. The Queen of Night's arias were anything but simple, and spanned a fantastic vocal range, for this character was sung by Constanze's sister, Josepha Hofer, *née* Weber, who was renowned in Vienna for her range and agility.

The opera was an immense success from the very beginning, and was performed almost nightly throughout October, which, even for the Theater auf der Wieden, was remarkable. Count Zinzendorf noted that he attended the twenty-fourth performance on 6 November: 'The music and the stage-designs are pretty, the rest an incredible farce; a huge audience.'[1] The playbill for the first night informed the audience that Mozart, 'out of respect for a gracious and honourable public, and from friendship for the author of the piece, will today direct the orchestra in person', and that 'the book of the opera, furnished with two copper-plates, on which is engraved Herr Schikaneder in the costume he wears for the role of Papageno, may be had at the box office for 30 kreutzer'. Schikaneder is credited as sole author both on the playbill and on the libretto, whose frontispiece is a symbolic engraving of the Masonic Cabinet of Reflection.

Mozart attended several of the early performances. After that of 7 October, he wrote to Constanze: 'I have just returned from the opera which was just as full as ever. As usual, the duet "Mann und Weib" and

[1] Zinzendorf: op. cit.

Papageno's glockenspiel in Act I had to be repeated, and the trio of the boys in Act II. But what always gives me the most pleasure is the *silent approval*. You can tell that this opera is becoming more and more esteemed.'[1] The following night, which was the occasion when he himself played Papageno's glockenspiel backstage (see. p. 333), he complained to Constanze of the behaviour of 'a thorough Bavarian' with whom he shared a box: 'Unfortunately I was there just when the second act began, that is, at the serious scene. But he made fun of everything. At first I restricted myself to drawing his attention to certain speeches. But he laughed at everything until I could stand it no longer. I called him a Papageno, and cleared out.'[2] The composer of *Die Zauberflöte* obviously appreciated both the farce and the solemnity of his curious masterpiece.

Let me attempt here to put an end to the persistent misinformation, still to be found at least in English-language books and magazines, that *Die Zauberflöte* was written for and first performed not at the Theater auf der Wieden but at a totally different theatre which did not even exist in Mozart's lifetime, called the Theater an der Wien. The Theater auf der Wieden, in the grounds of the Starhemberg residence in the Wieden district of Vienna, where *Die Zauberflöte* was first performed, is no longer standing. It was built in 1787, and was managed for some years by Schikaneder and his wife. It closed on 12 June, 1801, and was later demolished. The Theater an der Wien, on a site in the same suburb but about half a mile away, was built by Schikaneder in the years 1799–1801. The day after the Theater auf der Wieden closed, the new theatre opened its doors with an opera, *Alexander*, with music by Franz Teyber and libretto by Schikaneder. But this was ten years after both the première of *Die Zauberflöte* and the death of its composer. Of course, Mozart's opera was played there in the nineteenth century, but the Theater an der Wien, still in service in Vienna as a theatre for opera and operetta, does not need to have the première of *Die Zauberflöte* falsely assigned to it, for it has its own list of distinguished premières. It was here that Beethoven's *Fidelio* was first performed, as well as Johann Strauss's *Die Fledermaus*, and Franz Lehár's *Merry Widow*.

II

The first scene of Act I takes place in a rocky desert, with trees and hills in the distance. The young prince, Tamino, dressed in Japanese hunting costume, enters carrying a bow, but no arrows. He is pursued by a serpent, and calls on the gods to protect him. He then immediately faints from exhaustion, and three veiled women, the Ladies of the Queen of Night, appear with silver spears and kill the serpent. The Ladies, observing how handsome the prince is, proceed to quarrel

---

[1] Letter of 7 October, 1791.   [2] Letter of 8 October.

about who shall stand guard over him while the others report to the Queen. They resolve the problem by going off together.

Tamino revives, and is relieved to find the serpent dead. He hears the sound of pan-pipes, and, seeing a man approaching from the distance, quickly hides. Papageno, a comical-looking creature, wearing a garment of feathers and carrying on his back a cage full of birds, enters and announces himself, in a song, as a birdcatcher. He hopes one day to ensnare a wife just as he now ensnares birds. Tamino accosts him, and Papageno explains that he makes his living by catching birds for the 'star-flaming Queen' as he describes her, and that, in return, the three Ladies provide him with food and wine. When Tamino asks if it is he who has killed the serpent, Papageno is momentarily terrified, for he had not noticed it. Once assured that it is dead, however, he begins to boast of his prowess in having slain it with his bare hands. Immediately the three Ladies reappear and place a padlock on his lips as a punishment for lying.

The Ladies depart again, after presenting Tamino with a gift from their Queen: a miniature portrait of her daughter, Pamina. Tamino gazes at the portrait, enraptured. Clearly, he has already fallen in love with Pamina. The Ladies return, to announce the arrival of the Queen of Night, and the rocks suddenly divide to reveal her. She explains that her daughter has been abducted by a villainous enemy, and that, if Tamino will rescue her, he may claim her as his bride. The Queen leaves to the sound of thunder, and her three Ladies unlock Papageno's mouth, and persuade him to accompany Tamino on his perilous mission by giving him a chime of magic bells for his protection. To Tamino they give a flute with magical powers. Tamino and Papageno are to proceed to the castle of the evil Sarastro, where Pamina is being held prisoner. The way to the castle will be revealed to them by three genii in the form of boys, 'young, fair, kind and wise'. 'Follow their counsel alone,' the Ladies advise as they bid farewell to Tamino and Papageno.

The scene changes to a room in Sarastro's palace. Pamina has attempted to escape, but is brought back by Monostatos, a Moor in the service of Sarastro. Monostatos calls on slaves to bind Pamina securely. Then, left alone with her, he makes it clear that he intends to rape her. He is thwarted by the entrance of Papageno: each convinced that the other is the Devil, both men rush off in opposite directions. But Papageno immediately returns, having reasoned that, since there are black birds, there may well be black men. He informs Pamina that he is a messenger from the Queen, her mother, and that a prince who loves her will shortly be arriving to rescue her. They leave to go in search of Tamino, but not before singing a duet in which Pamina consoles Papageno who has complained that he has neither wife nor sweetheart.

Act I, Scene III takes place in front of a temple with three doors. Tamino enters, led by the three Boys who leave, after enjoining him to be patient, tolerant and silent. Tamino observes that the legends above the doors reveal that the temple is dedicated to Wisdom, Industry and Art. He approaches the first door, but voices from within order him back. He is similarly repulsed at the second door. As he approaches the third door it opens and a priest emerges (described in the cast of characters as the Speaker or Orator). The priest questions Tamino, and explains that he has been misled by a woman's idle words. Sarastro, the ruler of this domain, is no villain. All will be revealed to Tamino as soon as the hand of friendship leads him to become an initiate of the temple. The priest then re-enters the temple, leaving Tamino in a state of confusion and despair. He wonders aloud when this seemingly eternal night will end, and is answered by voices: 'Soon or never.' When he asks the voices if Pamina is still alive, they answer 'Yes'. Joyfully, Tamino plays his flute, and wild animals of every description gather around him, enchanted by the music. Suddenly he hears Papageno's pipes, and rushes off in search of him.

Pamina and Papageno enter from the opposite direction. He plays his chimes and is answered by Tamino's flute. They are about to hurry in the direction of the sound when they are surprised by Monostatos who approaches with slaves carrying chains. Papageno suddenly remembers the magic chimes he was given by the Ladies of the Queen of Night. He plays upon the bells, whereupon Monostatos and the slaves, bewitched, begin to dance to his tune, retreating as they do so. Papageno and Pamina observe that, if all honest men possessed such bells, they could live together in harmony and happiness.

Suddenly an off-stage chorus is heard, offering a salutation to Sarastro, whose approach is imminent. Terrified, Papageno asks Pamina what they should say to him. 'The truth,' she replies, 'even though to tell it were a crime.' Sarastro and his priests enter. Pamina kneels and confesses she meant to escape, but only because she was being molested by the wicked Moor. Sarastro bids her rise. He understands her great love for Tamino, but he cannot yet allow her to go free, for misfortune would befall her were she to return to her mother. A man must guide her, for without men women lack direction.

Monostatos enters with Tamino whom he has captured. Tamino and Pamina immediately embrace, but are separated. Sarastro orders that Monostatos be given a sound whipping, and then instructs that Tamino and Papageno, their heads veiled, should be led into the temple for the beginning of their initiation into the Brotherhood. A chorus extolling virtue and justice brings Act I to an end.

Act II begins in a porch of the temple. The priests assemble and are addressed by Sarastro. From his words we learn that their religion is that of Isis and Osiris. He informs the priest that Tamino, the son of a king, waits at the north door of the temple, desirous of emerging from the darkness of ignorance into the light of holiness. He is virtuous, discreet and benevolent. The priests agree that Tamino, for whom Pamina has been chosen by the gods, should be prepared for the trials he must undergo, and that Papageno should accompany him. Sarastro leads the priests in a prayer to Isis and Osiris, and they depart.

The scene changes to the crypt of the temple. Tamino and Papageno are led in by two priests who put certain ritual questions to them. Tamino gives satisfactory answers, but Papageno's desire is for food, drink and a wife. One of the priests assures him that, if he submits to the trials, he will gain a young and beautiful wife whose name is Papagena. In the first of the trials, Tamino will see his Pamina and Papageno his Papagena, but they must not speak. Death and despair await the man who is deceived by the intrigues of women.

As soon as the two priests have gone, the three Ladies of the Queen of Night miraculously appear and attempt to persuade Tamino and Papageno that they are being deceived by Sarastro. Their Queen is now within the temple precincts. Papageno is inclined to chatter amiably to the Ladies, and has to be continually reminded by Tamino to keep silent. As a chorus of voices off-stage raises the alarm, the three Ladies quickly disappear. The two priests return to lead Tamino and Papageno to a further stage in their spiritual journey.

The third scene of Act II is a garden in which Pamina lies sleeping. Monostatos, who still lusts after her, now sees his chance. As he approaches Pamina, however, there is a sound of thunder, and the Queen of Night suddenly appears. Dismissing Monostatos, who nevertheless hides nearby in order to eavesdrop, the Queen asks Pamina what has happened to the youth she sent. Told that he has dedicated himself to the brotherhood of priests, the Queen exclaims that Pamina is then lost to her forever. Pamina suggests that they flee, for under her mother's protection she can face any danger. The Queen explains that her power came to an end with the death of Pamina's father. He had voluntarily surrendered to the priests the circle of the sun with its seven compartments, and this powerful circle was now worn by Sarastro. Their only hope now is for Pamina to kill Sarastro and return the sacred circle to her mother. She hands a dagger to Pamina, vows she will have nothing further to do with her if she does not kill Sarastro, and then disappears again. Pamina exclaims that she could never perform such a deed, but Monostatos suddenly emerges from his hiding-place and seizes the dagger. He has overheard everything, he says. Pamina can save herself and her mother only by submitting to him. Pamina prefers death, and is saved from it by the immediate appearance of Sarastro. Contemptuously he dismisses Monostatos, who leaves muttering that, since the daughter won't have him he must try the mother.

Sarastro explains to Pamina that he knows all about her mother's ideas of revenge, but that the brotherhood of the sacred temple knows nothing of vengeance, for they are activated only by love. Within these holy walls men love one another, and if a traitor should be found he is forgiven. He who cannot accept these teachings is not worthy to be called a man.

Act II, Scene IV is set in a hall of the temple. Again the two priests remind Tamino and Papageno of their vow of silence, and again Papageno finds it impossible not to talk. When an aged crone appears and offers him water to drink, he chatters away to her, for want of better company. He is amused when she tells him she has a young sweetheart, but greatly disturbed to learn that his name is Papageno. When he asks her to reveal her name, there is a clap of thunder and she runs away.

The three Boys enter, bringing food and wine, and also the magic flute and the chimes which Sarastro has ordered to be returned to them both. The Boys leave, and Papageno attacks the food heartily. Pamina enters but is distressed to find that Tamino will not speak to her. Even Papageno keeps silent. Heartbroken, she wanders away, and trumpets summon Tamino and Papageno onward.

In the next scene, in the temple, Sarastro and the priests pray to their gods. Tamino and Papageno are brought in, and Tamino is assured that he has done well so far but that he has two more perilous trials to undergo. Pamina is led in, and Sarastro tells the loving couple that they must now say farewell to each other. All depart except Papageno who is told he will never experience the heavenly joys of the brotherhood. He replies that he would rather have a glass of wine. This is provided, and as he drinks it he begins to feel a longing for a wife of his own. The old woman whom he had previously encountered enters and advises him to accept her as his wife if he does not want to be imprisoned for ever on a diet of bread and water. Unenthusiastically, Papageno consents to marry her, at which she is instantly transformed into a young girl.

'Papagena', he exclaims before a priest bears her away with the remark that Papageno is not yet worthy of her.

Act II, Scene VI takes place in the garden. The three Boys sing optimistically of the golden sun which will soon rise to banish superstition and darkness. When a distraught Pamina enters, about to kill herself with her mother's dagger, they prevent her by assuring her that Tamino loves her and is even now facing death for her sake. They offer to take her to Tamino.

The scene changes to a rocky place where two men in armour guard a doorway. Tamino is brought in, and the men in armour inform him that the mysteries of Isis will be revealed to him if he follows the path beyond, to be purified by fire, water, air and earth. Tamino is about to take the path, but Pamina's voice is heard calling on him to wait, for she will undergo the trials with him. She tells him that he should play the magic flute, which was carved by her father from a thousand-year-old oak tree, for it will lead them both through the dangers of the trials.

Tamino and Pamina go through a hall of fire, and he plays the flute which brings them safely back. They then go through another door, again with the flute, and walk through water. As they return, the gates of the temple are thrown open, revealing Sarastro and the priests who welcome them inside.

The penultimate scene of the opera takes place in the garden. Papageno, having lost his Papagena, is in despair. He intends to hang himself unless someone takes pity on him by the time he counts three. He counts, and is saying a final farewell to the cruel world when the three Boys enter with the suggestion that he should play his magic chimes, which he had completely forgotten about. He plays, Papagena appears, and in a cheerful duet they begin to count the many little Papagenos and Papagenas they intend to raise.

Act II, Scene IX returns us to the entrance of the temple. The Queen of Night and her Ladies are being shown how to gain entrance by Monostatos, to whom the Queen has promised Pamina should their plan to overthrow Sarastro succeed. But suddenly there is a deafening crash of thunder, and the Queen and her followers disappear into eternal darkness. The temple doors open, and a blazing light reveals Sarastro, the priests, the three Boys, Tamino and Pamina. Sarastro announces the victory of light over darkness, and the opera ends with a chorus of thanksgiving to Isis and Osiris.

III

The plot of *Die Zauberflöte*, outlined in the previous section, bears more resemblance to pantomine, of whose tradition it is firmly a part, than to *opera seria* or *opera buffa*. It expounds a serious moral, but it also contains scenes of light relief. Surely it will not bear close critical examination? Yet it has been subjected to a very great amount of examination by Mozart scholars, and innumerable meanings have been read into it. It is not my intention to add to the speculation, except to the extent necessary for enjoyment of the opera. Mozart and Schikaneder were both members of Viennese Masonic lodges. That the plot is riddled with Masonic symbolism is obvious; but I am not a Mason, nor, I imagine, are the majority of people who love and appreciate *Die Zauberflöte*. So I can comment on that aspect of the work only from the outside.

Who wrote the libretto? Most books, scores and programmes today credit Schikaneder and Giesecke. The original playbills mention only Schikaneder, for Giesecke's contribution did not become known until nearly half a century later. Karl Ludwig Giesecke, whose real name was Johann Georg Metzler, was a member of Schikaneder's company at the time of the première of *Die Zauberflöte*: he was stage manager, and played a minor speaking role as first slave. He too was a Mason, and had various other professions and interests in addition to the theatre. He had been a playwright, had translated from Italian, and had written for

Schikaneder's company the libretto for Wranitzky's *Oberon der Elfenkönig* in 1789, two years before *Die Zauberflöte*, taking his plot from a story in *Dschinnistan*, an anthology of Oriental stories edited by Christoph Martin Wieland, the German poet and novelist, which had been published in 1786. In 1794 Giesecke gave up the theatre; in 1813 he became Professor of Mineralogy at the University of Dublin and, four years later, a member of the Irish Academy. He returned to Vienna in 1818 in connection with his gift of a scientific collection to the Imperial Natural History Museum, when he accidentally met some of his former musical and theatrical colleagues at an inn. In 1849, one of them, the tenor Julius Cornet, published a book, *Die Oper in Deutschland*, in which he described his 1818 re-encounter with Giesecke:

> Poor Giesecke led a penurious existence in Schikaneder's theatre as a member of the chorus and in small parts. After a time he disappeared; whither, no one knew. One day in the summer of 1818, an elegant old gentleman in a blue coat and white cravat, and wearing a decoration, sat down at the table in the tavern in Vienna at which Ignaz von Seyfried, Korntheuer, Julius Laroche, Küstner, Gned and I met for luncheon each day. His venerable, snow-white head, his meticulous way of speaking, and his whole bearing, made a favourable impression on us all. It was the former chorus singer Giesecke, now a Professor at Dublin University; he had come from Iceland and Lapland straight to Vienna with a natural history collection formed from the plant, mineral and animal kingdoms, which he intended to present to the Imperial Natural History Collection. Seyfried was the only one to recognize him. The old gentleman's joy at being in Vienna and at the Emperor Francis's recognition (he gave him a really valuable gold snuffbox shining with solitaires and filled with brand-new Kremnitz ducats) was the recompense for many years of privation and suffering. On this occasion we learnt so much about the old days; among other things we learnt that he (who was at that time a member of the banned order of Freemasons) was the real author of *Die Zauberflöte* (although Seyfried already had a suspicion of this). I relate this according to his own statement, which we had no reason to doubt. . . . Many thought that the prompter Helmböck had been Schikaneder's collaborator. But in this Giesecke also disabused us; Giesecke attributed to Schikaneder only the figures of Papageno and his wife.

In 1818, Julius Cornet and his companions at luncheon were all members of the Theater an der Wien. Schikaneder had been dead for six years, so it would have been difficult enough then to check the truth of Giesecke's assertion. Thirty-one years later, when Cornet published his book, Seyfried was the only one of those lunchtime companions still alive. He appears to have made no public comment: he had earlier claimed to have watched Mozart at work on the composition of *Die Zauberflöte* in the wooden hut. Seyfried, said to have studied piano with Mozart, would have been no more than fifteen years of age in 1791. It was not until 1799 that he joined Schikaneder's company as second Kapellmeister.

No doubt, as a literate and even reasonably literary member of the company, Giesecke may have played a part in the writing of *Die Zauberflöte*: he may also, after Schikaneder was safely dead, have somewhat exaggerated that part in talking of the past to his old Viennese friends. There is, however, a third person involved, though he did not contribute lines of dialogue but merely exerted an influence. This was Baron Ignaz von Born, the Grand Secretary of the *Loge zur Wahren Eintracht* (Lodge of True Unity) in Vienna. Born in Transylvania in 1742, he had come to Vienna at the invitation of the Empress Maria Theresa to continue his studies in mineralogy. He was one of the champions of the Enlightenment, and much respected in Vienna as a leading theoretician of Freemasonry. Although Mozart belonged to a different Viennese Lodge, he frequently attended Born's, and Born was an admirer and supporter of Mozart's music. He published in a Masonic journal a long article on Masonic ritual which was certainly drawn on by Schikaneder (or whoever) in the writing of the libretto of *Die Zauberflöte*. Born died in July, 1791, while the opera was being written, and the rumour spread not only that he had inspired the work, but that he had been used by librettist and composer as a model for the wise and benevolent Sarastro. It must surely have been Born himself who drew the attention of Mozart not only to his own writings but also to *Sethos*, the hoax novel on which Born constructed much of his Masonic philosophy and ritual and which, for many years, was apparently considered by Masons to be a holy book.

One still comes across the assertion that, after Schikaneder and Mozart had begun to write *Die Zauberflöte*, they were disconcerted to find that a rival theatre had produced an opera based, like theirs, on a story, *Lulu, oder Die Zauberflöte*, from Wieland's *Dschinnistan*. The rival opera was *Die Zauberzither, oder Kaspar der Fagottist*, with libretto by Joachim Perinet and music by Wenzel Müller. The suggestion is that, as a result, Schikaneder changed plot in mid-stream, and that the evil Sarastro became the embodiment of good while the Queen of Night was turned into the villainess of the piece. This seems scarcely likely. In a letter to Constanze,[1] Mozart wrote: 'To cheer myself up I then went to the Kasperle Theater[2] to see the new opera, *Der Fagottist*, which is making such a sensation. But there is absolutely nothing to it.'

That Schikaneder may have re-written his libretto, injecting more Masonic symbolism into it, is not only possible but most probable. However, there is no good reason to suppose that the finished libretto consists of two plots grafted together, or that it changes its intentions

---

[1] Letter of 12 June, 1791.

[2] The Leopoldstadttheater. Kaspar was a traditional clown in popular Viennese theatre, and to refer to a 'Kasperle Theater' is like saying 'a cheap variety theatre'.

owards the end of Act I. On its own ill-motivated, clumsily constructed
evel, the plot is not inconsistent. Tamino believes the Queen of Night to
ɔe the personification of wronged innocence, until his eyes are opened
ɔy initiation into the mysteries of Isis and Osiris, but we, the audience do
not have to think so. She is, after all, the Queen of Night, not of Day, and,
:hough to Wagner and his Tristan night was romantic and day banal, the
words bore a different connotation to the Viennese children of the
Enlightenment in the late eighteenth century, and especially to the
Masons with their sun symbolism. It is easier to believe the Queen of
Night to be Maria Theresa who persecuted the Masons, and the noble
Sarastro her successor Joseph II, than to accept that Mozart and
Schikaneder could possibly intend a character called Queen of Night to
be anything but an apostle of darkness and delusion.

The question of sources of the libretto of *Die Zauberflöte* is even more
complicated than the question of how many people had a hand in
actually writing it. There is no possibility of establishing an *Urtext* of
the libretto itself, for the text must have begun to be corrupted the
moment Schikaneder uttered his first ad lib on 30 September, 1791. (In
the last thirty years, more than one addition by Erich Kunz, the *echt-
Wienerisch* Papageno of the fifties and sixties, has been taken over by
his successors in Vienna, and may well creep into future printed
editions.)

We know that Schikaneder had found the plot of *Oberon der Elfenkönig*
in Wieland's Oriental anthology *Dschinnistan*. The anthology also
contains a story by A. J. Liebeskind, *Lulu, or The Magic Flute*. Here is a
summary of its plot:

The good fairy Perifirime, called the Radiant Fairy, lives in an old enchanted
castle in the Kingdom of Khurasan. During a hunt, Prince Lulu, son of the
king, ventures near the castle, a place normally avoided. There the fairy
appears to him in all her splendour and promises him a large reward if he will
submit to her orders. She confides to him that the evil magician Dilsengbuin,
helped by his perfidious servant Barsin, has stolen her finest talisman from
her: a fiery golden sword that all the spirits and elements of all countries
obey, because every being struck by its sparks at once becomes an obedient
servant of its possessor. But only a young man who has never known the power
of love could, by guile, take possession of the talisman. The fairy designates
Lulu as her saviour, and promises to give him the most precious of her
possessions if he will only obey her instructions. They refer to the beautiful
Sidi, whose father is Sabalem, King of Kashmir, then under the control of the
magician. The latter overwhelms Sidi with his attentions, but she defends
herself thanks to the power that has been given her, which allows her to resist
all outside power as long as her heart is not touched by love. The fairy gives
Lulu two magic gifts: a flute that conquers the hearts of all that hear it,
awakes or calms all passion as desired, and a ring that, when it is merely
turned allows its possessor to change himself into the personage of his

choice. Furthermore, when the ring is thrown to the ground, it brings the fairy to the help of whoever has so thrown it down.

Lulu, thus equipped, transforms himself into an old man and approaches the magician's castle, built on a rock. At once, by the sound of his flute, he attracts the forest animals, then the magician himself, who leads him into the castle, where he will try to awaken the love of the reticent beauty. Lulu succeeds in winning the confidence of the magician and of his son, the dwarf Barka, whose mother is none other than Barsin. He also wins the love of the beautiful Sidi. During a feast, he succeeds in putting both of them to sleep and seizing the sword. With the help of the spirits, and finally thanks to the appearance of the fairy, he overcomes all the obstacles set by the magician, who flees in the form of an owl, his son taking on that of a barn owl. The fairy demolishes the castle on the rock and takes the lovers in her chariot to her own castle, where the Kings of Khurasan and Kashmir bless their union.[1]

It is easy to see in this the beginnings of Schikaneder's *Zauberflöte*, whose plot, however, develops quite differently. A précis of the plot of *Kaspar der Fagottist, oder Die Zauberzither*[2] reveals such wide divergences from the original story, but along lines completely different from those of *Die Zauberflöte*, that there can be no possibility of Schikaneder having felt threatened by it.

Clearly, Schikaneder had a source or sources other than *Dschinnistan*. There are similarities between *Die Zauberflöte* and two earlier works by Mozart: Gebler's drama *Thamos, König in Ägypten*, for which he had provided incidental music and choruses, and *Zaide*. Thamos deals with the Masonic conflict between light and darkness, while *Zaide* contains a scene in which Gomatz finds a portrait of Zaide, immediately falls in love with her, and sings a love song not unlike Tamino's in a parallel scene in *Die Zauberflöte*. Schikaneder had already written in 1790, a libretto, *Der Stein der Weisen*, which includes several *Zauberflöte* elements, including a trial by fire and water.

The work of which Schikaneder made most use was a lengthy French novel, *Sethos*, first published in 1731, and later translated into many languages. There were two German translations: the first in 1732 and another in 1778. Purporting to be a work 'dans lequel on trouve la description des initiations aux Mystères Egyptiens, traduit d'un manuscrit Grec', *Sethos* was in fact, written by the Abbé Jean Terrasson, Professor of Greek and Latin Philosophy at the Collège de France. Sethos is an Egyptian prince, and the first part of the novel deals with his initiation into the mysteries of Isis and Osiris. Many of the details in *Die Zauberflöte* come directly from *Sethos*, and in Sarastro's first aria and the chorale for the Men in Armour, the novel is quoted almost verbatim.

That *Die Zauberflöte* was more than just a silly pantomine with the bonus of sublime music by Mozart was recognized from the beginning. As early as 1794, articles began to be written on the significance of the

[1] In Jahn: op. cit.   [2] Also in Jahn: op. cit.

work. It was described as a parable of the struggle between good and evil, and as a political allegory with the Queen of Night representing Louis XIV, Tamino the French populace and Pamina 'la liberté'. It was not until the mid-nineteenth century, however, that the opera's Masonic connections began to be publicly discussed, and it was in 1866 that Moritz Alexander Zille, a Leipzig Freemason, decided that Pamina was the Austrian people, Maria Theresa the Queen of Night and Tamino (not Sarastro) the Emperor Joseph II (himself a Mason). Not until 1914 did anything appear in print cautiously identifying parts of the libretto with aspects of the Masons' secret ritual. At the time of the first production of *Die Zauberflöte*, and for many years afterwards, Masons presumably responded to the real significance of the work, while non-Masons could appreciate the drama in general terms without relating the mysteries of Isis and Osiris to those of Freemasonry. Goethe, a Mason, is known to have referred to the two levels on which the work could be approached. He produced the opera in Weimar in 1794, and planned, and began to write, a sequel some fragments of which have survived, for which he intended that Wranitzky should compose the music. Schikaneder actually wrote and in 1798 staged a sequel, *Das Labirint, oder Der Kampf mit den Elementen*, with music by Peter von Winter.

In 1968, Professor Jacques Chailley wrote a book[1] which in very convincing detail, supported by a great deal of information about Freemasonry in eighteenth-century Vienna, makes the case for *Die Zauberflöte* as a work whose composer and librettist quite consciously set out to construct a symbolic story with a hidden meaning, a work whose Masonic ideals are vitally woven into its fabric, not merely added as inessential trimmings. No one ignorant of Professor Chailley's arguments need feel that his enjoyment of *Die Zauberflöte* is necessarily superficial. But anyone who takes the trouble to read the book will certainly find his appreciation of the opera enhanced when he next encounters it in the theatre. Every age, since 1791, has found its own ideas, desires and aspirations in this opera: historical allegory, Egyptian ritual, social satire, as well as the symbolic ceremony of Freemasonry. But Professor Chailley exhaustively demonstrates that the libretto of *Die Zauberflöte*, far from being the hastily flung-together vaudeville concoction many people take it to be,[2] makes perfect sense as Masonic ritual. This, of course, is not a startlingly original thought. What is new is the detail with which Chailley supports his case, presents his evidence and reaches his conclusions. He has subjected not only the libretto but also the music to extremely close examination. The struggle, as he sees it, is not between good and evil but between Man (Sarastro) and Woman

[1] *The Magic Flute, Masonic Opera* (Gollancz, 1972).

[2] Chailley (op. cit., p. 297), quotes Goethe's admonitory words: 'More knowledge is required to understand the value of this libretto than to mock it.'

(The Queen of Night). Let two examples suffice here to demonstrate his method. The very first scene of the opera, he tells us, 'bristles with allusions to the feminine ritual of the Lodges of Adoption', a ritual in which, for instance, the inspectress applies a padlock to the mouth of the future Companion, to guard her against the dangers of pointless chatter. This is exactly what happens to Papageno. Although he is a man, he is nevertheless in the service of a woman, the Queen of the Night.

The initiatory trials of the second act, according to Chailley, are modelled very closely upon the so-called 'journeys' of Masonic initiation into the first, or 'Apprentice' degree, and they successively evoke the four elements, Earth, Air, Water and Fire. These Masonic trials are apparently accompanied by a strict injunction to silence. In the second scene of Act II of the opera, Tamino is being tested for his knowledge, and for his intentions with regard to the Order into which he is asking admission. That, Chailley tells us, is why the Three Ladies, here representing the social aspect of the feminine world, rise up from under the stage – or the Earth – trying to discredit the Initiates in Tamino's eyes. This gives rise to a scene full of what were then contemporary allusions, and permits Schikaneder and Mozart to protest publicly against the accusations then being levelled at Freemasonry.

If Professor Chailley has his Masonic facts right, and I must assume that he has, then this is really very convincing. Convincing, that is, on *one* level. We know that Mozart and Schikaneder were Masons, and if their opera makes sense in Masonic terms, then it would be absurd to deny that this is because both composer and librettist consciously intended it to. However, although *Die Zauberflöte* may be a Masonic opera, it is not only that. It is both a suburban Viennese farce and a masterpiece of transcendental spirituality. The line between the ridiculous and the sublime is as thin as the line between most other apparent opposites. If *Die Zauberflöte* is about the struggle between masculine and feminine elements, it is also about the union of those elements in a greater, freer creativity. For 'struggle', perhaps read 'creative tension'. The great final chorus, ostensibly praising Isis and Osiris for having penetrated the recesses of darkness with their radiant light, is a hymn of praise to virtue and wisdom of whatever religious or philosophic persuasion.

The opera is invariably shortened in performance, not by the omission of any of Mozart's music, but by truncating Schikaneder's text. This, especially in performance in German before a non-German-speaking audience, is perhaps understandable. But I once attended a student performance in which the libretto was performed without cuts, and I was made to realize how different the work appears when the proportions of music to speech are drastically altered. Clearly, *Die Zauberflöte*, in Schikaneder's Viennese suburban theatre in the autumn of 1791, was more like a play with occasional music than an opera with dialogue, and as much of the Freemasonry is to be found in the spoken dialogue as in the words which are sung.

IV

Although, in *Die Zauberflöte*, Mozart's task was ostensibly only to provide musical numbers to be inserted into a spoken play, he wrote a full-scale overture of great weight and solemnity. Its basic tempo is an *allegro*, preceded by fifteen bars of *adagio* and interrupted once by three bars of solemn chords, but it is the solemnity of these *adagio* passages which pervades the entire Overture. I am in no position to interpret what many commentators refer to as Masonic symbolism here and throughout the opera, and I hope I have made it clear in the preceding section that I do not regard knowledge of Masonic ritual as essential to enjoyment and understanding of *Die Zauberflöte*. But, for what it is worth, I dutifully pass on the information that the first three bars of the Overture [Ex. 69] are

Ex. 69

said to represent the three knocks by which members were or are admitted to the Masonic initiation ceremony. Whether or not this is true (and it probably is), what is more to the point is that they relate to Tamino's attempt, in the opera, to gain admittance to Sarastro's temple. The fugal severity of the overture prepares us for one aspect of the work, its moral earnestness, but it does not prepare us for what one might call the Schikanederisch element of clowning which is equally a part of *Die Zauberflöte*.

In the Introduction (No. 1), Tamino calls for help and then falls unconscious, to be rescued by the three Ladies of the Queen of Night. Most of the Introduction, therefore, is a trio for the Ladies, and the tone is one of lyrical comedy as they quarrel over the handsome youth. The Overture and this first number must have surprised Schikaneder's first audience, for here was music of greater complexity than they were used to being offered in a *Zauberposse*. How relieved they must momentarily have felt next, when Schikaneder himself entered as Papageno and sang his simple and engaging entrance number (No. 2), 'Der Vogelfänger bin ich ja', a strophic song in three stanzas, with all the directness and appeal of a folk-song, which it has now virtually become. The little phrase, five notes of an ascending scale, which occurs as a refrain throughout the song, is played by Papageno on his pan-pipes (a simple instrument, known in French as 'flûte de Pan', but sometimes referred to in German now as a 'Papagenoflöte'). Papageno's phrase will be put to dramatic effect on several occasions later in the opera.

Tamino's aria, (No. 3: 'Dies Bildnis ist bezaubernd schön'), an ardent expression of love, is a miracle of form, and hardly less remarkable in its combination of romantic ardour with an inner, spiritual poise. What Tamino expresses is not the first physical passion of youth, though he is a young man, but a mature depth of feeling, what one might almost call the 'ideal' condition of love, as distinct from the 'real'. The aria's opening phrase [Ex. 70], based on a simple descending scale, is an

Ex. 70

Dies Bild - nis ist be-zau-bernd schön,   wie noch kein Au-ge je ge - seh'n!

example of that extraordinary *multum in parvo* which we frequently encounter in Verdi. Indeed, its similarity to the beginning of 'Caro nome' in *Rigoletto*, in which Gilda expresses a like feeling, is remarkable. The music of *Die Zauberflöte* is written in a bewildering variety of styles, with elements from the old *opera seria*, as well as from popular song and from religious music. The recitative and aria of the Queen of Night (No. 4: 'Zum Leiden bin ich auserkoren') derives principally from *opera seria*, but its recitative ('O zittre nicht, mein lieber Sohn') has a directness and simplicity which make it sound very modern and dramatic. The Queen's utterance is terse and to the point. The orchestral introduction preceding it is more portentous, but then it is intended to parallel the visual effect of the Queen's awesome appearance. The formal two-part aria reveals the ambiguity of the Queen of Night's character, for the opening *larghetto* is an affecting lament while the *allegro* has an icy glitter which should prepare us for her overt malevolence in Act II. The coloratura is strangely inhuman both in its rigidity and in the dizzy heights (up to the soprano's F in alt) to which it ascends [Ex. 71]. This,

Ex. 71

together with the Queen of Night's Act II aria, is the most dramatic use of coloratura in the operas of Mozart and, one is tempted to add, in anyone else's.

In several numbers in the opera, the differing musical styles merge. The Quintet (No. 5: 'Hm, hm, hm, hm') begun by Papageno humming, as his mouth had been padlocked, contains elements of the popular in Papageno's solo passages, though the overriding tone is lyrical, and full of charm. The orchestra's woodwind is always used to great effect, whether it is the bassoon mocking Papageno's temporary affliction or the oboe gently underlining the words of the three Ladies.

It is in the trio, 'Du feines Täubchen, nur herein' (No. 6), that we first encounter Pamina, as she struggles in vain to free herself from Monostatos. The lines sung by Papageno as he enters ('Schön Mädchen jung und fein, viel weisser noch als Kreide') can hardly refer to Pamina, as he has not yet seen her. Either he is singing them to Pamina's portrait which he carries or, more likely, is quoting (musically, as well) a popular Viennese song of 1791. In the trio, the melody advances the action, while, in the duet which follows between Pamina and Papageno (No. 7: 'Bei Männern, welche Liebe fühlen'), action is momentarily stilled to allow this ill-matched pair, heroine and comedian, to preach a tender sermon on love. In its last bars, simplicity appears to have been abandoned, as Pamina indulges in a repeated flourish [Ex. 72], though

Ex. 72

this, including the leap from middle C to the A flat above the stave, is expressive of deep feeling, as a sensitive performance by the soprano clearly reveals. There existed, apparently, an earlier version of this duet, less popular in style, which Schikaneder rejected, but which he may have reinstated when the opera was performed in 1802 at the new Theater an der Wien.[1]

The Finale to Act I (No. 8) is an extended piece of music, lasting about twenty-five minutes in performance, and ranging through all the differing styles which go to make up *Die Zauberflöte*. Comprising three major sections, it subdivides into smaller compartments within those sections. The first section, which is begun by the three Boys with Tamino, includes the great scene of Tamino and the Speaker; the second involves Pamina, Papageno and Monostatos, while the third introduces Sarastro. It is with the very first bars of the Finale that we encounter the solemn, quasi-Masonic aspect of the opera, for the orchestration has now taken on a quite different colouring. The three trombones, the muted trumpets, the muffled drums, these and the pure voices of the three Boys, bring a gravity of tone unlike anything in earlier operas by

[1] Schenk: op. cit., p. 567.

Mozart or in earlier scenes of this opera. It is important that the treble and alto voices be those of boys, and not, as so often happens outside Vienna, mature female voices.

Tamino's scene with the Speaker is remarkable for two reasons. The first is that, in it, we find Mozart anticipating the *durchkomponiert* opera developed by Wagner and Verdi in the mid-nineteenth century, and composing a scene which divides neither into recitative and melody nor into dialogue and music. The dramatic action is carried on in dialogue between tenor and bass, and though the dialogue can formally be labelled as recitative it in fact consists of a number of melodic units. A second reason for remarking on this scene is the musical quality of those melodic phrases. Mozart has infused into this exchange between Tamino and one of Sarastro's priests a quality of pure spirituality which distinguishes it, in its earnestness and solemnity, from its surroundings. Tamino's soliloquy which follows the scene with the Speaker begins with a phrase of almost unbearable despair [Ex. 73], and continues, first in

Ex. 73

O ew'-ge Nacht! wann wirst du schwin-den? Wann wird das Licht mein Au-ge fin-den?

richly thematic recitative and then in melodic aria ('Wie stark ist nicht dein Zauberton') as he plays his flute and sings, and is eventually answered by Papageno's pipes and the appearance of Papageno and Pamina. This leads to the second section of the Finale, in which Papageno and Pamina are apprehended by Monostatos. He and the other slaves are charmed into dancing by the magic silver bells on which Papageno plays a simple, polka-like tune. Papageno and Pamina then celebrate the effectiveness of the magic bells in a little duet whose opening phrase [Ex. 74] oddly anticipates the beginning of Schubert's song, 'Heidenröslein'.

Ex. 74

Könn-te je-der bra-ve Mann

An off-stage chorus announces the imminent arrival of Sarastro and begins the third section of the Finale. When Papageno, in terror of his life, asks Pamina what they should say to Sarastro, her brave reply, 'Die Wahrheit . . .' is set to phrases which combine the simplicity and naturalness of speech rhythms and inflections with the memorability of great music [Ex. 75]. (This quality of melodic declamation is what Verdi praised in Rossini, when he cited as an example the phrase 'Signor,

Ex. 75

giudizio, per carita', in *The Barber of Seville*.)[1] The expressive beauty and
dramatic rightness of phrase after phrase of this kind make *Die
Zauberflöte* more than just a very fine opera. Like *Fidelio*, it is an
affirmation of the highest aspects of humanity as well. This inspired
simplicity which we find pervading the utterances of Tamino, Pamina,
and now Sarastro, defies analysis. But it is immediately recognizable, and
the Finale to Act I is rich in examples of it. The act is brought to an end
with a joyous C major chorus in praise of Sarastro.

Act II begins with a slow march for the priests (No. 9). Jahn[2] tells that,
in answer to the accusation of a friend that he had stolen it from the
march in Act I, Scene III of Gluck's *Alceste*, 'Mozart laughingly replied
that that was impossible, as it still stood there'. The similarity between
the two pieces is one of mood only, for the orchestral colour Mozart
obtains with his single flute above strings, horns, basset-horns, bassoons
and trombones is unique in its awesome solemnity. When Sarastro
invites the priests to accept Tamino as an initiate, they answer with their
three B flat chords which we first heard in the Overture. Sarastro's aria
(No. 10: 'O Isis und Osiris') is a prayer of great beauty and majesty,
imbued with a human warmth which frees the music of any suspicion of
religiosity. (Was it not Bernard Shaw who said that Sarastro's two arias
were the only music he could imagine issuing from the voice of God?)
At the end of each of the aria's two stanzas, the chorus of priests quietly
repeats Sarastro's last phrase an octave higher, and the effect is one of a
radiantly unearthly ease.

The brief duet (No. 11: 'Bewahret euch vor Weibertücken') for two
priests, tenor and bass, is uncharacteristically jaunty, especially in view
of its message of warning against the wiles of women. It is followed by a
superb quintet (No. 12: 'Wie? Wie? Wie?') in which Tamino, Papageno
and the Queen of Night's three Ladies each contribute in their own
characteristic way, to form a unity out of a number of dissimilar
elements. The conversational ease, and the dovetailing of the Ladies'
admonitory tone, Tamino's dignified sense of purpose, and Papageno's
chattering, are sheer delight. Following on such charming music, the
effect of the final bars is electrifying. 'Thunder and lightning' are called
for by the stage directions, and Mozart produces appropriately terrifying chords to accompany the sudden disappearance of the Ladies,
followed by a descending arpeggio as Papageno, too, flings himself to
the ground in fear.

[1] *Letters of Giuseppe Verdi* (ed. Charles Osborne, 1971); pp. 217–218.
[2] Jahn: op. cit.

The brief, swift, song-like aria which Monostatos sings as he approaches the sleeping Pamina (No. 13: 'Alles fühlt der Liebe Freuden') is a fine piece of musical characterization; while it is quite simple melodically, its urgent, pauseless motion, pianissimo throughout, conveys a sense of stealth, added to by the unusual timbre of the piccolo which doubles the first violins. This is the only appearance of the piccolo in *Die Zauberflöte*. Evil of a more formidable kind is conveyed by the Queen of Night's second aria (No. 14: 'Der Hölle Rache kocht in meinem Herzen'), a brilliant 'revenge-aria' of the old *opera seria* type, in which the menacing coloratura takes the singer up to F in alt, and the relentless forward motion of the D minor music seems to emphasize the Queen's obsessive hatred of Sarastro. The stabbing staccato is like a series of fierce dagger-thrusts [Ex. 76].

Ex. 76

Even more affecting than Sarastro's first aria is his second (No. 15: 'In diesen heil'gen Hallen kennt man die Rache nicht'), in whose two stanzas of noble *larghetto* the High Priest expounds his Christian-humanist philosophy. (Its simplicity of utterance is damaged when basses sometimes end the second stanza by descending to the lower octave and singing a final E below the stave.) The *allegretto* trio for the three Boys (No. 16: 'Seid uns zum zweitenmal wilkommen') is lightly graceful, the simple vocal line decorated by a delicate, tripping figure for the violins. It is followed by the tragic grief of Pamina's G minor lament, 'Ach, ich fühl's' (No. 17), one of the most moving arias Mozart ever wrote. This extraordinary outburst of despair, desperate even in its restraint, is expressed in a vocal line of simplicity and a muted accompaniment, the orchestra commenting and consoling only in four bars of postlude, in a phrase of great tenderness.

In the next scene, the Priests' Chorus (No. 18: 'O Isis und Osiris'), a firm, confident prayer of grave beauty, is followed by a trio for Tamino, Pamina and Sarastro (No. 19: 'Soll ich dich, Teurer, nicht mehr seh'n?'). The mood of the trio is complex: Tamino and Pamina are being parted, but Sarastro can afford to express a guarded optimism as he, presumably, knows what the outcome of the lovers' trials will be. The restless arpeggios of the accompaniment convey the agitation and unease of the situation, while the two male voices breathe confidence and the soprano voice anxiously questions.

The refrain of Papageno's 'Ein Mädchen oder Weibchen' (No. 20) [Ex. 77], a simple, strophic song of great charm, introduced and punctuated by his magic chime of bells, has achieved in Austria the status of folk-song (with different words, beginning 'Üb' immer Treu

Ex. 77

Ein Mäd-chen o - der Weib - chen wünscht Pa - pa - ge - no sich,   o

so ein sanf - tes Täub - chen wär' Se - lig - keit für mich,

und Redlichkeit bis an dein kühles Grab').[1] An off-stage glockenspiel (nowadays usually a celeste) provides the music for Papageno's chime of bells, and Mozart in a letter to his wife while she was convalescing at Baden tells how, one evening at the Theater auf der Wieden, he had some fun at his old friend Schikaneder's expense:

> During Papageno's aria with the glockenspiel I went behind the scenes as I felt a sort of urge today to play it myself. Just for fun, at the point where Schikaneder has a pause, I played an arpeggio. He was startled, looked into the wings and saw me. When he came to his next pause I played no arpeggio. This time he stopped and refused to go on. I guessed what he was thinking and played another chord. He then hit the glockenspiel and shouted 'Shut up!' Whereupon everybody laughed. I rather think this joke taught a number of people in the audience that Papageno doesn't play the instrument himself.[2]

Though the Finale (No. 21) is an extended movement, occupying the last half-hour or so of the opera, it encompasses five separate scenes, and divides correspondingly into five musical sections: (i) the Three Boys and Pamina; (ii) the trials of Tamino and Pamina; (iii) Papageno and Papagena; (iv) the Queen of Night and her followers, leading into (v) the final chorus of victory over evil and darkness. The scene changes are, or should be, accomplished without breaks in the music: from the beginning of the Finale there is no further dialogue in the opera.

The scene of the three Boys and Pamina begins with the Boys' solemn trio, its rhythm and mood moving from serenity to urgency as they see the distraught Pamina approaching. After they have dissuaded Pamina from suicide, the tempo and key both brighten and the final passage for all four voices is positively joyous. The music comes to a full close; as the scene changes, it begins again, but as from a completely different, more austere world. Trombones are prominent in the *adagio* introductory bars [Ex. 78] which lead to a *fugato* at a steady tempo, over which two men, tenor and bass an octave apart, sing of the mysteries of Isis to the tune of an old German chorale, 'Ach Gott, von Himmel sieh darein' (Martin Luther's versification of Psalm 12). When Tamino and Pamina

---

[1] Jahn (op. cit.) quotes a few bars from a sixteenth-century chorale, 'Nun lob mein Seel' der Herren' which is identical with the beginning of Papageno's song.

[2] Letter written in October, 1791.

Ex. 78

are united, before undergoing together the trials of fire and water, they greet each other in phrases of the most moving simplicty. Pamina's 'Tamino mein' is very close to Ex. 70, the opening phrase of Tamino's aria in Act I as he gazes on her portrait. Here, we are at the very heart of *Die Zauberflöte* [Ex. 79]. The slow march with its solo (magic) flute, as

Ex. 79

Tamino and Pamina undergo the trials, is curiously divorced from the fire and water of those trials, exuding an air of spiritual tranquillity. When the lovers emerge from the second trial, an off-stage chorus celebrates their triumph in a joyous *allegro*. Again, the music comes to a full close. Now we return to the earthier sound of Papageno's world. He, too, contemplates suicide, and his farewell to the world, in Mozart's tragic key of G minor, has a touching dignity of its own [Ex. 80]. Like

Ex. 80

Pamina, he is saved by the three Boys, and his scene ends in an ecstatic mating-duet for him and his Papagena. Now the final section begins, in which the Queen of Night, her Ladies and Monostatos are dispatched to eternal darkness, and Sarastro, in six bars of confident *arioso*, introduces the chorus with which the opera ends, a joyous assertion in E flat of the triumph of light.

Die Zauberflöte is, without doubt, the apotheosis of the *Zauberoper*, but I think it should always be remembered that it *is* a *Zauberoper*, a magic opera, and that this Viennese genre existed well before Mozart's masterpiece and continued into the nineteenth century when it dwindled into the *Zauberpossen* of Raimund, Nestroy and their followers. Following the success of Mozart's opera, dozens of imitations of *Die Zauberflöte* were produced in the Viennese suburban theatres by Schikaneder and others. A Berlin journal complained: 'Everything is turned to magic at these theatres, there are the magic flute, the magic ring, the magic arrow, the magic mirror, the magic crown, and many other wretched magic affairs. Words and music are equally contemptible, except for *The Magic Flute*, so that one does not know whether to award the palm of silliness to the poet or the composer. Added to this, these miserable productions are still more miserably performed.'[1] Amongst the plays with music, plays by Raimund, Nestroy and others, one must remember to include Georg Ernst von Hofmann's melodrama, *Die Zauberharfe*, with music by Schubert, performed at the Theater an der Wien in 1820. (There may have been an opera, by Philipp Riotte, called *Mozart's Zauberflöte*, produced in Prague about 1820; there may, on the other hand, simply have been some confusion regarding a performance of Mozart's opera with which Riotte was connected.) Traces of the genre are still to be discerned as late as Ödön von Horvath's *Geschichten aus dem Wienerwald* in 1930. An immediate forerunner of *Die Zauberflöte* is the magic opera, *Oberon, König der Elfen* by Paul Wranitzky, produced by Schikaneder at his Theater auf der Wieden in 1789. Wenzel Müller, conductor and composer at the rival Theater in der Leopoldstadt, had his *Kaspar der Fagottist, oder die Zauberzither* produced there only a few months before the première of *Die Zauberflöte*, and it provided Schikaneder with a few ideas. (Müller remained at the Theater in der Leopoldstadt until his death in 1835. In 1818 he composed a parody of *Die Zauberflöte*, entitled *Die travestierte Zauberflöte*, and in the 1820s wrote music for the magic plays of Raimund.) Mozart's opera, of course, transcended the genre, but it remains a transcendent Viennese pantomime,'and the most successful productions are those which base it securely in that tradition rather than attempt to force it into a mould of Germanic religio-philosophical High Moral Purpose. The music is the message.

v

On the morning of 15 October, 1791, Mozart and the seven-year-old Karl brought Constanze back to Vienna from Baden. Mozart was still working on the Requiem, but broke off to compose a little Masonic Cantata (Eine kleine Freimaurer-Kantate, K. 623) to a text by Schikaneder, for the dedication of the temple of the Neugekrönte Hoffnung (Newly crowned hope) Lodge on 18 November. His health was deteriorating rapidly. During a walk in the Prater with Constanze he burst into tears as he spoke of his premonitions of approaching death

[1] *Berlin Musikalische Zeitung*, 1793, p. 142.

and his suspicion that he had been poisoned. He was well enough to conduct his Masonic cantata but two days later had to take to his bed. His hands and feet had become swollen, and he was subject to fits of vomiting. On 28 November his doctor, Dr Thomas Closset, called a consultation with Dr Matthias von Sallaba, chief physician of the Vienna General Hospital, but there was little that they could do. On 3 December, his condition seemed to improve slightly, though he was now suffering from dropsy and could move very little and only with great pain. The following afternoon, with two of his *Zauberflöte* cast and his brother-in-law Franz Hofer gathered around his bedside, he attempted a run-through of as much of the Requiem as he had finished.[1] The tenor Benedikt Schack sang falsetto, Hofer sang tenor and Franz Gerl bass. Mozart himself sang the alto part but wept as they reached the Lacrimosa, and was unable to continue. Later, he said he would like to have heard his *Zauberflöte* once more, and tried to hum Papageno's 'Vogelfänger' song to himself. In his final delirium, he imagined he was present at a performance of *Die Zauberflöte*. Almost his last words, murmured to his wife, were: 'Listen! Hofer is taking her top F. Now, how strongly she takes and holds the B flat. "Hört! hört! hört! der Mutter Schwur!"'[2] He died fifty-five minutes after midnight on 4 December. The cause of his death was described as 'severe miliary fever', but is now thought most likely to have been a uraemic coma following a lengthy kidney disease.

At 3 p.m. on 6 December, 1791, Mozart's funeral procession left St Stephen's Cathedral for the St Marx Cemetery, where he was buried in a common grave. Much that is misleading has been written about his funeral. It was not a pauper's funeral, but simply the cheapest available, and the fact that neither Constanze, who was ill and overwrought with grief, nor any of the mourners, followed the procession to Mozart's last resting place may well have had something to do with a decree of the late Emperor Joseph II, not then repealed, that the dead should not be buried in coffins, but merely sewn into sacks and covered with quicklime before being interred, and that ostentatious expressions of grief at funerals should be avoided. But Mozart's brothers-in-law and a number of friends and colleagues were present at the ceremony at St Stephen's. We have also been told countless times that the weather was dreadful, and that a snowstorm caused the members of the procession to disperse until there were none to witness the actual burial in St Marx's cemetery. But here Count Zinzendorf proves unexpectedly helpful. His diary entry for 5 December, 1791, records 'mild weather, mist three or four times a day for some time'. The following evening, for Zinzendorf noted the weather every evening, it was 'mild weather and frequent mist'.[3] Où sont

---

[1] It was later completed by Süssmayr.
[2] Letter by Seyfried. Now in the Mozarteum, Salzburg.
[3] To clinch the matter, O. E. Deutsch (op. cit.) quotes the barometric readings for 6

les neiges d'antan? In any case, one does not need to invoke a snowstorm to explain the failure of Mozart's friends to follow his coffin to its grave. Not only were public expressions of mourning frowned upon, there had been a cholera epidemic in Vienna, and the police regulations discouraged large and lengthy funeral processions.

Common graves at that time in Vienna were about seven and a half feet deep, and coffins, when they were used, were buried in three layers. The graves were not marked, and when Constanze visited the cemetery for the first time (apparently not until seventeen years later, which *is* difficult to explain), a new grave-digger was unable to tell her even the approximate place of burial. To this day it is not known, though a persistent Viennese story has it that the grave was on the right of the churchyard cross, in the third or fourth row of graves, near a willow-tree.

A week after Mozart's death the Prague correspondent of a Viennese journal wrote that 'the swelling of his body after his death led to the suspicion of his having been poisoned.' The rumour proved a persistent one. Thirty-two years later, Mozart's old rival Salieri attempted to cut his own throat, and later became completely deranged. In his ravings, he continually stated that he had poisoned Mozart and wished to confess to the crime. In the mid-eighteen-twenties Salieri's statement was widely discussed in Vienna, and believed by many. Another legend blames not Salieri but the Viennese Masons, in revenge for the composer having betrayed some of their secrets in *Die Zauberflöte*. According to this particular story, which appears to have emanated from Nazi Germany,[1] Mozart was assassinated, 'like Luther, Lessing, Schiller, and many others', for having invaded 'den Tempel Salomos, das heisst die Judenherrschaft'.[2] Salieri, Masons, Jewish Masons, or a disease of the kidneys: it hardly matters now. Mozart was the greatest composer of his century, and he is immortal.

Mozart was within weeks of his thirty-sixth birthday when he died. At that age Verdi had not yet written *Rigoletto*, but only those operas we think of as 'early Verdi'. Wagner had just completed *Lohengrin*: the great works of his maturity were many years away. If Mozart had lived to Verdi's age, he would have died in 1844. What kind of music would he have written? The operas we have are all early works, yet in them Mozart raised three different genres to greatness: *opera seria* with *Idomeneo*, *opera buffa* with the Da Ponte comedies, and the German *Singspiel* with *Die Zauberflöte*.

December from the *Wiener Zeitung* of 14 December. They support Zinzendorf. The records of the Vienna Observatory show there was a light easterly wind throughout the day.

[1] Mathilde Ludendorff: *Mozarts Leben und gewalsamer Tod* (Munich, 1936). Quoted in Jacques Chailley: *The Magic Flute, Masonic Opera* (Gollancz, 1972).

[2] 'Solomon's temple or Jewish dominance'.

Some Books Consulted
Index

Some Books Consulted

(This list contains titles of general interest. Details of others will be found throughout the volume, in footnotes to the text.)

Die Briefe Mozarts und seine Familie (5 vols.; ed. L. Schiedermair; Munich, 1914)

The Letters of Mozart and his Family (2 vols.; ed. E. Anderson; London, 1966)

Chailley, Jacques: *The Magic Flute, Masonic Opera* (London, 1966)

Da Ponte, Lorenzo: *Memoirs* (New York, 1929)

Dent, Edward J.: *Mozart's Operas* (Oxford, 1947)

Deutsch, Otto Erich: *Mozart, a Documentary Biography* (London, 1965)

Einstein, Alfred: *Mozart: His Character, His Work* (London, 1946)

Hughes, Spike: *Famous Mozart Operas* (London, 1957)

Jahn, Otto: *Wolfgang Amadeus Mozart* (4 vols.; Leipzig 1856–59; English translation, 3 vols.; London, 1882)

Jouve, Jean Pierre: *Mozart's Don Juan* (London, 1957)

Levey, Michael: *The Life and Death of Mozart* (London, 1971)

Liebner, János: *Mozart on the Stage* (London, 1972)

Newman, Ernest: *Opera Nights* (London, 1943)

—— *More Opera Nights*, (London, 1954)

Sadie, Stanley: *Mozart* (London, 1965)

Schenk, Erich: *Wolfgang Amadeus Mozart: Eine Biographie* (Vienna, 1955; English translation, *Mozart and his Times*, London, 1960)

Turner, W. J.: *Mozart, the Man and His Works* (London, 1938)

Had it been published before my own volume was substantially written, I would doubtless have consulted William Mann's *The Operas of Mozart* (London, 1977).

Index

Page numbers in italics refer to the principal references to the operas in question

CHARLES OSBORNE, well-known British musicologist, critic and broadcaster, lives in London, where he is a Director of the Arts Council of Great Britain. He spent his early years in Australia where he studied composition and singing. He composed several songs, and in his twenties toured as an actor. At this time he also wrote and published poetry. Since 1958 he has concentrated on writing about music. His *The Complete Operas of Verdi* (1970) has become the definitive guide to Verdi, and has been successfully translated into Italian. He lives in a large apartment in central London, with several thousand books, scores and gramophone records. His principal hobby is travel; he has traveled extensively in Europe, North Africa, the Middle East and Australia, with occasional forays to the U.S. He also directs an annual Poetry Festival in London, and has given poetry readings in company with Vincent Price, John Gielgud, Michael York, Irene Worth. He is a popular lecturer on musical and literary subjects.